W9-ALM-964

PRAISE FOR *PYTHON CRASH COURSE*

"It has been interesting to see No Starch Press producing future classics that should be alongside the more traditional programming books. *Python Crash Course* is one of those books."
—GREG LADEN, SCIENCEBLOGS

"Deals with some rather complex projects and lays them out in a consistent, logical, and pleasant manner that draws the reader into the subject."
—FULL CIRCLE MAGAZINE

"Well presented with good explanations of the code snippets. The book works with you, one small step at a time, building more complex code, explaining what's going on all the way."
—FLICKTHROUGH REVIEWS

"Learning Python with *Python Crash Course* was an extremely positive experience! A great choice if you're new to Python."
—MIKKE GOES CODING

"Does what it says on the tin, and does it really well. . . . Presents a large number of useful exercises as well as three challenging and entertaining projects."
—REALPYTHON.COM

"A fast-paced but comprehensive introduction to programming with Python, *Python Crash Course* is another superb book to add to your library and help you finally master Python."
—TUTORIALEDGE.NET

"A brilliant option for complete beginners without any coding experience. If you're looking for a solid, uncomplicated intro to this very deep language, I have to recommend this book."
—WHATPIXEL.COM

"Contains literally everything you need to know about Python and even more."
—FIREBEARSTUDIO.COM

PYTHON CRASH COURSE

2ND EDITION

A Hands-On, Project-Based Introduction to Programming

by Eric Matthes

no starch press

San Francisco

PYTHON CRASH COURSE, 2ND EDITION. Copyright © 2019 by Eric Matthes.

Printed in USA

Fourth printing

24 23 22 21 20   4 5 6 7 8 9

ISBN-10: 1-59327-928-0
ISBN-13: 978-1-59327-928-8

Publisher: William Pollock
Production Editor: Riley Hoffman
Cover Illustration: Josh Ellingson
Cover and Interior Design: Octopod Studios
Developmental Editor: Liz Chadwick
Technical Reviewer: Kenneth Love
Copyeditor: Anne Marie Walker
Compositors: Riley Hoffman and Happenstance Type-O-Rama
Proofreader: James Fraleigh

For information on distribution, translations, or bulk sales, please contact No Starch Press, Inc. directly:

No Starch Press, Inc.
245 8th Street, San Francisco, CA 94103
phone: 1.415.863.9900; info@nostarch.com
www.nostarch.com

The Library of Congress has catalogued the first edition as follows:

Matthes, Eric, 1972-
   Python crash course : a hands-on, project-based introduction to programming / by Eric Matthes.
       pages cm
   Includes index.
   Summary: "A project-based introduction to programming in Python, with exercises. Covers general programming concepts, Python fundamentals, and problem solving. Includes three projects - how to create a simple video game, use data visualization techniques to make graphs and charts, and build an interactive web application"-- Provided by publisher.
   ISBN 978-1-59327-603-4 -- ISBN 1-59327-603-6
   1. Python (Computer program language) I. Title.
   QA76.73.P98M38 2015
   005.13'3--dc23
                                                        2015018135

About the Author

Eric Matthes is a high school science and math teacher living in Alaska, where he teaches an introductory Python course. He has been writing programs since he was five years old. Eric currently focuses on writing software that addresses inefficiencies in education and brings the benefits of open source software to the field of education. In his spare time he enjoys climbing mountains and spending time with his family.

About the Technical Reviewer

Kenneth Love has been a Python programmer, teacher, and conference organizer for many years. He has spoken and taught at many conferences, been a Python and Django freelancer, and is currently a software engineer for O'Reilly Media. Kenneth is co-creator of the django-braces package, which provides several handy mixins for Django's class-based views. You can keep up with him on Twitter at @kennethlove.

For my father, who always made time to
answer my questions about programming,
and for Ever, who is just beginning to ask me
his questions

BRIEF CONTENTS

Project 2: Data Visualization

Project 3: Web Applications

CONTENTS IN DETAIL

5
IF STATEMENTS
71

6
DICTIONARIES
91

8
FUNCTIONS 129

9
CLASSES
157

10
FILES AND EXCEPTIONS
183

PART II: PROJECTS

PROJECT 1: ALIEN INVASION

12
A SHIP THAT FIRES BULLETS

13
ALIENS!   255

14
SCORING   279

PROJECT 2: DATA VISUALIZATION

15
GENERATING DATA   305

AFTERWORD   465

A
INSTALLATION AND TROUBLESHOOTING   467

B
TEXT EDITORS AND IDEs   473

C
GETTING HELP   479

D
USING GIT FOR VERSION CONTROL   485

INDEX   495

PREFACE TO
THE SECOND EDITION

The response to the first edition of *Python Crash Course* has been overwhelmingly positive. More than 500,000 copies are in print, including translations in eight languages. I've received letters and emails from readers as young as 10, as well as from retirees who want to learn to program in their free time. *Python Crash Course* is being used in middle schools and high schools, and also in college classes. Students who are assigned more advanced textbooks are using *Python Crash Course* as a companion text for their classes and finding it a worthwhile supplement. People are using it to enhance their skills on the job and to start working on their own side projects. In short, people are using the book for the full range of purposes I had hoped they would.

The opportunity to write a second edition of *Python Crash Course* has been thoroughly enjoyable. Although Python is a mature language, it continues to evolve as every language does. My goal in revising the book was to make it leaner and simpler. There is no longer any reason to learn Python 2, so this edition focuses on Python 3 only. Many Python packages have become easier to install, so setup and installation instructions are easier. I've added a few topics that I've realized readers would benefit from, and I've updated some sections to reflect new, simpler ways of doing things in Python. I've also clarified some sections where certain details of the language were not presented as accurately as they could have been. All the projects have been completely updated using popular, well-maintained libraries that you can confidently use to build your own projects.

The following is a summary of specific changes that have been made in the second edition:

- In Chapter 1, the instructions for installing Python have been simplified for users of all major operating systems. I now recommend the text editor Sublime Text, which is popular among beginner and professional programmers and works well on all operating systems.

- Chapter 2 includes a more accurate description of how variables are implemented in Python. Variables are described as *labels* for values, which leads to a better understanding of how variables behave in Python. The book now uses f-strings, introduced in Python 3.6. This is a much simpler way to use variable values in strings. The use of underscores to represent large numbers, such as 1_000_000, was also introduced in Python 3.6 and is included in this edition. Multiple assignment of variables was previously introduced in one of the projects, and that description has been generalized and moved to Chapter 2 for the benefit of all readers. Finally, a clear convention for representing constant values in Python is included in this chapter.

- In Chapter 6, I introduce the get() method for retrieving values from a dictionary, which can return a default value if a key does not exist.

- The Alien Invasion project (Chapters 12–14) is now entirely class-based. The game itself is a class, rather than a series of functions. This greatly simplifies the overall structure of the game, vastly reducing the number of function calls and parameters required. Readers familiar with the first edition will appreciate the simplicity this new class-based approach provides. Pygame can now be installed in one line on all systems, and readers are given the option of running the game in fullscreen mode or in a windowed mode.

- In the data visualization projects, the installation instructions for Matplotlib are simpler for all operating systems. The visualizations featuring Matplotlib use the subplots() function, which will be easier to build upon as you learn to create more complex visualizations. The Rolling Dice project in Chapter 15 uses Plotly, a well-maintained visualization library that features a clean syntax and beautiful, fully customizable output.

- In Chapter 16, the weather project is based on data from NOAA, which should be more stable over the next few years than the site used in the first edition. The mapping project focuses on global earthquake activity; by the end of this project you'll have a stunning visualization showing Earth's tectonic plate boundaries through a focus on the locations of all earthquakes over a given time period. You'll learn to plot any data set involving geographic points.

- Chapter 17 uses Plotly to visualize Python-related activity in open source projects on GitHub.

- The Learning Log project (Chapters 18–20) is built using the latest version of Django and styled using the latest version of Bootstrap. The process of deploying the project to Heroku has been simplified using the django-heroku package, and uses environment variables rather than modifying the *settings.py* files. This is a simpler approach and is more consistent with how professional programmers deploy modern Django projects.

- Appendix A has been fully updated to recommend current best practices in installing Python. Appendix B includes detailed instructions for setting up Sublime Text and brief descriptions of most of the major text editors and IDEs in current use. Appendix C directs readers to newer, more popular online resources for getting help, and Appendix D continues to offer a mini crash course in using Git for version control.

- The index has been thoroughly updated to allow you to use *Python Crash Course* as a reference for all of your future Python projects.

Thank you for reading *Python Crash Course*! If you have any feedback or questions, please feel free to get in touch.

ACKNOWLEDGMENTS

This book would not have been possible without the wonderful and extremely professional staff at No Starch Press. Bill Pollock invited me to write an introductory book, and I deeply appreciate that original offer. Tyler Ortman helped shape my thinking in the early stages of drafting. Liz Chadwick's and Leslie Shen's initial feedback on each chapter was invaluable, and Anne Marie Walker helped to clarify many parts of the book. Riley Hoffman answered every question I had about the process of assembling a complete book and patiently turned my work into a beautiful finished product.

I'd like to thank Kenneth Love, the technical reviewer for *Python Crash Course*. I met Kenneth at PyCon one year, and his enthusiasm for the language and the Python community has been a constant source of professional inspiration ever since. Kenneth went beyond simple fact-checking and reviewed the book with the goal of helping beginning programmers develop a solid understanding of the Python language and programming in general. That said, any inaccuracies that remain are completely my own.

I'd like to thank my father for introducing me to programming at a young age and for not being afraid that I'd break his equipment. I'd like to thank my wife, Erin, for supporting and encouraging me through the writing of this book, and I'd like to thank my son, Ever, whose curiosity inspires me every single day.

INTRODUCTION

Every programmer has a story about how they learned to write their first program. I started programming as a child when my father was working for Digital Equipment Corporation, one of the pioneering companies of the modern computing era. I wrote my first program on a kit computer that my dad had assembled in our basement. The computer consisted of nothing more than a bare motherboard connected to a keyboard without a case, and its monitor was a bare cathode ray tube. My initial program was a simple number guessing game, which looked something like this:

```
I'm thinking of a number! Try to guess the number I'm thinking of: 25
Too low! Guess again: 50
Too high! Guess again: 42
That's it! Would you like to play again? (yes/no) no
Thanks for playing!
```

I'll always remember how satisfied I felt watching my family play a game that I created and that worked as I intended it to.

That early experience had a lasting impact. There is real satisfaction in building something with a purpose, something that solves a problem. The software I write now meets a more significant need than my childhood efforts, but the sense of satisfaction I get from creating a program that works is still largely the same.

Who Is This Book For?

The goal of this book is to bring you up to speed with Python as quickly as possible so you can build programs that work—games, data visualizations, and web applications—while developing a foundation in programming that will serve you well for the rest of your life. *Python Crash Course* is written for people of any age who have never before programmed in Python or have never programmed at all. This book is for those who want to learn the basics of programming quickly so they can focus on interesting projects, and those who like to test their understanding of new concepts by solving meaningful problems. *Python Crash Course* is also perfect for middle school and high school teachers who want to offer their students a project-based introduction to programming. If you're taking a college class and want a friendlier introduction to Python than the text you've been assigned, this book could make your class easier as well.

What Can You Expect to Learn?

The purpose of this book is to make you a good programmer in general and a good Python programmer in particular. You'll learn efficiently and adopt good habits as I provide you with a solid foundation in general programming concepts. After working your way through *Python Crash Course*, you should be ready to move on to more advanced Python techniques, and your next programming language will be even easier to grasp.

In the first part of this book, you'll learn basic programming concepts you need to know to write Python programs. These concepts are the same as those you'd learn when starting out in almost any programming language. You'll learn about different kinds of data and the ways you can store data in lists and dictionaries within your programs. You'll learn to build collections of data and work through those collections in efficient ways. You'll learn to use while loops and if statements to test for certain conditions so you can run specific sections of code while those conditions are true and run other sections when they're not—a technique that greatly helps you automate processes.

You'll learn to accept input from users to make your programs interactive and to keep your programs running as long as the user is active. You'll explore how to write functions to make parts of your program reusable, so you only have to write blocks of code that perform certain actions once and then use that code as many times as you like. You'll then extend this concept to more complicated behavior with classes, making fairly simple programs respond to a variety of situations. You'll learn to write programs that handle common errors gracefully. After working through each of these basic concepts, you'll write a few short programs that solve some well-defined problems. Finally, you'll take your first step toward intermediate programming by learning how to write tests for your code so you can develop your programs further without worrying about introducing bugs. All the information in Part I will prepare you for taking on larger, more complex projects.

In Part II, you'll apply what you learned in Part I to three projects. You can do any or all of these projects in whichever order works best for you. In the first project (Chapters 12–14), you'll create a *Space Invaders*–style shooting game called *Alien Invasion*, which consists of levels of increasing difficulty. After you've completed this project, you should be well on your way to being able to develop your own 2D games.

The second project (Chapters 15–17) introduces you to data visualization. Data scientists aim to make sense of the vast amount of information available to them through a variety of visualization techniques. You'll work with data sets that you generate through code, data sets that you download from online sources, and data sets your programs download automatically. After you've completed this project, you'll be able to write programs that sift through large data sets and make visual representations of that stored information.

In the third project (Chapters 18–20), you'll build a small web application called Learning Log. This project allows you to keep a journal of ideas and concepts you've learned about a specific topic. You'll be able to keep separate logs for different topics and allow others to create an account and start their own journals. You'll also learn how to deploy your project so anyone can access it online from anywhere.

Online Resources

You can find all the supplementary resources for the book online at *https://nostarch.com/pythoncrashcourse2e/* or *http://ehmatthes.github.io/pcc_2e/*. These resources include:

Setup instructions   These instructions are identical to what's in the book but include active links you can click for all the different pieces. If you're having any setup issues, refer to this resource.

Updates   Python, like all languages, is constantly evolving. I maintain a thorough set of updates, so if anything isn't working, check here to see whether instructions have changed.

Solutions to exercises   You should spend significant time on your own attempting the exercises in the "Try It Yourself" sections. But if you're stuck and can't make any progress, solutions to most of the exercises are online.

Cheat sheets   A full set of downloadable cheat sheets for a quick reference to major concepts is also online.

Why Python?

Every year I consider whether to continue using Python or whether to move on to a different language—perhaps one that's newer to the programming world. But I continue to focus on Python for many reasons. Python is an incredibly efficient language: your programs will do more in fewer lines of code than many other languages would require. Python's syntax will also help you write "clean" code. Your code will be easy to read, easy to debug, and easy to extend and build upon compared to other languages.

People use Python for many purposes: to make games, build web applications, solve business problems, and develop internal tools at all kinds of interesting companies. Python is also used heavily in scientific fields for academic research and applied work.

One of the most important reasons I continue to use Python is because of the Python community, which includes an incredibly diverse and welcoming group of people. Community is essential to programmers because programming isn't a solitary pursuit. Most of us, even the most experienced programmers, need to ask advice from others who have already solved similar problems. Having a well-connected and supportive community is critical in helping you solve problems, and the Python community is fully supportive of people like you who are learning Python as your first programming language.

Python is a great language to learn, so let's get started!

PART I

BASICS

Part I of this book teaches you the basic concepts you'll need to write Python programs. Many of these concepts are common to all programming languages, so they'll be useful throughout your life as a programmer.

In **Chapter 1** you'll install Python on your computer and run your first program, which prints the message *Hello world!* to the screen.

In **Chapter 2** you'll learn to store information in variables and work with text and numerical values.

Chapters 3 and **4** introduce lists. Lists can store as much information as you want in one variable, allowing you to work with that data efficiently. You'll be able to work with hundreds, thousands, and even millions of values in just a few lines of code.

In **Chapter 5** you'll use if statements to write code that responds one way if certain conditions are true, and responds in a different way if those conditions are not true.

Chapter 6 shows you how to use Python's dictionaries, which let you make connections between different pieces of information. Like lists, dictionaries can contain as much information as you need to store.

In **Chapter 7** you'll learn how to accept input from users to make your programs interactive. You'll also learn about while loops, which run blocks of code repeatedly as long as certain conditions remain true.

In **Chapter 8** you'll write functions, which are named blocks of code that perform a specific task and can be run whenever you need them.

Chapter 9 introduces classes, which allow you to model real-world objects, such as dogs, cats, people, cars, rockets, and much more, so your code can represent anything real or abstract.

Chapter 10 shows you how to work with files and handle errors so your programs won't crash unexpectedly. You'll store data before your program closes, and read the data back in when the program runs again. You'll learn about Python's exceptions, which allow you to anticipate errors, and make your programs handle those errors gracefully.

In **Chapter 11** you'll learn to write tests for your code to check that your programs work the way you intend them to. As a result, you'll be able to expand your programs without worrying about introducing new bugs. Testing your code is one of the first skills that will help you transition from beginner to intermediate programmer.

1

GETTING STARTED

In this chapter, you'll run your first Python program, *hello_world.py*. First, you'll need to check whether a recent version of Python is installed on your computer; if it isn't, you'll install it. You'll also install a text editor to work with your Python programs. Text editors recognize Python code and highlight sections as you write, making it easy to understand your code's structure.

Setting Up Your Programming Environment

Python differs slightly on different operating systems, so you'll need to keep a few considerations in mind. In the following sections, we'll make sure Python is set up correctly on your system.

Python Versions

Every programming language evolves as new ideas and technologies emerge, and the developers of Python have continually made the language more versatile and powerful. As of this writing, the latest version is Python 3.7, but everything in this book should run on Python 3.6 or later. In this section, we'll find out if Python is already installed on your system and whether you need to install a newer version. Appendix A contains a comprehensive guide to installing the latest version of Python on each major operating system as well.

Some old Python projects still use Python 2, but you should use Python 3. If Python 2 is installed on your system, it's probably there to support some older programs that your system needs. We'll leave this installation as is, and make sure you have a more recent version to work with.

Running Snippets of Python Code

You can run Python's interpreter in a terminal window, allowing you to try bits of Python code without having to save and run an entire program.

Throughout this book, you'll see code snippets that look like this:

```
❶ >>> print("Hello Python interpreter!")
Hello Python interpreter!
```

The >>> prompt indicates that you should be using the terminal window, and the bold text is the code you should type in and then execute by pressing ENTER. Most of the examples in the book are small, self-contained programs that you'll run from your text editor rather than the terminal, because you'll write most of your code in the text editor. But sometimes basic concepts will be shown in a series of snippets run through a Python terminal session to demonstrate particular concepts more efficiently. When you see three angle brackets in a code listing ❶, you're looking at code and output from a terminal session. We'll try coding in the interpreter on your system in a moment.

We'll also use a text editor to create a simple program called *Hello World!* that has become a staple of learning to program. There's a long-held tradition in the programming world that printing a Hello world! message to the screen as your first program in a new language will bring you good luck. Such a simple program serves a very real purpose. If it runs correctly on your system, any Python program you write should work as well.

About the Sublime Text Editor

Sublime Text is a simple text editor that can be installed on all modern operating systems. Sublime Text lets you run almost all of your programs directly from the editor instead of through a terminal. Your code runs in a terminal session embedded in the Sublime Text window, which makes it easy to see the output.

Sublime Text is a beginner-friendly editor, but many professional programmers use it as well. If you become comfortable using it while learning Python, you can continue using it as you progress to larger and more complicated projects. Sublime Text has a very liberal licensing policy: you can use the editor free of charge as long as you want, but the developers request that you purchase a license if you like it and want to keep using it.

Appendix B provides information on other text editors. If you're curious about the other options, you might want to skim that appendix at this point. If you want to begin programming quickly, you can use Sublime Text to start and consider other editors once you've gained some experience as a programmer. In this chapter, I'll walk you through installing Sublime Text on your operating system.

Python on Different Operating Systems

Python is a cross-platform programming language, which means it runs on all the major operating systems. Any Python program you write should run on any modern computer that has Python installed. However, the methods for setting up Python on different operating systems vary slightly.

In this section, you'll learn how to set up Python on your system. You'll first check whether a recent version of Python is installed on your system and install it if it's not. Then you'll install Sublime Text. These are the only two steps that are different for each operating system.

In the sections that follow, you'll run the *Hello World!* program and troubleshoot anything that didn't work. I'll walk you through this process for each operating system, so you'll have a beginner-friendly Python programming environment.

Python on Windows

Windows doesn't always come with Python, so you'll probably need to install it, and then install Sublime Text.

Installing Python

First, check whether Python is installed on your system. Open a command window by entering command into the Start menu or by holding down the SHIFT key while right-clicking on your desktop and selecting **Open command window here** from the menu. In the terminal window, enter python in lowercase. If you get a Python prompt (>>>) in response, Python is installed on your system. If you see an error message telling you that python is not a recognized command, Python isn't installed.

In that case, or if you see a version of Python earlier than Python 3.6, you need to download a Python installer for Windows. Go to *https://python .org/* and hover over the **Downloads** link. You should see a button for downloading the latest version of Python. Click the button, which should automatically start downloading the correct installer for your system. After you've downloaded the file, run the installer. Make sure you select the option **Add Python to PATH**, which will make it easier to configure your system correctly. Figure 1-1 shows this option selected.

Figure 1-1: Make sure you select the checkbox labeled Add Python to PATH.

Running Python in a Terminal Session

Open a command window and enter **python** in lowercase. You should see a Python prompt (>>>), which means Windows has found the version of Python you just installed.

```
C:\> python
Python 3.7.2 (v3.7.2:9a3ffc0492, Dec 23 2018, 23:09:28) [MSC v.1916 64 bit
(AMD64)] on win32
Type "help", "copyright", "credits" or "license" for more information.
>>>
```

NOTE *If you don't see this output or something similar, see the more detailed setup instructions in Appendix A.*

Enter the following line in your Python session, and make sure you see the output Hello Python interpreter!

```
>>> print("Hello Python interpreter!")
Hello Python interpreter!
>>>
```

Any time you want to run a snippet of Python code, open a command window and start a Python terminal session. To close the terminal session, press CTRL-Z and then press ENTER, or enter the command exit().

Installing Sublime Text

You can download an installer for Sublime Text at *https://sublimetext.com/*. Click the download link and look for a Windows installer. After downloading the installer, run the installer and accept all of its defaults.

Python on macOS

Python is already installed on most macOS systems, but it's most likely an outdated version that you won't want to learn on. In this section, you'll install the latest version of Python, and then you'll install Sublime Text and make sure it's configured correctly.

Checking Whether Python 3 Is Installed

Open a terminal window by going to **Applications ▸ Utilities ▸ Terminal**. You can also press ⌘-spacebar, type **terminal**, and then press ENTER. To see which version of Python is installed, enter **python** with a lowercase *p*—this also starts the Python interpreter within the terminal, allowing you to enter Python commands. You should see output telling you which Python version is installed on your system and a >>> prompt where you can start entering Python commands, like this:

```
$ python
Python 2.7.15 (default, Aug 17 2018, 22:39:05)
[GCC 4.2.1 Compatible Apple LLVM 9.1.0 (clang-902.0.39.2)] on darwin
Type "help", "copyright", "credits", or "license" for more information.
>>>
```

This output indicates that Python 2.7.15 is currently the default version installed on this computer. Once you've seen this output, press CTRL-D or enter **exit()** to leave the Python prompt and return to a terminal prompt.

To check whether you have Python 3 installed, enter the command **python3**. You'll probably get an error message, meaning you don't have any versions of Python 3 installed. If the output shows you have Python 3.6 or a later version installed, you can skip ahead to "Running Python in a Terminal Session" on page 8. If Python 3 isn't installed by default, you'll need to install it manually. Note that whenever you see the python command in this book, you need to use the python3 command instead to make sure you're using Python 3, not Python 2; they differ significantly enough that you'll run into trouble trying to run the code in this book using Python 2.

If you see any version earlier than Python 3.6, follow the instructions in the next section to install the latest version.

Installing the Latest Version of Python

You can find a Python installer for your system at *https://python.org/*. Hover over the **Download** link, and you should see a button for downloading the latest Python version. Click the button, which should automatically start downloading the correct installer for your system. After the file downloads, run the installer.

When you're finished, enter the following at a terminal prompt:

```
$ python3 --version
Python 3.7.2
```

You should see output similar to this, in which case, you're ready to try out Python. Whenever you see the command **python**, make sure you use **python3**.

Running Python in a Terminal Session

You can now try running snippets of Python code by opening a terminal and typing **python3**. Enter the following line in the terminal session:

```
>>> print("Hello Python interpreter!")
Hello Python interpreter!
>>>
```

Your message should print directly in the current terminal window. Remember that you can close the Python interpreter by pressing CTRL-D or by entering the command exit().

Installing Sublime Text

To install the Sublime Text editor, you need to download the installer at *https://sublimetext.com/*. Click the **Download** link and look for an installer for macOS. After the installer downloads, open it and then drag the Sublime Text icon into your *Applications* folder.

Python on Linux

Linux systems are designed for programming, so Python is already installed on most Linux computers. The people who write and maintain Linux expect you to do your own programming at some point and encourage you to do so. For this reason, there's very little to install and only a few settings to change to start programming.

Checking Your Version of Python

Open a terminal window by running the Terminal application on your system (in Ubuntu, you can press CTRL-ALT-T). To find out which version of Python is installed, enter **python3** with a lowercase *p*. When Python is installed, this command starts the Python interpreter. You should see output indicating which version of Python is installed and a >>> prompt where you can start entering Python commands, like this:

```
$ python3
Python 3.7.2 (default, Dec 27 2018, 04:01:51)
[GCC 7.3.0] on linux
```

```
Type "help", "copyright", "credits" or "license" for more information.
>>>
```

This output indicates that Python 3.7.2 is currently the default version of Python installed on this computer. When you've seen this output, press CTRL-D or enter **exit()** to leave the Python prompt and return to a terminal prompt. Whenever you see the **python** command in this book, enter **python3** instead.

You'll need Python 3.6 or later to run the code in this book. If the Python version installed on your system is earlier than Python 3.6, refer to Appendix A to install the latest version.

Running Python in a Terminal Session

You can try running snippets of Python code by opening a terminal and entering **python3**, as you did when checking your version. Do this again, and when you have Python running, enter the following line in the terminal session:

```
>>> print("Hello Python interpreter!")
Hello Python interpreter!
>>>
```

The message should print directly in the current terminal window. Remember that you can close the Python interpreter by pressing CTRL-D or by entering the command exit().

Installing Sublime Text

On Linux, you can install Sublime Text from the Ubuntu Software Center. Click the Ubuntu Software icon in your menu, and search for **Sublime Text**. Click to install it, and then launch it.

Running a Hello World Program

With a recent version of Python and Sublime Text installed, you're almost ready to run your first Python program written in a text editor. But before doing so, you need to make sure Sublime Text is set up to use the correct version of Python on your system. Then you'll write the *Hello World!* program and run it.

Configuring Sublime Text to Use the Correct Python Version

If the python command on your system runs Python 3, you won't need to configure anything and can skip to the next section. If you use the python3 command, you'll need to configure Sublime Text to use the correct Python version when it runs your programs.

Click the Sublime Text icon to launch it, or search for Sublime Text in your system's search bar and then launch it. Go to **Tools ▸ Build System ▸ New Build System**, which will open a new configuration file for you. Delete what you see and enter the following:

Python3 .sublime-build

```
{
    "cmd": ["python3", "-u", "$file"],
}
```

This code tells Sublime Text to use your system's python3 command when running your Python program files. Save the file as *Python3.sublime-build* in the default directory that Sublime Text opens when you choose Save.

Running hello_world.py

Before you write your first program, make a folder called *python_work* somewhere on your system for your projects. It's best to use lowercase letters and underscores for spaces in file and folder names, because Python uses these naming conventions.

Open Sublime Text, and save an empty Python file (**File ▸ Save As**) called *hello_world.py* in your *python_work* folder. The extension *.py* tells Sublime Text that the code in your file is written in Python, which tells it how to run the program and highlight the text in a helpful way.

After you've saved your file, enter the following line in the text editor:

hello_world.py

```
print("Hello Python world!")
```

If the python command works on your system, you can run your program by selecting **Tools ▸ Build** in the menu or by pressing CTRL-B (⌘-B on macOS). If you had to configure Sublime Text in the previous section, select **Tools ▸ Build System** and then select **Python 3**. From now on you'll be able to select **Tools ▸ Build** or just press CTRL-B (or ⌘-B) to run your programs.

A terminal screen should appear at the bottom of the Sublime Text window, showing the following output:

```
Hello Python world!
[Finished in 0.1s]
```

If you don't see this output, something might have gone wrong in the program. Check every character on the line you entered. Did you accidentally capitalize print? Did you forget one or both of the quotation marks or parentheses? Programming languages expect very specific syntax, and if you don't provide that, you'll get errors. If you can't get the program to run, see the suggestions in the next section.

Troubleshooting

If you can't get *hello_world.py* to run, here are a few remedies you can try that are also good general solutions for any programming problem:

- When a program contains a significant error, Python displays a *traceback*, which is an error report. Python looks through the file and tries to identify the problem. Check the traceback; it might give you a clue as to what issue is preventing the program from running.

- Step away from your computer, take a short break, and then try again. Remember that syntax is very important in programming, so even a missing colon, a mismatched quotation mark, or mismatched parentheses can prevent a program from running properly. Reread the relevant parts of this chapter, look over your code, and try to find the mistake.

- Start over again. You probably don't need to uninstall any software, but it might make sense to delete your *hello_world.py* file and re-create it from scratch.

- Ask someone else to follow the steps in this chapter, on your computer or a different one, and watch what they do carefully. You might have missed one small step that someone else happens to catch.

- Find someone who knows Python and ask them to help you get set up. If you ask around, you might find that you unexpectedly know someone who uses Python.

- The setup instructions in this chapter are also available through the book's companion website at *https://nostarch.com/pythoncrashcourse2e/*. The online version of these instructions might work better for you because you can simply cut and paste code.

- Ask for help online. Appendix C provides a number of resources, such as forums and live chat sites, where you can ask for solutions from people who've already worked through the issue you're currently facing.

Never worry that you're bothering experienced programmers. Every programmer has been stuck at some point, and most programmers are happy to help you set up your system correctly. As long as you can state clearly what you're trying to do, what you've already tried, and the results you're getting, there's a good chance someone will be able to help you. As mentioned in the Introduction, the Python community is very friendly and welcoming to beginners.

Python should run well on any modern computer. Early setup issues can be frustrating, but they're well worth sorting out. Once you get *hello_world.py* running, you can start to learn Python, and your programming work will become more interesting and satisfying.

Running Python Programs from a Terminal

Most of the programs you write in your text editor you'll run directly from the editor. But sometimes it's useful to run programs from a terminal instead. For example, you might want to run an existing program without opening it for editing.

You can do this on any system with Python installed if you know how to access the directory where the program file is stored. To try this, make sure you've saved the *hello_world.py* file in the *python_work* folder on your desktop.

On Windows

You can use the terminal command cd, for *change directory*, to navigate through your filesystem in a command window. The command dir, for *directory*, shows you all the files that exist in the current directory.

Open a new terminal window and enter the following commands to run *hello_world.py*:

```
❶ C:\> cd Desktop\python_work
❷ C:\Desktop\python_work> dir
  hello_world.py
❸ C:\Desktop\python_work> python hello_world.py
  Hello Python world!
```

At ❶ you use the cd command to navigate to the *python_work* folder, which is in the *Desktop* folder. Next, you use the dir command to make sure *hello_world.py* is in this folder ❷. Then you run the file using the command python hello_world.py ❸.

Most of your programs will run fine directly from your editor. But as your work becomes more complex, you'll want to run some of your programs from a terminal.

On macOS and Linux

Running a Python program from a terminal session is the same on Linux and macOS. You can use the terminal command cd, for *change directory*, to navigate through your filesystem in a terminal session. The command ls, for *list*, shows you all the nonhidden files that exist in the current directory.

Open a new terminal window and enter the following commands to run *hello_world.py*:

```
❶ ~$ cd Desktop/python_work/
❷ ~/Desktop/python_work$ ls
  hello_world.py
❸ ~/Desktop/python_work$ python hello_world.py
  Hello Python world!
```

At ❶ you use the `cd` command to navigate to the *python_work* folder, which is in the *Desktop* folder. Next, you use the `ls` command to make sure *hello_world.py* is in this folder ❷. Then you run the file using the command `python hello_world.py` ❸.

It's that simple. You just use the `python` (or `python3`) command to run Python programs.

TRY IT YOURSELF

The exercises in this chapter are exploratory in nature. Starting in Chapter 2, the challenges you'll solve will be based on what you've learned.

1-1. python.org: Explore the Python home page (*https://python.org/*) to find topics that interest you. As you become familiar with Python, different parts of the site will be more useful to you.

1-2. Hello World Typos: Open the *hello_world.py* file you just created. Make a typo somewhere in the line and run the program again. Can you make a typo that generates an error? Can you make sense of the error message? Can you make a typo that doesn't generate an error? Why do you think it didn't make an error?

1-3. Infinite Skills: If you had infinite programming skills, what would you build? You're about to learn how to program. If you have an end goal in mind, you'll have an immediate use for your new skills; now is a great time to draft descriptions of what you want to create. It's a good habit to keep an "ideas" notebook that you can refer to whenever you want to start a new project. Take a few minutes now to describe three programs you want to create.

Summary

In this chapter, you learned a bit about Python in general, and you installed Python on your system if it wasn't already there. You also installed a text editor to make it easier to write Python code. You ran snippets of Python code in a terminal session, and you ran your first program, *hello_world.py*. You probably learned a bit about troubleshooting as well.

In the next chapter, you'll learn about the different kinds of data you can work with in your Python programs, and you'll use variables as well.

2

VARIABLES AND
SIMPLE DATA TYPES

In this chapter you'll learn about the different kinds of data you can work with in your Python programs. You'll also learn how to use variables to represent data in your programs.

What Really Happens When You Run hello_world.py

Let's take a closer look at what Python does when you run *hello_world.py*. As it turns out, Python does a fair amount of work, even when it runs a simple program:

hello_world.py
```
print("Hello Python world!")
```

When you run this code, you should see this output:

```
Hello Python world!
```

When you run the file *hello_world.py*, the ending *.py* indicates that the file is a Python program. Your editor then runs the file through the *Python interpreter*, which reads through the program and determines what each word in the program means. For example, when the interpreter sees the word `print` followed by parentheses, it prints to the screen whatever is inside the parentheses.

As you write your programs, your editor highlights different parts of your program in different ways. For example, it recognizes that `print()` is the name of a function and displays that word in one color. It recognizes that `"Hello Python world!"` is not Python code and displays that phrase in a different color. This feature is called *syntax highlighting* and is quite useful as you start to write your own programs.

Variables

Let's try using a variable in *hello_world.py*. Add a new line at the beginning of the file, and modify the second line:

hello_world.py
```
message = "Hello Python world!"
print(message)
```

Run this program to see what happens. You should see the same output you saw previously:

```
Hello Python world!
```

We've added a *variable* named `message`. Every variable is connected to a *value*, which is the information associated with that variable. In this case the value is the `"Hello Python world!"` text.

Adding a variable makes a little more work for the Python interpreter. When it processes the first line, it associates the variable `message` with the `"Hello Python world!"` text. When it reaches the second line, it prints the value associated with `message` to the screen.

Let's expand on this program by modifying *hello_world.py* to print a second message. Add a blank line to *hello_world.py*, and then add two new lines of code:

```
message = "Hello Python world!"
print(message)

message = "Hello Python Crash Course world!"
print(message)
```

Now when you run *hello_world.py*, you should see two lines of output:

```
Hello Python world!
Hello Python Crash Course world!
```

You can change the value of a variable in your program at any time, and Python will always keep track of its current value.

Naming and Using Variables

When you're using variables in Python, you need to adhere to a few rules and guidelines. Breaking some of these rules will cause errors; other guidelines just help you write code that's easier to read and understand. Be sure to keep the following variable rules in mind:

- Variable names can contain only letters, numbers, and underscores. They can start with a letter or an underscore, but not with a number. For instance, you can call a variable *message_1* but not *1_message*.
- Spaces are not allowed in variable names, but underscores can be used to separate words in variable names. For example, *greeting_message* works, but *greeting message* will cause errors.
- Avoid using Python keywords and function names as variable names; that is, do not use words that Python has reserved for a particular programmatic purpose, such as the word print. (See "Python Keywords and Built-in Functions" on page 471.)
- Variable names should be short but descriptive. For example, *name* is better than *n*, *student_name* is better than *s_n*, and *name_length* is better than *length_of_persons_name*.
- Be careful when using the lowercase letter *l* and the uppercase letter *O* because they could be confused with the numbers *1* and *0*.

It can take some practice to learn how to create good variable names, especially as your programs become more interesting and complicated. As you write more programs and start to read through other people's code, you'll get better at coming up with meaningful names.

NOTE   *The Python variables you're using at this point should be lowercase. You won't get errors if you use uppercase letters, but uppercase letters in variable names have special meanings that we'll discuss in later chapters.*

Avoiding Name Errors When Using Variables

Every programmer makes mistakes, and most make mistakes every day. Although good programmers might create errors, they also know how to respond to those errors efficiently. Let's look at an error you're likely to make early on and learn how to fix it.

We'll write some code that generates an error on purpose. Enter the following code, including the misspelled word *mesage* shown in bold:

```
message = "Hello Python Crash Course reader!"
print(mesage)
```

When an error occurs in your program, the Python interpreter does its best to help you figure out where the problem is. The interpreter provides a traceback when a program cannot run successfully. A *traceback* is a record of where the interpreter ran into trouble when trying to execute your code. Here's an example of the traceback that Python provides after you've accidentally misspelled a variable's name:

```
Traceback (most recent call last):
❶   File "hello_world.py", line 2, in <module>
❷     print(mesage)
❸ NameError: name 'mesage' is not defined
```

The output at ❶ reports that an error occurs in line 2 of the file *hello_world.py*. The interpreter shows this line ❷ to help us spot the error quickly and tells us what kind of error it found ❸. In this case it found a *name error* and reports that the variable being printed, message, has not been defined. Python can't identify the variable name provided. A name error usually means we either forgot to set a variable's value before using it, or we made a spelling mistake when entering the variable's name.

Of course, in this example we omitted the letter *s* in the variable name message in the second line. The Python interpreter doesn't spellcheck your code, but it does ensure that variable names are spelled consistently. For example, watch what happens when we spell *message* incorrectly in another place in the code as well:

```
mesage = "Hello Python Crash Course reader!"
print(mesage)
```

In this case, the program runs successfully!

```
Hello Python Crash Course reader!
```

Programming languages are strict, but they disregard good and bad spelling. As a result, you don't need to consider English spelling and grammar rules when you're trying to create variable names and writing code.

Many programming errors are simple, single-character typos in one line of a program. If you're spending a long time searching for one of these errors, know that you're in good company. Many experienced and talented programmers spend hours hunting down these kinds of tiny errors. Try to laugh about it and move on, knowing it will happen frequently throughout your programming life.

Variables Are Labels

Variables are often described as boxes you can store values in. This idea can be helpful the first few times you use a variable, but it isn't an accurate way to describe how variables are represented internally in Python. It's much better to think of variables as labels that you can assign to values. You can also say that a variable references a certain value.

This distinction probably won't matter much in your initial programs, but it's worth learning earlier rather than later. At some point, you'll see unexpected behavior from a variable, and an accurate understanding of how variables work will help you identify what's happening in your code.

NOTE   *The best way to understand new programming concepts is to try using them in your programs. If you get stuck while working on an exercise in this book, try doing something else for a while. If you're still stuck, review the relevant part of that chapter. If you still need help, see the suggestions in Appendix C.*

TRY IT YOURSELF

Write a separate program to accomplish each of these exercises. Save each program with a filename that follows standard Python conventions, using lowercase letters and underscores, such as *simple_message.py* and *simple _messages.py*.

2-1. Simple Message: Assign a message to a variable, and then print that message.

2-2. Simple Messages: Assign a message to a variable, and print that message. Then change the value of the variable to a new message, and print the new message.

Strings

Because most programs define and gather some sort of data, and then do something useful with it, it helps to classify different types of data. The first data type we'll look at is the string. Strings are quite simple at first glance, but you can use them in many different ways.

A *string* is a series of characters. Anything inside quotes is considered a string in Python, and you can use single or double quotes around your strings like this:

```
"This is a string."
'This is also a string.'
```

This flexibility allows you to use quotes and apostrophes within your strings:

```
'I told my friend, "Python is my favorite language!"'
"The language 'Python' is named after Monty Python, not the snake."
"One of Python's strengths is its diverse and supportive community."
```

Let's explore some of the ways you can use strings.

Changing Case in a String with Methods

One of the simplest tasks you can do with strings is change the case of the words in a string. Look at the following code, and try to determine what's happening:

name.py
```
name = "ada lovelace"
print(name.title())
```

Save this file as *name.py*, and then run it. You should see this output:

```
Ada Lovelace
```

In this example, the variable name refers to the lowercase string "ada lovelace". The method title() appears after the variable in the print() call. A *method* is an action that Python can perform on a piece of data. The dot (.) after name in name.title() tells Python to make the title() method act on the variable name. Every method is followed by a set of parentheses, because methods often need additional information to do their work. That information is provided inside the parentheses. The title() function doesn't need any additional information, so its parentheses are empty.

The title() method changes each word to title case, where each word begins with a capital letter. This is useful because you'll often want to think of a name as a piece of information. For example, you might want your program to recognize the input values Ada, ADA, and ada as the same name, and display all of them as Ada.

Several other useful methods are available for dealing with case as well. For example, you can change a string to all uppercase or all lowercase letters like this:

```
name = "Ada Lovelace"
print(name.upper())
print(name.lower())
```

This will display the following:

```
ADA LOVELACE
ada lovelace
```

The lower() method is particularly useful for storing data. Many times you won't want to trust the capitalization that your users provide, so you'll convert strings to lowercase before storing them. Then when you want to display the information, you'll use the case that makes the most sense for each string.

Using Variables in Strings

In some situations, you'll want to use a variable's value inside a string. For example, you might want two variables to represent a first name and a last name respectively, and then want to combine those values to display someone's full name:

full_name.py

```
first_name = "ada"
last_name = "lovelace"
❶ full_name = f"{first_name} {last_name}"
print(full_name)
```

To insert a variable's value into a string, place the letter f immediately before the opening quotation mark ❶. Put braces around the name or names of any variable you want to use inside the string. Python will replace each variable with its value when the string is displayed.

These strings are called *f-strings*. The *f* is for *format*, because Python formats the string by replacing the name of any variable in braces with its value. The output from the previous code is:

```
ada lovelace
```

You can do a lot with f-strings. For example, you can use f-strings to compose complete messages using the information associated with a variable, as shown here:

```
first_name = "ada"
last_name = "lovelace"
full_name = f"{first_name} {last_name}"
❶ print(f"Hello, {full_name.title()}!")
```

The full name is used in a sentence that greets the user ❶, and the title() method changes the name to title case. This code returns a simple but nicely formatted greeting:

```
Hello, Ada Lovelace!
```

You can also use f-strings to compose a message, and then assign the entire message to a variable:

```
first_name = "ada"
last_name = "lovelace"
full_name = f"{first_name} {last_name}"
❶ message = f"Hello, {full_name.title()}!"
❷ print(message)
```

This code displays the message Hello, Ada Lovelace! as well, but by assigning the message to a variable ❶ we make the final print() call much simpler ❷.

NOTE *F-strings were first introduced in Python 3.6. If you're using Python 3.5 or earlier, you'll need to use the format() method rather than this f syntax. To use format(), list the variables you want to use in the string inside the parentheses following format. Each variable is referred to by a set of braces; the braces will be filled by the values listed in parentheses in the order provided:*

```
full_name = "{} {}".format(first_name, last_name)
```

Adding Whitespace to Strings with Tabs or Newlines

In programming, *whitespace* refers to any nonprinting character, such as spaces, tabs, and end-of-line symbols. You can use whitespace to organize your output so it's easier for users to read.

To add a tab to your text, use the character combination \t as shown at ❶:

```
>>> print("Python")
Python
❶ >>> print("\tPython")
    Python
```

To add a newline in a string, use the character combination \n:

```
>>> print("Languages:\nPython\nC\nJavaScript")
Languages:
Python
C
JavaScript
```

You can also combine tabs and newlines in a single string. The string "\n\t" tells Python to move to a new line, and start the next line with a tab. The following example shows how you can use a one-line string to generate four lines of output:

```
>>> print("Languages:\n\tPython\n\tC\n\tJavaScript")
Languages:
    Python
    C
    JavaScript
```

Newlines and tabs will be very useful in the next two chapters when you start to produce many lines of output from just a few lines of code.

Stripping Whitespace

Extra whitespace can be confusing in your programs. To programmers 'python' and 'python ' look pretty much the same. But to a program, they are two different strings. Python detects the extra space in 'python ' and considers it significant unless you tell it otherwise.

It's important to think about whitespace, because often you'll want to compare two strings to determine whether they are the same. For example, one important instance might involve checking people's usernames when they log in to a website. Extra whitespace can be confusing in much simpler situations as well. Fortunately, Python makes it easy to eliminate extraneous whitespace from data that people enter.

Python can look for extra whitespace on the right and left sides of a string. To ensure that no whitespace exists at the right end of a string, use the rstrip() method.

```
❶ >>> favorite_language = 'python '
❷ >>> favorite_language
  'python '
❸ >>> favorite_language.rstrip()
  'python'
❹ >>> favorite_language
  'python '
```

The value associated with favorite_language at ❶ contains extra whitespace at the end of the string. When you ask Python for this value in a terminal session, you can see the space at the end of the value ❷. When the rstrip() method acts on the variable favorite_language at ❸, this extra space is removed. However, it is only removed temporarily. If you ask for the value of favorite_language again, you can see that the string looks the same as when it was entered, including the extra whitespace ❹.

To remove the whitespace from the string permanently, you have to associate the stripped value with the variable name:

```
  >>> favorite_language = 'python '
❶ >>> favorite_language = favorite_language.rstrip()
  >>> favorite_language
  'python'
```

To remove the whitespace from the string, you strip the whitespace from the right side of the string and then associate this new value with the original variable, as shown at ❶. Changing a variable's value is done often in programming. This is how a variable's value can be updated as a program is executed or in response to user input.

You can also strip whitespace from the left side of a string using the lstrip() method, or from both sides at once using strip():

```
❶ >>> favorite_language = ' python '
❷ >>> favorite_language.rstrip()
  ' python'
❸ >>> favorite_language.lstrip()
  'python '
❹ >>> favorite_language.strip()
  'python'
```

In this example, we start with a value that has whitespace at the beginning and the end ❶. We then remove the extra space from the right side at ❷, from the left side at ❸, and from both sides at ❹. Experimenting with these stripping functions can help you become familiar with manipulating strings. In the real world, these stripping functions are used most often to clean up user input before it's stored in a program.

Avoiding Syntax Errors with Strings

One kind of error that you might see with some regularity is a syntax error. A *syntax error* occurs when Python doesn't recognize a section of your program as valid Python code. For example, if you use an apostrophe within single quotes, you'll produce an error. This happens because Python interprets everything between the first single quote and the apostrophe as a string. It then tries to interpret the rest of the text as Python code, which causes errors.

Here's how to use single and double quotes correctly. Save this program as *apostrophe.py* and then run it:

apostrophe.py
```
message = "One of Python's strengths is its diverse community."
print(message)
```

The apostrophe appears inside a set of double quotes, so the Python interpreter has no trouble reading the string correctly:

```
One of Python's strengths is its diverse community.
```

However, if you use single quotes, Python can't identify where the string should end:

```
message = 'One of Python's strengths is its diverse community.'
print(message)
```

You'll see the following output:

```
  File "apostrophe.py", line 1
    message = 'One of Python's strengths is its diverse community.'
                            ^❶
SyntaxError: invalid syntax
```

In the output you can see that the error occurs at ❶ right after the second single quote. This syntax error indicates that the interpreter doesn't recognize something in the code as valid Python code. Errors can come from a variety of sources, and I'll point out some common ones as they arise. You might see syntax errors often as you learn to write proper Python code. Syntax errors are also the least specific kind of error, so they can be difficult and frustrating to identify and correct. If you get stuck on a particularly stubborn error, see the suggestions in Appendix C.

NOTE *Your editor's syntax highlighting feature should help you spot some syntax errors quickly as you write your programs. If you see Python code highlighted as if it's English or English highlighted as if it's Python code, you probably have a mismatched quotation mark somewhere in your file.*

TRY IT YOURSELF

Save each of the following exercises as a separate file with a name like *name_cases.py*. If you get stuck, take a break or see the suggestions in Appendix C.

2-3. Personal Message: Use a variable to represent a person's name, and print a message to that person. Your message should be simple, such as, "Hello Eric, would you like to learn some Python today?"

2-4. Name Cases: Use a variable to represent a person's name, and then print that person's name in lowercase, uppercase, and title case.

2-5. Famous Quote: Find a quote from a famous person you admire. Print the quote and the name of its author. Your output should look something like the following, including the quotation marks:

> Albert Einstein once said, "A person who never made a mistake never tried anything new."

2-6. Famous Quote 2: Repeat Exercise 2-5, but this time, represent the famous person's name using a variable called famous_person. Then compose your message and represent it with a new variable called message. Print your message.

2-7. Stripping Names: Use a variable to represent a person's name, and include some whitespace characters at the beginning and end of the name. Make sure you use each character combination, "\t" and "\n", at least once.

Print the name once, so the whitespace around the name is displayed. Then print the name using each of the three stripping functions, lstrip(), rstrip(), and strip().

Numbers

Numbers are used quite often in programming to keep score in games, represent data in visualizations, store information in web applications, and so on. Python treats numbers in several different ways, depending on how they're being used. Let's first look at how Python manages integers, because they're the simplest to work with.

Integers

You can add (+), subtract (-), multiply (*), and divide (/) integers in Python.

```
>>> 2 + 3
5
>>> 3 - 2
1
>>> 2 * 3
6
>>> 3 / 2
1.5
```

In a terminal session, Python simply returns the result of the operation. Python uses two multiplication symbols to represent exponents:

```
>>> 3 ** 2
9
>>> 3 ** 3
27
>>> 10 ** 6
1000000
```

Python supports the order of operations too, so you can use multiple operations in one expression. You can also use parentheses to modify the order of operations so Python can evaluate your expression in the order you specify. For example:

```
>>> 2 + 3*4
14
>>> (2 + 3) * 4
20
```

The spacing in these examples has no effect on how Python evaluates the expressions; it simply helps you more quickly spot the operations that have priority when you're reading through the code.

Floats

Python calls any number with a decimal point a *float*. This term is used in most programming languages, and it refers to the fact that a decimal point can appear at any position in a number. Every programming language must be carefully designed to properly manage decimal numbers so numbers behave appropriately no matter where the decimal point appears.

For the most part, you can use decimals without worrying about how they behave. Simply enter the numbers you want to use, and Python will most likely do what you expect:

```
>>> 0.1 + 0.1
0.2
>>> 0.2 + 0.2
0.4
>>> 2 * 0.1
0.2
>>> 2 * 0.2
0.4
```

But be aware that you can sometimes get an arbitrary number of decimal places in your answer:

```
>>> 0.2 + 0.1
0.30000000000000004
>>> 3 * 0.1
0.30000000000000004
```

This happens in all languages and is of little concern. Python tries to find a way to represent the result as precisely as possible, which is sometimes difficult given how computers have to represent numbers internally. Just ignore the extra decimal places for now; you'll learn ways to deal with the extra places when you need to in the projects in Part II.

Integers and Floats

When you divide any two numbers, even if they are integers that result in a whole number, you'll always get a float:

```
>>> 4/2
2.0
```

If you mix an integer and a float in any other operation, you'll get a float as well:

```
>>> 1 + 2.0
3.0
>>> 2 * 3.0
6.0
>>> 3.0 ** 2
9.0
```

Python defaults to a float in any operation that uses a float, even if the output is a whole number.

Underscores in Numbers

When you're writing long numbers, you can group digits using underscores to make large numbers more readable:

```
>>> universe_age = 14_000_000_000
```

When you print a number that was defined using underscores, Python prints only the digits:

```
>>> print(universe_age)
14000000000
```

Python ignores the underscores when storing these kinds of values. Even if you don't group the digits in threes, the value will still be unaffected. To Python, 1000 is the same as 1_000, which is the same as 10_00. This feature works for integers and floats, but it's only available in Python 3.6 and later.

Multiple Assignment

You can assign values to more than one variable using just a single line. This can help shorten your programs and make them easier to read; you'll use this technique most often when initializing a set of numbers.

For example, here's how you can initialize the variables x, y, and z to zero:

```
>>> x, y, z = 0, 0, 0
```

You need to separate the variable names with commas, and do the same with the values, and Python will assign each value to its respectively positioned variable. As long as the number of values matches the number of variables, Python will match them up correctly.

Constants

A *constant* is like a variable whose value stays the same throughout the life of a program. Python doesn't have built-in constant types, but Python programmers use all capital letters to indicate a variable should be treated as a constant and never be changed:

```
MAX_CONNECTIONS = 5000
```

When you want to treat a variable as a constant in your code, make the name of the variable all capital letters.

Comments

Comments are an extremely useful feature in most programming languages. Everything you've written in your programs so far is Python code. As your programs become longer and more complicated, you should add notes within your programs that describe your overall approach to the problem you're solving. A *comment* allows you to write notes in English within your programs.

How Do You Write Comments?

In Python, the hash mark (#) indicates a comment. Anything following a hash mark in your code is ignored by the Python interpreter. For example:

comment.py
```
# Say hello to everyone.
print("Hello Python people!")
```

Python ignores the first line and executes the second line.

```
Hello Python people!
```

What Kind of Comments Should You Write?

The main reason to write comments is to explain what your code is supposed to do and how you are making it work. When you're in the middle of working on a project, you understand how all of the pieces fit together. But when you return to a project after some time away, you'll likely have forgotten some of the details. You can always study your code for a while and figure out how segments were supposed to work, but writing good comments can save you time by summarizing your overall approach in clear English.

If you want to become a professional programmer or collaborate with other programmers, you should write meaningful comments. Today, most software is written collaboratively, whether by a group of employees at one company or a group of people working together on an open source project. Skilled programmers expect to see comments in code, so it's best to start adding descriptive comments to your programs now. Writing clear, concise comments in your code is one of the most beneficial habits you can form as a new programmer.

When you're determining whether to write a comment, ask yourself if you had to consider several approaches before coming up with a reasonable way to make something work; if so, write a comment about your solution. It's much easier to delete extra comments later on than it is to go back and write comments for a sparsely commented program. From now on, I'll use comments in examples throughout this book to help explain sections of code.

The Zen of Python

Experienced Python programmers will encourage you to avoid complexity and aim for simplicity whenever possible. The Python community's philosophy is contained in "The Zen of Python" by Tim Peters. You can access this brief set of principles for writing good Python code by entering `import this` into your interpreter. I won't reproduce the entire "Zen of Python" here, but I'll share a few lines to help you understand why they should be important to you as a beginning Python programmer.

```
>>> import this
The Zen of Python, by Tim Peters
Beautiful is better than ugly.
```

Python programmers embrace the notion that code can be beautiful and elegant. In programming, people solve problems. Programmers have always respected well-designed, efficient, and even beautiful solutions to problems. As you learn more about Python and use it to write more code, someone might look over your shoulder one day and say, "Wow, that's some beautiful code!"

`Simple is better than complex.`

If you have a choice between a simple and a complex solution, and both work, use the simple solution. Your code will be easier to maintain, and it will be easier for you and others to build on that code later on.

`Complex is better than complicated.`

Real life is messy, and sometimes a simple solution to a problem is unattainable. In that case, use the simplest solution that works.

`Readability counts.`

Even when your code is complex, aim to make it readable. When you're working on a project that involves complex coding, focus on writing informative comments for that code.

`There should be one-- and preferably only one --obvious way to do it.`

If two Python programmers are asked to solve the same problem, they should come up with fairly compatible solutions. This is not to say there's no room for creativity in programming. On the contrary! But much of programming consists of using small, common approaches to simple situations within a larger, more creative project. The nuts and bolts of your programs should make sense to other Python programmers.

`Now is better than never.`

You could spend the rest of your life learning all the intricacies of Python and of programming in general, but then you'd never complete any projects. Don't try to write perfect code; write code that works, and then decide whether to improve your code for that project or move on to something new.

As you continue to the next chapter and start digging into more involved topics, try to keep this philosophy of simplicity and clarity in mind. Experienced programmers will respect your code more and will be happy to give you feedback and collaborate with you on interesting projects.

TRY IT YOURSELF

2-11. Zen of Python: Enter `import this` into a Python terminal session and skim through the additional principles.

Summary

In this chapter you learned to work with variables. You learned to use descriptive variable names and how to resolve name errors and syntax errors when they arise. You learned what strings are and how to display strings using lowercase, uppercase, and title case. You started using whitespace to organize output neatly, and you learned to strip unneeded whitespace from different parts of a string. You started working with integers and floats, and learned some of the ways you can work with numerical data. You also learned to write explanatory comments to make your code easier for you and others to read. Finally, you read about the philosophy of keeping your code as simple as possible, whenever possible.

In Chapter 3 you'll learn to store collections of information in data structures called *lists*. You'll learn to work through a list, manipulating any information in that list.

3

INTRODUCING LISTS

In this chapter and the next you'll learn what lists are and how to start working with the elements in a list. Lists allow you to store sets of information in one place, whether you have just a few items or millions of items. Lists are one of Python's most powerful features readily accessible to new programmers, and they tie together many important concepts in programming.

What Is a List?

A *list* is a collection of items in a particular order. You can make a list that includes the letters of the alphabet, the digits from 0–9, or the names of all the people in your family. You can put anything you want into a list, and the items in your list don't have to be related in any particular way. Because a list usually contains more than one element, it's a good idea to make the name of your list plural, such as letters, digits, or names.

In Python, square brackets ([]) indicate a list, and individual elements in the list are separated by commas. Here's a simple example of a list that contains a few kinds of bicycles:

bicycles.py
```
bicycles = ['trek', 'cannondale', 'redline', 'specialized']
print(bicycles)
```

If you ask Python to print a list, Python returns its representation of the list, including the square brackets:

```
['trek', 'cannondale', 'redline', 'specialized']
```

Because this isn't the output you want your users to see, let's learn how to access the individual items in a list.

Accessing Elements in a List

Lists are ordered collections, so you can access any element in a list by telling Python the position, or *index*, of the item desired. To access an element in a list, write the name of the list followed by the index of the item enclosed in square brackets.

For example, let's pull out the first bicycle in the list bicycles:

```
  bicycles = ['trek', 'cannondale', 'redline', 'specialized']
❶ print(bicycles[0])
```

The syntax for this is shown at ❶. When we ask for a single item from a list, Python returns just that element without square brackets:

```
trek
```

This is the result you want your users to see—clean, neatly formatted output.

You can also use the string methods from Chapter 2 on any element in this list. For example, you can format the element 'trek' more neatly by using the title() method:

```
bicycles = ['trek', 'cannondale', 'redline', 'specialized']
print(bicycles[0].title())
```

This example produces the same output as the preceding example except 'Trek' is capitalized.

Index Positions Start at 0, Not 1

Python considers the first item in a list to be at position 0, not position 1. This is true of most programming languages, and the reason has to do with how the list operations are implemented at a lower level. If you're receiving unexpected results, determine whether you are making a simple off-by-one error.

The second item in a list has an index of 1. Using this counting system, you can get any element you want from a list by subtracting one from its position in the list. For instance, to access the fourth item in a list, you request the item at index 3.

The following asks for the bicycles at index 1 and index 3:

```
bicycles = ['trek', 'cannondale', 'redline', 'specialized']
print(bicycles[1])
print(bicycles[3])
```

This code returns the second and fourth bicycles in the list:

```
cannondale
specialized
```

Python has a special syntax for accessing the last element in a list. By asking for the item at index -1, Python always returns the last item in the list:

```
bicycles = ['trek', 'cannondale', 'redline', 'specialized']
print(bicycles[-1])
```

This code returns the value 'specialized'. This syntax is quite useful, because you'll often want to access the last items in a list without knowing exactly how long the list is. This convention extends to other negative index values as well. The index -2 returns the second item from the end of the list, the index -3 returns the third item from the end, and so forth.

Using Individual Values from a List

You can use individual values from a list just as you would any other variable. For example, you can use f-strings to create a message based on a value from a list.

Let's try pulling the first bicycle from the list and composing a message using that value.

```
bicycles = ['trek', 'cannondale', 'redline', 'specialized']
❶ message = f"My first bicycle was a {bicycles[0].title()}."

print(message)
```

At ❶, we build a sentence using the value at `bicycles[0]` and assign it to the variable `message`. The output is a simple sentence about the first bicycle in the list:

```
My first bicycle was a Trek.
```

TRY IT YOURSELF

Try these short programs to get some firsthand experience with Python's lists. You might want to create a new folder for each chapter's exercises to keep them organized.

3-1. Names: Store the names of a few of your friends in a list called names. Print each person's name by accessing each element in the list, one at a time.

3-2. Greetings: Start with the list you used in Exercise 3-1, but instead of just printing each person's name, print a message to them. The text of each message should be the same, but each message should be personalized with the person's name.

3-3. Your Own List: Think of your favorite mode of transportation, such as a motorcycle or a car, and make a list that stores several examples. Use your list to print a series of statements about these items, such as "I would like to own a Honda motorcycle."

Changing, Adding, and Removing Elements

Most lists you create will be dynamic, meaning you'll build a list and then add and remove elements from it as your program runs its course. For example, you might create a game in which a player has to shoot aliens out of the sky. You could store the initial set of aliens in a list and then remove an alien from the list each time one is shot down. Each time a new alien appears on the screen, you add it to the list. Your list of aliens will increase and decrease in length throughout the course of the game.

Modifying Elements in a List

The syntax for modifying an element is similar to the syntax for accessing an element in a list. To change an element, use the name of the list followed by the index of the element you want to change, and then provide the new value you want that item to have.

For example, let's say we have a list of motorcycles, and the first item in the list is 'honda'. How would we change the value of this first item?

motorcycles.py ❶
```
motorcycles = ['honda', 'yamaha', 'suzuki']
print(motorcycles)
```

❷
```
motorcycles[0] = 'ducati'
print(motorcycles)
```

The code at ❶ defines the original list, with 'honda' as the first element. The code at ❷ changes the value of the first item to 'ducati'. The output shows that the first item has indeed been changed, and the rest of the list stays the same:

```
['honda', 'yamaha', 'suzuki']
['ducati', 'yamaha', 'suzuki']
```

You can change the value of any item in a list, not just the first item.

Adding Elements to a List

You might want to add a new element to a list for many reasons. For example, you might want to make new aliens appear in a game, add new data to a visualization, or add new registered users to a website you've built. Python provides several ways to add new data to existing lists.

Appending Elements to the End of a List

The simplest way to add a new element to a list is to *append* the item to the list. When you append an item to a list, the new element is added to the end of the list. Using the same list we had in the previous example, we'll add the new element 'ducati' to the end of the list:

```
motorcycles = ['honda', 'yamaha', 'suzuki']
print(motorcycles)
```

❶
```
motorcycles.append('ducati')
print(motorcycles)
```

The append() method at ❶ adds 'ducati' to the end of the list without affecting any of the other elements in the list:

```
['honda', 'yamaha', 'suzuki']
['honda', 'yamaha', 'suzuki', 'ducati']
```

The append() method makes it easy to build lists dynamically. For example, you can start with an empty list and then add items to the list using a series of append() calls. Using an empty list, let's add the elements 'honda', 'yamaha', and 'suzuki' to the list:

```
motorcycles = []

motorcycles.append('honda')
motorcycles.append('yamaha')
motorcycles.append('suzuki')

print(motorcycles)
```

The resulting list looks exactly the same as the lists in the previous examples:

```
['honda', 'yamaha', 'suzuki']
```

Building lists this way is very common, because you often won't know the data your users want to store in a program until after the program is running. To put your users in control, start by defining an empty list that will hold the users' values. Then append each new value provided to the list you just created.

Inserting Elements into a List

You can add a new element at any position in your list by using the insert() method. You do this by specifying the index of the new element and the value of the new item.

```
motorcycles = ['honda', 'yamaha', 'suzuki']

❶ motorcycles.insert(0, 'ducati')
print(motorcycles)
```

In this example, the code at ❶ inserts the value 'ducati' at the beginning of the list. The insert() method opens a space at position 0 and stores the value 'ducati' at that location. This operation shifts every other value in the list one position to the right:

```
['ducati', 'honda', 'yamaha', 'suzuki']
```

Removing Elements from a List

Often, you'll want to remove an item or a set of items from a list. For example, when a player shoots down an alien from the sky, you'll most likely want to remove it from the list of active aliens. Or when a user decides to cancel their account on a web application you created, you'll want to remove that user from the list of active users. You can remove an item according to its position in the list or according to its value.

Removing an Item Using the del Statement

If you know the position of the item you want to remove from a list, you can use the del statement.

```
motorcycles = ['honda', 'yamaha', 'suzuki']
print(motorcycles)
```

❶ `del motorcycles[0]`
```
print(motorcycles)
```

The code at ❶ uses del to remove the first item, 'honda', from the list of motorcycles:

```
['honda', 'yamaha', 'suzuki']
['yamaha', 'suzuki']
```

You can remove an item from any position in a list using the del statement if you know its index. For example, here's how to remove the second item, 'yamaha', in the list:

```
motorcycles = ['honda', 'yamaha', 'suzuki']
print(motorcycles)

del motorcycles[1]
print(motorcycles)
```

The second motorcycle is deleted from the list:

```
['honda', 'yamaha', 'suzuki']
['honda', 'suzuki']
```

In both examples, you can no longer access the value that was removed from the list after the del statement is used.

Removing an Item Using the pop() Method

Sometimes you'll want to use the value of an item after you remove it from a list. For example, you might want to get the *x* and *y* position of an alien that was just shot down, so you can draw an explosion at that position. In a web application, you might want to remove a user from a list of active members and then add that user to a list of inactive members.

The pop() method removes the last item in a list, but it lets you work with that item after removing it. The term *pop* comes from thinking of a list as a stack of items and popping one item off the top of the stack. In this analogy, the top of a stack corresponds to the end of a list.

Let's pop a motorcycle from the list of motorcycles:

```
❶ motorcycles = ['honda', 'yamaha', 'suzuki']
  print(motorcycles)

❷ popped_motorcycle = motorcycles.pop()
❸ print(motorcycles)
❹ print(popped_motorcycle)
```

We start by defining and printing the list motorcycles at ❶. At ❷ we pop a value from the list and store that value in the variable popped_motorcycle. We print the list at ❸ to show that a value has been removed from the list. Then we print the popped value at ❹ to prove that we still have access to the value that was removed.

The output shows that the value 'suzuki' was removed from the end of the list and is now assigned to the variable popped_motorcycle:

```
['honda', 'yamaha', 'suzuki']
['honda', 'yamaha']
suzuki
```

How might this pop() method be useful? Imagine that the motorcycles in the list are stored in chronological order according to when we owned them. If this is the case, we can use the pop() method to print a statement about the last motorcycle we bought:

```
motorcycles = ['honda', 'yamaha', 'suzuki']

last_owned = motorcycles.pop()
print(f"The last motorcycle I owned was a {last_owned.title()}.")
```

The output is a simple sentence about the most recent motorcycle we owned:

```
The last motorcycle I owned was a Suzuki.
```

Popping Items from any Position in a List

You can use pop() to remove an item from any position in a list by including the index of the item you want to remove in parentheses.

```
  motorcycles = ['honda', 'yamaha', 'suzuki']

❶ first_owned = motorcycles.pop(0)
❷ print(f"The first motorcycle I owned was a {first_owned.title()}.")
```

We start by popping the first motorcycle in the list at ❶, and then we print a message about that motorcycle at ❷. The output is a simple sentence describing the first motorcycle I ever owned:

```
The first motorcycle I owned was a Honda.
```

Remember that each time you use pop(), the item you work with is no longer stored in the list.

If you're unsure whether to use the del statement or the pop() method, here's a simple way to decide: when you want to delete an item from a list and not use that item in any way, use the del statement; if you want to use an item as you remove it, use the pop() method.

Removing an Item by Value

Sometimes you won't know the position of the value you want to remove from a list. If you only know the value of the item you want to remove, you can use the remove() method.

For example, let's say we want to remove the value 'ducati' from the list of motorcycles.

```
motorcycles = ['honda', 'yamaha', 'suzuki', 'ducati']
print(motorcycles)
```

```
❶ motorcycles.remove('ducati')
  print(motorcycles)
```

The code at ❶ tells Python to figure out where 'ducati' appears in the list and remove that element:

```
['honda', 'yamaha', 'suzuki', 'ducati']
['honda', 'yamaha', 'suzuki']
```

You can also use the remove() method to work with a value that's being removed from a list. Let's remove the value 'ducati' and print a reason for removing it from the list:

```
❶ motorcycles = ['honda', 'yamaha', 'suzuki', 'ducati']
  print(motorcycles)

❷ too_expensive = 'ducati'
❸ motorcycles.remove(too_expensive)
  print(motorcycles)
❹ print(f"\nA {too_expensive.title()} is too expensive for me.")
```

After defining the list at ❶, we assign the value 'ducati' to a variable called too_expensive ❷. We then use this variable to tell Python which value to remove from the list at ❸. At ❹ the value 'ducati' has been removed

from the list but is still accessible through the variable too_expensive, allowing us to print a statement about why we removed 'ducati' from the list of
motorcycles:

```
['honda', 'yamaha', 'suzuki', 'ducati']
['honda', 'yamaha', 'suzuki']

A Ducati is too expensive for me.
```

NOTE   *The remove() method deletes only the first occurrence of the value you specify. If there's
a possibility the value appears more than once in the list, you'll need to use a loop
to make sure all occurrences of the value are removed. You'll learn how to do this in
Chapter 7.*

TRY IT YOURSELF

The following exercises are a bit more complex than those in Chapter 2, but
they give you an opportunity to use lists in all of the ways described.

3-4. Guest List: If you could invite anyone, living or deceased, to dinner, who
would you invite? Make a list that includes at least three people you'd like to
invite to dinner. Then use your list to print a message to each person, inviting
them to dinner.

3-5. Changing Guest List: You just heard that one of your guests can't make the
dinner, so you need to send out a new set of invitations. You'll have to think of
someone else to invite.

- Start with your program from Exercise 3-4. Add a print() call at the end
  of your program stating the name of the guest who can't make it.

- Modify your list, replacing the name of the guest who can't make it with
  the name of the new person you are inviting.

- Print a second set of invitation messages, one for each person who is still
  in your list.

3-6. More Guests: You just found a bigger dinner table, so now more space is
available. Think of three more guests to invite to dinner.

- Start with your program from Exercise 3-4 or Exercise 3-5. Add a print()
  call to the end of your program informing people that you found a bigger
  dinner table.

- Use insert() to add one new guest to the beginning of your list.

- Use insert() to add one new guest to the middle of your list.

- Use append() to add one new guest to the end of your list.

- Print a new set of invitation messages, one for each person in your list.

3-7. Shrinking Guest List: You just found out that your new dinner table won't arrive in time for the dinner, and you have space for only two guests.

- Start with your program from Exercise 3-6. Add a new line that prints a message saying that you can invite only two people for dinner.
- Use pop() to remove guests from your list one at a time until only two names remain in your list. Each time you pop a name from your list, print a message to that person letting them know you're sorry you can't invite them to dinner.
- Print a message to each of the two people still on your list, letting them know they're still invited.
- Use del to remove the last two names from your list, so you have an empty list. Print your list to make sure you actually have an empty list at the end of your program.

Organizing a List

Often, your lists will be created in an unpredictable order, because you can't always control the order in which your users provide their data. Although this is unavoidable in most circumstances, you'll frequently want to present your information in a particular order. Sometimes you'll want to preserve the original order of your list, and other times you'll want to change the original order. Python provides a number of different ways to organize your lists, depending on the situation.

Sorting a List Permanently with the sort() Method

Python's sort() method makes it relatively easy to sort a list. Imagine we have a list of cars and want to change the order of the list to store them alphabetically. To keep the task simple, let's assume that all the values in the list are lowercase.

cars.py

```
cars = ['bmw', 'audi', 'toyota', 'subaru']
❶ cars.sort()
print(cars)
```

The sort() method, shown at ❶, changes the order of the list permanently. The cars are now in alphabetical order, and we can never revert to the original order:

```
['audi', 'bmw', 'subaru', 'toyota']
```

You can also sort this list in reverse alphabetical order by passing the argument reverse=True to the sort() method. The following example sorts the list of cars in reverse alphabetical order:

```
cars = ['bmw', 'audi', 'toyota', 'subaru']
cars.sort(reverse=True)
print(cars)
```

Again, the order of the list is permanently changed:

```
['toyota', 'subaru', 'bmw', 'audi']
```

Sorting a List Temporarily with the sorted() Function

To maintain the original order of a list but present it in a sorted order, you can use the sorted() function. The sorted() function lets you display your list in a particular order but doesn't affect the actual order of the list.

Let's try this function on the list of cars.

```
cars = ['bmw', 'audi', 'toyota', 'subaru']

❶ print("Here is the original list:")
print(cars)

❷ print("\nHere is the sorted list:")
print(sorted(cars))

❸ print("\nHere is the original list again:")
print(cars)
```

We first print the list in its original order at ❶ and then in alphabetical order at ❷. After the list is displayed in the new order, we show that the list is still stored in its original order at ❸.

```
Here is the original list:
['bmw', 'audi', 'toyota', 'subaru']

Here is the sorted list:
['audi', 'bmw', 'subaru', 'toyota']

❹ Here is the original list again:
['bmw', 'audi', 'toyota', 'subaru']
```

Notice that the list still exists in its original order at ❹ after the sorted() function has been used. The sorted() function can also accept a reverse=True argument if you want to display a list in reverse alphabetical order.

NOTE *Sorting a list alphabetically is a bit more complicated when all the values are not in lowercase. There are several ways to interpret capital letters when determining a sort order, and specifying the exact order can be more complex than we want to deal with at this time. However, most approaches to sorting will build directly on what you learned in this section.*

Printing a List in Reverse Order

To reverse the original order of a list, you can use the reverse() method. If we originally stored the list of cars in chronological order according to when we owned them, we could easily rearrange the list into reverse chronological order:

```
cars = ['bmw', 'audi', 'toyota', 'subaru']
print(cars)

cars.reverse()
print(cars)
```

Notice that reverse() doesn't sort backward alphabetically; it simply reverses the order of the list:

```
['bmw', 'audi', 'toyota', 'subaru']
['subaru', 'toyota', 'audi', 'bmw']
```

The reverse() method changes the order of a list permanently, but you can revert to the original order anytime by applying reverse() to the same list a second time.

Finding the Length of a List

You can quickly find the length of a list by using the len() function. The list in this example has four items, so its length is 4:

```
>>> cars = ['bmw', 'audi', 'toyota', 'subaru']
>>> len(cars)
4
```

You'll find len() useful when you need to identify the number of aliens that still need to be shot down in a game, determine the amount of data you have to manage in a visualization, or figure out the number of registered users on a website, among other tasks.

NOTE *Python counts the items in a list starting with one, so you shouldn't run into any off-by-one errors when determining the length of a list.*

3-8. Seeing the World: Think of at least five places in the world you'd like to visit.

- Store the locations in a list. Make sure the list is not in alphabetical order.

- Print your list in its original order. Don't worry about printing the list neatly, just print it as a raw Python list.

- Use sorted() to print your list in alphabetical order without modifying the actual list.

- Show that your list is still in its original order by printing it.

- Use sorted() to print your list in reverse alphabetical order without changing the order of the original list.

- Show that your list is still in its original order by printing it again.

- Use reverse() to change the order of your list. Print the list to show that its order has changed.

- Use reverse() to change the order of your list again. Print the list to show it's back to its original order.

- Use sort() to change your list so it's stored in alphabetical order. Print the list to show that its order has been changed.

- Use sort() to change your list so it's stored in reverse alphabetical order. Print the list to show that its order has changed.

3-9. Dinner Guests: Working with one of the programs from Exercises 3-4 through 3-7 (page 42), use len() to print a message indicating the number of people you are inviting to dinner.

3-10. Every Function: Think of something you could store in a list. For example, you could make a list of mountains, rivers, countries, cities, languages, or anything else you'd like. Write a program that creates a list containing these items and then uses each function introduced in this chapter at least once.

Avoiding Index Errors When Working with Lists

One type of error is common to see when you're working with lists for the first time. Let's say you have a list with three items, and you ask for the fourth item:

motorcycles.py
```
motorcycles = ['honda', 'yamaha', 'suzuki']
print(motorcycles[3])
```

This example results in an *index error*:

```
Traceback (most recent call last):
  File "motorcycles.py", line 2, in <module>
    print(motorcycles[3])
IndexError: list index out of range
```

Python attempts to give you the item at index 3. But when it searches the list, no item in motorcycles has an index of 3. Because of the off-by-one nature of indexing in lists, this error is typical. People think the third item is item number 3, because they start counting at 1. But in Python the third item is number 2, because it starts indexing at 0.

An index error means Python can't find an item at the index you requested. If an index error occurs in your program, try adjusting the index you're asking for by one. Then run the program again to see if the results are correct.

Keep in mind that whenever you want to access the last item in a list you use the index -1. This will always work, even if your list has changed size since the last time you accessed it:

```
motorcycles = ['honda', 'yamaha', 'suzuki']
print(motorcycles[-1])
```

The index -1 always returns the last item in a list, in this case the value 'suzuki':

```
'suzuki'
```

The only time this approach will cause an error is when you request the last item from an empty list:

```
motorcycles = []
print(motorcycles[-1])
```

No items are in motorcycles, so Python returns another index error:

```
Traceback (most recent call last):
  File "motorcyles.py", line 3, in <module>
    print(motorcycles[-1])
IndexError: list index out of range
```

NOTE *If an index error occurs and you can't figure out how to resolve it, try printing your list or just printing the length of your list. Your list might look much different than you thought it did, especially if it has been managed dynamically by your program. Seeing the actual list, or the exact number of items in your list, can help you sort out such logical errors.*

Summary

In this chapter you learned what lists are and how to work with the individual items in a list. You learned how to define a list and how to add and remove elements. You learned to sort lists permanently and temporarily for display purposes. You also learned how to find the length of a list and how to avoid index errors when you're working with lists.

In Chapter 4 you'll learn how to work with items in a list more efficiently. By looping through each item in a list using just a few lines of code you'll be able to work efficiently, even when your list contains thousands or millions of items.

4

WORKING WITH LISTS

In Chapter 3 you learned how to make a simple list, and you learned to work with the individual elements in a list. In this chapter you'll learn how to *loop* through an entire list using just a few lines of code regardless of how long the list is. Looping allows you to take the same action, or set of actions, with every item in a list. As a result, you'll be able to work efficiently with lists of any length, including those with thousands or even millions of items.

Looping Through an Entire List

You'll often want to run through all entries in a list, performing the same task with each item. For example, in a game you might want to move every element on the screen by the same amount, or in a list of numbers you might want to perform the same statistical operation on every element. Or perhaps you'll want to display each headline from a list of articles on a website. When you want to do the same action with every item in a list, you can use Python's for loop.

Let's say we have a list of magicians' names, and we want to print out each name in the list. We could do this by retrieving each name from the list individually, but this approach could cause several problems. For one, it would be repetitive to do this with a long list of names. Also, we'd have to change our code each time the list's length changed. A for loop avoids both of these issues by letting Python manage these issues internally.

Let's use a for loop to print out each name in a list of magicians:

magicians.py
```
❶ magicians = ['alice', 'david', 'carolina']
❷ for magician in magicians:
❸     print(magician)
```

We begin by defining a list at ❶, just as we did in Chapter 3. At ❷, we define a for loop. This line tells Python to pull a name from the list magicians, and associate it with the variable magician. At ❸ we tell Python to print the name that's just been assigned to magician. Python then repeats lines ❷ and ❸, once for each name in the list. It might help to read this code as "For every magician in the list of magicians, print the magician's name." The output is a simple printout of each name in the list:

```
alice
david
carolina
```

A Closer Look at Looping

The concept of looping is important because it's one of the most common ways a computer automates repetitive tasks. For example, in a simple loop like we used in *magicians.py*, Python initially reads the first line of the loop:

```
for magician in magicians:
```

This line tells Python to retrieve the first value from the list magicians and associate it with the variable magician. This first value is 'alice'. Python then reads the next line:

```
    print(magician)
```

Python prints the current value of magician, which is still 'alice'. Because the list contains more values, Python returns to the first line of the loop:

```
for magician in magicians:
```

Python retrieves the next name in the list, 'david', and associates that value with the variable magician. Python then executes the line:

```
    print(magician)
```

Python prints the current value of `magician` again, which is now `'david'`. Python repeats the entire loop once more with the last value in the list, `'carolina'`. Because no more values are in the list, Python moves on to the next line in the program. In this case nothing comes after the `for` loop, so the program simply ends.

When you're using loops for the first time, keep in mind that the set of steps is repeated once for each item in the list, no matter how many items are in the list. If you have a million items in your list, Python repeats these steps a million times—and usually very quickly.

Also keep in mind when writing your own `for` loops that you can choose any name you want for the temporary variable that will be associated with each value in the list. However, it's helpful to choose a meaningful name that represents a single item from the list. For example, here's a good way to start a `for` loop for a list of cats, a list of dogs, and a general list of items:

```
for cat in cats:
for dog in dogs:
for item in list_of_items:
```

These naming conventions can help you follow the action being done on each item within a `for` loop. Using singular and plural names can help you identify whether a section of code is working with a single element from the list or the entire list.

Doing More Work Within a for Loop

You can do just about anything with each item in a `for` loop. Let's build on the previous example by printing a message to each magician, telling them that they performed a great trick:

magicians.py
```
magicians = ['alice', 'david', 'carolina']
for magician in magicians:
❶    print(f"{magician.title()}, that was a great trick!")
```

The only difference in this code is at ❶ where we compose a message to each magician, starting with that magician's name. The first time through the loop the value of magician is `'alice'`, so Python starts the first message with the name `'Alice'`. The second time through the message will begin with `'David'`, and the third time through the message will begin with `'Carolina'`.

The output shows a personalized message for each magician in the list:

```
Alice, that was a great trick!
David, that was a great trick!
Carolina, that was a great trick!
```

You can also write as many lines of code as you like in the `for` loop. Every indented line following the line `for magician in magicians` is considered *inside the loop*, and each indented line is executed once for each value in the list. Therefore, you can do as much work as you like with each value in the list.

Let's add a second line to our message, telling each magician that we're looking forward to their next trick:

```
magicians = ['alice', 'david', 'carolina']
for magician in magicians:
    print(f"{magician.title()}, that was a great trick!")
❶    print(f"I can't wait to see your next trick, {magician.title()}.\n")
```

Because we have indented both calls to print(), each line will be executed once for every magician in the list. The newline ("\n") in the second print() call ❶ inserts a blank line after each pass through the loop. This creates a set of messages that are neatly grouped for each person in the list:

```
Alice, that was a great trick!
I can't wait to see your next trick, Alice.

David, that was a great trick!
I can't wait to see your next trick, David.

Carolina, that was a great trick!
I can't wait to see your next trick, Carolina.
```

You can use as many lines as you like in your for loops. In practice you'll often find it useful to do a number of different operations with each item in a list when you use a for loop.

Doing Something After a for Loop

What happens once a for loop has finished executing? Usually, you'll want to summarize a block of output or move on to other work that your program must accomplish.

Any lines of code after the for loop that are not indented are executed once without repetition. Let's write a thank you to the group of magicians as a whole, thanking them for putting on an excellent show. To display this group message after all of the individual messages have been printed, we place the thank you message after the for loop without indentation:

```
magicians = ['alice', 'david', 'carolina']
for magician in magicians:
    print(f"{magician.title()}, that was a great trick!")
    print(f"I can't wait to see your next trick, {magician.title()}.\n")

❶ print("Thank you, everyone. That was a great magic show!")
```

The first two calls to print() are repeated once for each magician in the list, as you saw earlier. However, because the line at ❶ is not indented, it's printed only once:

```
Alice, that was a great trick!
I can't wait to see your next trick, Alice.

David, that was a great trick!
I can't wait to see your next trick, David.

Carolina, that was a great trick!
I can't wait to see your next trick, Carolina.

Thank you, everyone. That was a great magic show!
```

When you're processing data using a for loop, you'll find that this is a good way to summarize an operation that was performed on an entire data set. For example, you might use a for loop to initialize a game by running through a list of characters and displaying each character on the screen. You might then write some additional code after this loop that displays a *Play Now* button after all the characters have been drawn to the screen.

Avoiding Indentation Errors

Python uses indentation to determine how a line, or group of lines, is related to the rest of the program. In the previous examples, the lines that printed messages to individual magicians were part of the for loop because they were indented. Python's use of indentation makes code very easy to read. Basically, it uses whitespace to force you to write neatly formatted code with a clear visual structure. In longer Python programs, you'll notice blocks of code indented at a few different levels. These indentation levels help you gain a general sense of the overall program's organization.

As you begin to write code that relies on proper indentation, you'll need to watch for a few common *indentation errors*. For example, people sometimes indent lines of code that don't need to be indented or forget to indent lines that need to be indented. Seeing examples of these errors now will help you avoid them in the future and correct them when they do appear in your own programs.

Let's examine some of the more common indentation errors.

Forgetting to Indent

Always indent the line after the for statement in a loop. If you forget, Python will remind you:

magicians.py
```
magicians = ['alice', 'david', 'carolina']
for magician in magicians:
❶ print(magician)
```

The call to print() ❶ should be indented, but it's not. When Python expects an indented block and doesn't find one, it lets you know which line it had a problem with.

```
File "magicians.py", line 3
    print(magician)
        ^
IndentationError: expected an indented block
```

You can usually resolve this kind of indentation error by indenting the line or lines immediately after the for statement.

Forgetting to Indent Additional Lines

Sometimes your loop will run without any errors but won't produce the expected result. This can happen when you're trying to do several tasks in a loop and you forget to indent some of its lines.

For example, this is what happens when we forget to indent the second line in the loop that tells each magician we're looking forward to their next trick:

```
magicians = ['alice', 'david', 'carolina']
for magician in magicians:
    print(f"{magician.title()}, that was a great trick!")
❶ print(f"I can't wait to see your next trick, {magician.title()}.\n")
```

The call to print() ❶ is supposed to be indented, but because Python finds at least one indented line after the for statement, it doesn't report an error. As a result, the first print() call is executed once for each name in the list because it is indented. The second print() call is not indented, so it is executed only once after the loop has finished running. Because the final value associated with magician is 'carolina', she is the only one who receives the "looking forward to the next trick" message:

```
Alice, that was a great trick!
David, that was a great trick!
Carolina, that was a great trick!
I can't wait to see your next trick, Carolina.
```

This is a *logical error*. The syntax is valid Python code, but the code does not produce the desired result because a problem occurs in its logic. If you expect to see a certain action repeated once for each item in a list and it's executed only once, determine whether you need to simply indent a line or a group of lines.

Indenting Unnecessarily

If you accidentally indent a line that doesn't need to be indented, Python informs you about the unexpected indent:

hello_world.py

❶
```
message = "Hello Python world!"
    print(message)
```

We don't need to indent the print() call ❶, because it isn't part of a loop; hence, Python reports that error:

```
File "hello_world.py", line 2
    print(message)
    ^
IndentationError: unexpected indent
```

You can avoid unexpected indentation errors by indenting only when you have a specific reason to do so. In the programs you're writing at this point, the only lines you should indent are the actions you want to repeat for each item in a for loop.

Indenting Unnecessarily After the Loop

If you accidentally indent code that should run after a loop has finished, that code will be repeated once for each item in the list. Sometimes this prompts Python to report an error, but often this will result in a logical error.

For example, let's see what happens when we accidentally indent the line that thanked the magicians as a group for putting on a good show:

magicians.py

❶
```
magicians = ['alice', 'david', 'carolina']
for magician in magicians:
    print(f"{magician.title()}, that was a great trick!")
    print(f"I can't wait to see your next trick, {magician.title()}.\n")

    print("Thank you everyone, that was a great magic show!")
```

Because the line at ❶ is indented, it's printed once for each person in the list, as shown here:

```
Alice, that was a great trick!
I can't wait to see your next trick, Alice.

Thank you everyone, that was a great magic show!
David, that was a great trick!
I can't wait to see your next trick, David.

Thank you everyone, that was a great magic show!
Carolina, that was a great trick!
I can't wait to see your next trick, Carolina.

Thank you everyone, that was a great magic show!
```

This is another logical error, similar to the one in "Forgetting to Indent Additional Lines" on page 54. Because Python doesn't know what you're trying to accomplish with your code, it will run all code that is written in valid syntax. If an action is repeated many times when it should be executed only once, you probably need to unindent the code for that action.

Forgetting the Colon

The colon at the end of a for statement tells Python to interpret the next line as the start of a loop.

```
magicians = ['alice', 'david', 'carolina']
❶ for magician in magicians
      print(magician)
```

If you accidentally forget the colon, as shown at ❶, you'll get a syntax error because Python doesn't know what you're trying to do. Although this is an easy error to fix, it's not always an easy error to find. You'd be surprised by the amount of time programmers spend hunting down single-character errors like this. Such errors are difficult to find because we often just see what we expect to see.

TRY IT YOURSELF

4-1. Pizzas: Think of at least three kinds of your favorite pizza. Store these pizza names in a list, and then use a for loop to print the name of each pizza.

- Modify your for loop to print a sentence using the name of the pizza instead of printing just the name of the pizza. For each pizza you should have one line of output containing a simple statement like *I like pepperoni pizza*.

- Add a line at the end of your program, outside the for loop, that states how much you like pizza. The output should consist of three or more lines about the kinds of pizza you like and then an additional sentence, such as *I really love pizza!*

4-2. Animals: Think of at least three different animals that have a common characteristic. Store the names of these animals in a list, and then use a for loop to print out the name of each animal.

- Modify your program to print a statement about each animal, such as *A dog would make a great pet*.

- Add a line at the end of your program stating what these animals have in common. You could print a sentence such as *Any of these animals would make a great pet!*

Making Numerical Lists

Many reasons exist to store a set of numbers. For example, you'll need to keep track of the positions of each character in a game, and you might want to keep track of a player's high scores as well. In data visualizations, you'll almost always work with sets of numbers, such as temperatures, distances, population sizes, or latitude and longitude values, among other types of numerical sets.

Lists are ideal for storing sets of numbers, and Python provides a variety of tools to help you work efficiently with lists of numbers. Once you understand how to use these tools effectively, your code will work well even when your lists contain millions of items.

Using the range() Function

Python's range() function makes it easy to generate a series of numbers. For example, you can use the range() function to print a series of numbers like this:

*first
_numbers.py*

```
for value in range(1, 5):
    print(value)
```

Although this code looks like it should print the numbers from 1 to 5, it doesn't print the number 5:

```
1
2
3
4
```

In this example, range() prints only the numbers 1 through 4. This is another result of the off-by-one behavior you'll see often in programming languages. The range() function causes Python to start counting at the first value you give it, and it stops when it reaches the second value you provide. Because it stops at that second value, the output never contains the end value, which would have been 5 in this case.

To print the numbers from 1 to 5, you would use range(1, 6):

```
for value in range(1, 6):
    print(value)
```

This time the output starts at 1 and ends at 5:

```
1
2
3
4
5
```

If your output is different than what you expect when you're using range(), try adjusting your end value by 1.

You can also pass range() only one argument, and it will start the sequence of numbers at 0. For example, range(6) would return the numbers from 0 through 5.

Using range() to Make a List of Numbers

If you want to make a list of numbers, you can convert the results of range() directly into a list using the list() function. When you wrap list() around a call to the range() function, the output will be a list of numbers.

In the example in the previous section, we simply printed out a series of numbers. We can use list() to convert that same set of numbers into a list:

```
numbers = list(range(1, 6))
print(numbers)
```

And this is the result:

```
[1, 2, 3, 4, 5]
```

We can also use the range() function to tell Python to skip numbers in a given range. If you pass a third argument to range(), Python uses that value as a step size when generating numbers.

For example, here's how to list the even numbers between 1 and 10:

even_numbers.py
```
even_numbers = list(range(2, 11, 2))
print(even_numbers)
```

In this example, the range() function starts with the value 2 and then adds 2 to that value. It adds 2 repeatedly until it reaches or passes the end value, 11, and produces this result:

```
[2, 4, 6, 8, 10]
```

You can create almost any set of numbers you want to using the range() function. For example, consider how you might make a list of the first 10 square numbers (that is, the square of each integer from 1 through 10). In Python, two asterisks (**) represent exponents. Here's how you might put the first 10 square numbers into a list:

squares.py
```
❶ squares = []
❷ for value in range(1, 11):
❸     square = value ** 2
❹     squares.append(square)

❺ print(squares)
```

We start with an empty list called squares ❶. At ❷, we tell Python to loop through each value from 1 to 10 using the range() function. Inside the loop, the current value is raised to the second power and assigned to the variable square ❸. At ❹, each new value of square is appended to the list squares. Finally, when the loop has finished running, the list of squares is printed ❺:

```
[1, 4, 9, 16, 25, 36, 49, 64, 81, 100]
```

To write this code more concisely, omit the temporary variable square and append each new value directly to the list:

```
squares = []
for value in range(1,11):
❶    squares.append(value**2)

print(squares)
```

The code at ❶ does the same work as the lines at ❸ and ❹ in *squares.py*. Each value in the loop is raised to the second power and then immediately appended to the list of squares.

You can use either of these two approaches when you're making more complex lists. Sometimes using a temporary variable makes your code easier to read; other times it makes the code unnecessarily long. Focus first on writing code that you understand clearly, which does what you want it to do. Then look for more efficient approaches as you review your code.

Simple Statistics with a List of Numbers

A few Python functions are helpful when working with lists of numbers. For example, you can easily find the minimum, maximum, and sum of a list of numbers:

```
>>> digits = [1, 2, 3, 4, 5, 6, 7, 8, 9, 0]
>>> min(digits)
0
>>> max(digits)
9
>>> sum(digits)
45
```

NOTE   *The examples in this section use short lists of numbers in order to fit easily on the page. They would work just as well if your list contained a million or more numbers.*

List Comprehensions

The approach described earlier for generating the list squares consisted of using three or four lines of code. A *list comprehension* allows you to generate this same list in just one line of code. A list comprehension combines the for loop and the creation of new elements into one line, and automatically appends each new element. List comprehensions are not always presented to beginners, but I have included them here because you'll most likely see them as soon as you start looking at other people's code.

The following example builds the same list of square numbers you saw earlier but uses a list comprehension:

squares.py
```
squares = [value**2 for value in range(1, 11)]
print(squares)
```

To use this syntax, begin with a descriptive name for the list, such as squares. Next, open a set of square brackets and define the expression for the values you want to store in the new list. In this example the expression is value**2, which raises the value to the second power. Then, write a for loop to generate the numbers you want to feed into the expression, and close the square brackets. The for loop in this example is for value in range(1, 11), which feeds the values 1 through 10 into the expression value**2. Notice that no colon is used at the end of the for statement.

The result is the same list of square numbers you saw earlier:

```
[1, 4, 9, 16, 25, 36, 49, 64, 81, 100]
```

It takes practice to write your own list comprehensions, but you'll find them worthwhile once you become comfortable creating ordinary lists. When you're writing three or four lines of code to generate lists and it begins to feel repetitive, consider writing your own list comprehensions.

TRY IT YOURSELF

4-3. Counting to Twenty: Use a for loop to print the numbers from 1 to 20, inclusive.

4-4. One Million: Make a list of the numbers from one to one million, and then use a for loop to print the numbers. (If the output is taking too long, stop it by pressing CTRL-C or by closing the output window.)

4-5. Summing a Million: Make a list of the numbers from one to one million, and then use min() and max() to make sure your list actually starts at one and ends at one million. Also, use the sum() function to see how quickly Python can add a million numbers.

4-6. Odd Numbers: Use the third argument of the range() function to make a list of the odd numbers from 1 to 20. Use a for loop to print each number.

4-7. Threes: Make a list of the multiples of 3 from 3 to 30. Use a for loop to print the numbers in your list.

4-8. Cubes: A number raised to the third power is called a *cube*. For example, the cube of 2 is written as 2**3 in Python. Make a list of the first 10 cubes (that is, the cube of each integer from 1 through 10), and use a for loop to print out the value of each cube.

4-9. Cube Comprehension: Use a list comprehension to generate a list of the first 10 cubes.

Working with Part of a List

In Chapter 3 you learned how to access single elements in a list, and in this chapter you've been learning how to work through all the elements in a list. You can also work with a specific group of items in a list, which Python calls a *slice*.

Slicing a List

To make a slice, you specify the index of the first and last elements you want to work with. As with the range() function, Python stops one item before the second index you specify. To output the first three elements in a list, you would request indices 0 through 3, which would return elements 0, 1, and 2.

The following example involves a list of players on a team:

players.py
```
players = ['charles', 'martina', 'michael', 'florence', 'eli']
❶ print(players[0:3])
```

The code at ❶ prints a slice of this list, which includes just the first three players. The output retains the structure of the list and includes the first three players in the list:

```
['charles', 'martina', 'michael']
```

You can generate any subset of a list. For example, if you want the second, third, and fourth items in a list, you would start the slice at index 1 and end at index 4:

```
players = ['charles', 'martina', 'michael', 'florence', 'eli']
print(players[1:4])
```

This time the slice starts with 'martina' and ends with 'florence':

```
['martina', 'michael', 'florence']
```

If you omit the first index in a slice, Python automatically starts your slice at the beginning of the list:

```
players = ['charles', 'martina', 'michael', 'florence', 'eli']
print(players[:4])
```

Without a starting index, Python starts at the beginning of the list:

```
['charles', 'martina', 'michael', 'florence']
```

A similar syntax works if you want a slice that includes the end of a list. For example, if you want all items from the third item through the last item, you can start with index 2 and omit the second index:

```
players = ['charles', 'martina', 'michael', 'florence', 'eli']
print(players[2:])
```

Python returns all items from the third item through the end of the list:

```
['michael', 'florence', 'eli']
```

This syntax allows you to output all of the elements from any point in your list to the end regardless of the length of the list. Recall that a negative index returns an element a certain distance from the end of a list; therefore, you can output any slice from the end of a list. For example, if we want to output the last three players on the roster, we can use the slice players[-3:]:

```
players = ['charles', 'martina', 'michael', 'florence', 'eli']
print(players[-3:])
```

This prints the names of the last three players and would continue to work as the list of players changes in size.

NOTE *You can include a third value in the brackets indicating a slice. If a third value is included, this tells Python how many items to skip between items in the specified range.*

Looping Through a Slice

You can use a slice in a for loop if you want to loop through a subset of the elements in a list. In the next example we loop through the first three players and print their names as part of a simple roster:

```
players = ['charles', 'martina', 'michael', 'florence', 'eli']

print("Here are the first three players on my team:")
❶ for player in players[:3]:
    print(player.title())
```

Instead of looping through the entire list of players at ❶, Python loops through only the first three names:

```
Here are the first three players on my team:
Charles
Martina
Michael
```

Slices are very useful in a number of situations. For instance, when you're creating a game, you could add a player's final score to a list every time that player finishes playing. You could then get a player's top three scores by sorting the list in decreasing order and taking a slice that includes just the first three scores. When you're working with data, you can use slices to process your data in chunks of a specific size. Or, when you're building a web application, you could use slices to display information in a series of pages with an appropriate amount of information on each page.

Copying a List

Often, you'll want to start with an existing list and make an entirely new list based on the first one. Let's explore how copying a list works and examine one situation in which copying a list is useful.

To copy a list, you can make a slice that includes the entire original list by omitting the first index and the second index ([:]). This tells Python to make a slice that starts at the first item and ends with the last item, producing a copy of the entire list.

For example, imagine we have a list of our favorite foods and want to make a separate list of foods that a friend likes. This friend likes everything in our list so far, so we can create their list by copying ours:

foods.py
```
❶ my_foods = ['pizza', 'falafel', 'carrot cake']
❷ friend_foods = my_foods[:]

print("My favorite foods are:")
print(my_foods)

print("\nMy friend's favorite foods are:")
print(friend_foods)
```

At ❶ we make a list of the foods we like called my_foods. At ❷ we make a new list called friend_foods. We make a copy of my_foods by asking for a slice of my_foods without specifying any indices and store the copy in friend_foods. When we print each list, we see that they both contain the same foods:

```
My favorite foods are:
['pizza', 'falafel', 'carrot cake']

My friend's favorite foods are:
['pizza', 'falafel', 'carrot cake']
```

To prove that we actually have two separate lists, we'll add a new food to each list and show that each list keeps track of the appropriate person's favorite foods:

```
  my_foods = ['pizza', 'falafel', 'carrot cake']
❶ friend_foods = my_foods[:]

❷ my_foods.append('cannoli')
❸ friend_foods.append('ice cream')
```

```
print("My favorite foods are:")
print(my_foods)

print("\nMy friend's favorite foods are:")
print(friend_foods)
```

At ❶ we copy the original items in my_foods to the new list friend_foods, as we did in the previous example. Next, we add a new food to each list: at ❷ we add 'cannoli' to my_foods, and at ❸ we add 'ice cream' to friend_foods. We then print the two lists to see whether each of these foods is in the appropriate list.

```
My favorite foods are:
❹ ['pizza', 'falafel', 'carrot cake', 'cannoli']

My friend's favorite foods are:
❺ ['pizza', 'falafel', 'carrot cake', 'ice cream']
```

The output at ❹ shows that 'cannoli' now appears in our list of favorite foods but 'ice cream' doesn't. At ❺ we can see that 'ice cream' now appears in our friend's list but 'cannoli' doesn't. If we had simply set friend_foods equal to my_foods, we would not produce two separate lists. For example, here's what happens when you try to copy a list without using a slice:

```
my_foods = ['pizza', 'falafel', 'carrot cake']

# This doesn't work:
❶ friend_foods = my_foods

my_foods.append('cannoli')
friend_foods.append('ice cream')

print("My favorite foods are:")
print(my_foods)

print("\nMy friend's favorite foods are:")
print(friend_foods)
```

Instead of storing a copy of my_foods in friend_foods at ❶, we set friend _foods equal to my_foods. This syntax actually tells Python to associate the new variable friend_foods with the list that is already associated with my_foods, so now both variables point to the same list. As a result, when we add 'cannoli' to my_foods, it will also appear in friend_foods. Likewise 'ice cream' will appear in both lists, even though it appears to be added only to friend_foods.

The output shows that both lists are the same now, which is not what we wanted:

```
My favorite foods are:
['pizza', 'falafel', 'carrot cake', 'cannoli', 'ice cream']
```

```
My friend's favorite foods are:
['pizza', 'falafel', 'carrot cake', 'cannoli', 'ice cream']
```

NOTE *Don't worry about the details in this example for now. Basically, if you're trying to work with a copy of a list and you see unexpected behavior, make sure you are copying the list using a slice, as we did in the first example.*

TRY IT YOURSELF

4-10. Slices: Using one of the programs you wrote in this chapter, add several lines to the end of the program that do the following:

- Print the message *The first three items in the list are:*. Then use a slice to print the first three items from that program's list.
- Print the message *Three items from the middle of the list are:*. Use a slice to print three items from the middle of the list.
- Print the message *The last three items in the list are:*. Use a slice to print the last three items in the list.

4-11. My Pizzas, Your Pizzas: Start with your program from Exercise 4-1 (page 56). Make a copy of the list of pizzas, and call it friend_pizzas. Then, do the following:

- Add a new pizza to the original list.
- Add a different pizza to the list friend_pizzas.
- Prove that you have two separate lists. Print the message *My favorite pizzas are:*, and then use a for loop to print the first list. Print the message *My friend's favorite pizzas are:*, and then use a for loop to print the second list. Make sure each new pizza is stored in the appropriate list.

4-12. More Loops: All versions of *foods.py* in this section have avoided using for loops when printing to save space. Choose a version of *foods.py*, and write two for loops to print each list of foods.

Tuples

Lists work well for storing collections of items that can change throughout the life of a program. The ability to modify lists is particularly important when you're working with a list of users on a website or a list of characters in a game. However, sometimes you'll want to create a list of items that cannot change. Tuples allow you to do just that. Python refers to values that cannot change as *immutable*, and an immutable list is called a *tuple*.

Defining a Tuple

A tuple looks just like a list except you use parentheses instead of square brackets. Once you define a tuple, you can access individual elements by using each item's index, just as you would for a list.

For example, if we have a rectangle that should always be a certain size, we can ensure that its size doesn't change by putting the dimensions into a tuple:

dimensions.py
```
❶ dimensions = (200, 50)
❷ print(dimensions[0])
   print(dimensions[1])
```

We define the tuple `dimensions` at ❶, using parentheses instead of square brackets. At ❷ we print each element in the tuple individually, using the same syntax we've been using to access elements in a list:

```
200
50
```

Let's see what happens if we try to change one of the items in the tuple `dimensions`:

```
   dimensions = (200, 50)
❶ dimensions[0] = 250
```

The code at ❶ tries to change the value of the first dimension, but Python returns a type error. Basically, because we're trying to alter a tuple, which can't be done to that type of object, Python tells us we can't assign a new value to an item in a tuple:

```
Traceback (most recent call last):
  File "dimensions.py", line 2, in <module>
    dimensions[0] = 250
TypeError: 'tuple' object does not support item assignment
```

This is beneficial because we want Python to raise an error when a line of code tries to change the dimensions of the rectangle.

NOTE   *Tuples are technically defined by the presence of a comma; the parentheses make them look neater and more readable. If you want to define a tuple with one element, you need to include a trailing comma:*

```
my_t = (3,)
```

It doesn't often make sense to build a tuple with one element, but this can happen when tuples are generated automatically.

Looping Through All Values in a Tuple

You can loop over all the values in a tuple using a for loop, just as you did with a list:

```
dimensions = (200, 50)
for dimension in dimensions:
    print(dimension)
```

Python returns all the elements in the tuple, just as it would for a list:

```
200
50
```

Writing over a Tuple

Although you can't modify a tuple, you can assign a new value to a variable that represents a tuple. So if we wanted to change our dimensions, we could redefine the entire tuple:

```
❶ dimensions = (200, 50)
  print("Original dimensions:")
  for dimension in dimensions:
      print(dimension)

❷ dimensions = (400, 100)
❸ print("\nModified dimensions:")
  for dimension in dimensions:
      print(dimension)
```

The lines starting at ❶ define the original tuple and print the initial dimensions. At ❷, we associate a new tuple with the variable dimensions. We then print the new dimensions at ❸. Python doesn't raise any errors this time, because reassigning a variable is valid:

```
Original dimensions:
200
50

Modified dimensions:
400
100
```

When compared with lists, tuples are simple data structures. Use them when you want to store a set of values that should not be changed throughout the life of a program.

4-13. Buffet: A buffet-style restaurant offers only five basic foods. Think of five simple foods, and store them in a tuple.

- Use a for loop to print each food the restaurant offers.
- Try to modify one of the items, and make sure that Python rejects the change.
- The restaurant changes its menu, replacing two of the items with different foods. Add a line that rewrites the tuple, and then use a for loop to print each of the items on the revised menu.

Styling Your Code

Now that you're writing longer programs, ideas about how to style your code are worthwhile to know. Take the time to make your code as easy as possible to read. Writing easy-to-read code helps you keep track of what your programs are doing and helps others understand your code as well.

Python programmers have agreed on a number of styling conventions to ensure that everyone's code is structured in roughly the same way. Once you've learned to write clean Python code, you should be able to understand the overall structure of anyone else's Python code, as long as they follow the same guidelines. If you're hoping to become a professional programmer at some point, you should begin following these guidelines as soon as possible to develop good habits.

The Style Guide

When someone wants to make a change to the Python language, they write a *Python Enhancement Proposal (PEP)*. One of the oldest PEPs is *PEP 8*, which instructs Python programmers on how to style their code. PEP 8 is fairly lengthy, but much of it relates to more complex coding structures than what you've seen so far.

The Python style guide was written with the understanding that code is read more often than it is written. You'll write your code once and then start reading it as you begin debugging. When you add features to a program, you'll spend more time reading your code. When you share your code with other programmers, they'll read your code as well.

Given the choice between writing code that's easier to write or code that's easier to read, Python programmers will almost always encourage you to write code that's easier to read. The following guidelines will help you write clear code from the start.

Indentation

PEP 8 recommends that you use four spaces per indentation level. Using four spaces improves readability while leaving room for multiple levels of indentation on each line.

In a word processing document, people often use tabs rather than spaces to indent. This works well for word processing documents, but the Python interpreter gets confused when tabs are mixed with spaces. Every text editor provides a setting that lets you use the TAB key but then converts each tab to a set number of spaces. You should definitely use your TAB key, but also make sure your editor is set to insert spaces rather than tabs into your document.

Mixing tabs and spaces in your file can cause problems that are very difficult to diagnose. If you think you have a mix of tabs and spaces, you can convert all tabs in a file to spaces in most editors.

Line Length

Many Python programmers recommend that each line should be less than 80 characters. Historically, this guideline developed because most computers could fit only 79 characters on a single line in a terminal window. Currently, people can fit much longer lines on their screens, but other reasons exist to adhere to the 79-character standard line length. Professional programmers often have several files open on the same screen, and using the standard line length allows them to see entire lines in two or three files that are open side by side onscreen. PEP 8 also recommends that you limit all of your comments to 72 characters per line, because some of the tools that generate automatic documentation for larger projects add formatting characters at the beginning of each commented line.

The PEP 8 guidelines for line length are not set in stone, and some teams prefer a 99-character limit. Don't worry too much about line length in your code as you're learning, but be aware that people who are working collaboratively almost always follow the PEP 8 guidelines. Most editors allow you to set up a visual cue, usually a vertical line on your screen, that shows you where these limits are.

NOTE   *Appendix B shows you how to configure your text editor so it always inserts four spaces each time you press the TAB key and shows a vertical guideline to help you follow the 79-character limit.*

Blank Lines

To group parts of your program visually, use blank lines. You should use blank lines to organize your files, but don't do so excessively. By following the examples provided in this book, you should strike the right balance. For example, if you have five lines of code that build a list, and then another three lines that do something with that list, it's appropriate to place a blank line between the two sections. However, you should not place three or four blank lines between the two sections.

Blank lines won't affect how your code runs, but they will affect the readability of your code. The Python interpreter uses horizontal indentation to interpret the meaning of your code, but it disregards vertical spacing.

Other Style Guidelines

PEP 8 has many additional styling recommendations, but most of the guidelines refer to more complex programs than what you're writing at this point. As you learn more complex Python structures, I'll share the relevant parts of the PEP 8 guidelines.

TRY IT YOURSELF

4-14. PEP 8: Look through the original PEP 8 style guide at *https://python.org/dev/peps/pep-0008/*. You won't use much of it now, but it might be interesting to skim through it.

4-15. Code Review: Choose three of the programs you've written in this chapter and modify each one to comply with PEP 8:

- Use four spaces for each indentation level. Set your text editor to insert four spaces every time you press TAB, if you haven't already done so (see Appendix B for instructions on how to do this).

- Use less than 80 characters on each line, and set your editor to show a vertical guideline at the 80th character position.

- Don't use blank lines excessively in your program files.

Summary

In this chapter you learned how to work efficiently with the elements in a list. You learned how to work through a list using a for loop, how Python uses indentation to structure a program, and how to avoid some common indentation errors. You learned to make simple numerical lists, as well as a few operations you can perform on numerical lists. You learned how to slice a list to work with a subset of items and how to copy lists properly using a slice. You also learned about tuples, which provide a degree of protection to a set of values that shouldn't change, and how to style your increasingly complex code to make it easy to read.

In Chapter 5, you'll learn to respond appropriately to different conditions by using if statements. You'll learn to string together relatively complex sets of conditional tests to respond appropriately to exactly the kind of situation or information you're looking for. You'll also learn to use if statements while looping through a list to take specific actions with selected elements from a list.

5

IF STATEMENTS

Programming often involves examining a set of conditions and deciding which action to take based on those conditions. Python's `if` statement allows you to examine the current state of a program and respond appropriately to that state.

In this chapter you'll learn to write conditional tests, which allow you to check any condition of interest. You'll learn to write simple `if` statements, and you'll learn how to create a more complex series of `if` statements to identify when the exact conditions you want are present. You'll then apply this concept to lists, so you'll be able to write a `for` loop that handles most items in a list one way but handles certain items with specific values in a different way.

A Simple Example

The following short example shows how if tests let you respond to special situations correctly. Imagine you have a list of cars and you want to print out the name of each car. Car names are proper names, so the names of most cars should be printed in title case. However, the value 'bmw' should be printed in all uppercase. The following code loops through a list of car names and looks for the value 'bmw'. Whenever the value is 'bmw', it's printed in uppercase instead of title case:

cars.py

```
cars = ['audi', 'bmw', 'subaru', 'toyota']

for car in cars:
❶    if car == 'bmw':
        print(car.upper())
    else:
        print(car.title())
```

The loop in this example first checks if the current value of car is 'bmw' ❶. If it is, the value is printed in uppercase. If the value of car is anything other than 'bmw', it's printed in title case:

```
Audi
BMW
Subaru
Toyota
```

This example combines a number of the concepts you'll learn about in this chapter. Let's begin by looking at the kinds of tests you can use to examine the conditions in your program.

Conditional Tests

At the heart of every if statement is an expression that can be evaluated as True or False and is called a *conditional test*. Python uses the values True and False to decide whether the code in an if statement should be executed. If a conditional test evaluates to True, Python executes the code following the if statement. If the test evaluates to False, Python ignores the code following the if statement.

Checking for Equality

Most conditional tests compare the current value of a variable to a specific value of interest. The simplest conditional test checks whether the value of a variable is equal to the value of interest:

```
❶ >>> car = 'bmw'
❷ >>> car == 'bmw'
   True
```

The line at ❶ sets the value of car to 'bmw' using a single equal sign, as you've seen many times already. The line at ❷ checks whether the value of car is 'bmw' using a double equal sign (==). This *equality operator* returns True if the values on the left and right side of the operator match, and False if they don't match. The values in this example match, so Python returns True.

When the value of car is anything other than 'bmw', this test returns False:

```
❶ >>> car = 'audi'
❷ >>> car == 'bmw'
   False
```

A single equal sign is really a statement; you might read the code at ❶ as "Set the value of car equal to 'audi'." On the other hand, a double equal sign, like the one at ❷, asks a question: "Is the value of car equal to 'bmw'?" Most programming languages use equal signs in this way.

Ignoring Case When Checking for Equality

Testing for equality is case sensitive in Python. For example, two values with different capitalization are not considered equal:

```
>>> car = 'Audi'
>>> car == 'audi'
False
```

If case matters, this behavior is advantageous. But if case doesn't matter and instead you just want to test the value of a variable, you can convert the variable's value to lowercase before doing the comparison:

```
>>> car = 'Audi'
>>> car.lower() == 'audi'
True
```

This test would return True no matter how the value 'Audi' is formatted because the test is now case insensitive. The lower() function doesn't change the value that was originally stored in car, so you can do this kind of comparison without affecting the original variable:

```
❶ >>> car = 'Audi'
❷ >>> car.lower() == 'audi'
   True
❸ >>> car
   'Audi'
```

At ❶ we assign the capitalized string 'Audi' to the variable car. At ❷ we convert the value of car to lowercase and compare the lowercase value to the string `'audi'`. The two strings match, so Python returns `True`. At ❸ we can see that the value stored in car has not been affected by the `lower()` method.

Websites enforce certain rules for the data that users enter in a manner similar to this. For example, a site might use a conditional test like this to ensure that every user has a truly unique username, not just a variation on the capitalization of another person's username. When someone submits a new username, that new username is converted to lowercase and compared to the lowercase versions of all existing usernames. During this check, a username like `'John'` will be rejected if any variation of `'john'` is already in use.

Checking for Inequality

When you want to determine whether two values are not equal, you can combine an exclamation point and an equal sign (!=). The exclamation point represents *not*, as it does in many programming languages.

Let's use another `if` statement to examine how to use the inequality operator. We'll store a requested pizza topping in a variable and then print a message if the person did not order anchovies:

toppings.py

```
requested_topping = 'mushrooms'

❶ if requested_topping != 'anchovies':
      print("Hold the anchovies!")
```

The line at ❶ compares the value of `requested_topping` to the value `'anchovies'`. If these two values do not match, Python returns `True` and executes the code following the `if` statement. If the two values match, Python returns `False` and does not run the code following the `if` statement.

Because the value of `requested_topping` is not `'anchovies'`, the `print()` function is executed:

```
Hold the anchovies!
```

Most of the conditional expressions you write will test for equality, but sometimes you'll find it more efficient to test for inequality.

Numerical Comparisons

Testing numerical values is pretty straightforward. For example, the following code checks whether a person is 18 years old:

```
>>> age = 18
>>> age == 18
True
```

You can also test to see if two numbers are not equal. For example, the following code prints a message if the given answer is not correct:

magic _number.py

```
answer = 17

❶ if answer != 42:
    print("That is not the correct answer. Please try again!")
```

The conditional test at ❶ passes, because the value of answer (17) is not equal to 42. Because the test passes, the indented code block is executed:

```
That is not the correct answer. Please try again!
```

You can include various mathematical comparisons in your conditional statements as well, such as less than, less than or equal to, greater than, and greater than or equal to:

```
>>> age = 19
>>> age < 21
True
>>> age <= 21
True
>>> age > 21
False
>>> age >= 21
False
```

Each mathematical comparison can be used as part of an if statement, which can help you detect the exact conditions of interest.

Checking Multiple Conditions

You may want to check multiple conditions at the same time. For example, sometimes you might need two conditions to be True to take an action. Other times you might be satisfied with just one condition being True. The keywords and and or can help you in these situations.

Using and to Check Multiple Conditions

To check whether two conditions are both True simultaneously, use the keyword and to combine the two conditional tests; if each test passes, the overall expression evaluates to True. If either test fails or if both tests fail, the expression evaluates to False.

For example, you can check whether two people are both over 21 using the following test:

```
❶ >>> age_0 = 22
   >>> age_1 = 18
❷ >>> age_0 >= 21 and age_1 >= 21
   False
```

❸ ```
>>> age_1 = 22
>>> age_0 >= 21 and age_1 >= 21
True
```

At ❶ we define two ages, age_0 and age_1. At ❷ we check whether both ages are 21 or older. The test on the left passes, but the test on the right fails, so the overall conditional expression evaluates to False. At ❸ we change age_1 to 22. The value of age_1 is now greater than 21, so both individual tests pass, causing the overall conditional expression to evaluate as True.

To improve readability, you can use parentheses around the individual tests, but they are not required. If you use parentheses, your test would look like this:

```
(age_0 >= 21) and (age_1 >= 21)
```

Using or to Check Multiple Conditions

The keyword or allows you to check multiple conditions as well, but it passes when either or both of the individual tests pass. An or expression fails only when both individual tests fail.

Let's consider two ages again, but this time we'll look for only one person to be over 21:

❶ ```
>>> age_0 = 22
>>> age_1 = 18
```
❷ ```
>>> age_0 >= 21 or age_1 >= 21
True
```
❸ ```
>>> age_0 = 18
>>> age_0 >= 21 or age_1 >= 21
False
```

We start with two age variables again at ❶. Because the test for age_0 at ❷ passes, the overall expression evaluates to True. We then lower age_0 to 18. In the test at ❸, both tests now fail and the overall expression evaluates to False.

Checking Whether a Value Is in a List

Sometimes it's important to check whether a list contains a certain value before taking an action. For example, you might want to check whether a new username already exists in a list of current usernames before completing someone's registration on a website. In a mapping project, you might want to check whether a submitted location already exists in a list of known locations.

To find out whether a particular value is already in a list, use the keyword in. Let's consider some code you might write for a pizzeria. We'll make a list of toppings a customer has requested for a pizza and then check whether certain toppings are in the list.

```
>>> requested_toppings = ['mushrooms', 'onions', 'pineapple']
❶ >>> 'mushrooms' in requested_toppings
True
❷ >>> 'pepperoni' in requested_toppings
False
```

At ❶ and ❷, the keyword in tells Python to check for the existence of 'mushrooms' and 'pepperoni' in the list requested_toppings. This technique is quite powerful because you can create a list of essential values, and then easily check whether the value you're testing matches one of the values in the list.

Checking Whether a Value Is Not in a List

Other times, it's important to know if a value does not appear in a list. You can use the keyword not in this situation. For example, consider a list of users who are banned from commenting in a forum. You can check whether a user has been banned before allowing that person to submit a comment:

banned
_users.py
```
banned_users = ['andrew', 'carolina', 'david']
user = 'marie'

❶ if user not in banned_users:
    print(f"{user.title()}, you can post a response if you wish.")
```

The line at ❶ reads quite clearly. If the value of user is not in the list banned_users, Python returns True and executes the indented line.

The user 'marie' is not in the list banned_users, so she sees a message inviting her to post a response:

```
Marie, you can post a response if you wish.
```

Boolean Expressions

As you learn more about programming, you'll hear the term *Boolean expression* at some point. A Boolean expression is just another name for a conditional test. A *Boolean value* is either True or False, just like the value of a conditional expression after it has been evaluated.

Boolean values are often used to keep track of certain conditions, such as whether a game is running or whether a user can edit certain content on a website:

```
game_active = True
can_edit = False
```

Boolean values provide an efficient way to track the state of a program or a particular condition that is important in your program.

5-1. Conditional Tests: Write a series of conditional tests. Print a statement describing each test and your prediction for the results of each test. Your code should look something like this:

```
car = 'subaru'
print("Is car == 'subaru'? I predict True.")
print(car == 'subaru')

print("\nIs car == 'audi'? I predict False.")
print(car == 'audi')
```

- Look closely at your results, and make sure you understand why each line evaluates to True or False.
- Create at least ten tests. Have at least five tests evaluate to True and another five tests evaluate to False.

5-2. More Conditional Tests: You don't have to limit the number of tests you create to ten. If you want to try more comparisons, write more tests and add them to *conditional_tests.py*. Have at least one True and one False result for each of the following:

- Tests for equality and inequality with strings
- Tests using the lower() method
- Numerical tests involving equality and inequality, greater than and less than, greater than or equal to, and less than or equal to
- Tests using the and keyword and the or keyword
- Test whether an item is in a list
- Test whether an item is not in a list

if Statements

When you understand conditional tests, you can start writing if statements. Several different kinds of if statements exist, and your choice of which to use depends on the number of conditions you need to test. You saw several examples of if statements in the discussion about conditional tests, but now let's dig deeper into the topic.

Simple if Statements

The simplest kind of if statement has one test and one action:

```
if conditional_test:
    do something
```

You can put any conditional test in the first line and just about any action in the indented block following the test. If the conditional test evaluates to True, Python executes the code following the if statement. If the test evaluates to False, Python ignores the code following the if statement.

Let's say we have a variable representing a person's age, and we want to know if that person is old enough to vote. The following code tests whether the person can vote:

voting.py

```
  age = 19
❶ if age >= 18:
❷     print("You are old enough to vote!")
```

At ❶ Python checks to see whether the value of age is greater than or equal to 18. It is, so Python executes the indented print() call at ❷:

```
You are old enough to vote!
```

Indentation plays the same role in if statements as it did in for loops. All indented lines after an if statement will be executed if the test passes, and the entire block of indented lines will be ignored if the test does not pass.

You can have as many lines of code as you want in the block following the if statement. Let's add another line of output if the person is old enough to vote, asking if the individual has registered to vote yet:

```
age = 19
if age >= 18:
    print("You are old enough to vote!")
    print("Have you registered to vote yet?")
```

The conditional test passes, and both print() calls are indented, so both lines are printed:

```
You are old enough to vote!
Have you registered to vote yet?
```

If the value of age is less than 18, this program would produce no output.

if-else Statements

Often, you'll want to take one action when a conditional test passes and a different action in all other cases. Python's if-else syntax makes this possible. An if-else block is similar to a simple if statement, but the else statement allows you to define an action or set of actions that are executed when the conditional test fails.

We'll display the same message we had previously if the person is old enough to vote, but this time we'll add a message for anyone who is not old enough to vote:

```
age = 17
❶ if age >= 18:
       print("You are old enough to vote!")
       print("Have you registered to vote yet?")
❷ else:
       print("Sorry, you are too young to vote.")
       print("Please register to vote as soon as you turn 18!")
```

If the conditional test at ❶ passes, the first block of indented print() calls is executed. If the test evaluates to False, the else block at ❷ is executed. Because age is less than 18 this time, the conditional test fails and the code in the else block is executed:

```
Sorry, you are too young to vote.
Please register to vote as soon as you turn 18!
```

This code works because it has only two possible situations to evaluate: a person is either old enough to vote or not old enough to vote. The if-else structure works well in situations in which you want Python to always execute one of two possible actions. In a simple if-else chain like this, one of the two actions will always be executed.

The if-elif-else Chain

Often, you'll need to test more than two possible situations, and to evaluate these you can use Python's if-elif-else syntax. Python executes only one block in an if-elif-else chain. It runs each conditional test in order until one passes. When a test passes, the code following that test is executed and Python skips the rest of the tests.

Many real-world situations involve more than two possible conditions. For example, consider an amusement park that charges different rates for different age groups:

- Admission for anyone under age 4 is free.
- Admission for anyone between the ages of 4 and 18 is $25.
- Admission for anyone age 18 or older is $40.

How can we use an if statement to determine a person's admission rate? The following code tests for the age group of a person and then prints an admission price message:

amusement _park.py

```
age = 12

❶ if age < 4:
       print("Your admission cost is $0.")
```

```
❷ elif age < 18:
        print("Your admission cost is $25.")
❸ else:
        print("Your admission cost is $40.")
```

The if test at ❶ tests whether a person is under 4 years old. If the test passes, an appropriate message is printed and Python skips the rest of the tests. The elif line at ❷ is really another if test, which runs only if the previous test failed. At this point in the chain, we know the person is at least 4 years old because the first test failed. If the person is under 18, an appropriate message is printed and Python skips the else block. If both the if and elif tests fail, Python runs the code in the else block at ❸.

In this example the test at ❶ evaluates to False, so its code block is not executed. However, the second test evaluates to True (12 is less than 18) so its code is executed. The output is one sentence, informing the user of the admission cost:

```
Your admission cost is $25.
```

Any age greater than 17 would cause the first two tests to fail. In these situations, the else block would be executed and the admission price would be $40.

Rather than printing the admission price within the if-elif-else block, it would be more concise to set just the price inside the if-elif-else chain and then have a simple print() call that runs after the chain has been evaluated:

```
age = 12

if age < 4:
❶     price = 0
elif age < 18:
❷     price = 25
else:
❸     price = 40

❹ print(f"Your admission cost is ${price}.")
```

The lines at ❶, ❷, and ❸ set the value of price according to the person's age, as in the previous example. After the price is set by the if-elif-else chain, a separate unindented print() call ❹ uses this value to display a message reporting the person's admission price.

This code produces the same output as the previous example, but the purpose of the if-elif-else chain is narrower. Instead of determining a price and displaying a message, it simply determines the admission price. In addition to being more efficient, this revised code is easier to modify than the original approach. To change the text of the output message, you would need to change only one print() call rather than three separate print() calls.

Using Multiple elif Blocks

You can use as many `elif` blocks in your code as you like. For example, if the amusement park were to implement a discount for seniors, you could add one more conditional test to the code to determine whether someone qualified for the senior discount. Let's say that anyone 65 or older pays half the regular admission, or $20:

```
age = 12

if age < 4:
    price = 0
elif age < 18:
    price = 25
❶ elif age < 65:
    price = 40
❷ else:
    price = 20

print(f"Your admission cost is ${price}.")
```

Most of this code is unchanged. The second `elif` block at ❶ now checks to make sure a person is less than age 65 before assigning them the full admission rate of $40. Notice that the value assigned in the `else` block at ❷ needs to be changed to $20, because the only ages that make it to this block are people 65 or older.

Omitting the else Block

Python does not require an `else` block at the end of an `if-elif` chain. Sometimes an `else` block is useful; sometimes it is clearer to use an additional `elif` statement that catches the specific condition of interest:

```
age = 12

if age < 4:
    price = 0
elif age < 18:
    price = 25
elif age < 65:
    price = 40
❶ elif age >= 65:
    price = 20

print(f"Your admission cost is ${price}.")
```

The extra `elif` block at ❶ assigns a price of $20 when the person is 65 or older, which is a bit clearer than the general `else` block. With this change, every block of code must pass a specific test in order to be executed.

The else block is a catchall statement. It matches any condition that wasn't matched by a specific if or elif test, and that can sometimes include invalid or even malicious data. If you have a specific final condition you are testing for, consider using a final elif block and omit the else block. As a result, you'll gain extra confidence that your code will run only under the correct conditions.

Testing Multiple Conditions

The if-elif-else chain is powerful, but it's only appropriate to use when you just need one test to pass. As soon as Python finds one test that passes, it skips the rest of the tests. This behavior is beneficial, because it's efficient and allows you to test for one specific condition.

However, sometimes it's important to check all of the conditions of interest. In this case, you should use a series of simple if statements with no elif or else blocks. This technique makes sense when more than one condition could be True, and you want to act on every condition that is True.

Let's reconsider the pizzeria example. If someone requests a two-topping pizza, you'll need to be sure to include both toppings on their pizza:

toppings.py

```
❶ requested_toppings = ['mushrooms', 'extra cheese']

❷ if 'mushrooms' in requested_toppings:
      print("Adding mushrooms.")
❸ if 'pepperoni' in requested_toppings:
      print("Adding pepperoni.")
❹ if 'extra cheese' in requested_toppings:
      print("Adding extra cheese.")

  print("\nFinished making your pizza!")
```

We start at ❶ with a list containing the requested toppings. The if statement at ❷ checks to see whether the person requested mushrooms on their pizza. If so, a message is printed confirming that topping. The test for pepperoni at ❸ is another simple if statement, not an elif or else statement, so this test is run regardless of whether the previous test passed or not. The code at ❹ checks whether extra cheese was requested regardless of the results from the first two tests. These three independent tests are executed every time this program is run.

Because every condition in this example is evaluated, both mushrooms and extra cheese are added to the pizza:

```
Adding mushrooms.
Adding extra cheese.

Finished making your pizza!
```

This code would not work properly if we used an `if-elif-else` block, because the code would stop running after only one test passes. Here's what that would look like:

```
requested_toppings = ['mushrooms', 'extra cheese']

if 'mushrooms' in requested_toppings:
    print("Adding mushrooms.")
elif 'pepperoni' in requested_toppings:
    print("Adding pepperoni.")
elif 'extra cheese' in requested_toppings:
    print("Adding extra cheese.")

print("\nFinished making your pizza!")
```

The test for `'mushrooms'` is the first test to pass, so mushrooms are added to the pizza. However, the values `'extra cheese'` and `'pepperoni'` are never checked, because Python doesn't run any tests beyond the first test that passes in an `if-elif-else` chain. The customer's first topping will be added, but all of their other toppings will be missed:

```
Adding mushrooms.

Finished making your pizza!
```

In summary, if you want only one block of code to run, use an `if-elif-else` chain. If more than one block of code needs to run, use a series of independent `if` statements.

TRY IT YOURSELF

5-3. Alien Colors #1: Imagine an alien was just shot down in a game. Create a variable called `alien_color` and assign it a value of `'green'`, `'yellow'`, or `'red'`.

- Write an `if` statement to test whether the alien's color is green. If it is, print a message that the player just earned 5 points.
- Write one version of this program that passes the `if` test and another that fails. (The version that fails will have no output.)

5-4. Alien Colors #2: Choose a color for an alien as you did in Exercise 5-3, and write an `if-else` chain.

- If the alien's color is green, print a statement that the player just earned 5 points for shooting the alien.
- If the alien's color isn't green, print a statement that the player just earned 10 points.
- Write one version of this program that runs the `if` block and another that runs the `else` block.

5-5. Alien Colors #3: Turn your `if-else` chain from Exercise 5-4 into an `if-elif-else` chain.

- If the alien is green, print a message that the player earned 5 points.
- If the alien is yellow, print a message that the player earned 10 points.
- If the alien is red, print a message that the player earned 15 points.
- Write three versions of this program, making sure each message is printed for the appropriate color alien.

5-6. Stages of Life: Write an `if-elif-else` chain that determines a person's stage of life. Set a value for the variable age, and then:

- If the person is less than 2 years old, print a message that the person is a baby.
- If the person is at least 2 years old but less than 4, print a message that the person is a toddler.
- If the person is at least 4 years old but less than 13, print a message that the person is a kid.
- If the person is at least 13 years old but less than 20, print a message that the person is a teenager.
- If the person is at least 20 years old but less than 65, print a message that the person is an adult.
- If the person is age 65 or older, print a message that the person is an elder.

5-7. Favorite Fruit: Make a list of your favorite fruits, and then write a series of independent `if` statements that check for certain fruits in your list.

- Make a list of your three favorite fruits and call it `favorite_fruits`.
- Write five `if` statements. Each should check whether a certain kind of fruit is in your list. If the fruit is in your list, the `if` block should print a statement, such as *You really like bananas!*

Using if Statements with Lists

You can do some interesting work when you combine lists and `if` statements. You can watch for special values that need to be treated differently than other values in the list. You can manage changing conditions efficiently, such as the availability of certain items in a restaurant throughout a shift. You can also begin to prove that your code works as you expect it to in all possible situations.

Checking for Special Items

This chapter began with a simple example that showed how to handle a special value like `'bmw'`, which needed to be printed in a different format than other values in the list. Now that you have a basic understanding of conditional tests and `if` statements, let's take a closer look at how you can watch for special values in a list and handle those values appropriately.

Let's continue with the pizzeria example. The pizzeria displays a message whenever a topping is added to your pizza, as it's being made. The code for this action can be written very efficiently by making a list of toppings the customer has requested and using a loop to announce each topping as it's added to the pizza:

toppings.py

```
requested_toppings = ['mushrooms', 'green peppers', 'extra cheese']

for requested_topping in requested_toppings:
    print(f"Adding {requested_topping}.")

print("\nFinished making your pizza!")
```

The output is straightforward because this code is just a simple for loop:

```
Adding mushrooms.
Adding green peppers.
Adding extra cheese.

Finished making your pizza!
```

But what if the pizzeria runs out of green peppers? An if statement inside the for loop can handle this situation appropriately:

```
requested_toppings = ['mushrooms', 'green peppers', 'extra cheese']

for requested_topping in requested_toppings:
❶    if requested_topping == 'green peppers':
        print("Sorry, we are out of green peppers right now.")
❷    else:
        print(f"Adding {requested_topping}.")

print("\nFinished making your pizza!")
```

This time we check each requested item before adding it to the pizza. The code at ❶ checks to see if the person requested green peppers. If so, we display a message informing them why they can't have green peppers. The else block at ❷ ensures that all other toppings will be added to the pizza.

The output shows that each requested topping is handled appropriately.

```
Adding mushrooms.
Sorry, we are out of green peppers right now.
Adding extra cheese.

Finished making your pizza!
```

Checking That a List Is Not Empty

We've made a simple assumption about every list we've worked with so far; we've assumed that each list has at least one item in it. Soon we'll let users provide the information that's stored in a list, so we won't be able to assume that a list has any items in it each time a loop is run. In this situation, it's useful to check whether a list is empty before running a for loop.

As an example, let's check whether the list of requested toppings is empty before building the pizza. If the list is empty, we'll prompt the user and make sure they want a plain pizza. If the list is not empty, we'll build the pizza just as we did in the previous examples:

```
❶ requested_toppings = []

❷ if requested_toppings:
        for requested_topping in requested_toppings:
            print(f"Adding {requested_topping}.")
        print("\nFinished making your pizza!")
❸ else:
        print("Are you sure you want a plain pizza?")
```

This time we start out with an empty list of requested toppings at ❶. Instead of jumping right into a for loop, we do a quick check at ❷. When the name of a list is used in an if statement, Python returns True if the list contains at least one item; an empty list evaluates to False. If requested_toppings passes the conditional test, we run the same for loop we used in the previous example. If the conditional test fails, we print a message asking the customer if they really want a plain pizza with no toppings ❸.

The list is empty in this case, so the output asks if the user really wants a plain pizza:

```
Are you sure you want a plain pizza?
```

If the list is not empty, the output will show each requested topping being added to the pizza.

Using Multiple Lists

People will ask for just about anything, especially when it comes to pizza toppings. What if a customer actually wants french fries on their pizza? You can use lists and if statements to make sure your input makes sense before you act on it.

Let's watch out for unusual topping requests before we build a pizza. The following example defines two lists. The first is a list of available toppings at the pizzeria, and the second is the list of toppings that the user has requested. This time, each item in requested_toppings is checked against the list of available toppings before it's added to the pizza:

```
❶ available_toppings = ['mushrooms', 'olives', 'green peppers',
                        'pepperoni', 'pineapple', 'extra cheese']

❷ requested_toppings = ['mushrooms', 'french fries', 'extra cheese']

❸ for requested_topping in requested_toppings:
❹     if requested_topping in available_toppings:
           print(f"Adding {requested_topping}.")
❺     else:
           print(f"Sorry, we don't have {requested_topping}.")

print("\nFinished making your pizza!")
```

At ❶ we define a list of available toppings at this pizzeria. Note that this could be a tuple if the pizzeria has a stable selection of toppings. At ❷, we make a list of toppings that a customer has requested. Note the unusual request, 'french fries'. At ❸ we loop through the list of requested toppings. Inside the loop, we first check to see if each requested topping is actually in the list of available toppings ❹. If it is, we add that topping to the pizza. If the requested topping is not in the list of available toppings, the else block will run ❺. The else block prints a message telling the user which toppings are unavailable.

This code syntax produces clean, informative output:

```
Adding mushrooms.
Sorry, we don't have french fries.
Adding extra cheese.

Finished making your pizza!
```

In just a few lines of code, we've managed a real-world situation pretty effectively!

TRY IT YOURSELF

5-8. Hello Admin: Make a list of five or more usernames, including the name 'admin'. Imagine you are writing code that will print a greeting to each user after they log in to a website. Loop through the list, and print a greeting to each user:

- If the username is 'admin', print a special greeting, such as *Hello admin, would you like to see a status report?*
- Otherwise, print a generic greeting, such as *Hello Jaden, thank you for logging in again.*

5-9. No Users: Add an if test to *hello_admin.py* to make sure the list of users is not empty.

- If the list is empty, print the message *We need to find some users!*
- Remove all of the usernames from your list, and make sure the correct message is printed.

5-10. Checking Usernames: Do the following to create a program that simulates how websites ensure that everyone has a unique username.

- Make a list of five or more usernames called current_users.
- Make another list of five usernames called new_users. Make sure one or two of the new usernames are also in the current_users list.
- Loop through the new_users list to see if each new username has already been used. If it has, print a message that the person will need to enter a new username. If a username has not been used, print a message saying that the username is available.
- Make sure your comparison is case insensitive. If 'John' has been used, 'JOHN' should not be accepted. (To do this, you'll need to make a copy of current_users containing the lowercase versions of all existing users.)

5-11. Ordinal Numbers: Ordinal numbers indicate their position in a list, such as *1st* or *2nd*. Most ordinal numbers end in *th*, except 1, 2, and 3.

- Store the numbers 1 through 9 in a list.
- Loop through the list.
- Use an if-elif-else chain inside the loop to print the proper ordinal ending for each number. Your output should read "1st 2nd 3rd 4th 5th 6th 7th 8th 9th", and each result should be on a separate line.

Styling Your if Statements

In every example in this chapter, you've seen good styling habits. The only recommendation PEP 8 provides for styling conditional tests is to use a single space around comparison operators, such as ==, >=, <=. For example:

```
if age < 4:
```

is better than:

```
if age<4:
```

Such spacing does not affect the way Python interprets your code; it just makes your code easier for you and others to read.

TRY IT YOURSELF

5-12. Styling if statements: Review the programs you wrote in this chapter, and make sure you styled your conditional tests appropriately.

5-13. Your Ideas: At this point, you're a more capable programmer than you were when you started this book. Now that you have a better sense of how real-world situations are modeled in programs, you might be thinking of some problems you could solve with your own programs. Record any new ideas you have about problems you might want to solve as your programming skills continue to improve. Consider games you might want to write, data sets you might want to explore, and web applications you'd like to create.

Summary

In this chapter you learned how to write conditional tests, which always evaluate to True or False. You learned to write simple if statements, if-else chains, and if-elif-else chains. You began using these structures to identify particular conditions you needed to test and to know when those conditions have been met in your programs. You learned to handle certain items in a list differently than all other items while continuing to utilize the efficiency of a for loop. You also revisited Python's style recommendations to ensure that your increasingly complex programs are still relatively easy to read and understand.

In Chapter 6 you'll learn about Python's dictionaries. A dictionary is similar to a list, but it allows you to connect pieces of information. You'll learn to build dictionaries, loop through them, and use them in combination with lists and if statements. Learning about dictionaries will enable you to model an even wider variety of real-world situations.

6

DICTIONARIES

In this chapter you'll learn how to use
Python's dictionaries, which allow you to
connect pieces of related information. You'll
learn how to access the information once it's
in a dictionary and how to modify that information.
Because dictionaries can store an almost limitless
amount of information, I'll show you how to loop
through the data in a dictionary. Additionally, you'll learn to nest dictionaries inside lists, lists inside dictionaries, and even dictionaries inside other
dictionaries.

Understanding dictionaries allows you to model a variety of real-world
objects more accurately. You'll be able to create a dictionary representing a person and then store as much information as you want about that
person. You can store their name, age, location, profession, and any other
aspect of a person you can describe. You'll be able to store any two kinds of

information that can be matched up, such as a list of words and their meanings, a list of people's names and their favorite numbers, a list of mountains and their elevations, and so forth.

A Simple Dictionary

Consider a game featuring aliens that can have different colors and point values. This simple dictionary stores information about a particular alien:

alien.py
```
alien_0 = {'color': 'green', 'points': 5}

print(alien_0['color'])
print(alien_0['points'])
```

The dictionary alien_0 stores the alien's color and point value. The last two lines access and display that information, as shown here:

```
green
5
```

As with most new programming concepts, using dictionaries takes practice. Once you've worked with dictionaries for a bit you'll soon see how effectively they can model real-world situations.

Working with Dictionaries

A *dictionary* in Python is a collection of *key-value pairs*. Each *key* is connected to a value, and you can use a key to access the value associated with that key. A key's value can be a number, a string, a list, or even another dictionary. In fact, you can use any object that you can create in Python as a value in a dictionary.

In Python, a dictionary is wrapped in braces, {}, with a series of key-value pairs inside the braces, as shown in the earlier example:

```
alien_0 = {'color': 'green', 'points': 5}
```

A *key-value pair* is a set of values associated with each other. When you provide a key, Python returns the value associated with that key. Every key is connected to its value by a colon, and individual key-value pairs are separated by commas. You can store as many key-value pairs as you want in a dictionary.

The simplest dictionary has exactly one key-value pair, as shown in this modified version of the alien_0 dictionary:

```
alien_0 = {'color': 'green'}
```

This dictionary stores one piece of information about alien_0, namely the alien's color. The string 'color' is a key in this dictionary, and its associated value is 'green'.

Accessing Values in a Dictionary

To get the value associated with a key, give the name of the dictionary and then place the key inside a set of square brackets, as shown here:

alien.py
```
alien_0 = {'color': 'green'}
print(alien_0['color'])
```

This returns the value associated with the key 'color' from the dictionary alien_0:

```
green
```

You can have an unlimited number of key-value pairs in a dictionary. For example, here's the original alien_0 dictionary with two key-value pairs:

```
alien_0 = {'color': 'green', 'points': 5}
```

Now you can access either the color or the point value of alien_0. If a player shoots down this alien, you can look up how many points they should earn using code like this:

```
alien_0 = {'color': 'green', 'points': 5}

❶ new_points = alien_0['points']
❷ print(f"You just earned {new_points} points!")
```

Once the dictionary has been defined, the code at ❶ pulls the value associated with the key 'points' from the dictionary. This value is then assigned to the variable new_points. The line at ❷ prints a statement about how many points the player just earned:

```
You just earned 5 points!
```

If you run this code every time an alien is shot down, the alien's point value will be retrieved.

Adding New Key-Value Pairs

Dictionaries are dynamic structures, and you can add new key-value pairs to a dictionary at any time. For example, to add a new key-value pair, you would give the name of the dictionary followed by the new key in square brackets along with the new value.

Let's add two new pieces of information to the alien_0 dictionary: the alien's x- and y-coordinates, which will help us display the alien in a particular position on the screen. Let's place the alien on the left edge of the screen, 25 pixels down from the top. Because screen coordinates usually start at the upper-left corner of the screen, we'll place the alien on the left edge of the screen by setting the x-coordinate to 0 and 25 pixels from the top by setting its y-coordinate to positive 25, as shown here:

alien.py
```
alien_0 = {'color': 'green', 'points': 5}
print(alien_0)

❶ alien_0['x_position'] = 0
❷ alien_0['y_position'] = 25
print(alien_0)
```

We start by defining the same dictionary that we've been working with. We then print this dictionary, displaying a snapshot of its information. At ❶ we add a new key-value pair to the dictionary: key 'x_position' and value 0. We do the same for key 'y_position' at ❷. When we print the modified dictionary, we see the two additional key-value pairs:

```
{'color': 'green', 'points': 5}
{'color': 'green', 'points': 5, 'y_position': 25, 'x_position': 0}
```

The final version of the dictionary contains four key-value pairs. The original two specify color and point value, and two more specify the alien's position.

NOTE *As of Python 3.7, dictionaries retain the order in which they were defined. When you print a dictionary or loop through its elements, you will see the elements in the same order in which they were added to the dictionary.*

Starting with an Empty Dictionary

It's sometimes convenient, or even necessary, to start with an empty dictionary and then add each new item to it. To start filling an empty dictionary, define a dictionary with an empty set of braces and then add each key-value pair on its own line. For example, here's how to build the alien_0 dictionary using this approach:

alien.py
```
alien_0 = {}

alien_0['color'] = 'green'
alien_0['points'] = 5

print(alien_0)
```

Here we define an empty alien_0 dictionary, and then add color and point values to it. The result is the dictionary we've been using in previous examples:

```
{'color': 'green', 'points': 5}
```

Typically, you'll use empty dictionaries when storing user-supplied data in a dictionary or when you write code that generates a large number of key-value pairs automatically.

Modifying Values in a Dictionary

To modify a value in a dictionary, give the name of the dictionary with the key in square brackets and then the new value you want associated with that key. For example, consider an alien that changes from green to yellow as a game progresses:

alien.py

```
alien_0 = {'color': 'green'}
print(f"The alien is {alien_0['color']}.")

alien_0['color'] = 'yellow'
print(f"The alien is now {alien_0['color']}.")
```

We first define a dictionary for alien_0 that contains only the alien's color; then we change the value associated with the key 'color' to 'yellow'. The output shows that the alien has indeed changed from green to yellow:

```
The alien is green.
The alien is now yellow.
```

For a more interesting example, let's track the position of an alien that can move at different speeds. We'll store a value representing the alien's current speed and then use it to determine how far to the right the alien should move:

```
alien_0 = {'x_position': 0, 'y_position': 25, 'speed': 'medium'}
print(f"Original position: {alien_0['x_position']}")

# Move the alien to the right.
# Determine how far to move the alien based on its current speed.
❶ if alien_0['speed'] == 'slow':
      x_increment = 1
  elif alien_0['speed'] == 'medium':
      x_increment = 2
  else:
      # This must be a fast alien.
      x_increment = 3

# The new position is the old position plus the increment.
❷ alien_0['x_position'] = alien_0['x_position'] + x_increment

print(f"New position: {alien_0['x_position']}")
```

We start by defining an alien with an initial *x* position and *y* position, and a speed of 'medium'. We've omitted the color and point values for the sake of simplicity, but this example would work the same way if you included those key-value pairs as well. We also print the original value of x_position to see how far the alien moves to the right.

At ❶, an if-elif-else chain determines how far the alien should move to the right and assigns this value to the variable x_increment. If the alien's speed is 'slow', it moves one unit to the right; if the speed is 'medium', it moves two units to the right; and if it's 'fast', it moves three units to the right. Once the increment has been calculated, it's added to the value of x_position at ❷, and the result is stored in the dictionary's x_position.

Because this is a medium-speed alien, its position shifts two units to the right:

```
Original x-position: 0
New x-position: 2
```

This technique is pretty cool: by changing one value in the alien's dictionary, you can change the overall behavior of the alien. For example, to turn this medium-speed alien into a fast alien, you would add the line:

```
alien_0['speed'] = 'fast'
```

The if-elif-else block would then assign a larger value to x_increment the next time the code runs.

Removing Key-Value Pairs

When you no longer need a piece of information that's stored in a dictionary, you can use the del statement to completely remove a key-value pair. All del needs is the name of the dictionary and the key that you want to remove.

For example, let's remove the key 'points' from the alien_0 dictionary along with its value:

alien.py
```
alien_0 = {'color': 'green', 'points': 5}
print(alien_0)
```
❶
```
del alien_0['points']
print(alien_0)
```

The line at ❶ tells Python to delete the key 'points' from the dictionary alien_0 and to remove the value associated with that key as well. The output shows that the key 'points' and its value of 5 are deleted from the dictionary, but the rest of the dictionary is unaffected:

```
{'color': 'green', 'points': 5}
{'color': 'green'}
```

NOTE *Be aware that the deleted key-value pair is removed permanently.*

A Dictionary of Similar Objects

The previous example involved storing different kinds of information about one object, an alien in a game. You can also use a dictionary to store one kind of information about many objects. For example, say you want to poll a number of people and ask them what their favorite programming language is. A dictionary is useful for storing the results of a simple poll, like this:

```
favorite_languages = {
    'jen': 'python',
    'sarah': 'c',
    'edward': 'ruby',
    'phil': 'python',
    }
```

As you can see, we've broken a larger dictionary into several lines. Each key is the name of a person who responded to the poll, and each value is their language choice. When you know you'll need more than one line to define a dictionary, press ENTER after the opening brace. Then indent the next line one level (four spaces), and write the first key-value pair, followed by a comma. From this point forward when you press ENTER, your text editor should automatically indent all subsequent key-value pairs to match the first key-value pair.

Once you've finished defining the dictionary, add a closing brace on a new line after the last key-value pair and indent it one level so it aligns with the keys in the dictionary. It's good practice to include a comma after the last key-value pair as well, so you're ready to add a new key-value pair on the next line.

NOTE *Most editors have some functionality that helps you format extended lists and dictionaries in a similar manner to this example. Other acceptable ways to format long dictionaries are available as well, so you may see slightly different formatting in your editor, or in other sources.*

To use this dictionary, given the name of a person who took the poll, you can easily look up their favorite language:

*favorite
_languages.py*

```
favorite_languages = {
    'jen': 'python',
    'sarah': 'c',
    'edward': 'ruby',
    'phil': 'python',
    }
```

❶ ```
language = favorite_languages['sarah'].title()
print(f"Sarah's favorite language is {language}.")
```

To see which language Sarah chose, we ask for the value at:

```
favorite_languages['sarah']
```
```

We use this syntax to pull Sarah's favorite language from the dictionary at ❶ and assign it to the variable `language`. Creating a new variable here makes for a much cleaner `print()` call. The output shows Sarah's favorite language:

```
Sarah's favorite language is C.
```

You could use this same syntax with any individual represented in the dictionary.

Using get() to Access Values

Using keys in square brackets to retrieve the value you're interested in from a dictionary might cause one potential problem: if the key you ask for doesn't exist, you'll get an error.

Let's see what happens when you ask for the point value of an alien that doesn't have a point value set:

alien_no_points.py
```
alien_0 = {'color': 'green', 'speed': 'slow'}
print(alien_0['points'])
```

This results in a traceback, showing a `KeyError`:

```
Traceback (most recent call last):
  File "alien_no_points.py", line 2, in <module>
    print(alien_0['points'])
KeyError: 'points'
```

You'll learn more about how to handle errors like this in general in Chapter 10. For dictionaries, specifically, you can use the get() method to set a default value that will be returned if the requested key doesn't exist.

The get() method requires a key as a first argument. As a second optional argument, you can pass the value to be returned if the key doesn't exist:

```
alien_0 = {'color': 'green', 'speed': 'slow'}

point_value = alien_0.get('points', 'No point value assigned.')
print(point_value)
```

If the key 'points' exists in the dictionary, you'll get the corresponding value. If it doesn't, you get the default value. In this case, points doesn't exist, and we get a clean message instead of an error:

```
No point value assigned.
```

If there's a chance the key you're asking for might not exist, consider using the get() method instead of the square bracket notation.

NOTE
If you leave out the second argument in the call to get() *and the key doesn't exist, Python will return the value* None*. The special value* None *means "no value exists." This is not an error: it's a special value meant to indicate the absence of a value. You'll see more uses for* None *in Chapter 8.*

TRY IT YOURSELF

6-1. Person: Use a dictionary to store information about a person you know. Store their first name, last name, age, and the city in which they live. You should have keys such as first_name, last_name, age, and city. Print each piece of information stored in your dictionary.

6-2. Favorite Numbers: Use a dictionary to store people's favorite numbers. Think of five names, and use them as keys in your dictionary. Think of a favorite number for each person, and store each as a value in your dictionary. Print each person's name and their favorite number. For even more fun, poll a few friends and get some actual data for your program.

6-3. Glossary: A Python dictionary can be used to model an actual dictionary. However, to avoid confusion, let's call it a glossary.

- Think of five programming words you've learned about in the previous chapters. Use these words as the keys in your glossary, and store their meanings as values.

- Print each word and its meaning as neatly formatted output. You might print the word followed by a colon and then its meaning, or print the word on one line and then print its meaning indented on a second line. Use the newline character (\n) to insert a blank line between each word-meaning pair in your output.

Looping Through a Dictionary

A single Python dictionary can contain just a few key-value pairs or millions of pairs. Because a dictionary can contain large amounts of data, Python lets you loop through a dictionary. Dictionaries can be used to store information in a variety of ways; therefore, several different ways exist to loop through them. You can loop through all of a dictionary's key-value pairs, through its keys, or through its values.

Looping Through All Key-Value Pairs

Before we explore the different approaches to looping, let's consider a new dictionary designed to store information about a user on a website. The following dictionary would store one person's username, first name, and last name:

```
user_0 = {
    'username': 'efermi',
    'first': 'enrico',
    'last': 'fermi',
    }
```

You can access any single piece of information about user_0 based on what you've already learned in this chapter. But what if you wanted to see everything stored in this user's dictionary? To do so, you could loop through the dictionary using a for loop:

user.py
```
user_0 = {
    'username': 'efermi',
    'first': 'enrico',
    'last': 'fermi',
    }

❶ for key, value in user_0.items():
❷     print(f"\nKey: {key}")
❸     print(f"Value: {value}")
```

As shown at ❶, to write a for loop for a dictionary, you create names for the two variables that will hold the key and value in each key-value pair. You can choose any names you want for these two variables. This code would work just as well if you had used abbreviations for the variable names, like this:

```
for k, v in user_0.items()
```

The second half of the for statement at ❶ includes the name of the dictionary followed by the method items(), which returns a list of key-value pairs. The for loop then assigns each of these pairs to the two variables provided. In the preceding example, we use the variables to print each key ❷, followed by the associated value ❸. The "\n" in the first print() call ensures that a blank line is inserted before each key-value pair in the output:

```
Key: username
Value: efermi

Key: first
Value: enrico

Key: last
Value: fermi
```

Looping through all key-value pairs works particularly well for dictionaries like the *favorite_languages.py* example on page 97, which stores the same kind of information for many different keys. If you loop through the favorite_languages dictionary, you get the name of each person in the dictionary and their favorite programming language. Because the keys always refer to a person's name and the value is always a language, we'll use the variables name and language in the loop instead of key and value. This will make it easier to follow what's happening inside the loop:

favorite _languages.py

```
favorite_languages = {
    'jen': 'python',
    'sarah': 'c',
    'edward': 'ruby',
    'phil': 'python',
    }
```

❶ for name, language in favorite_languages.items():
❷   print(f"{name.title()}'s favorite language is {language.title()}.")

The code at ❶ tells Python to loop through each key-value pair in the dictionary. As it works through each pair the key is assigned to the variable name, and the value is assigned to the variable language. These descriptive names make it much easier to see what the print() call at ❷ is doing.

Now, in just a few lines of code, we can display all of the information from the poll:

```
Jen's favorite language is Python.
Sarah's favorite language is C.
Edward's favorite language is Ruby.
Phil's favorite language is Python.
```

This type of looping would work just as well if our dictionary stored the results from polling a thousand or even a million people.

Looping Through All the Keys in a Dictionary

The keys() method is useful when you don't need to work with all of the values in a dictionary. Let's loop through the favorite_languages dictionary and print the names of everyone who took the poll:

```
favorite_languages = {
    'jen': 'python',
    'sarah': 'c',
    'edward': 'ruby',
    'phil': 'python',
    }
```

❶ for name in favorite_languages.keys():
    print(name.title())

The line at ❶ tells Python to pull all the keys from the dictionary favorite_languages and assign them one at a time to the variable name. The output shows the names of everyone who took the poll:

```
Jen
Sarah
Edward
Phil
```

Looping through the keys is actually the default behavior when looping through a dictionary, so this code would have exactly the same output if you wrote . . .

```
for name in favorite_languages:
```

rather than . . .

```
for name in favorite_languages.keys():
```

You can choose to use the keys() method explicitly if it makes your code easier to read, or you can omit it if you wish.

You can access the value associated with any key you care about inside the loop by using the current key. Let's print a message to a couple of friends about the languages they chose. We'll loop through the names in the dictionary as we did previously, but when the name matches one of our friends, we'll display a message about their favorite language:

```
favorite_languages = {
    --snip--
    }

❶ friends = ['phil', 'sarah']
  for name in favorite_languages.keys():
      print(f"Hi {name.title()}.")

❷     if name in friends:
❸         language = favorite_languages[name].title()
          print(f"\t{name.title()}, I see you love {language}!")
```

At ❶ we make a list of friends that we want to print a message to. Inside the loop, we print each person's name. Then at ❷ we check whether the name we're working with is in the list friends. If it is, we determine the person's favorite language using the name of the dictionary and the current value of name as the key ❸. We then print a special greeting, including a reference to their language of choice.

Everyone's name is printed, but our friends receive a special message:

```
Hi Jen.
Hi Sarah.
    Sarah, I see you love C!
Hi Edward.
```

```
Hi Phil.
    Phil, I see you love Python!
```

You can also use the keys() method to find out if a particular person was polled. This time, let's find out if Erin took the poll:

```
favorite_languages = {
    'jen': 'python',
    'sarah': 'c',
    'edward': 'ruby',
    'phil': 'python',
    }
```

❶ if 'erin' not in favorite_languages.keys():
       print("Erin, please take our poll!")

The keys() method isn't just for looping: it actually returns a list of all the keys, and the line at ❶ simply checks if 'erin' is in this list. Because she's not, a message is printed inviting her to take the poll:

```
Erin, please take our poll!
```

Looping Through a Dictionary's Keys in a Particular Order

Starting in Python 3.7, looping through a dictionary returns the items in the same order they were inserted. Sometimes, though, you'll want to loop through a dictionary in a different order.

One way to do this is to sort the keys as they're returned in the for loop. You can use the sorted() function to get a copy of the keys in order:

```
favorite_languages = {
    'jen': 'python',
    'sarah': 'c',
    'edward': 'ruby',
    'phil': 'python',
    }

for name in sorted(favorite_languages.keys()):
    print(f"{name.title()}, thank you for taking the poll.")
```

This for statement is like other for statements except that we've wrapped the sorted() function around the dictionary.keys() method. This tells Python to list all keys in the dictionary and sort that list before looping through it. The output shows everyone who took the poll, with the names displayed in order:

```
Edward, thank you for taking the poll.
Jen, thank you for taking the poll.
Phil, thank you for taking the poll.
Sarah, thank you for taking the poll.
```

Looping Through All Values in a Dictionary

If you are primarily interested in the values that a dictionary contains, you can use the values() method to return a list of values without any keys. For example, say we simply want a list of all languages chosen in our programming language poll without the name of the person who chose each language:

```
favorite_languages = {
    'jen': 'python',
    'sarah': 'c',
    'edward': 'ruby',
    'phil': 'python',
    }

print("The following languages have been mentioned:")
for language in favorite_languages.values():
    print(language.title())
```

The for statement here pulls each value from the dictionary and assigns it to the variable language. When these values are printed, we get a list of all chosen languages:

```
The following languages have been mentioned:
Python
C
Ruby
Python
```

This approach pulls all the values from the dictionary without checking for repeats. That might work fine with a small number of values, but in a poll with a large number of respondents, this would result in a very repetitive list. To see each language chosen without repetition, we can use a set. A *set* is a collection in which each item must be unique:

```
favorite_languages = {
    --snip--
    }

  print("The following languages have been mentioned:")
❶ for language in set(favorite_languages.values()):
      print(language.title())
```

When you wrap set() around a list that contains duplicate items, Python identifies the unique items in the list and builds a set from those items. At ❶ we use set() to pull out the unique languages in favorite_languages.values().

The result is a nonrepetitive list of languages that have been mentioned by people taking the poll:

```
The following languages have been mentioned:
Python
```

As you continue learning about Python, you'll often find a built-in feature of the language that helps you do exactly what you want with your data.

NOTE *You can build a set directly using braces and separating the elements with commas:*

```
>>> languages = {'python', 'ruby', 'python', 'c'}
>>> languages
{'ruby', 'python', 'c'}
```

It's easy to mistake sets for dictionaries because they're both wrapped in braces. When you see braces but no key-value pairs, you're probably looking at a set. Unlike lists and dictionaries, sets do not retain items in any specific order.

TRY IT YOURSELF

6-4. Glossary 2: Now that you know how to loop through a dictionary, clean up the code from Exercise 6-3 (page 99) by replacing your series of print() calls with a loop that runs through the dictionary's keys and values. When you're sure that your loop works, add five more Python terms to your glossary. When you run your program again, these new words and meanings should automatically be included in the output.

6-5. Rivers: Make a dictionary containing three major rivers and the country each river runs through. One key-value pair might be 'nile': 'egypt'.

- Use a loop to print a sentence about each river, such as *The Nile runs through Egypt.*

- Use a loop to print the name of each river included in the dictionary.

- Use a loop to print the name of each country included in the dictionary.

6-6. Polling: Use the code in *favorite_languages.py* (page 97).

- Make a list of people who should take the favorite languages poll. Include some names that are already in the dictionary and some that are not.

- Loop through the list of people who should take the poll. If they have already taken the poll, print a message thanking them for responding. If they have not yet taken the poll, print a message inviting them to take the poll.

Nesting

Sometimes you'll want to store multiple dictionaries in a list, or a list of items as a value in a dictionary. This is called *nesting*. You can nest dictionaries inside a list, a list of items inside a dictionary, or even a dictionary inside another dictionary. Nesting is a powerful feature, as the following examples will demonstrate.

A List of Dictionaries

The `alien_0` dictionary contains a variety of information about one alien, but it has no room to store information about a second alien, much less a screen full of aliens. How can you manage a fleet of aliens? One way is to make a list of aliens in which each alien is a dictionary of information about that alien. For example, the following code builds a list of three aliens:

aliens.py
```
alien_0 = {'color': 'green', 'points': 5}
alien_1 = {'color': 'yellow', 'points': 10}
alien_2 = {'color': 'red', 'points': 15}

❶ aliens = [alien_0, alien_1, alien_2]

for alien in aliens:
    print(alien)
```

We first create three dictionaries, each representing a different alien. At ❶ we store each of these dictionaries in a list called aliens. Finally, we loop through the list and print out each alien:

```
{'color': 'green', 'points': 5}
{'color': 'yellow', 'points': 10}
{'color': 'red', 'points': 15}
```

A more realistic example would involve more than three aliens with code that automatically generates each alien. In the following example we use range() to create a fleet of 30 aliens:

```
# Make an empty list for storing aliens.
aliens = []

# Make 30 green aliens.
❶ for alien_number in range(30):
❷     new_alien = {'color': 'green', 'points': 5, 'speed': 'slow'}
❸     aliens.append(new_alien)

# Show the first 5 aliens.
❹ for alien in aliens[:5]:
        print(alien)
    print("...")

# Show how many aliens have been created.
❺ print(f"Total number of aliens: {len(aliens)}")
```

This example begins with an empty list to hold all of the aliens that will be created. At ❶ range() returns a series of numbers, which just tells Python how many times we want the loop to repeat. Each time the loop runs we create a new alien ❷ and then append each new alien to the list aliens ❸. At ❹ we use a slice to print the first five aliens, and then at ❺ we print the length of the list to prove we've actually generated the full fleet of 30 aliens:

```
{'color': 'green', 'points': 5, 'speed': 'slow'}
{'color': 'green', 'points': 5, 'speed': 'slow'}
{'color': 'green', 'points': 5, 'speed': 'slow'}
{'color': 'green', 'points': 5, 'speed': 'slow'}
{'color': 'green', 'points': 5, 'speed': 'slow'}
...

Total number of aliens: 30
```

These aliens all have the same characteristics, but Python considers each one a separate object, which allows us to modify each alien individually.

How might you work with a group of aliens like this? Imagine that one aspect of a game has some aliens changing color and moving faster as the game progresses. When it's time to change colors, we can use a for loop and an if statement to change the color of aliens. For example, to change the first three aliens to yellow, medium-speed aliens worth 10 points each, we could do this:

```
# Make an empty list for storing aliens.
aliens = []

# Make 30 green aliens.
for alien_number in range (30):
    new_alien = {'color': 'green', 'points': 5, 'speed': 'slow'}
    aliens.append(new_alien)

for alien in aliens[:3]:
    if alien['color'] == 'green':
        alien['color'] = 'yellow'
        alien['speed'] = 'medium'
        alien['points'] = 10

# Show the first 5 aliens.
for alien in aliens[:5]:
    print(alien)
print("...")
```

Because we want to modify the first three aliens, we loop through a slice that includes only the first three aliens. All of the aliens are green now but that won't always be the case, so we write an if statement to make sure we're only modifying green aliens. If the alien is green, we change the color to `'yellow'`, the speed to `'medium'`, and the point value to 10, as shown in the following output:

```
{'color': 'yellow', 'points': 10, 'speed': 'medium'}
{'color': 'yellow', 'points': 10, 'speed': 'medium'}
{'color': 'yellow', 'points': 10, 'speed': 'medium'}
{'color': 'green', 'points': 5, 'speed': 'slow'}
{'color': 'green', 'points': 5, 'speed': 'slow'}
...
```

You could expand this loop by adding an `elif` block that turns yellow aliens into red, fast-moving ones worth 15 points each. Without showing the entire program again, that loop would look like this:

```
for alien in aliens[0:3]:
    if alien['color'] == 'green':
        alien['color'] = 'yellow'
        alien['speed'] = 'medium'
        alien['points'] = 10
    elif alien['color'] == 'yellow':
        alien['color'] = 'red'
        alien['speed'] = 'fast'
        alien['points'] = 15
```

It's common to store a number of dictionaries in a list when each dictionary contains many kinds of information about one object. For example, you might create a dictionary for each user on a website, as we did in *user.py* on page 100, and store the individual dictionaries in a list called users. All of the dictionaries in the list should have an identical structure so you can loop through the list and work with each dictionary object in the same way.

A List in a Dictionary

Rather than putting a dictionary inside a list, it's sometimes useful to put a list inside a dictionary. For example, consider how you might describe a pizza that someone is ordering. If you were to use only a list, all you could really store is a list of the pizza's toppings. With a dictionary, a list of toppings can be just one aspect of the pizza you're describing.

In the following example, two kinds of information are stored for each pizza: a type of crust and a list of toppings. The list of toppings is a value associated with the key `'toppings'`. To use the items in the list, we give the name of the dictionary and the key `'toppings'`, as we would any value in the dictionary. Instead of returning a single value, we get a list of toppings:

pizza.py
```
# Store information about a pizza being ordered.
❶ pizza = {
    'crust': 'thick',
    'toppings': ['mushrooms', 'extra cheese'],
    }
```

```
   # Summarize the order.
❷ print(f"You ordered a {pizza['crust']}-crust pizza "
       "with the following toppings:")

❸ for topping in pizza['toppings']:
       print(f"\t{topping}")
```

We begin at ❶ with a dictionary that holds information about a pizza that has been ordered. One key in the dictionary is 'crust', and the associated value is the string 'thick'. The next key, 'toppings', has a list as its value that stores all requested toppings. At ❷ we summarize the order before building the pizza. When you need to break up a long line in a print() call, choose an appropriate point at which to break the line being printed, and end the line with a quotation mark. Indent the next line, add an opening quotation mark, and continue the string. Python will automatically combine all of the strings it finds inside the parentheses. To print the toppings, we write a for loop ❸. To access the list of toppings, we use the key 'toppings', and Python grabs the list of toppings from the dictionary.

The following output summarizes the pizza that we plan to build:

```
You ordered a thick-crust pizza with the following toppings:
    mushrooms
    extra cheese
```

You can nest a list inside a dictionary any time you want more than one value to be associated with a single key in a dictionary. In the earlier example of favorite programming languages, if we were to store each person's responses in a list, people could choose more than one favorite language. When we loop through the dictionary, the value associated with each person would be a list of languages rather than a single language. Inside the dictionary's for loop, we use another for loop to run through the list of languages associated with each person:

favorite ❶ `favorite_languages = {`
_languages.py   `    'jen': ['python', 'ruby'],`
    `    'sarah': ['c'],`
    `    'edward': ['ruby', 'go'],`
    `    'phil': ['python', 'haskell'],`
    `    }`

```
❷ for name, languages in favorite_languages.items():
       print(f"\n{name.title()}'s favorite languages are:")
❸      for language in languages:
           print(f"\t{language.title()}")
```

As you can see at ❶ the value associated with each name is now a list. Notice that some people have one favorite language and others have multiple favorites. When we loop through the dictionary at ❷, we use the variable name languages to hold each value from the dictionary, because we know that each value will be a list. Inside the main dictionary loop, we use another for loop ❸ to run through each person's list of favorite languages. Now each person can list as many favorite languages as they like:

```
Jen's favorite languages are:
    Python
    Ruby

Sarah's favorite languages are:
    C

Edward's favorite languages are:
    Ruby
    Go

Phil's favorite languages are:
    Python
    Haskell
```

To refine this program even further, you could include an if statement at the beginning of the dictionary's for loop to see whether each person has more than one favorite language by examining the value of len(languages). If a person has more than one favorite, the output would stay the same. If the person has only one favorite language, you could change the wording to reflect that. For example, you could say Sarah's favorite language is C.

NOTE *You should not nest lists and dictionaries too deeply. If you're nesting items much deeper than what you see in the preceding examples or you're working with someone else's code with significant levels of nesting, most likely a simpler way to solve the problem exists.*

A Dictionary in a Dictionary

You can nest a dictionary inside another dictionary, but your code can get complicated quickly when you do. For example, if you have several users for a website, each with a unique username, you can use the usernames as the keys in a dictionary. You can then store information about each user by using a dictionary as the value associated with their username. In the following listing, we store three pieces of information about each user: their first name, last name, and location. We'll access this information by looping through the usernames and the dictionary of information associated with each username:

many_users.py
```
users = {
    'aeinstein': {
        'first': 'albert',
```

```
            'last': 'einstein',
            'location': 'princeton',
            },

        'mcurie': {
            'first': 'marie',
            'last': 'curie',
            'location': 'paris',
            },

        }

❶ for username, user_info in users.items():
❷     print(f"\nUsername: {username}")
❸     full_name = f"{user_info['first']} {user_info['last']}"
        location = user_info['location']

❹     print(f"\tFull name: {full_name.title()}")
        print(f"\tLocation: {location.title()}")
```

We first define a dictionary called users with two keys: one each for the usernames 'aeinstein' and 'mcurie'. The value associated with each key is a dictionary that includes each user's first name, last name, and location. At ❶ we loop through the users dictionary. Python assigns each key to the variable username, and the dictionary associated with each username is assigned to the variable user_info. Once inside the main dictionary loop, we print the username at ❷.

At ❸ we start accessing the inner dictionary. The variable user_info, which contains the dictionary of user information, has three keys: 'first', 'last', and 'location'. We use each key to generate a neatly formatted full name and location for each person, and then print a summary of what we know about each user ❹:

```
Username: aeinstein
    Full name: Albert Einstein
    Location: Princeton

Username: mcurie
    Full name: Marie Curie
    Location: Paris
```

Notice that the structure of each user's dictionary is identical. Although not required by Python, this structure makes nested dictionaries easier to work with. If each user's dictionary had different keys, the code inside the for loop would be more complicated.

6-7. People: Start with the program you wrote for Exercise 6-1 (page 99). Make two new dictionaries representing different people, and store all three dictionaries in a list called people. Loop through your list of people. As you loop through the list, print everything you know about each person.

6-8. Pets: Make several dictionaries, where each dictionary represents a different pet. In each dictionary, include the kind of animal and the owner's name. Store these dictionaries in a list called pets. Next, loop through your list and as you do, print everything you know about each pet.

6-9. Favorite Places: Make a dictionary called favorite_places. Think of three names to use as keys in the dictionary, and store one to three favorite places for each person. To make this exercise a bit more interesting, ask some friends to name a few of their favorite places. Loop through the dictionary, and print each person's name and their favorite places.

6-10. Favorite Numbers: Modify your program from Exercise 6-2 (page 99) so each person can have more than one favorite number. Then print each person's name along with their favorite numbers.

6-11. Cities: Make a dictionary called cities. Use the names of three cities as keys in your dictionary. Create a dictionary of information about each city and include the country that the city is in, its approximate population, and one fact about that city. The keys for each city's dictionary should be something like country, population, and fact. Print the name of each city and all of the information you have stored about it.

6-12. Extensions: We're now working with examples that are complex enough that they can be extended in any number of ways. Use one of the example programs from this chapter, and extend it by adding new keys and values, changing the context of the program or improving the formatting of the output.

Summary

In this chapter you learned how to define a dictionary and how to work with the information stored in a dictionary. You learned how to access and modify individual elements in a dictionary, and how to loop through all of the information in a dictionary. You learned to loop through a dictionary's key-value pairs, its keys, and its values. You also learned how to nest multiple dictionaries in a list, nest lists in a dictionary, and nest a dictionary inside a dictionary.

In the next chapter you'll learn about while loops and how to accept input from people who are using your programs. This will be an exciting chapter, because you'll learn to make all of your programs interactive: they'll be able to respond to user input.

7

USER INPUT AND WHILE LOOPS

Most programs are written to solve an end user's problem. To do so, you usually need to get some information from the user. For a simple example, let's say someone wants to find out whether they're old enough to vote. If you write a program to answer this question, you need to know the user's age before you can provide an answer. The program will need to ask the user to enter, or *input*, their age; once the program has this input, it can compare it to the voting age to determine if the user is old enough and then report the result.

In this chapter you'll learn how to accept user input so your program can then work with it. When your program needs a name, you'll be able to prompt the user for a name. When your program needs a list of names, you'll be able to prompt the user for a series of names. To do this, you'll use the input() function.

You'll also learn how to keep programs running as long as users want them to, so they can enter as much information as they need to; then, your program can work with that information. You'll use Python's while loop to keep programs running as long as certain conditions remain true.

With the ability to work with user input and the ability to control how long your programs run, you'll be able to write fully interactive programs.

How the input() Function Works

The input() function pauses your program and waits for the user to enter some text. Once Python receives the user's input, it assigns that input to a variable to make it convenient for you to work with.

For example, the following program asks the user to enter some text, then displays that message back to the user:

parrot.py

```
message = input("Tell me something, and I will repeat it back to you: ")
print(message)
```

The input() function takes one argument: the *prompt*, or instructions, that we want to display to the user so they know what to do. In this example, when Python runs the first line, the user sees the prompt Tell me something, and I will repeat it back to you: . The program waits while the user enters their response and continues after the user presses ENTER. The response is assigned to the variable message, then print(message) displays the input back to the user:

```
Tell me something, and I will repeat it back to you: Hello everyone!
Hello everyone!
```

NOTE   *Sublime Text and many other editors don't run programs that prompt the user for input. You can use these editors to write programs that prompt for input, but you'll need to run these programs from a terminal. See "Running Python Programs from a Terminal" on page 12.*

Writing Clear Prompts

Each time you use the input() function, you should include a clear, easy-to-follow prompt that tells the user exactly what kind of information you're looking for. Any statement that tells the user what to enter should work. For example:

greeter.py

```
name = input("Please enter your name: ")
print(f"\nHello, {name}!")
```

Add a space at the end of your prompts (after the colon in the preceding example) to separate the prompt from the user's response and to make it clear to your user where to enter their text. For example:

```
Please enter your name: Eric
Hello, Eric!
```

Sometimes you'll want to write a prompt that's longer than one line. For example, you might want to tell the user why you're asking for certain input. You can assign your prompt to a variable and pass that variable to the input() function. This allows you to build your prompt over several lines, then write a clean input() statement.

greeter.py

```
prompt = "If you tell us who you are, we can personalize the messages you see."
prompt += "\nWhat is your first name? "

name = input(prompt)
print(f"\nHello, {name}!")
```

This example shows one way to build a multi-line string. The first line assigns the first part of the message to the variable prompt. In the second line, the operator += takes the string that was assigned to prompt and adds the new string onto the end.

The prompt now spans two lines, again with space after the question mark for clarity:

```
If you tell us who you are, we can personalize the messages you see.
What is your first name? Eric

Hello, Eric!
```

Using int() to Accept Numerical Input

When you use the input() function, Python interprets everything the user enters as a string. Consider the following interpreter session, which asks for the user's age:

```
>>> age = input("How old are you? ")
How old are you? 21
>>> age
'21'
```

The user enters the number 21, but when we ask Python for the value of age, it returns '21', the string representation of the numerical value entered. We know Python interpreted the input as a string because the number is now enclosed in quotes. If all you want to do is print the input, this works well. But if you try to use the input as a number, you'll get an error:

```
>>> age = input("How old are you? ")
How old are you? 21
❶ >>> age >= 18
Traceback (most recent call last):
  File "<stdin>", line 1, in <module>
❷ TypeError: unorderable types: str() >= int()
```

When you try to use the input to do a numerical comparison ❶, Python produces an error because it can't compare a string to an integer: the string '21' that's assigned to age can't be compared to the numerical value 18 ❷.

We can resolve this issue by using the int() function, which tells Python to treat the input as a numerical value. The int() function converts a string representation of a number to a numerical representation, as shown here:

```
>>> age = input("How old are you? ")
How old are you? 21
❶ >>> age = int(age)
>>> age >= 18
True
```

In this example, when we enter 21 at the prompt, Python interprets the number as a string, but the value is then converted to a numerical representation by int() ❶. Now Python can run the conditional test: it compares age (which now represents the numerical value 21) and 18 to see if age is greater than or equal to 18. This test evaluates to True.

How do you use the int() function in an actual program? Consider a program that determines whether people are tall enough to ride a roller coaster:

rollercoaster.py
```
height = input("How tall are you, in inches? ")
height = int(height)

if height >= 48:
    print("\nYou're tall enough to ride!")
else:
    print("\nYou'll be able to ride when you're a little older.")
```

The program can compare height to 48 because height = int(height) converts the input value to a numerical representation before the comparison is made. If the number entered is greater than or equal to 48, we tell the user that they're tall enough:

```
How tall are you, in inches? 71

You're tall enough to ride!
```

When you use numerical input to do calculations and comparisons, be sure to convert the input value to a numerical representation first.

The Modulo Operator

A useful tool for working with numerical information is the *modulo operator* (%), which divides one number by another number and returns the remainder:

```
>>> 4 % 3
1
```

```
>>> 5 % 3
2
>>> 6 % 3
0
>>> 7 % 3
1
```

The modulo operator doesn't tell you how many times one number fits into another; it just tells you what the remainder is.

When one number is divisible by another number, the remainder is 0, so the modulo operator always returns 0. You can use this fact to determine if a number is even or odd:

even_or_odd.py
```
number = input("Enter a number, and I'll tell you if it's even or odd: ")
number = int(number)

if number % 2 == 0:
    print(f"\nThe number {number} is even.")
else:
    print(f"\nThe number {number} is odd.")
```

Even numbers are always divisible by two, so if the modulo of a number and two is zero (here, if number % 2 == 0) the number is even. Otherwise, it's odd.

```
Enter a number, and I'll tell you if it's even or odd: 42

The number 42 is even.
```

TRY IT YOURSELF

7-1. Rental Car: Write a program that asks the user what kind of rental car they would like. Print a message about that car, such as "Let me see if I can find you a Subaru."

7-2. Restaurant Seating: Write a program that asks the user how many people are in their dinner group. If the answer is more than eight, print a message saying they'll have to wait for a table. Otherwise, report that their table is ready.

7-3. Multiples of Ten: Ask the user for a number, and then report whether the number is a multiple of 10 or not.

Introducing while Loops

The for loop takes a collection of items and executes a block of code once for each item in the collection. In contrast, the while loop runs as long as, or *while*, a certain condition is true.

The while Loop in Action

You can use a while loop to count up through a series of numbers. For example, the following while loop counts from 1 to 5:

counting.py

```
current_number = 1
while current_number <= 5:
    print(current_number)
    current_number += 1
```

In the first line, we start counting from 1 by assigning current_number the value 1. The while loop is then set to keep running as long as the value of current_number is less than or equal to 5. The code inside the loop prints the value of current_number and then adds 1 to that value with current_number += 1. (The += operator is shorthand for current_number = current_number + 1.)

Python repeats the loop as long as the condition current_number <= 5 is true. Because 1 is less than 5, Python prints 1 and then adds 1, making the current number 2. Because 2 is less than 5, Python prints 2 and adds 1 again, making the current number 3, and so on. Once the value of current_number is greater than 5, the loop stops running and the program ends:

```
1
2
3
4
5
```

The programs you use every day most likely contain while loops. For example, a game needs a while loop to keep running as long as you want to keep playing, and so it can stop running as soon as you ask it to quit. Programs wouldn't be fun to use if they stopped running before we told them to or kept running even after we wanted to quit, so while loops are quite useful.

Letting the User Choose When to Quit

We can make the *parrot.py* program run as long as the user wants by putting most of the program inside a while loop. We'll define a *quit value* and then keep the program running as long as the user has not entered the quit value:

parrot.py ❶
```
prompt = "\nTell me something, and I will repeat it back to you:"
prompt += "\nEnter 'quit' to end the program. "
```

```
❷ message = ""
❸ while message != 'quit':
      message = input(prompt)
      print(message)
```

At ❶, we define a prompt that tells the user their two options: entering a message or entering the quit value (in this case, 'quit'). Then we set up a variable message ❷ to keep track of whatever value the user enters. We define message as an empty string, "", so Python has something to check the first time it reaches the while line. The first time the program runs and Python reaches the while statement, it needs to compare the value of message to 'quit', but no user input has been entered yet. If Python has nothing to compare, it won't be able to continue running the program. To solve this problem, we make sure to give message an initial value. Although it's just an empty string, it will make sense to Python and allow it to perform the comparison that makes the while loop work. This while loop ❸ runs as long as the value of message is not 'quit'.

The first time through the loop, message is just an empty string, so Python enters the loop. At message = input(prompt), Python displays the prompt and waits for the user to enter their input. Whatever they enter is assigned to message and printed; then, Python reevaluates the condition in the while statement. As long as the user has not entered the word 'quit', the prompt is displayed again and Python waits for more input. When the user finally enters 'quit', Python stops executing the while loop and the program ends:

```
Tell me something, and I will repeat it back to you:
Enter 'quit' to end the program. Hello everyone!
Hello everyone!

Tell me something, and I will repeat it back to you:
Enter 'quit' to end the program. Hello again.
Hello again.

Tell me something, and I will repeat it back to you:
Enter 'quit' to end the program. quit
quit
```

This program works well, except that it prints the word 'quit' as if it were an actual message. A simple if test fixes this:

```
prompt = "\nTell me something, and I will repeat it back to you:"
prompt += "\nEnter 'quit' to end the program. "

message = ""
while message != 'quit':
    message = input(prompt)

    if message != 'quit':
        print(message)
```

Now the program makes a quick check before displaying the message and only prints the message if it does not match the quit value:

```
Tell me something, and I will repeat it back to you:
Enter 'quit' to end the program. Hello everyone!
Hello everyone!

Tell me something, and I will repeat it back to you:
Enter 'quit' to end the program. Hello again.
Hello again.

Tell me something, and I will repeat it back to you:
Enter 'quit' to end the program. quit
```

Using a Flag

In the previous example, we had the program perform certain tasks while a given condition was true. But what about more complicated programs in which many different events could cause the program to stop running?

For example, in a game, several different events can end the game. When the player runs out of ships, their time runs out, or the cities they were supposed to protect are all destroyed, the game should end. It needs to end if any one of these events happens. If many possible events might occur to stop the program, trying to test all these conditions in one while statement becomes complicated and difficult.

For a program that should run only as long as many conditions are true, you can define one variable that determines whether or not the entire program is active. This variable, called a *flag*, acts as a signal to the program. We can write our programs so they run while the flag is set to True and stop running when any of several events sets the value of the flag to False. As a result, our overall while statement needs to check only one condition: whether or not the flag is currently True. Then, all our other tests (to see if an event has occurred that should set the flag to False) can be neatly organized in the rest of the program.

Let's add a flag to *parrot.py* from the previous section. This flag, which we'll call active (though you can call it anything), will monitor whether or not the program should continue running:

```
prompt = "\nTell me something, and I will repeat it back to you:"
prompt += "\nEnter 'quit' to end the program. "
```
```
❶ active = True
❷ while active:
       message = input(prompt)

❸     if message == 'quit':
           active = False
❹     else:
           print(message)
```

We set the variable active to True ❶ so the program starts in an active state. Doing so makes the while statement simpler because no comparison is made in the while statement itself; the logic is taken care of in other parts of the program. As long as the active variable remains True, the loop will continue running ❷.

In the if statement inside the while loop, we check the value of message once the user enters their input. If the user enters 'quit' ❸, we set active to False, and the while loop stops. If the user enters anything other than 'quit' ❹, we print their input as a message.

This program has the same output as the previous example where we placed the conditional test directly in the while statement. But now that we have a flag to indicate whether the overall program is in an active state, it would be easy to add more tests (such as elif statements) for events that should cause active to become False. This is useful in complicated programs like games in which there may be many events that should each make the program stop running. When any of these events causes the active flag to become False, the main game loop will exit, a *Game Over* message can be displayed, and the player can be given the option to play again.

Using break to Exit a Loop

To exit a while loop immediately without running any remaining code in the loop, regardless of the results of any conditional test, use the break statement. The break statement directs the flow of your program; you can use it to control which lines of code are executed and which aren't, so the program only executes code that you want it to, when you want it to.

For example, consider a program that asks the user about places they've visited. We can stop the while loop in this program by calling break as soon as the user enters the 'quit' value:

cities.py
```
prompt = "\nPlease enter the name of a city you have visited:"
prompt += "\n(Enter 'quit' when you are finished.) "

❶ while True:
    city = input(prompt)

    if city == 'quit':
        break
    else:
        print(f"I'd love to go to {city.title()}!")
```

A loop that starts with while True ❶ will run forever unless it reaches a break statement. The loop in this program continues asking the user to enter the names of cities they've been to until they enter 'quit'. When they enter 'quit', the break statement runs, causing Python to exit the loop:

```
Please enter the name of a city you have visited:
(Enter 'quit' when you are finished.) New York
I'd love to go to New York!
```

```
Please enter the name of a city you have visited:
(Enter 'quit' when you are finished.) San Francisco
I'd love to go to San Francisco!

Please enter the name of a city you have visited:
(Enter 'quit' when you are finished.) quit
```

NOTE   *You can use the break statement in any of Python's loops. For example, you could use break to quit a for loop that's working through a list or a dictionary.*

Using continue in a Loop

Rather than breaking out of a loop entirely without executing the rest of its code, you can use the continue statement to return to the beginning of the loop based on the result of a conditional test. For example, consider a loop that counts from 1 to 10 but prints only the odd numbers in that range:

counting.py
```
current_number = 0
while current_number < 10:
❶    current_number += 1
     if current_number % 2 == 0:
         continue

    print(current_number)
```

First we set current_number to 0. Because it's less than 10, Python enters the while loop. Once inside the loop, we increment the count by 1 at ❶, so current_number is 1. The if statement then checks the modulo of current_number and 2. If the modulo is 0 (which means current_number is divisible by 2), the continue statement tells Python to ignore the rest of the loop and return to the beginning. If the current number is not divisible by 2, the rest of the loop is executed and Python prints the current number:

```
1
3
5
7
9
```

Avoiding Infinite Loops

Every while loop needs a way to stop running so it won't continue to run forever. For example, this counting loop should count from 1 to 5:

counting.py
```
x = 1
while x <= 5:
    print(x)
    x += 1
```

But if you accidentally omit the line x += 1 (as shown next), the loop will run forever:

```
# This loop runs forever!
x = 1
while x <= 5:
    print(x)
```

Now the value of x will start at 1 but never change. As a result, the conditional test x <= 5 will always evaluate to True and the while loop will run forever, printing a series of 1s, like this:

```
1
1
1
1
--snip--
```

Every programmer accidentally writes an infinite while loop from time to time, especially when a program's loops have subtle exit conditions. If your program gets stuck in an infinite loop, press CTRL-C or just close the terminal window displaying your program's output.

To avoid writing infinite loops, test every while loop and make sure the loop stops when you expect it to. If you want your program to end when the user enters a certain input value, run the program and enter that value. If the program doesn't end, scrutinize the way your program handles the value that should cause the loop to exit. Make sure at least one part of the program can make the loop's condition False or cause it to reach a break statement.

NOTE   *Sublime Text and some other editors have an embedded output window. This can make it difficult to stop an infinite loop, and you might have to close the editor to end the loop. Try clicking in the output area of the editor before pressing CTRL-C, and you should be able to cancel an infinite loop.*

TRY IT YOURSELF

7-4. Pizza Toppings: Write a loop that prompts the user to enter a series of pizza toppings until they enter a 'quit' value. As they enter each topping, print a message saying you'll add that topping to their pizza.

7-5. Movie Tickets: A movie theater charges different ticket prices depending on a person's age. If a person is under the age of 3, the ticket is free; if they are between 3 and 12, the ticket is $10; and if they are over age 12, the ticket is $15. Write a loop in which you ask users their age, and then tell them the cost of their movie ticket.

(continued)

Using a while Loop with Lists and Dictionaries

So far, we've worked with only one piece of user information at a time. We received the user's input and then printed the input or a response to it. The next time through the while loop, we'd receive another input value and respond to that. But to keep track of many users and pieces of information, we'll need to use lists and dictionaries with our while loops.

A for loop is effective for looping through a list, but you shouldn't modify a list inside a for loop because Python will have trouble keeping track of the items in the list. To modify a list as you work through it, use a while loop. Using while loops with lists and dictionaries allows you to collect, store, and organize lots of input to examine and report on later.

Moving Items from One List to Another

Consider a list of newly registered but unverified users of a website. After we verify these users, how can we move them to a separate list of confirmed users? One way would be to use a while loop to pull users from the list of unconfirmed users as we verify them and then add them to a separate list of confirmed users. Here's what that code might look like:

confirmed _users.py
```
# Start with users that need to be verified,
#  and an empty list to hold confirmed users.
❶ unconfirmed_users = ['alice', 'brian', 'candace']
confirmed_users = []

# Verify each user until there are no more unconfirmed users.
#  Move each verified user into the list of confirmed users.
❷ while unconfirmed_users:
❸     current_user = unconfirmed_users.pop()

    print(f"Verifying user: {current_user.title()}")
❹     confirmed_users.append(current_user)
```

```
# Display all confirmed users.
print("\nThe following users have been confirmed:")
for confirmed_user in confirmed_users:
    print(confirmed_user.title())
```

We begin with a list of unconfirmed users at ❶ (Alice, Brian, and Candace) and an empty list to hold confirmed users. The while loop at ❷ runs as long as the list unconfirmed_users is not empty. Within this loop, the pop() method at ❸ removes unverified users one at a time from the end of unconfirmed_users. Here, because Candace is last in the unconfirmed_users list, her name will be the first to be removed, assigned to current_user, and added to the confirmed_users list at ❹. Next is Brian, then Alice.

We simulate confirming each user by printing a verification message and then adding them to the list of confirmed users. As the list of unconfirmed users shrinks, the list of confirmed users grows. When the list of unconfirmed users is empty, the loop stops and the list of confirmed users is printed:

```
Verifying user: Candace
Verifying user: Brian
Verifying user: Alice

The following users have been confirmed:
Candace
Brian
Alice
```

Removing All Instances of Specific Values from a List

In Chapter 3 we used remove() to remove a specific value from a list. The remove() function worked because the value we were interested in appeared only once in the list. But what if you want to remove all instances of a value from a list?

Say you have a list of pets with the value 'cat' repeated several times. To remove all instances of that value, you can run a while loop until 'cat' is no longer in the list, as shown here:

pets.py
```
pets = ['dog', 'cat', 'dog', 'goldfish', 'cat', 'rabbit', 'cat']
print(pets)

while 'cat' in pets:
    pets.remove('cat')

print(pets)
```

We start with a list containing multiple instances of 'cat'. After printing the list, Python enters the while loop because it finds the value 'cat' in the list at least once. Once inside the loop, Python removes the first instance of 'cat', returns to the while line, and then reenters the loop when it finds that 'cat' is still in the list. It removes each instance of 'cat' until the value is no longer in the list, at which point Python exits the loop and prints the list again:

```
['dog', 'cat', 'dog', 'goldfish', 'cat', 'rabbit', 'cat']
['dog', 'dog', 'goldfish', 'rabbit']
```

Filling a Dictionary with User Input

You can prompt for as much input as you need in each pass through a while loop. Let's make a polling program in which each pass through the loop prompts for the participant's name and response. We'll store the data we gather in a dictionary, because we want to connect each response with a particular user:

mountain _poll.py

```
responses = {}

# Set a flag to indicate that polling is active.
polling_active = True

while polling_active:
    # Prompt for the person's name and response.
❶    name = input("\nWhat is your name? ")
    response = input("Which mountain would you like to climb someday? ")

    # Store the response in the dictionary.
❷    responses[name] = response

    # Find out if anyone else is going to take the poll.
❸    repeat = input("Would you like to let another person respond? (yes/ no) ")
    if repeat == 'no':
        polling_active = False

# Polling is complete. Show the results.
print("\n--- Poll Results ---")
❹ for name, response in responses.items():
    print(f"{name} would like to climb {response}.")
```

The program first defines an empty dictionary (responses) and sets a flag (polling_active) to indicate that polling is active. As long as polling_active is True, Python will run the code in the while loop.

Within the loop, the user is prompted to enter their name and a mountain they'd like to climb ❶. That information is stored in the responses dictionary ❷, and the user is asked whether or not to keep the poll running ❸. If they enter yes, the program enters the while loop again. If they enter no, the polling_active flag is set to False, the while loop stops running, and the final code block at ❹ displays the results of the poll.

If you run this program and enter sample responses, you should see output like this:

```
What is your name? Eric
Which mountain would you like to climb someday? Denali
Would you like to let another person respond? (yes/ no) yes

What is your name? Lynn
Which mountain would you like to climb someday? Devil's Thumb
Would you like to let another person respond? (yes/ no) no

--- Poll Results ---
Eric would like to climb Denali.
Lynn would like to climb Devil's Thumb.
```

TRY IT YOURSELF

7-8. Deli: Make a list called sandwich_orders and fill it with the names of various sandwiches. Then make an empty list called finished_sandwiches. Loop through the list of sandwich orders and print a message for each order, such as I made your tuna sandwich. As each sandwich is made, move it to the list of finished sandwiches. After all the sandwiches have been made, print a message listing each sandwich that was made.

7-9. No Pastrami: Using the list sandwich_orders from Exercise 7-8, make sure the sandwich 'pastrami' appears in the list at least three times. Add code near the beginning of your program to print a message saying the deli has run out of pastrami, and then use a while loop to remove all occurrences of 'pastrami' from sandwich_orders. Make sure no pastrami sandwiches end up in finished_sandwiches.

7-10. Dream Vacation: Write a program that polls users about their dream vacation. Write a prompt similar to *If you could visit one place in the world, where would you go?* Include a block of code that prints the results of the poll.

Summary

In this chapter you learned how to use input() to allow users to provide their own information in your programs. You learned to work with both text and numerical input and how to use while loops to make your programs run as long as your users want them to. You saw several ways to control the flow of a while loop by setting an active flag, using the break statement, and using the continue statement. You learned how to use a while loop to move items from one list to another and how to remove all instances of a value from a list. You also learned how while loops can be used with dictionaries.

In Chapter 8 you'll learn about *functions*. Functions allow you to break your programs into small parts, each of which does one specific job. You can call a function as many times as you want, and you can store your functions in separate files. By using functions, you'll be able to write more efficient code that's easier to troubleshoot and maintain and that can be reused in many different programs.

8

FUNCTIONS

In this chapter you'll learn to write *functions*, which are named blocks of code that are designed to do one specific job. When you want to perform a particular task that you've defined in a function, you *call* the function responsible for it. If you need to perform that task multiple times throughout your program, you don't need to type all the code for the same task again and again; you just call the function dedicated to handling that task, and the call tells Python to run the code inside the function. You'll find that using functions makes your programs easier to write, read, test, and fix.

In this chapter you'll also learn ways to pass information to functions. You'll learn how to write certain functions whose primary job is to display information and other functions designed to process data and return a value or set of values. Finally, you'll learn to store functions in separate files called *modules* to help organize your main program files.

Defining a Function

Here's a simple function named greet_user() that prints a greeting:

greeter.py
```
❶ def greet_user():
❷     """Display a simple greeting."""
❸     print("Hello!")

❹ greet_user()
```

This example shows the simplest structure of a function. The line at ❶ uses the keyword def to inform Python that you're defining a function. This is the *function definition*, which tells Python the name of the function and, if applicable, what kind of information the function needs to do its job. The parentheses hold that information. In this case, the name of the function is greet_user(), and it needs no information to do its job, so its parentheses are empty. (Even so, the parentheses are required.) Finally, the definition ends in a colon.

Any indented lines that follow def greet_user(): make up the *body* of the function. The text at ❷ is a comment called a *docstring*, which describes what the function does. Docstrings are enclosed in triple quotes, which Python looks for when it generates documentation for the functions in your programs.

The line print("Hello!") ❸ is the only line of actual code in the body of this function, so greet_user() has just one job: print("Hello!").

When you want to use this function, you call it. A *function call* tells Python to execute the code in the function. To *call* a function, you write the name of the function, followed by any necessary information in parentheses, as shown at ❹. Because no information is needed here, calling our function is as simple as entering greet_user(). As expected, it prints Hello!:

```
Hello!
```

Passing Information to a Function

Modified slightly, the function greet_user() can not only tell the user Hello! but also greet them by name. For the function to do this, you enter username in the parentheses of the function's definition at def greet_user(). By adding username here you allow the function to accept any value of username you specify. The function now expects you to provide a value for username each time you call it. When you call greet_user(), you can pass it a name, such as 'jesse', inside the parentheses:

```
def greet_user(username):
    """Display a simple greeting."""
    print(f"Hello, {username.title()}!")

greet_user('jesse')
```

Entering greet_user('jesse') calls greet_user() and gives the function the information it needs to execute the print() call. The function accepts the name you passed it and displays the greeting for that name:

```
Hello, Jesse!
```

Likewise, entering greet_user('sarah') calls greet_user(), passes it 'sarah', and prints Hello, Sarah! You can call greet_user() as often as you want and pass it any name you want to produce a predictable output every time.

Arguments and Parameters

In the preceding greet_user() function, we defined greet_user() to require a value for the variable username. Once we called the function and gave it the information (a person's name), it printed the right greeting.

The variable username in the definition of greet_user() is an example of a *parameter*, a piece of information the function needs to do its job. The value 'jesse' in greet_user('jesse') is an example of an *argument*. An argument is a piece of information that's passed from a function call to a function. When we call the function, we place the value we want the function to work with in parentheses. In this case the argument 'jesse' was passed to the function greet_user(), and the value was assigned to the parameter username.

NOTE *People sometimes speak of arguments and parameters interchangeably. Don't be surprised if you see the variables in a function definition referred to as arguments or the variables in a function call referred to as parameters.*

TRY IT YOURSELF

8-1. Message: Write a function called display_message() that prints one sentence telling everyone what you are learning about in this chapter. Call the function, and make sure the message displays correctly.

8-2. Favorite Book: Write a function called favorite_book() that accepts one parameter, title. The function should print a message, such as One of my favorite books is Alice in Wonderland. Call the function, making sure to include a book title as an argument in the function call.

Passing Arguments

Because a function definition can have multiple parameters, a function call may need multiple arguments. You can pass arguments to your functions in a number of ways. You can use *positional arguments*, which need to be in the same order the parameters were written; *keyword arguments*, where each argument consists of a variable name and a value; and lists and dictionaries of values. Let's look at each of these in turn.

Positional Arguments

When you call a function, Python must match each argument in the function call with a parameter in the function definition. The simplest way to do this is based on the order of the arguments provided. Values matched up this way are called *positional arguments*.

To see how this works, consider a function that displays information about pets. The function tells us what kind of animal each pet is and the pet's name, as shown here:

pets.py ❶
```python
def describe_pet(animal_type, pet_name):
    """Display information about a pet."""
    print(f"\nI have a {animal_type}.")
    print(f"My {animal_type}'s name is {pet_name.title()}.")
```

❷
```python
describe_pet('hamster', 'harry')
```

The definition shows that this function needs a type of animal and the animal's name ❶. When we call describe_pet(), we need to provide an animal type and a name, in that order. For example, in the function call, the argument 'hamster' is assigned to the parameter animal_type and the argument 'harry' is assigned to the parameter pet_name ❷. In the function body, these two parameters are used to display information about the pet being described.

The output describes a hamster named Harry:

```
I have a hamster.
My hamster's name is Harry.
```

Multiple Function Calls

You can call a function as many times as needed. Describing a second, different pet requires just one more call to describe_pet():

```python
def describe_pet(animal_type, pet_name):
    """Display information about a pet."""
    print(f"\nI have a {animal_type}.")
    print(f"My {animal_type}'s name is {pet_name.title()}.")

describe_pet('hamster', 'harry')
describe_pet('dog', 'willie')
```

In this second function call, we pass describe_pet() the arguments 'dog' and 'willie'. As with the previous set of arguments we used, Python matches 'dog' with the parameter animal_type and 'willie' with the parameter pet_name.

As before, the function does its job, but this time it prints values for a dog named Willie. Now we have a hamster named Harry and a dog named Willie:

```
I have a hamster.
My hamster's name is Harry.

I have a dog.
My dog's name is Willie.
```

Calling a function multiple times is a very efficient way to work. The code describing a pet is written once in the function. Then, anytime you want to describe a new pet, you call the function with the new pet's information. Even if the code for describing a pet were to expand to ten lines, you could still describe a new pet in just one line by calling the function again.

You can use as many positional arguments as you need in your functions. Python works through the arguments you provide when calling the function and matches each one with the corresponding parameter in the function's definition.

Order Matters in Positional Arguments

You can get unexpected results if you mix up the order of the arguments in a function call when using positional arguments:

```
def describe_pet(animal_type, pet_name):
    """Display information about a pet."""
    print(f"\nI have a {animal_type}.")
    print(f"My {animal_type}'s name is {pet_name.title()}.")

describe_pet('harry', 'hamster')
```

In this function call we list the name first and the type of animal second. Because the argument 'harry' is listed first this time, that value is assigned to the parameter animal_type. Likewise, 'hamster' is assigned to pet_name. Now we have a "harry" named "Hamster":

```
I have a harry.
My harry's name is Hamster.
```

If you get funny results like this, check to make sure the order of the arguments in your function call matches the order of the parameters in the function's definition.

Keyword Arguments

A *keyword argument* is a name-value pair that you pass to a function. You directly associate the name and the value within the argument, so when you pass the argument to the function, there's no confusion (you won't end up with a harry named Hamster). Keyword arguments free you from having to worry about correctly ordering your arguments in the function call, and they clarify the role of each value in the function call.

Let's rewrite *pets.py* using keyword arguments to call `describe_pet()`:

```
def describe_pet(animal_type, pet_name):
    """Display information about a pet."""
    print(f"\nI have a {animal_type}.")
    print(f"My {animal_type}'s name is {pet_name.title()}.")

describe_pet(animal_type='hamster', pet_name='harry')
```

The function `describe_pet()` hasn't changed. But when we call the function, we explicitly tell Python which parameter each argument should be matched with. When Python reads the function call, it knows to assign the argument 'hamster' to the parameter `animal_type` and the argument 'harry' to `pet_name`. The output correctly shows that we have a hamster named Harry.

The order of keyword arguments doesn't matter because Python knows where each value should go. The following two function calls are equivalent:

```
describe_pet(animal_type='hamster', pet_name='harry')
describe_pet(pet_name='harry', animal_type='hamster')
```

NOTE   *When you use keyword arguments, be sure to use the exact names of the parameters in the function's definition.*

Default Values

When writing a function, you can define a *default value* for each parameter. If an argument for a parameter is provided in the function call, Python uses the argument value. If not, it uses the parameter's default value. So when you define a default value for a parameter, you can exclude the corresponding argument you'd usually write in the function call. Using default values can simplify your function calls and clarify the ways in which your functions are typically used.

For example, if you notice that most of the calls to `describe_pet()` are being used to describe dogs, you can set the default value of `animal_type` to 'dog'. Now anyone calling `describe_pet()` for a dog can omit that information:

```
def describe_pet(pet_name, animal_type='dog'):
    """Display information about a pet."""
    print(f"\nI have a {animal_type}.")
    print(f"My {animal_type}'s name is {pet_name.title()}.")

describe_pet(pet_name='willie')
```

We changed the definition of describe_pet() to include a default value, 'dog', for animal_type. Now when the function is called with no animal_type specified, Python knows to use the value 'dog' for this parameter:

```
I have a dog.
My dog's name is Willie.
```

Note that the order of the parameters in the function definition had to be changed. Because the default value makes it unnecessary to specify a type of animal as an argument, the only argument left in the function call is the pet's name. Python still interprets this as a positional argument, so if the function is called with just a pet's name, that argument will match up with the first parameter listed in the function's definition. This is the reason the first parameter needs to be pet_name.

The simplest way to use this function now is to provide just a dog's name in the function call:

```
describe_pet('willie')
```

This function call would have the same output as the previous example. The only argument provided is 'willie', so it is matched up with the first parameter in the definition, pet_name. Because no argument is provided for animal_type, Python uses the default value 'dog'.

To describe an animal other than a dog, you could use a function call like this:

```
describe_pet(pet_name='harry', animal_type='hamster')
```

Because an explicit argument for animal_type is provided, Python will ignore the parameter's default value.

NOTE *When you use default values, any parameter with a default value needs to be listed after all the parameters that don't have default values. This allows Python to continue interpreting positional arguments correctly.*

Equivalent Function Calls

Because positional arguments, keyword arguments, and default values can all be used together, often you'll have several equivalent ways to call a function. Consider the following definition for describe_pet() with one default value provided:

```
def describe_pet(pet_name, animal_type='dog'):
```

With this definition, an argument always needs to be provided for pet_name, and this value can be provided using the positional or keyword format. If the animal being described is not a dog, an argument for animal_type must be included in the call, and this argument can also be specified using the positional or keyword format.

All of the following calls would work for this function:

```
# A dog named Willie.
describe_pet('willie')
describe_pet(pet_name='willie')

# A hamster named Harry.
describe_pet('harry', 'hamster')
describe_pet(pet_name='harry', animal_type='hamster')
describe_pet(animal_type='hamster', pet_name='harry')
```

Each of these function calls would have the same output as the previous examples.

NOTE *It doesn't really matter which calling style you use. As long as your function calls produce the output you want, just use the style you find easiest to understand.*

Avoiding Argument Errors

When you start to use functions, don't be surprised if you encounter errors about unmatched arguments. Unmatched arguments occur when you provide fewer or more arguments than a function needs to do its work. For example, here's what happens if we try to call describe_pet() with no arguments:

```
def describe_pet(animal_type, pet_name):
    """Display information about a pet."""
    print(f"\nI have a {animal_type}.")
    print(f"My {animal_type}'s name is {pet_name.title()}.")

describe_pet()
```

Python recognizes that some information is missing from the function call, and the traceback tells us that:

```
Traceback (most recent call last):
❶   File "pets.py", line 6, in <module>
❷     describe_pet()
❸ TypeError: describe_pet() missing 2 required positional arguments: 'animal_
type' and 'pet_name'
```

At ❶ the traceback tells us the location of the problem, allowing us to look back and see that something went wrong in our function call. At ❷ the offending function call is written out for us to see. At ❸ the traceback tells us the call is missing two arguments and reports the names of the missing arguments. If this function were in a separate file, we could probably rewrite the call correctly without having to open that file and read the function code.

Python is helpful in that it reads the function's code for us and tells us the names of the arguments we need to provide. This is another motivation for giving your variables and functions descriptive names. If you do, Python's error messages will be more useful to you and anyone else who might use your code.

If you provide too many arguments, you should get a similar traceback that can help you correctly match your function call to the function definition.

TRY IT YOURSELF

8-3. T-Shirt: Write a function called make_shirt() that accepts a size and the text of a message that should be printed on the shirt. The function should print a sentence summarizing the size of the shirt and the message printed on it.

Call the function once using positional arguments to make a shirt. Call the function a second time using keyword arguments.

8-4. Large Shirts: Modify the make_shirt() function so that shirts are large by default with a message that reads *I love Python*. Make a large shirt and a medium shirt with the default message, and a shirt of any size with a different message.

8-5. Cities: Write a function called describe_city() that accepts the name of a city and its country. The function should print a simple sentence, such as Reykjavik is in Iceland. Give the parameter for the country a default value. Call your function for three different cities, at least one of which is not in the default country.

Return Values

A function doesn't always have to display its output directly. Instead, it can process some data and then return a value or set of values. The value the function returns is called a *return value*. The return statement takes a value from inside a function and sends it back to the line that called the function. Return values allow you to move much of your program's grunt work into functions, which can simplify the body of your program.

Returning a Simple Value

Let's look at a function that takes a first and last name, and returns a neatly formatted full name:

formatted ❶
_name.py

```
❶ def get_formatted_name(first_name, last_name):
      """Return a full name, neatly formatted."""
❷     full_name = f"{first_name} {last_name}"
❸     return full_name.title()

❹ musician = get_formatted_name('jimi', 'hendrix')
  print(musician)
```

The definition of get_formatted_name() takes as parameters a first and last name ❶. The function combines these two names, adds a space between them, and assigns the result to full_name ❷. The value of full_name is converted to title case, and then returned to the calling line at ❸.

When you call a function that returns a value, you need to provide a variable that the return value can be assigned to. In this case, the returned value is assigned to the variable musician at ❹. The output shows a neatly formatted name made up of the parts of a person's name:

```
Jimi Hendrix
```

This might seem like a lot of work to get a neatly formatted name when we could have just written:

```
print("Jimi Hendrix")
```

But when you consider working with a large program that needs to store many first and last names separately, functions like get_formatted_name() become very useful. You store first and last names separately and then call this function whenever you want to display a full name.

Making an Argument Optional

Sometimes it makes sense to make an argument optional so that people using the function can choose to provide extra information only if they want to. You can use default values to make an argument optional.

For example, say we want to expand get_formatted_name() to handle middle names as well. A first attempt to include middle names might look like this:

```
def get_formatted_name(first_name, middle_name, last_name):
    """Return a full name, neatly formatted."""
    full_name = f"{first_name} {middle_name} {last_name}"
    return full_name.title()

musician = get_formatted_name('john', 'lee', 'hooker')
print(musician)
```

This function works when given a first, middle, and last name. The function takes in all three parts of a name and then builds a string out of them. The function adds spaces where appropriate and converts the full name to title case:

John Lee Hooker

But middle names aren't always needed, and this function as written would not work if you tried to call it with only a first name and a last name. To make the middle name optional, we can give the `middle_name` argument an empty default value and ignore the argument unless the user provides a value. To make `get_formatted_name()` work without a middle name, we set the default value of `middle_name` to an empty string and move it to the end of the list of parameters:

```
❶ def get_formatted_name(first_name, last_name, middle_name=''):
       """Return a full name, neatly formatted."""
❷     if middle_name:
           full_name = f"{first_name} {middle_name} {last_name}"
❸     else:
           full_name = f"{first_name} {last_name}"
       return full_name.title()

   musician = get_formatted_name('jimi', 'hendrix')
   print(musician)

❹ musician = get_formatted_name('john', 'hooker', 'lee')
   print(musician)
```

In this example, the name is built from three possible parts. Because there's always a first and last name, these parameters are listed first in the function's definition. The middle name is optional, so it's listed last in the definition, and its default value is an empty string ❶.

In the body of the function, we check to see if a middle name has been provided. Python interprets non-empty strings as `True`, so `if middle_name` evaluates to `True` if a middle name argument is in the function call ❷. If a middle name is provided, the first, middle, and last names are combined to form a full name. This name is then changed to title case and returned to the function call line where it's assigned to the variable `musician` and printed. If no middle name is provided, the empty string fails the `if` test and the `else` block runs ❸. The full name is made with just a first and last name, and the formatted name is returned to the calling line where it's assigned to `musician` and printed.

Calling this function with a first and last name is straightforward. If we're using a middle name, however, we have to make sure the middle name is the last argument passed so Python will match up the positional arguments correctly ❹.

This modified version of our function works for people with just a first and last name, and it works for people who have a middle name as well:

```
Jimi Hendrix
John Lee Hooker
```

Optional values allow functions to handle a wide range of use cases while letting function calls remain as simple as possible.

Returning a Dictionary

A function can return any kind of value you need it to, including more complicated data structures like lists and dictionaries. For example, the following function takes in parts of a name and returns a dictionary representing a person:

person.py
```
def build_person(first_name, last_name):
    """Return a dictionary of information about a person."""
❶   person = {'first': first_name, 'last': last_name}
❷   return person

musician = build_person('jimi', 'hendrix')
❸ print(musician)
```

The function build_person() takes in a first and last name, and puts these values into a dictionary at ❶. The value of first_name is stored with the key 'first', and the value of last_name is stored with the key 'last'. The entire dictionary representing the person is returned at ❷. The return value is printed at ❸ with the original two pieces of textual information now stored in a dictionary:

```
{'first': 'jimi', 'last': 'hendrix'}
```

This function takes in simple textual information and puts it into a more meaningful data structure that lets you work with the information beyond just printing it. The strings 'jimi' and 'hendrix' are now labeled as a first name and last name. You can easily extend this function to accept optional values like a middle name, an age, an occupation, or any other information you want to store about a person. For example, the following change allows you to store a person's age as well:

```
def build_person(first_name, last_name, age=None):
    """Return a dictionary of information about a person."""
    person = {'first': first_name, 'last': last_name}
    if age:
        person['age'] = age
    return person

musician = build_person('jimi', 'hendrix', age=27)
print(musician)
```

We add a new optional parameter age to the function definition and assign the parameter the special value None, which is used when a variable has no specific value assigned to it. You can think of None as a placeholder value. In conditional tests, None evaluates to False. If the function call includes a value for age, that value is stored in the dictionary. This function always stores a person's name, but it can also be modified to store any other information you want about a person.

Using a Function with a while Loop

You can use functions with all the Python structures you've learned about so far. For example, let's use the get_formatted_name() function with a while loop to greet users more formally. Here's a first attempt at greeting people using their first and last names:

greeter.py
```
def get_formatted_name(first_name, last_name):
    """Return a full name, neatly formatted."""
    full_name = f"{first_name} {last_name}"
    return full_name.title()

# This is an infinite loop!
while True:
❶   print("\nPlease tell me your name:")
    f_name = input("First name: ")
    l_name = input("Last name: ")

    formatted_name = get_formatted_name(f_name, l_name)
    print(f"\nHello, {formatted_name}!")
```

For this example, we use a simple version of get_formatted_name() that doesn't involve middle names. The while loop asks the user to enter their name, and we prompt for their first and last name separately ❶.

But there's one problem with this while loop: We haven't defined a quit condition. Where do you put a quit condition when you ask for a series of inputs? We want the user to be able to quit as easily as possible, so each prompt should offer a way to quit. The break statement offers a straightforward way to exit the loop at either prompt:

```
def get_formatted_name(first_name, last_name):
    """Return a full name, neatly formatted."""
    full_name = f"{first_name} {last_name}"
    return full_name.title()

while True:
    print("\nPlease tell me your name:")
    print("(enter 'q' at any time to quit)")

    f_name = input("First name: ")
    if f_name == 'q':
        break
```

```
l_name = input("Last name: ")
if l_name == 'q':
    break

formatted_name = get_formatted_name(f_name, l_name)
print(f"\nHello, {formatted_name}!")
```

We add a message that informs the user how to quit, and then we break out of the loop if the user enters the quit value at either prompt. Now the program will continue greeting people until someone enters 'q' for either name:

```
Please tell me your name:
(enter 'q' at any time to quit)
First name: eric
Last name: matthes

Hello, Eric Matthes!

Please tell me your name:
(enter 'q' at any time to quit)
First name: q
```

TRY IT YOURSELF

8-6. City Names: Write a function called city_country() that takes in the name of a city and its country. The function should return a string formatted like this:

```
"Santiago, Chile"
```

Call your function with at least three city-country pairs, and print the values that are returned.

8-7. Album: Write a function called make_album() that builds a dictionary describing a music album. The function should take in an artist name and an album title, and it should return a dictionary containing these two pieces of information. Use the function to make three dictionaries representing different albums. Print each return value to show that the dictionaries are storing the album information correctly.

Use None to add an optional parameter to make_album() that allows you to store the number of songs on an album. If the calling line includes a value for the number of songs, add that value to the album's dictionary. Make at least one new function call that includes the number of songs on an album.

8-8. User Albums: Start with your program from Exercise 8-7. Write a while loop that allows users to enter an album's artist and title. Once you have that information, call make_album() with the user's input and print the dictionary that's created. Be sure to include a quit value in the while loop.

Passing a List

You'll often find it useful to pass a list to a function, whether it's a list of names, numbers, or more complex objects, such as dictionaries. When you pass a list to a function, the function gets direct access to the contents of the list. Let's use functions to make working with lists more efficient.

Say we have a list of users and want to print a greeting to each. The following example sends a list of names to a function called greet_users(), which greets each person in the list individually:

greet_users.py

```
def greet_users(names):
    """Print a simple greeting to each user in the list."""
    for name in names:
        msg = f"Hello, {name.title()}!"
        print(msg)

❶ usernames = ['hannah', 'ty', 'margot']
  greet_users(usernames)
```

We define greet_users() so it expects a list of names, which it assigns to the parameter names. The function loops through the list it receives and prints a greeting to each user. At ❶ we define a list of users and then pass the list usernames to greet_users() in our function call:

```
Hello, Hannah!
Hello, Ty!
Hello, Margot!
```

This is the output we wanted. Every user sees a personalized greeting, and you can call the function any time you want to greet a specific set of users.

Modifying a List in a Function

When you pass a list to a function, the function can modify the list. Any changes made to the list inside the function's body are permanent, allowing you to work efficiently even when you're dealing with large amounts of data.

Consider a company that creates 3D printed models of designs that users submit. Designs that need to be printed are stored in a list, and after being printed they're moved to a separate list. The following code does this without using functions:

printing _models.py

```
# Start with some designs that need to be printed.
unprinted_designs = ['phone case', 'robot pendant', 'dodecahedron']
completed_models = []

# Simulate printing each design, until none are left.
#  Move each design to completed_models after printing.
while unprinted_designs:
    current_design = unprinted_designs.pop()
```

```
        print(f"Printing model: {current_design}")
        completed_models.append(current_design)

# Display all completed models.
print("\nThe following models have been printed:")
for completed_model in completed_models:
    print(completed_model)
```

This program starts with a list of designs that need to be printed and an empty list called completed_models that each design will be moved to after it has been printed. As long as designs remain in unprinted_designs, the while loop simulates printing each design by removing a design from the end of the list, storing it in current_design, and displaying a message that the current design is being printed. It then adds the design to the list of completed models. When the loop is finished running, a list of the designs that have been printed is displayed:

```
Printing model: dodecahedron
Printing model: robot pendant
Printing model: phone case

The following models have been printed:
dodecahedron
robot pendant
phone case
```

We can reorganize this code by writing two functions, each of which does one specific job. Most of the code won't change; we're just making it more carefully structured. The first function will handle printing the designs, and the second will summarize the prints that have been made:

```
❶ def print_models(unprinted_designs, completed_models):
      """
      Simulate printing each design, until none are left.
      Move each design to completed_models after printing.
      """
      while unprinted_designs:
          current_design = unprinted_designs.pop()
          print(f"Printing model: {current_design}")
          completed_models.append(current_design)

❷ def show_completed_models(completed_models):
      """Show all the models that were printed."""
      print("\nThe following models have been printed:")
      for completed_model in completed_models:
          print(completed_model)

unprinted_designs = ['phone case', 'robot pendant', 'dodecahedron']
completed_models = []

print_models(unprinted_designs, completed_models)
show_completed_models(completed_models)
```

At ❶ we define the function print_models() with two parameters: a list of designs that need to be printed and a list of completed models. Given these two lists, the function simulates printing each design by emptying the list of unprinted designs and filling up the list of completed models. At ❷ we define the function show_completed_models() with one parameter: the list of completed models. Given this list, show_completed_models() displays the name of each model that was printed.

This program has the same output as the version without functions, but the code is much more organized. The code that does most of the work has been moved to two separate functions, which makes the main part of the program easier to understand. Look at the body of the program to see how much easier it is to understand what this program is doing:

```
unprinted_designs = ['phone case', 'robot pendant', 'dodecahedron']
completed_models = []

print_models(unprinted_designs, completed_models)
show_completed_models(completed_models)
```

We set up a list of unprinted designs and an empty list that will hold the completed models. Then, because we've already defined our two functions, all we have to do is call them and pass them the right arguments. We call print_models() and pass it the two lists it needs; as expected, print_models() simulates printing the designs. Then we call show_completed_models() and pass it the list of completed models so it can report the models that have been printed. The descriptive function names allow others to read this code and understand it, even without comments.

This program is easier to extend and maintain than the version without functions. If we need to print more designs later on, we can simply call print_models() again. If we realize the printing code needs to be modified, we can change the code once, and our changes will take place everywhere the function is called. This technique is more efficient than having to update code separately in several places in the program.

This example also demonstrates the idea that every function should have one specific job. The first function prints each design, and the second displays the completed models. This is more beneficial than using one function to do both jobs. If you're writing a function and notice the function is doing too many different tasks, try to split the code into two functions. Remember that you can always call a function from another function, which can be helpful when splitting a complex task into a series of steps.

Preventing a Function from Modifying a List

Sometimes you'll want to prevent a function from modifying a list. For example, say that you start with a list of unprinted designs and write a function to move them to a list of completed models, as in the previous example. You may decide that even though you've printed all the designs, you want to keep the original list of unprinted designs for your records.

But because you moved all the design names out of `unprinted_designs`, the list is now empty, and the empty list is the only version you have; the original is gone. In this case, you can address this issue by passing the function a copy of the list, not the original. Any changes the function makes to the list will affect only the copy, leaving the original list intact.

You can send a copy of a list to a function like this:

```
function_name(list_name[:])
```

The slice notation `[:]` makes a copy of the list to send to the function. If we didn't want to empty the list of unprinted designs in *printing_models.py*, we could call `print_models()` like this:

```
print_models(unprinted_designs[:], completed_models)
```

The function `print_models()` can do its work because it still receives the names of all unprinted designs. But this time it uses a copy of the original unprinted designs list, not the actual `unprinted_designs` list. The list `completed_models` will fill up with the names of printed models like it did before, but the original list of unprinted designs will be unaffected by the function.

Even though you can preserve the contents of a list by passing a copy of it to your functions, you should pass the original list to functions unless you have a specific reason to pass a copy. It's more efficient for a function to work with an existing list to avoid using the time and memory needed to make a separate copy, especially when you're working with large lists.

TRY IT YOURSELF

8-9. Messages: Make a list containing a series of short text messages. Pass the list to a function called `show_messages()`, which prints each text message.

8-10. Sending Messages: Start with a copy of your program from Exercise 8-9. Write a function called `send_messages()` that prints each text message and moves each message to a new list called `sent_messages` as it's printed. After calling the function, print both of your lists to make sure the messages were moved correctly.

8-11. Archived Messages: Start with your work from Exercise 8-10. Call the function `send_messages()` with a copy of the list of messages. After calling the function, print both of your lists to show that the original list has retained its messages.

Passing an Arbitrary Number of Arguments

Sometimes you won't know ahead of time how many arguments a function needs to accept. Fortunately, Python allows a function to collect an arbitrary number of arguments from the calling statement.

For example, consider a function that builds a pizza. It needs to accept a number of toppings, but you can't know ahead of time how many toppings a person will want. The function in the following example has one parameter, *toppings, but this parameter collects as many arguments as the calling line provides:

pizza.py

```
def make_pizza(*toppings):
    """Print the list of toppings that have been requested."""
    print(toppings)

make_pizza('pepperoni')
make_pizza('mushrooms', 'green peppers', 'extra cheese')
```

The asterisk in the parameter name *toppings tells Python to make an empty tuple called toppings and pack whatever values it receives into this tuple. The print() call in the function body produces output showing that Python can handle a function call with one value and a call with three values. It treats the different calls similarly. Note that Python packs the arguments into a tuple, even if the function receives only one value:

```
('pepperoni',)
('mushrooms', 'green peppers', 'extra cheese')
```

Now we can replace the print() call with a loop that runs through the list of toppings and describes the pizza being ordered:

```
def make_pizza(*toppings):
    """Summarize the pizza we are about to make."""
    print("\nMaking a pizza with the following toppings:")
    for topping in toppings:
        print(f"- {topping}")

make_pizza('pepperoni')
make_pizza('mushrooms', 'green peppers', 'extra cheese')
```

The function responds appropriately, whether it receives one value or three values:

```
Making a pizza with the following toppings:
- pepperoni

Making a pizza with the following toppings:
- mushrooms
- green peppers
- extra cheese
```

This syntax works no matter how many arguments the function receives.

Mixing Positional and Arbitrary Arguments

If you want a function to accept several different kinds of arguments, the parameter that accepts an arbitrary number of arguments must be placed last in the function definition. Python matches positional and keyword arguments first and then collects any remaining arguments in the final parameter.

For example, if the function needs to take in a size for the pizza, that parameter must come before the parameter *toppings:

```
def make_pizza(size, *toppings):
    """Summarize the pizza we are about to make."""
    print(f"\nMaking a {size}-inch pizza with the following toppings:")
    for topping in toppings:
        print(f"- {topping}")

make_pizza(16, 'pepperoni')
make_pizza(12, 'mushrooms', 'green peppers', 'extra cheese')
```

In the function definition, Python assigns the first value it receives to the parameter size. All other values that come after are stored in the tuple toppings. The function calls include an argument for the size first, followed by as many toppings as needed.

Now each pizza has a size and a number of toppings, and each piece of information is printed in the proper place, showing size first and toppings after:

```
Making a 16-inch pizza with the following toppings:
- pepperoni

Making a 12-inch pizza with the following toppings:
- mushrooms
- green peppers
- extra cheese
```

NOTE *You'll often see the generic parameter name *args, which collects arbitrary positional arguments like this.*

Using Arbitrary Keyword Arguments

Sometimes you'll want to accept an arbitrary number of arguments, but you won't know ahead of time what kind of information will be passed to the function. In this case, you can write functions that accept as many key-value pairs as the calling statement provides. One example involves building user profiles: you know you'll get information about a user, but you're not sure what kind of information you'll receive. The function build_profile() in the following example always takes in a first and last name, but it accepts an arbitrary number of keyword arguments as well:

user_profile.py

```
def build_profile(first, last, **user_info):
    """Build a dictionary containing everything we know about a user."""
❶  user_info['first_name'] = first
    user_info['last_name'] = last
    return user_info

user_profile = build_profile('albert', 'einstein',
                             location='princeton',
                             field='physics')
print(user_profile)
```

The definition of build_profile() expects a first and last name, and then it allows the user to pass in as many name-value pairs as they want. The double asterisks before the parameter **user_info cause Python to create an empty dictionary called user_info and pack whatever name-value pairs it receives into this dictionary. Within the function, you can access the key-value pairs in user_info just as you would for any dictionary.

In the body of build_profile(), we add the first and last names to the user_info dictionary because we'll always receive these two pieces of information from the user ❶, and they haven't been placed into the dictionary yet. Then we return the user_info dictionary to the function call line.

We call build_profile(), passing it the first name 'albert', the last name 'einstein', and the two key-value pairs location='princeton' and field='physics'. We assign the returned profile to user_profile and print user_profile:

```
{'location': 'princeton', 'field': 'physics',
 'first_name': 'albert', 'last_name': 'einstein'}
```

The returned dictionary contains the user's first and last names and, in this case, the location and field of study as well. The function would work no matter how many additional key-value pairs are provided in the function call.

You can mix positional, keyword, and arbitrary values in many different ways when writing your own functions. It's useful to know that all these argument types exist because you'll see them often when you start reading other people's code. It takes practice to learn to use the different types correctly and to know when to use each type. For now, remember to use the simplest approach that gets the job done. As you progress you'll learn to use the most efficient approach each time.

NOTE *You'll often see the parameter name **kwargs used to collect non-specific keyword arguments.*

8-12. Sandwiches: Write a function that accepts a list of items a person wants on a sandwich. The function should have one parameter that collects as many items as the function call provides, and it should print a summary of the sandwich that's being ordered. Call the function three times, using a different number of arguments each time.

8-13. User Profile: Start with a copy of *user_profile.py* from page 149. Build a profile of yourself by calling `build_profile()`, using your first and last names and three other key-value pairs that describe you.

8-14. Cars: Write a function that stores information about a car in a dictionary. The function should always receive a manufacturer and a model name. It should then accept an arbitrary number of keyword arguments. Call the function with the required information and two other name-value pairs, such as a color or an optional feature. Your function should work for a call like this one:

```
car = make_car('subaru', 'outback', color='blue', tow_package=True)
```

Print the dictionary that's returned to make sure all the information was stored correctly.

Storing Your Functions in Modules

One advantage of functions is the way they separate blocks of code from your main program. By using descriptive names for your functions, your main program will be much easier to follow. You can go a step further by storing your functions in a separate file called a *module* and then *importing* that module into your main program. An import statement tells Python to make the code in a module available in the currently running program file.

Storing your functions in a separate file allows you to hide the details of your program's code and focus on its higher-level logic. It also allows you to reuse functions in many different programs. When you store your functions in separate files, you can share those files with other programmers without having to share your entire program. Knowing how to import functions also allows you to use libraries of functions that other programmers have written.

There are several ways to import a module, and I'll show you each of these briefly.

Importing an Entire Module

To start importing functions, we first need to create a module. A *module* is a file ending in *.py* that contains the code you want to import into your program. Let's make a module that contains the function make_pizza(). To make this module, we'll remove everything from the file *pizza.py* except the function make_pizza():

pizza.py

```
def make_pizza(size, *toppings):
    """Summarize the pizza we are about to make."""
    print(f"\nMaking a {size}-inch pizza with the following toppings:")
    for topping in toppings:
        print(f"- {topping}")
```

Now we'll make a separate file called *making_pizzas.py* in the same directory as *pizza.py*. This file imports the module we just created and then makes two calls to make_pizza():

making _pizzas.py

```
import pizza

❶ pizza.make_pizza(16, 'pepperoni')
pizza.make_pizza(12, 'mushrooms', 'green peppers', 'extra cheese')
```

When Python reads this file, the line import pizza tells Python to open the file *pizza.py* and copy all the functions from it into this program. You don't actually see code being copied between files because Python copies the code behind the scenes just before the program runs. All you need to know is that any function defined in *pizza.py* will now be available in *making_pizzas.py*.

To call a function from an imported module, enter the name of the module you imported, pizza, followed by the name of the function, make_pizza(), separated by a dot ❶. This code produces the same output as the original program that didn't import a module:

```
Making a 16-inch pizza with the following toppings:
- pepperoni

Making a 12-inch pizza with the following toppings:
- mushrooms
- green peppers
- extra cheese
```

This first approach to importing, in which you simply write import followed by the name of the module, makes every function from the module available in your program. If you use this kind of import statement to import an entire module named *module_name.py*, each function in the module is available through the following syntax:

```
module_name.function_name()
```

Importing Specific Functions

You can also import a specific function from a module. Here's the general syntax for this approach:

```
from module_name import function_name
```

You can import as many functions as you want from a module by separating each function's name with a comma:

```
from module_name import function_0, function_1, function_2
```

The *making_pizzas.py* example would look like this if we want to import just the function we're going to use:

```
from pizza import make_pizza

make_pizza(16, 'pepperoni')
make_pizza(12, 'mushrooms', 'green peppers', 'extra cheese')
```

With this syntax, you don't need to use the dot notation when you call a function. Because we've explicitly imported the function make_pizza() in the import statement, we can call it by name when we use the function.

Using as to Give a Function an Alias

If the name of a function you're importing might conflict with an existing name in your program or if the function name is long, you can use a short, unique *alias*—an alternate name similar to a nickname for the function. You'll give the function this special nickname when you import the function.

Here we give the function make_pizza() an alias, mp(), by importing make_pizza as mp. The as keyword renames a function using the alias you provide:

```
from pizza import make_pizza as mp

mp(16, 'pepperoni')
mp(12, 'mushrooms', 'green peppers', 'extra cheese')
```

The import statement shown here renames the function make_pizza() to mp() in this program. Any time we want to call make_pizza() we can simply write mp() instead, and Python will run the code in make_pizza() while avoiding any confusion with another make_pizza() function you might have written in this program file.

The general syntax for providing an alias is:

```
from module_name import function_name as fn
```

Using as to Give a Module an Alias

You can also provide an alias for a module name. Giving a module a short alias, like p for pizza, allows you to call the module's functions more quickly. Calling p.make_pizza() is more concise than calling pizza.make_pizza():

```
import pizza as p

p.make_pizza(16, 'pepperoni')
p.make_pizza(12, 'mushrooms', 'green peppers', 'extra cheese')
```

The module pizza is given the alias p in the import statement, but all of the module's functions retain their original names. Calling the functions by writing p.make_pizza() is not only more concise than writing pizza.make_pizza(), but also redirects your attention from the module name and allows you to focus on the descriptive names of its functions. These function names, which clearly tell you what each function does, are more important to the readability of your code than using the full module name.

The general syntax for this approach is:

```
import module_name as mn
```

Importing All Functions in a Module

You can tell Python to import every function in a module by using the asterisk (*) operator:

```
from pizza import *

make_pizza(16, 'pepperoni')
make_pizza(12, 'mushrooms', 'green peppers', 'extra cheese')
```

The asterisk in the import statement tells Python to copy every function from the module pizza into this program file. Because every function is imported, you can call each function by name without using the dot notation. However, it's best not to use this approach when you're working with larger modules that you didn't write: if the module has a function name that matches an existing name in your project, you can get some unexpected results. Python may see several functions or variables with the same name, and instead of importing all the functions separately, it will overwrite the functions.

The best approach is to import the function or functions you want, or import the entire module and use the dot notation. This leads to clear code that's easy to read and understand. I include this section so you'll recognize import statements like the following when you see them in other people's code:

```
from module_name import *
```

Styling Functions

You need to keep a few details in mind when you're styling functions. Functions should have descriptive names, and these names should use lowercase letters and underscores. Descriptive names help you and others understand what your code is trying to do. Module names should use these conventions as well.

Every function should have a comment that explains concisely what the function does. This comment should appear immediately after the function definition and use the docstring format. In a well-documented function, other programmers can use the function by reading only the description in the docstring. They should be able to trust that the code works as described, and as long as they know the name of the function, the arguments it needs, and the kind of value it returns, they should be able to use it in their programs.

If you specify a default value for a parameter, no spaces should be used on either side of the equal sign:

```
def function_name(parameter_0, parameter_1='default value')
```

The same convention should be used for keyword arguments in function calls:

```
function_name(value_0, parameter_1='value')
```

PEP 8 (*https://www.python.org/dev/peps/pep-0008/*) recommends that you limit lines of code to 79 characters so every line is visible in a reasonably sized editor window. If a set of parameters causes a function's definition to be longer than 79 characters, press ENTER after the opening parenthesis on the definition line. On the next line, press TAB twice to separate the list of arguments from the body of the function, which will only be indented one level.

Most editors automatically line up any additional lines of parameters to match the indentation you have established on the first line:

```
def function_name(
        parameter_0, parameter_1, parameter_2,
        parameter_3, parameter_4, parameter_5):
    function body...
```

If your program or module has more than one function, you can separate each by two blank lines to make it easier to see where one function ends and the next one begins.

All import statements should be written at the beginning of a file. The only exception is if you use comments at the beginning of your file to describe the overall program.

Summary

In this chapter you learned how to write functions and to pass arguments so that your functions have access to the information they need to do their work. You learned how to use positional and keyword arguments, and how to accept an arbitrary number of arguments. You saw functions that display output and functions that return values. You learned how to use functions with lists, dictionaries, `if` statements, and `while` loops. You also saw how to store your functions in separate files called *modules*, so your program files will be simpler and easier to understand. Finally, you learned to style your functions so your programs will continue to be well-structured and as easy as possible for you and others to read.

One of your goals as a programmer should be to write simple code that does what you want it to, and functions help you do this. They allow you to write blocks of code and leave them alone once you know they work. When you know a function does its job correctly, you can trust that it will continue to work and move on to your next coding task.

Functions allow you to write code once and then reuse that code as many times as you want. When you need to run the code in a function, all you need to do is write a one-line call and the function does its job. When you need to modify a function's behavior, you only have to modify one block of code, and your change takes effect everywhere you've made a call to that function.

Using functions makes your programs easier to read, and good function names summarize what each part of a program does. Reading a series of function calls gives you a much quicker sense of what a program does than reading a long series of code blocks.

Functions also make your code easier to test and debug. When the bulk of your program's work is done by a set of functions, each of which has a specific job, it's much easier to test and maintain the code you've written. You can write a separate program that calls each function and tests whether each function works in all the situations it may encounter. When you do this, you can be confident that your functions will work properly each time you call them.

In Chapter 9 you'll learn to write classes. *Classes* combine functions and data into one neat package that can be used in flexible and efficient ways.

9

CLASSES

Object-oriented programming is one of the most effective approaches to writing software. In object-oriented programming you write *classes* that represent real-world things and situations, and you create *objects* based on these classes. When you write a class, you define the general behavior that a whole category of objects can have.

When you create individual objects from the class, each object is automatically equipped with the general behavior; you can then give each object whatever unique traits you desire. You'll be amazed how well real-world situations can be modeled with object-oriented programming.

Making an object from a class is called *instantiation*, and you work with *instances* of a class. In this chapter you'll write classes and create instances of those classes. You'll specify the kind of information that can be stored in instances, and you'll define actions that can be taken with these instances. You'll also write classes that extend the functionality of existing classes, so similar classes can share code efficiently. You'll store your classes in modules and import classes written by other programmers into your own program files.

Understanding object-oriented programming will help you see the world as a programmer does. It'll help you really know your code, not just what's happening line by line, but also the bigger concepts behind it. Knowing the logic behind classes will train you to think logically so you can write programs that effectively address almost any problem you encounter.

Classes also make life easier for you and the other programmers you'll work with as you take on increasingly complex challenges. When you and other programmers write code based on the same kind of logic, you'll be able to understand each other's work. Your programs will make sense to many collaborators, allowing everyone to accomplish more.

Creating and Using a Class

You can model almost anything using classes. Let's start by writing a simple class, Dog, that represents a dog—not one dog in particular, but any dog. What do we know about most pet dogs? Well, they all have a name and age. We also know that most dogs sit and roll over. Those two pieces of information (name and age) and those two behaviors (sit and roll over) will go in our Dog class because they're common to most dogs. This class will tell Python how to make an object representing a dog. After our class is written, we'll use it to make individual instances, each of which represents one specific dog.

Creating the Dog Class

Each instance created from the Dog class will store a name and an age, and we'll give each dog the ability to sit() and roll_over():

dog.py

```
❶ class Dog:
❷     """A simple attempt to model a dog."""

❸     def __init__(self, name, age):
          """Initialize name and age attributes."""
❹         self.name = name
          self.age = age

❺     def sit(self):
          """Simulate a dog sitting in response to a command."""
          print(f"{self.name} is now sitting.")

      def roll_over(self):
          """Simulate rolling over in response to a command."""
          print(f"{self.name} rolled over!")
```

There's a lot to notice here, but don't worry. You'll see this structure throughout this chapter and have lots of time to get used to it. At ❶ we define a class called Dog. By convention, capitalized names refer to classes in Python. There are no parentheses in the class definition because we're creating this class from scratch. At ❷ we write a docstring describing what this class does.

The __init__() Method

A function that's part of a class is a *method*. Everything you learned about functions applies to methods as well; the only practical difference for now is the way we'll call methods. The __init__() method at ❸ is a special method that Python runs automatically whenever we create a new instance based on the Dog class. This method has two leading underscores and two trailing underscores, a convention that helps prevent Python's default method names from conflicting with your method names. Make sure to use two underscores on each side of __init__(). If you use just one on each side, the method won't be called automatically when you use your class, which can result in errors that are difficult to identify.

We define the __init__() method to have three parameters: self, name, and age. The self parameter is required in the method definition, and it must come first before the other parameters. It must be included in the definition because when Python calls this method later (to create an instance of Dog), the method call will automatically pass the self argument. Every method call associated with an instance automatically passes self, which is a reference to the instance itself; it gives the individual instance access to the attributes and methods in the class. When we make an instance of Dog, Python will call the __init__() method from the Dog class. We'll pass Dog() a name and an age as arguments; self is passed automatically, so we don't need to pass it. Whenever we want to make an instance from the Dog class, we'll provide values for only the last two parameters, name and age.

The two variables defined at ❹ each have the prefix self. Any variable prefixed with self is available to every method in the class, and we'll also be able to access these variables through any instance created from the class. The line self.name = name takes the value associated with the parameter name and assigns it to the variable name, which is then attached to the instance being created. The same process happens with self.age = age. Variables that are accessible through instances like this are called *attributes*.

The Dog class has two other methods defined: sit() and roll_over() ❺. Because these methods don't need additional information to run, we just define them to have one parameter, self. The instances we create later will have access to these methods. In other words, they'll be able to sit and roll over. For now, sit() and roll_over() don't do much. They simply print a message saying the dog is sitting or rolling over. But the concept can be extended to realistic situations: if this class were part of an actual computer game, these methods would contain code to make an animated dog sit and roll over. If this class was written to control a robot, these methods would direct movements that cause a robotic dog to sit and roll over.

Making an Instance from a Class

Think of a class as a set of instructions for how to make an instance. The class Dog is a set of instructions that tells Python how to make individual instances representing specific dogs.

Let's make an instance representing a specific dog:

```
class Dog:
    --snip--

❶ my_dog = Dog('Willie', 6)

❷ print(f"My dog's name is {my_dog.name}.")
❸ print(f"My dog is {my_dog.age} years old.")
```

The Dog class we're using here is the one we just wrote in the previous example. At ❶ we tell Python to create a dog whose name is 'Willie' and whose age is 6. When Python reads this line, it calls the __init__() method in Dog with the arguments 'Willie' and 6. The __init__() method creates an instance representing this particular dog and sets the name and age attributes using the values we provided. Python then returns an instance representing this dog. We assign that instance to the variable my_dog. The naming convention is helpful here: we can usually assume that a capitalized name like Dog refers to a class, and a lowercase name like my_dog refers to a single instance created from a class.

Accessing Attributes

To access the attributes of an instance, you use dot notation. At ❷ we access the value of my_dog's attribute name by writing:

```
my_dog.name
```

Dot notation is used often in Python. This syntax demonstrates how Python finds an attribute's value. Here Python looks at the instance my_dog and then finds the attribute name associated with my_dog. This is the same attribute referred to as self.name in the class Dog. At ❸ we use the same approach to work with the attribute age.

The output is a summary of what we know about my_dog:

```
My dog's name is Willie.
My dog is 6 years old.
```

Calling Methods

After we create an instance from the class Dog, we can use dot notation to call any method defined in Dog. Let's make our dog sit and roll over:

```
class Dog:
    --snip--
```

```
my_dog = Dog('Willie', 6)
my_dog.sit()
my_dog.roll_over()
```

To call a method, give the name of the instance (in this case, my_dog)
and the method you want to call, separated by a dot. When Python reads
my_dog.sit(), it looks for the method sit() in the class Dog and runs that
code. Python interprets the line my_dog.roll_over() in the same way.

Now Willie does what we tell him to:

```
Willie is now sitting.
Willie rolled over!
```

This syntax is quite useful. When attributes and methods have been
given appropriately descriptive names like name, age, sit(), and roll_over(),
we can easily infer what a block of code, even one we've never seen before,
is supposed to do.

Creating Multiple Instances

You can create as many instances from a class as you need. Let's create a
second dog called your_dog:

```
class Dog:
    --snip--

my_dog = Dog('Willie', 6)
your_dog = Dog('Lucy', 3)

print(f"My dog's name is {my_dog.name}.")
print(f"My dog is {my_dog.age} years old.")
my_dog.sit()

print(f"\nYour dog's name is {your_dog.name}.")
print(f"Your dog is {your_dog.age} years old.")
your_dog.sit()
```

In this example we create a dog named Willie and a dog named Lucy.
Each dog is a separate instance with its own set of attributes, capable of the
same set of actions:

```
My dog's name is Willie.
My dog is 6 years old.
Willie is now sitting.

Your dog's name is Lucy.
Your dog is 3 years old.
Lucy is now sitting.
```

Even if we used the same name and age for the second dog, Python
would still create a separate instance from the Dog class. You can make

as many instances from one class as you need, as long as you give each instance a unique variable name or it occupies a unique spot in a list or dictionary.

Working with Classes and Instances

You can use classes to represent many real-world situations. Once you write a class, you'll spend most of your time working with instances created from that class. One of the first tasks you'll want to do is modify the attributes associated with a particular instance. You can modify the attributes of an instance directly or write methods that update attributes in specific ways.

The Car Class

Let's write a new class representing a car. Our class will store information about the kind of car we're working with, and it will have a method that summarizes this information:

car.py
```
class Car:
    """A simple attempt to represent a car."""

❶   def __init__(self, make, model, year):
        """Initialize attributes to describe a car."""
        self.make = make
```

```
        self.model = model
        self.year = year

❷    def get_descriptive_name(self):
        """Return a neatly formatted descriptive name."""
        long_name = f"{self.year} {self.make} {self.model}"
        return long_name.title()

❸ my_new_car = Car('audi', 'a4', 2019)
  print(my_new_car.get_descriptive_name())
```

At ❶ in the Car class, we define the __init__() method with the self parameter first, just like we did before with our Dog class. We also give it three other parameters: make, model, and year. The __init__() method takes in these parameters and assigns them to the attributes that will be associated with instances made from this class. When we make a new Car instance, we'll need to specify a make, model, and year for our instance.

At ❷ we define a method called get_descriptive_name() that puts a car's year, make, and model into one string neatly describing the car. This will spare us from having to print each attribute's value individually. To work with the attribute values in this method, we use self.make, self.model, and self.year. At ❸ we make an instance from the Car class and assign it to the variable my_new_car. Then we call get_descriptive_name() to show what kind of car we have:

```
2019 Audi A4
```

To make the class more interesting, let's add an attribute that changes over time. We'll add an attribute that stores the car's overall mileage.

Setting a Default Value for an Attribute

When an instance is created, attributes can be defined without being passed in as parameters. These attributes can be defined in the __init__() method, where they are assigned a default value.

Let's add an attribute called odometer_reading that always starts with a value of 0. We'll also add a method read_odometer() that helps us read each car's odometer:

```
class Car:

    def __init__(self, make, model, year):
        """Initialize attributes to describe a car."""
        self.make = make
        self.model = model
        self.year = year
❶       self.odometer_reading = 0

    def get_descriptive_name(self):
        --snip--
```

```
❷    def read_odometer(self):
        """Print a statement showing the car's mileage."""
        print(f"This car has {self.odometer_reading} miles on it.")

my_new_car = Car('audi', 'a4', 2019)
print(my_new_car.get_descriptive_name())
my_new_car.read_odometer()
```

This time when Python calls the __init__() method to create a new instance, it stores the make, model, and year values as attributes like it did in the previous example. Then Python creates a new attribute called odometer_reading and sets its initial value to 0 ❶. We also have a new method called read_odometer() at ❷ that makes it easy to read a car's mileage.

Our car starts with a mileage of 0:

```
2019 Audi A4
This car has 0 miles on it.
```

Not many cars are sold with exactly 0 miles on the odometer, so we need a way to change the value of this attribute.

Modifying Attribute Values

You can change an attribute's value in three ways: you can change the value directly through an instance, set the value through a method, or increment the value (add a certain amount to it) through a method. Let's look at each of these approaches.

Modifying an Attribute's Value Directly

The simplest way to modify the value of an attribute is to access the attribute directly through an instance. Here we set the odometer reading to 23 directly:

```
class Car:
    --snip--

my_new_car = Car('audi', 'a4', 2019)
print(my_new_car.get_descriptive_name())

❶ my_new_car.odometer_reading = 23
my_new_car.read_odometer()
```

At ❶ we use dot notation to access the car's odometer_reading attribute and set its value directly. This line tells Python to take the instance my_new_car, find the attribute odometer_reading associated with it, and set the value of that attribute to 23:

```
2019 Audi A4
This car has 23 miles on it.
```

Sometimes you'll want to access attributes directly like this, but other times you'll want to write a method that updates the value for you.

Modifying an Attribute's Value Through a Method

It can be helpful to have methods that update certain attributes for you. Instead of accessing the attribute directly, you pass the new value to a method that handles the updating internally.

Here's an example showing a method called update_odometer():

```
class Car:
    --snip--

❶   def update_odometer(self, mileage):
        """Set the odometer reading to the given value."""
        self.odometer_reading = mileage

my_new_car = Car('audi', 'a4', 2019)
print(my_new_car.get_descriptive_name())

❷ my_new_car.update_odometer(23)
my_new_car.read_odometer()
```

The only modification to Car is the addition of update_odometer() at ❶. This method takes in a mileage value and assigns it to self.odometer_reading. At ❷ we call update_odometer() and give it 23 as an argument (corresponding to the mileage parameter in the method definition). It sets the odometer reading to 23, and read_odometer() prints the reading:

```
2019 Audi A4
This car has 23 miles on it.
```

We can extend the method update_odometer() to do additional work every time the odometer reading is modified. Let's add a little logic to make sure no one tries to roll back the odometer reading:

```
class Car:
    --snip--

    def update_odometer(self, mileage):
        """
        Set the odometer reading to the given value.
        Reject the change if it attempts to roll the odometer back.
        """
❶       if mileage >= self.odometer_reading:
            self.odometer_reading = mileage
        else:
❷           print("You can't roll back an odometer!")
```

Now update_odometer() checks that the new reading makes sense before modifying the attribute. If the new mileage, mileage, is greater than or equal to the existing mileage, `self.odometer_reading`, you can update the odometer reading to the new mileage ❶. If the new mileage is less than the existing mileage, you'll get a warning that you can't roll back an odometer ❷.

Incrementing an Attribute's Value Through a Method

Sometimes you'll want to increment an attribute's value by a certain amount rather than set an entirely new value. Say we buy a used car and put 100 miles on it between the time we buy it and the time we register it. Here's a method that allows us to pass this incremental amount and add that value to the odometer reading:

```
class Car:
    --snip--

    def update_odometer(self, mileage):
        --snip--

❶   def increment_odometer(self, miles):
        """Add the given amount to the odometer reading."""
        self.odometer_reading += miles

❷ my_used_car = Car('subaru', 'outback', 2015)
  print(my_used_car.get_descriptive_name())

❸ my_used_car.update_odometer(23_500)
  my_used_car.read_odometer()

❹ my_used_car.increment_odometer(100)
  my_used_car.read_odometer()
```

The new method `increment_odometer()` at ❶ takes in a number of miles, and adds this value to `self.odometer_reading`. At ❷ we create a used car, `my_used_car`. We set its odometer to 23,500 by calling `update_odometer()` and passing it `23_500` at ❸. At ❹ we call `increment_odometer()` and pass it `100` to add the 100 miles that we drove between buying the car and registering it:

```
2015 Subaru Outback
This car has 23500 miles on it.
This car has 23600 miles on it.
```

You can easily modify this method to reject negative increments so no one uses this function to roll back an odometer.

NOTE   *You can use methods like this to control how users of your program update values such as an odometer reading, but anyone with access to the program can set the odometer reading to any value by accessing the attribute directly. Effective security takes extreme attention to detail in addition to basic checks like those shown here.*

9-4. Number Served: Start with your program from Exercise 9-1 (page 162). Add an attribute called number_served with a default value of 0. Create an instance called restaurant from this class. Print the number of customers the restaurant has served, and then change this value and print it again.

Add a method called set_number_served() that lets you set the number of customers that have been served. Call this method with a new number and print the value again.

Add a method called increment_number_served() that lets you increment the number of customers who've been served. Call this method with any number you like that could represent how many customers were served in, say, a day of business.

9-5. Login Attempts: Add an attribute called login_attempts to your User class from Exercise 9-3 (page 162). Write a method called increment_login _attempts() that increments the value of login_attempts by 1. Write another method called reset_login_attempts() that resets the value of login_attempts to 0.

Make an instance of the User class and call increment_login_attempts() several times. Print the value of login_attempts to make sure it was incremented properly, and then call reset_login_attempts(). Print login_attempts again to make sure it was reset to 0.

Inheritance

You don't always have to start from scratch when writing a class. If the class you're writing is a specialized version of another class you wrote, you can use *inheritance*. When one class *inherits* from another, it takes on the attributes and methods of the first class. The original class is called the *parent class*, and the new class is the *child class*. The child class can inherit any or all of the attributes and methods of its parent class, but it's also free to define new attributes and methods of its own.

The __init__() Method for a Child Class

When you're writing a new class based on an existing class, you'll often want to call the __init__() method from the parent class. This will initialize any attributes that were defined in the parent __init__() method and make them available in the child class.

As an example, let's model an electric car. An electric car is just a specific kind of car, so we can base our new ElectricCar class on the Car class we wrote earlier. Then we'll only have to write code for the attributes and behavior specific to electric cars.

Let's start by making a simple version of the `ElectricCar` class, which does everything the `Car` class does:

electric_car.py ❶
```
class Car:
    """A simple attempt to represent a car."""

    def __init__(self, make, model, year):
        self.make = make
        self.model = model
        self.year = year
        self.odometer_reading = 0

    def get_descriptive_name(self):
        long_name = f"{self.year} {self.make} {self.model}"
        return long_name.title()

    def read_odometer(self):
        print(f"This car has {self.odometer_reading} miles on it.")

    def update_odometer(self, mileage):
        if mileage >= self.odometer_reading:
            self.odometer_reading = mileage
        else:
            print("You can't roll back an odometer!")

    def increment_odometer(self, miles):
        self.odometer_reading += miles
```
❷
```
class ElectricCar(Car):
    """Represent aspects of a car, specific to electric vehicles."""
```
❸
```
    def __init__(self, make, model, year):
        """Initialize attributes of the parent class."""
```
❹
```
        super().__init__(make, model, year)
```

❺
```
my_tesla = ElectricCar('tesla', 'model s', 2019)
print(my_tesla.get_descriptive_name())
```

At ❶ we start with `Car`. When you create a child class, the parent class must be part of the current file and must appear before the child class in the file. At ❷ we define the child class, `ElectricCar`. The name of the parent class must be included in parentheses in the definition of a child class. The `__init__()` method at ❸ takes in the information required to make a `Car` instance.

The `super()` function at ❹ is a special function that allows you to call a method from the parent class. This line tells Python to call the `__init__()` method from `Car`, which gives an `ElectricCar` instance all the attributes defined in that method. The name *super* comes from a convention of calling the parent class a *superclass* and the child class a *subclass*.

We test whether inheritance is working properly by trying to create an electric car with the same kind of information we'd provide when making a regular car. At ❺ we make an instance of the ElectricCar class and assign it to my_tesla. This line calls the __init__() method defined in ElectricCar, which in turn tells Python to call the __init__() method defined in the parent class Car. We provide the arguments 'tesla', 'model s', and 2019.

Aside from __init__(), there are no attributes or methods yet that are particular to an electric car. At this point we're just making sure the electric car has the appropriate Car behaviors:

```
2019 Tesla Model S
```

The ElectricCar instance works just like an instance of Car, so now we can begin defining attributes and methods specific to electric cars.

Defining Attributes and Methods for the Child Class

Once you have a child class that inherits from a parent class, you can add any new attributes and methods necessary to differentiate the child class from the parent class.

Let's add an attribute that's specific to electric cars (a battery, for example) and a method to report on this attribute. We'll store the battery size and write a method that prints a description of the battery:

```
class Car:
    --snip--

class ElectricCar(Car):
    """Represent aspects of a car, specific to electric vehicles."""

    def __init__(self, make, model, year):
        """
        Initialize attributes of the parent class.
        Then initialize attributes specific to an electric car.
        """
        super().__init__(make, model, year)
❶       self.battery_size = 75

❷   def describe_battery(self):
        """Print a statement describing the battery size."""
        print(f"This car has a {self.battery_size}-kWh battery.")

my_tesla = ElectricCar('tesla', 'model s', 2019)
print(my_tesla.get_descriptive_name())
my_tesla.describe_battery()
```

At ❶ we add a new attribute self.battery_size and set its initial value to, say, 75. This attribute will be associated with all instances created from the ElectricCar class but won't be associated with any instances of Car. We also add a method called `describe_battery()` that prints information about the battery at ❷. When we call this method, we get a description that is clearly specific to an electric car:

```
2019 Tesla Model S
This car has a 75-kWh battery.
```

There's no limit to how much you can specialize the `ElectricCar` class. You can add as many attributes and methods as you need to model an electric car to whatever degree of accuracy you need. An attribute or method that could belong to any car, rather than one that's specific to an electric car, should be added to the `Car` class instead of the `ElectricCar` class. Then anyone who uses the `Car` class will have that functionality available as well, and the `ElectricCar` class will only contain code for the information and behavior specific to electric vehicles.

Overriding Methods from the Parent Class

You can override any method from the parent class that doesn't fit what you're trying to model with the child class. To do this, you define a method in the child class with the same name as the method you want to override in the parent class. Python will disregard the parent class method and only pay attention to the method you define in the child class.

Say the class `Car` had a method called `fill_gas_tank()`. This method is meaningless for an all-electric vehicle, so you might want to override this method. Here's one way to do that:

```
class ElectricCar(Car):
    --snip--

    def fill_gas_tank(self):
        """Electric cars don't have gas tanks."""
        print("This car doesn't need a gas tank!")
```

Now if someone tries to call `fill_gas_tank()` with an electric car, Python will ignore the method `fill_gas_tank()` in `Car` and run this code instead. When you use inheritance, you can make your child classes retain what you need and override anything you don't need from the parent class.

Instances as Attributes

When modeling something from the real world in code, you may find that you're adding more and more detail to a class. You'll find that you have a growing list of attributes and methods and that your files are becoming lengthy. In these situations, you might recognize that part of one class can be written as a separate class. You can break your large class into smaller classes that work together.

For example, if we continue adding detail to the `ElectricCar` class, we might notice that we're adding many attributes and methods specific to the car's battery. When we see this happening, we can stop and move those attributes and methods to a separate class called Battery. Then we can use a Battery instance as an attribute in the ElectricCar class:

```
class Car:
    --snip--

❶ class Battery:
    """A simple attempt to model a battery for an electric car."""

❷     def __init__(self, battery_size=75):
        """Initialize the battery's attributes."""
        self.battery_size = battery_size

❸     def describe_battery(self):
        """Print a statement describing the battery size."""
        print(f"This car has a {self.battery_size}-kWh battery.")


class ElectricCar(Car):
    """Represent aspects of a car, specific to electric vehicles."""

    def __init__(self, make, model, year):
        """
        Initialize attributes of the parent class.
        Then initialize attributes specific to an electric car.
        """
        super().__init__(make, model, year)
❹         self.battery = Battery()


my_tesla = ElectricCar('tesla', 'model s', 2019)

print(my_tesla.get_descriptive_name())
my_tesla.battery.describe_battery()
```

At ❶ we define a new class called Battery that doesn't inherit from any other class. The __init__() method at ❷ has one parameter, battery_size, in addition to self. This is an optional parameter that sets the battery's size to 75 if no value is provided. The method describe_battery() has been moved to this class as well ❸.

In the ElectricCar class, we now add an attribute called self.battery ❹. This line tells Python to create a new instance of Battery (with a default size of 75, because we're not specifying a value) and assign that instance to the attribute self.battery. This will happen every time the __init__() method is called; any ElectricCar instance will now have a Battery instance created automatically.

We create an electric car and assign it to the variable my_tesla. When we want to describe the battery, we need to work through the car's battery attribute:

```
my_tesla.battery.describe_battery()
```

This line tells Python to look at the instance `my_tesla`, find its `battery` attribute, and call the method `describe_battery()` that's associated with the Battery instance stored in the attribute.

The output is identical to what we saw previously:

```
2019 Tesla Model S
This car has a 75-kWh battery.
```

This looks like a lot of extra work, but now we can describe the battery in as much detail as we want without cluttering the `ElectricCar` class. Let's add another method to `Battery` that reports the range of the car based on the battery size:

```
class Car:
    --snip--

class Battery:
    --snip--

❶  def get_range(self):
        """Print a statement about the range this battery provides."""
        if self.battery_size == 75:
            range = 260
        elif self.battery_size == 100:
            range = 315

        print(f"This car can go about {range} miles on a full charge.")

class ElectricCar(Car):
    --snip--

my_tesla = ElectricCar('tesla', 'model s', 2019)
print(my_tesla.get_descriptive_name())
my_tesla.battery.describe_battery()
❷ my_tesla.battery.get_range()
```

The new method get_range() at ❶ performs some simple analysis. If the battery's capacity is 75 kWh, get_range() sets the range to 260 miles, and if the capacity is 100 kWh, it sets the range to 315 miles. It then reports this value. When we want to use this method, we again have to call it through the car's battery attribute at ❷.

The output tells us the range of the car based on its battery size:

```
2019 Tesla Model S
This car has a 75-kWh battery.
This car can go about 260 miles on a full charge.
```

Modeling Real-World Objects

As you begin to model more complicated things like electric cars, you'll wrestle with interesting questions. Is the range of an electric car a property of the battery or of the car? If we're only describing one car, it's probably fine to maintain the association of the method get_range() with the Battery class. But if we're describing a manufacturer's entire line of cars, we probably want to move get_range() to the ElectricCar class. The get_range() method would still check the battery size before determining the range, but it would report a range specific to the kind of car it's associated with. Alternatively, we could maintain the association of the get_range() method with the battery but pass it a parameter such as car_model. The get_range() method would then report a range based on the battery size and car model.

This brings you to an interesting point in your growth as a programmer. When you wrestle with questions like these, you're thinking at a higher logical level rather than a syntax-focused level. You're thinking not about Python, but about how to represent the real world in code. When you reach this point, you'll realize there are often no right or wrong approaches to modeling real-world situations. Some approaches are more efficient than others, but it takes practice to find the most efficient representations. If your code is working as you want it to, you're doing well! Don't be discouraged if you find you're ripping apart your classes and rewriting them several times using different approaches. In the quest to write accurate, efficient code, everyone goes through this process.

TRY IT YOURSELF

9-6. Ice Cream Stand: An ice cream stand is a specific kind of restaurant. Write a class called IceCreamStand that inherits from the Restaurant class you wrote in Exercise 9-1 (page 162) or Exercise 9-4 (page 167). Either version of the class will work; just pick the one you like better. Add an attribute called flavors that stores a list of ice cream flavors. Write a method that displays these flavors. Create an instance of IceCreamStand, and call this method.

9-7. Admin: An administrator is a special kind of user. Write a class called Admin that inherits from the User class you wrote in Exercise 9-3 (page 162) or Exercise 9-5 (page 167). Add an attribute, privileges, that stores a list of strings like "can add post", "can delete post", "can ban user", and so on. Write a method called show_privileges() that lists the administrator's set of privileges. Create an instance of Admin, and call your method.

9-8. Privileges: Write a separate Privileges class. The class should have one attribute, privileges, that stores a list of strings as described in Exercise 9-7. Move the show_privileges() method to this class. Make a Privileges instance as an attribute in the Admin class. Create a new instance of Admin and use your method to show its privileges.

(continued)

Importing Classes

As you add more functionality to your classes, your files can get long, even when you use inheritance properly. In keeping with the overall philosophy of Python, you'll want to keep your files as uncluttered as possible. To help, Python lets you store classes in modules and then import the classes you need into your main program.

Importing a Single Class

Let's create a module containing just the Car class. This brings up a subtle naming issue: we already have a file named *car.py* in this chapter, but this module should be named *car.py* because it contains code representing a car. We'll resolve this naming issue by storing the Car class in a module named *car.py*, replacing the *car.py* file we were previously using. From now on, any program that uses this module will need a more specific filename, such as *my_car.py*. Here's *car.py* with just the code from the class Car:

car.py ❶
```python
"""A class that can be used to represent a car."""

class Car:
    """A simple attempt to represent a car."""

    def __init__(self, make, model, year):
        """Initialize attributes to describe a car."""
        self.make = make
        self.model = model
        self.year = year
        self.odometer_reading = 0

    def get_descriptive_name(self):
        """Return a neatly formatted descriptive name."""
        long_name = f"{self.year} {self.make} {self.model}"
        return long_name.title()

    def read_odometer(self):
        """Print a statement showing the car's mileage."""
        print(f"This car has {self.odometer_reading} miles on it.")
```

```
        def update_odometer(self, mileage):
            """
            Set the odometer reading to the given value.
            Reject the change if it attempts to roll the odometer back.
            """
            if mileage >= self.odometer_reading:
                self.odometer_reading = mileage
            else:
                print("You can't roll back an odometer!")

        def increment_odometer(self, miles):
            """Add the given amount to the odometer reading."""
            self.odometer_reading += miles
```

At ❶ we include a module-level docstring that briefly describes the contents of this module. You should write a docstring for each module you create.

Now we make a separate file called *my_car.py*. This file will import the Car class and then create an instance from that class:

my_car.py ❶
```
from car import Car

my_new_car = Car('audi', 'a4', 2019)
print(my_new_car.get_descriptive_name())

my_new_car.odometer_reading = 23
my_new_car.read_odometer()
```

The `import` statement at ❶ tells Python to open the `car` module and import the class `Car`. Now we can use the `Car` class as if it were defined in this file. The output is the same as we saw earlier:

```
2019 Audi A4
This car has 23 miles on it.
```

Importing classes is an effective way to program. Picture how long this program file would be if the entire `Car` class were included. When you instead move the class to a module and import the module, you still get all the same functionality, but you keep your main program file clean and easy to read. You also store most of the logic in separate files; once your classes work as you want them to, you can leave those files alone and focus on the higher-level logic of your main program.

Storing Multiple Classes in a Module

You can store as many classes as you need in a single module, although each class in a module should be related somehow. The classes `Battery` and `ElectricCar` both help represent cars, so let's add them to the module *car.py*.

```
"""A set of classes used to represent gas and electric cars."""

class Car:
    --snip--

class Battery:
    """A simple attempt to model a battery for an electric car."""

    def __init__(self, battery_size=75):
        """Initialize the battery's attributes."""
        self.battery_size = battery_size

    def describe_battery(self):
        """Print a statement describing the battery size."""
        print(f"This car has a {self.battery_size}-kWh battery.")

    def get_range(self):
        """Print a statement about the range this battery provides."""
        if self.battery_size == 75:
            range = 260
        elif self.battery_size == 100:
            range = 315

        print(f"This car can go about {range} miles on a full charge.")

class ElectricCar(Car):
    """Models aspects of a car, specific to electric vehicles."""

    def __init__(self, make, model, year):
        """
        Initialize attributes of the parent class.
        Then initialize attributes specific to an electric car.
        """
        super().__init__(make, model, year)
        self.battery = Battery()
```

Now we can make a new file called *my_electric_car.py*, import the
ElectricCar class, and make an electric car:

```
from car import ElectricCar

my_tesla = ElectricCar('tesla', 'model s', 2019)

print(my_tesla.get_descriptive_name())
my_tesla.battery.describe_battery()
my_tesla.battery.get_range()
```

This has the same output we saw earlier, even though most of the logic
is hidden away in a module:

```
2019 Tesla Model S
This car has a 75-kWh battery.
This car can go about 260 miles on a full charge.
```

Importing Multiple Classes from a Module

You can import as many classes as you need into a program file. If we want to make a regular car and an electric car in the same file, we need to import both classes, Car and ElectricCar:

my_cars.py ❶ `from car import Car, ElectricCar`

❷
```
my_beetle = Car('volkswagen', 'beetle', 2019)
print(my_beetle.get_descriptive_name())
```

❸
```
my_tesla = ElectricCar('tesla', 'roadster', 2019)
print(my_tesla.get_descriptive_name())
```

You import multiple classes from a module by separating each class with a comma ❶. Once you've imported the necessary classes, you're free to make as many instances of each class as you need.

In this example we make a regular Volkswagen Beetle at ❷ and an electric Tesla Roadster at ❸:

```
2019 Volkswagen Beetle
2019 Tesla Roadster
```

Importing an Entire Module

You can also import an entire module and then access the classes you need using dot notation. This approach is simple and results in code that is easy to read. Because every call that creates an instance of a class includes the module name, you won't have naming conflicts with any names used in the current file.

Here's what it looks like to import the entire car module and then create a regular car and an electric car:

my_cars.py ❶ `import car`

❷
```
my_beetle = car.Car('volkswagen', 'beetle', 2019)
print(my_beetle.get_descriptive_name())
```

❸
```
my_tesla = car.ElectricCar('tesla', 'roadster', 2019)
print(my_tesla.get_descriptive_name())
```

At ❶ we import the entire car module. We then access the classes we need through the *module_name.ClassName* syntax. At ❷ we again create a Volkswagen Beetle, and at ❸ we create a Tesla Roadster.

Importing All Classes from a Module

You can import every class from a module using the following syntax:

```
from module_name import *
```

This method is not recommended for two reasons. First, it's helpful to be able to read the import statements at the top of a file and get a clear sense of which classes a program uses. With this approach it's unclear which classes you're using from the module. This approach can also lead to confusion with names in the file. If you accidentally import a class with the same name as something else in your program file, you can create errors that are hard to diagnose. I show this here because even though it's not a recommended approach, you're likely to see it in other people's code at some point.

If you need to import many classes from a module, you're better off importing the entire module and using the *module_name.ClassName* syntax. You won't see all the classes used at the top of the file, but you'll see clearly where the module is used in the program. You'll also avoid the potential naming conflicts that can arise when you import every class in a module.

Importing a Module into a Module

Sometimes you'll want to spread out your classes over several modules to keep any one file from growing too large and avoid storing unrelated classes in the same module. When you store your classes in several modules, you may find that a class in one module depends on a class in another module. When this happens, you can import the required class into the first module.

For example, let's store the Car class in one module and the ElectricCar and Battery classes in a separate module. We'll make a new module called *electric_car.py*—replacing the *electric_car.py* file we created earlier—and copy just the Battery and ElectricCar classes into this file:

electric_car.py

```
"""A set of classes that can be used to represent electric cars."""

❶ from car import Car

class Battery:
    --snip--

class ElectricCar(Car):
    --snip--
```

The class ElectricCar needs access to its parent class Car, so we import Car directly into the module at ❶. If we forget this line, Python will raise an error when we try to import the electric_car module. We also need to update the Car module so it contains only the Car class:

car.py

```
"""A class that can be used to represent a car."""

class Car:
    --snip--
```

Now we can import from each module separately and create whatever kind of car we need:

my_cars.py ❶
```
from car import Car
from electric_car import ElectricCar

my_beetle = Car('volkswagen', 'beetle', 2019)
print(my_beetle.get_descriptive_name())

my_tesla = ElectricCar('tesla', 'roadster', 2019)
print(my_tesla.get_descriptive_name())
```

At ❶ we import Car from its module, and ElectricCar from its module. We then create one regular car and one electric car. Both kinds of cars are created correctly:

```
2019 Volkswagen Beetle
2019 Tesla Roadster
```

Using Aliases

As you saw in Chapter 8, aliases can be quite helpful when using modules to organize your projects' code. You can use aliases when importing classes as well.

As an example, consider a program where you want to make a bunch of electric cars. It might get tedious to type (and read) ElectricCar over and over again. You can give ElectricCar an alias in the import statement:

```
from electric_car import ElectricCar as EC
```

Now you can use this alias whenever you want to make an electric car:

```
my_tesla = EC('tesla', 'roadster', 2019)
```

Finding Your Own Workflow

As you can see, Python gives you many options for how to structure code in a large project. It's important to know all these possibilities so you can determine the best ways to organize your projects as well as understand other people's projects.

When you're starting out, keep your code structure simple. Try doing everything in one file and moving your classes to separate modules once everything is working. If you like how modules and files interact, try storing your classes in modules when you start a project. Find an approach that lets you write code that works, and go from there.

The Python Standard Library

The *Python standard library* is a set of modules included with every Python installation. Now that you have a basic understanding of how functions and classes work, you can start to use modules like these that other programmers have written. You can use any function or class in the standard library by including a simple import statement at the top of your file. Let's look at one module, random, which can be useful in modeling many real-world situations.

One interesting function from the random module is randint(). This function takes two integer arguments and returns a randomly selected integer between (and including) those numbers.

Here's how to generate a random number between 1 and 6:

```
>>> from random import randint
>>> randint(1, 6)
3
```

Another useful function is choice(). This function takes in a list or tuple and returns a randomly chosen element:

```
>>> from random import choice
>>> players = ['charles', 'martina', 'michael', 'florence', 'eli']
>>> first_up = choice(players)
>>> first_up
'florence'
```

The `random` module shouldn't be used when building security-related applications, but it's good enough for many fun and interesting projects.

NOTE *You can also download modules from external sources. You'll see a number of these examples in Part II, where we'll need external modules to complete each project.*

TRY IT YOURSELF

9-13. Dice: Make a class `Die` with one attribute called `sides`, which has a default value of 6. Write a method called `roll_die()` that prints a random number between 1 and the number of sides the die has. Make a 6-sided die and roll it 10 times.

Make a 10-sided die and a 20-sided die. Roll each die 10 times.

9-14. Lottery: Make a list or tuple containing a series of 10 numbers and five letters. Randomly select four numbers or letters from the list and print a message saying that any ticket matching these four numbers or letters wins a prize.

9-15. Lottery Analysis: You can use a loop to see how hard it might be to win the kind of lottery you just modeled. Make a list or tuple called `my_ticket`. Write a loop that keeps pulling numbers until your ticket wins. Print a message reporting how many times the loop had to run to give you a winning ticket.

9-16. Python Module of the Week: One excellent resource for exploring the Python standard library is a site called *Python Module of the Week*. Go to *https://pymotw.com/* and look at the table of contents. Find a module that looks interesting to you and read about it, perhaps starting with the `random` module.

Styling Classes

A few styling issues related to classes are worth clarifying, especially as your programs become more complicated.

Class names should be written in *CamelCase*. To do this, capitalize the first letter of each word in the name, and don't use underscores. Instance and module names should be written in lowercase with underscores between words.

Every class should have a docstring immediately following the class definition. The docstring should be a brief description of what the class does, and you should follow the same formatting conventions you used for writing docstrings in functions. Each module should also have a docstring describing what the classes in a module can be used for.

You can use blank lines to organize code, but don't use them excessively. Within a class you can use one blank line between methods, and within a module you can use two blank lines to separate classes.

If you need to import a module from the standard library and a module that you wrote, place the import statement for the standard library module first. Then add a blank line and the import statement for the module you wrote. In programs with multiple import statements, this convention makes it easier to see where the different modules used in the program come from.

Summary

In this chapter you learned how to write your own classes. You learned how to store information in a class using attributes and how to write methods that give your classes the behavior they need. You learned to write __init__() methods that create instances from your classes with exactly the attributes you want. You saw how to modify the attributes of an instance directly and through methods. You learned that inheritance can simplify the creation of classes that are related to each other, and you learned to use instances of one class as attributes in another class to keep each class simple.

You saw how storing classes in modules and importing classes you need into the files where they'll be used can keep your projects organized. You started learning about the Python standard library, and you saw an example based on the random module. Finally, you learned to style your classes using Python conventions.

In Chapter 10 you'll learn to work with files so you can save the work you've done in a program and the work you've allowed users to do. You'll also learn about *exceptions*, a special Python class designed to help you respond to errors when they arise.

10

FILES AND EXCEPTIONS

Now that you've mastered the basic skills
you need to write organized programs
that are easy to use, it's time to think about
making your programs even more relevant and
usable. In this chapter you'll learn to work with files
so your programs can quickly analyze lots of data.

You'll learn to handle errors so your programs don't crash when they
encounter unexpected situations. You'll learn about *exceptions*, which are
special objects Python creates to manage errors that arise while a program
is running. You'll also learn about the json module, which allows you to save
user data so it isn't lost when your program stops running.

Learning to work with files and save data will make your programs
easier for people to use. Users will be able to choose what data to enter and
when to enter it. People can run your program, do some work, and then
close the program and pick up where they left off later. Learning to handle
exceptions will help you deal with situations in which files don't exist and
deal with other problems that can cause your programs to crash. This will
make your programs more robust when they encounter bad data, whether

it comes from innocent mistakes or from malicious attempts to break your programs. With the skills you'll learn in this chapter, you'll make your programs more applicable, usable, and stable.

Reading from a File

An incredible amount of data is available in text files. Text files can contain weather data, traffic data, socioeconomic data, literary works, and more. Reading from a file is particularly useful in data analysis applications, but it's also applicable to any situation in which you want to analyze or modify information stored in a file. For example, you can write a program that reads in the contents of a text file and rewrites the file with formatting that allows a browser to display it.

When you want to work with the information in a text file, the first step is to read the file into memory. You can read the entire contents of a file, or you can work through the file one line at a time.

Reading an Entire File

To begin, we need a file with a few lines of text in it. Let's start with a file that contains *pi* to 30 decimal places, with 10 decimal places per line:

pi_digits.txt
```
3.1415926535
  8979323846
  2643383279
```

To try the following examples yourself, you can enter these lines in an editor and save the file as *pi_digits.txt*, or you can download the file from the book's resources through *https://nostarch.com/pythoncrashcourse2e/*. Save the file in the same directory where you'll store this chapter's programs.

Here's a program that opens this file, reads it, and prints the contents of the file to the screen:

file_reader.py
```python
with open('pi_digits.txt') as file_object:
    contents = file_object.read()
print(contents)
```

The first line of this program has a lot going on. Let's start by looking at the open() function. To do any work with a file, even just printing its contents, you first need to *open* the file to access it. The open() function needs one argument: the name of the file you want to open. Python looks for this file in the directory where the program that's currently being executed is stored. In this example, *file_reader.py* is currently running, so Python looks for *pi_digits.txt* in the directory where *file_reader.py* is stored. The open() function returns an object representing the file. Here, open('pi_digits.txt') returns an object representing *pi_digits.txt*. Python assigns this object to file_object, which we'll work with later in the program.

The keyword with closes the file once access to it is no longer needed. Notice how we call open() in this program but not close(). You could open and close the file by calling open() and close(), but if a bug in your program prevents the close() method from being executed, the file may never close. This may seem trivial, but improperly closed files can cause data to be lost or corrupted. And if you call close() too early in your program, you'll find yourself trying to work with a *closed* file (a file you can't access), which leads to more errors. It's not always easy to know exactly when you should close a file, but with the structure shown here, Python will figure that out for you. All you have to do is open the file and work with it as desired, trusting that Python will close it automatically when the with block finishes execution.

Once we have a file object representing *pi_digits.txt*, we use the read() method in the second line of our program to read the entire contents of the file and store it as one long string in contents. When we print the value of contents, we get the entire text file back:

```
3.1415926535
  8979323846
  2643383279
```

The only difference between this output and the original file is the extra blank line at the end of the output. The blank line appears because read() returns an empty string when it reaches the end of the file; this empty string shows up as a blank line. If you want to remove the extra blank line, you can use rstrip() in the call to print():

```
with open('pi_digits.txt') as file_object:
    contents = file_object.read()

print(contents.rstrip())
```

Recall that Python's rstrip() method removes, or strips, any whitespace characters from the right side of a string. Now the output matches the contents of the original file exactly:

```
3.1415926535
  8979323846
  2643383279
```

File Paths

When you pass a simple filename like *pi_digits.txt* to the open() function, Python looks in the directory where the file that's currently being executed (that is, your *.py* program file) is stored.

Sometimes, depending on how you organize your work, the file you want to open won't be in the same directory as your program file. For example, you might store your program files in a folder called *python_work*; inside *python_work*, you might have another folder called *text_files* to distinguish your program files from the text files they're manipulating. Even though *text_files* is in *python_work*, just passing open() the name of a file in *text_files* won't work, because Python will only look in *python_work* and stop there; it won't go on and look in *text_files*. To get Python to open files from a directory other than the one where your program file is stored, you need to provide a *file path*, which tells Python to look in a specific location on your system.

Because *text_files* is inside *python_work*, you could use a relative file path to open a file from *text_files*. A *relative file path* tells Python to look for a given location relative to the directory where the currently running program file is stored. For example, you'd write:

```
with open('text_files/filename.txt') as file_object:
```

This line tells Python to look for the desired *.txt* file in the folder *text_files* and assumes that *text_files* is located inside *python_work* (which it is).

NOTE *Windows systems use a backslash (\) instead of a forward slash (/) when displaying file paths, but you can still use forward slashes in your code.*

You can also tell Python exactly where the file is on your computer regardless of where the program that's being executed is stored. This is called an *absolute file path*. You use an absolute path if a relative path doesn't work. For instance, if you've put *text_files* in some folder other than *python_work*—say, a folder called *other_files*—then just passing open() the path 'text_files/filename.txt' won't work because Python will only look for that location inside *python_work*. You'll need to write out a full path to clarify where you want Python to look.

Absolute paths are usually longer than relative paths, so it's helpful to assign them to a variable and then pass that variable to open():

```
file_path = '/home/ehmatthes/other_files/text_files/filename.txt'
with open(file_path) as file_object:
```

Using absolute paths, you can read files from any location on your system. For now it's easiest to store files in the same directory as your program files or in a folder such as *text_files* within the directory that stores your program files.

NOTE *If you try to use backslashes in a file path, you'll get an error because the backslash is used to escape characters in strings. For example, in the path "C:\path\to\file.txt", the sequence \t is interpreted as a tab. If you need to use backslashes, you can escape each one in the path, like this: "C:\\path\\to\\file.txt".*

Reading Line by Line

When you're reading a file, you'll often want to examine each line of the file. You might be looking for certain information in the file, or you might want to modify the text in the file in some way. For example, you might want to read through a file of weather data and work with any line that includes the word *sunny* in the description of that day's weather. In a news report, you might look for any line with the tag <headline> and rewrite that line with a specific kind of formatting.

You can use a for loop on the file object to examine each line from a file one at a time:

file_reader.py

```
❶ filename = 'pi_digits.txt'

❷ with open(filename) as file_object:
❸     for line in file_object:
        print(line)
```

At ❶ we assign the name of the file we're reading from to the variable filename. This is a common convention when working with files. Because the variable filename doesn't represent the actual file—it's just a string telling Python where to find the file—you can easily swap out 'pi_digits.txt' for the name of another file you want to work with. After we call open(), an object representing the file and its contents is assigned to the variable file_object ❷. We again use the with syntax to let Python open and close the file properly. To examine the file's contents, we work through each line in the file by looping over the file object ❸.

When we print each line, we find even more blank lines:

```
3.1415926535

  8979323846

  2643383279
```

These blank lines appear because an invisible newline character is at the end of each line in the text file. The print function adds its own newline each time we call it, so we end up with two newline characters at the end of each line: one from the file and one from print(). Using rstrip() on each line in the print() call eliminates these extra blank lines:

```
filename = 'pi_digits.txt'

with open(filename) as file_object:
    for line in file_object:
        print(line.rstrip())
```

Now the output matches the contents of the file once again:

```
3.1415926535
 8979323846
 2643383279
```

Making a List of Lines from a File

When you use with, the file object returned by open() is only available inside the with block that contains it. If you want to retain access to a file's contents outside the with block, you can store the file's lines in a list inside the block and then work with that list. You can process parts of the file immediately and postpone some processing for later in the program.

The following example stores the lines of *pi_digits.txt* in a list inside the with block and then prints the lines outside the with block:

```
filename = 'pi_digits.txt'

with open(filename) as file_object:
❶     lines = file_object.readlines()

❷ for line in lines:
    print(line.rstrip())
```

At ❶ the readlines() method takes each line from the file and stores it in a list. This list is then assigned to lines, which we can continue to work with after the with block ends. At ❷ we use a simple for loop to print each line from lines. Because each item in lines corresponds to each line in the file, the output matches the contents of the file exactly.

Working with a File's Contents

After you've read a file into memory, you can do whatever you want with that data, so let's briefly explore the digits of *pi*. First, we'll attempt to build a single string containing all the digits in the file with no whitespace in it:

pi_string.py
```
filename = 'pi_digits.txt'

with open(filename) as file_object:
    lines = file_object.readlines()

❶ pi_string = ''
❷ for line in lines:
    pi_string += line.rstrip()

❸ print(pi_string)
print(len(pi_string))
```

We start by opening the file and storing each line of digits in a list, just as we did in the previous example. At ❶ we create a variable, pi_string, to hold the digits of *pi*. We then create a loop that adds each line of digits to pi_string and removes the newline character from each line ❷. At ❸ we print this string and also show how long the string is:

```
3.1415926535  8979323846  2643383279
36
```

The variable pi_string contains the whitespace that was on the left side of the digits in each line, but we can get rid of that by using strip() instead of rstrip():

```
--snip--
for line in lines:
    pi_string += line.strip()

print(pi_string)
print(len(pi_string))
```

Now we have a string containing *pi* to 30 decimal places. The string is 32 characters long because it also includes the leading 3 and a decimal point:

```
3.14159265358979323846264338327 9
32
```

NOTE   *When Python reads from a text file, it interprets all text in the file as a string. If you read in a number and want to work with that value in a numerical context, you'll have to convert it to an integer using the int() function or convert it to a float using the float() function.*

Large Files: One Million Digits

So far we've focused on analyzing a text file that contains only three lines, but the code in these examples would work just as well on much larger files. If we start with a text file that contains *pi* to 1,000,000 decimal places instead of just 30, we can create a single string containing all these digits. We don't need to change our program at all except to pass it a different file. We'll also print just the first 50 decimal places, so we don't have to watch a million digits scroll by in the terminal:

pi_string.py
```
filename = 'pi_million_digits.txt'

with open(filename) as file_object:
    lines = file_object.readlines()
```

```
pi_string = ''
for line in lines:
    pi_string += line.strip()

print(f"{pi_string[:52]}...")
print(len(pi_string))
```

The output shows that we do indeed have a string containing *pi* to 1,000,000 decimal places:

```
3.14159265358979323846264338327950288419716939937510...
1000002
```

Python has no inherent limit to how much data you can work with; you can work with as much data as your system's memory can handle.

NOTE   *To run this program (and many of the examples that follow), you'll need to download the resources available at* https://nostarch.com/pythoncrashcourse2e/.

Is Your Birthday Contained in Pi?

I've always been curious to know if my birthday appears anywhere in the digits of *pi*. Let's use the program we just wrote to find out if someone's birthday appears anywhere in the first million digits of *pi*. We can do this by expressing each birthday as a string of digits and seeing if that string appears anywhere in pi_string:

```
--snip--
for line in lines:
    pi_string += line.strip()

❶ birthday = input("Enter your birthday, in the form mmddyy: ")
❷ if birthday in pi_string:
    print("Your birthday appears in the first million digits of pi!")
else:
    print("Your birthday does not appear in the first million digits of pi.")
```

At ❶ we prompt for the user's birthday, and then at ❷ we check if that string is in pi_string. Let's try it:

```
Enter your birthdate, in the form mmddyy: 120372
Your birthday appears in the first million digits of pi!
```

My birthday does appear in the digits of *pi*! Once you've read from a file, you can analyze its contents in just about any way you can imagine.

Writing to a File

One of the simplest ways to save data is to write it to a file. When you write text to a file, the output will still be available after you close the terminal containing your program's output. You can examine output after a program finishes running, and you can share the output files with others as well. You can also write programs that read the text back into memory and work with it again later.

Writing to an Empty File

To write text to a file, you need to call `open()` with a second argument telling Python that you want to write to the file. To see how this works, let's write a simple message and store it in a file instead of printing it to the screen:

*write
_message.py*

```
filename = 'programming.txt'

❶ with open(filename, 'w') as file_object:
❷     file_object.write("I love programming.")
```

The call to `open()` in this example has two arguments ❶. The first argument is still the name of the file we want to open. The second argument, `'w'`, tells Python that we want to open the file in *write mode.* You can open a file in *read mode* (`'r'`), *write mode* (`'w'`), *append mode* (`'a'`), or a mode that allows you to read and write to the file (`'r+'`). If you omit the mode argument, Python opens the file in read-only mode by default.

The open() function automatically creates the file you're writing to if it doesn't already exist. However, be careful opening a file in write mode (`'w'`) because if the file does exist, Python will erase the contents of the file before returning the file object.

At ❷ we use the write() method on the file object to write a string to the file. This program has no terminal output, but if you open the file *programming.txt*, you'll see one line:

programming.txt

```
I love programming.
```

This file behaves like any other file on your computer. You can open it, write new text in it, copy from it, paste to it, and so forth.

NOTE *Python can only write strings to a text file. If you want to store numerical data in a text file, you'll have to convert the data to string format first using the* str() *function.*

Writing Multiple Lines

The write() function doesn't add any newlines to the text you write. So if you write more than one line without including newline characters, your file may not look the way you want it to:

```
filename = 'programming.txt'

with open(filename, 'w') as file_object:
    file_object.write("I love programming.")
    file_object.write("I love creating new games.")
```

If you open *programming.txt*, you'll see the two lines squished together:

```
I love programming.I love creating new games.
```

Including newlines in your calls to write() makes each string appear on its own line:

```
filename = 'programming.txt'

with open(filename, 'w') as file_object:
    file_object.write("I love programming.\n")
    file_object.write("I love creating new games.\n")
```

The output now appears on separate lines:

```
I love programming.
I love creating new games.
```

You can also use spaces, tab characters, and blank lines to format your output, just as you've been doing with terminal-based output.

Appending to a File

If you want to add content to a file instead of writing over existing content, you can open the file in *append mode*. When you open a file in append mode, Python doesn't erase the contents of the file before returning the file object. Any lines you write to the file will be added at the end of the file. If the file doesn't exist yet, Python will create an empty file for you.

Let's modify *write_message.py* by adding some new reasons we love programming to the existing file *programming.txt*:

write _message.py

```
filename = 'programming.txt'

❶ with open(filename, 'a') as file_object:
❷     file_object.write("I also love finding meaning in large datasets.\n")
      file_object.write("I love creating apps that can run in a browser.\n")
```

At ❶ we use the 'a' argument to open the file for appending rather than writing over the existing file. At ❷ we write two new lines, which are added to *programming.txt*:

programming.txt

```
I love programming.
I love creating new games.
I also love finding meaning in large datasets.
I love creating apps that can run in a browser.
```

We end up with the original contents of the file, followed by the new content we just added.

TRY IT YOURSELF

10-3. Guest: Write a program that prompts the user for their name. When they respond, write their name to a file called *guest.txt*.

10-4. Guest Book: Write a while loop that prompts users for their name. When they enter their name, print a greeting to the screen and add a line recording their visit in a file called *guest_book.txt*. Make sure each entry appears on a new line in the file.

10-5. Programming Poll: Write a while loop that asks people why they like programming. Each time someone enters a reason, add their reason to a file that stores all the responses.

Exceptions

Python uses special objects called *exceptions* to manage errors that arise during a program's execution. Whenever an error occurs that makes Python unsure what to do next, it creates an exception object. If you write code that handles the exception, the program will continue running. If you don't handle the exception, the program will halt and show a *traceback*, which includes a report of the exception that was raised.

Exceptions are handled with try-except blocks. A try-except block asks Python to do something, but it also tells Python what to do if an exception is raised. When you use try-except blocks, your programs will continue running even if things start to go wrong. Instead of tracebacks, which can be confusing for users to read, users will see friendly error messages that you write.

Handling the ZeroDivisionError Exception

Let's look at a simple error that causes Python to raise an exception. You probably know that it's impossible to divide a number by zero, but let's ask Python to do it anyway:

division
_calculator.py
```
print(5/0)
```

Of course Python can't do this, so we get a traceback:

```
Traceback (most recent call last):
  File "division_calculator.py", line 1, in <module>
    print(5/0)
❶ ZeroDivisionError: division by zero
```

The error reported at ❶ in the traceback, `ZeroDivisionError`, is an exception object. Python creates this kind of object in response to a situation where it can't do what we ask it to. When this happens, Python stops the program and tells us the kind of exception that was raised. We can use this information to modify our program. We'll tell Python what to do when this kind of exception occurs; that way, if it happens again, we're prepared.

Using try-except Blocks

When you think an error may occur, you can write a try-except block to handle the exception that might be raised. You tell Python to try running some code, and you tell it what to do if the code results in a particular kind of exception.

Here's what a try-except block for handling the `ZeroDivisionError` exception looks like:

```
try:
    print(5/0)
except ZeroDivisionError:
    print("You can't divide by zero!")
```

We put `print(5/0)`, the line that caused the error, inside a try block. If the code in a try block works, Python skips over the except block. If the code in the try block causes an error, Python looks for an except block whose error matches the one that was raised and runs the code in that block.

In this example, the code in the try block produces a `ZeroDivisionError`, so Python looks for an except block telling it how to respond. Python then runs the code in that block, and the user sees a friendly error message instead of a traceback:

```
You can't divide by zero!
```

If more code followed the try-except block, the program would continue running because we told Python how to handle the error. Let's look at an example where catching an error can allow a program to continue running.

Using Exceptions to Prevent Crashes

Handling errors correctly is especially important when the program has more work to do after the error occurs. This happens often in programs that prompt users for input. If the program responds to invalid input appropriately, it can prompt for more valid input instead of crashing.

Let's create a simple calculator that does only division:

*division
_calculator.py*

```
print("Give me two numbers, and I'll divide them.")
print("Enter 'q' to quit.")

while True:
❶    first_number = input("\nFirst number: ")
     if first_number == 'q':
         break
❷    second_number = input("Second number: ")
     if second_number == 'q':
         break
❸    answer = int(first_number) / int(second_number)
     print(answer)
```

This program prompts the user to input a `first_number` ❶ and, if the user does not enter *q* to quit, a `second_number` ❷. We then divide these two numbers to get an `answer` ❸. This program does nothing to handle errors, so asking it to divide by zero causes it to crash:

```
Give me two numbers, and I'll divide them.
Enter 'q' to quit.

First number: 5
Second number: 0
Traceback (most recent call last):
  File "division_calculator.py", line 9, in <module>
    answer = int(first_number) / int(second_number)
ZeroDivisionError: division by zero
```

It's bad that the program crashed, but it's also not a good idea to let users see tracebacks. Nontechnical users will be confused by them, and in a malicious setting, attackers will learn more than you want them to know from a traceback. For example, they'll know the name of your program file, and they'll see a part of your code that isn't working properly. A skilled attacker can sometimes use this information to determine which kind of attacks to use against your code.

The else Block

We can make this program more error resistant by wrapping the line that might produce errors in a try-except block. The error occurs on the line that performs the division, so that's where we'll put the try-except block. This example also includes an else block. Any code that depends on the try block executing successfully goes in the else block:

```
--snip--
while True:
    --snip--
    if second_number == 'q':
        break
❶   try:
        answer = int(first_number) / int(second_number)
❷   except ZeroDivisionError:
        print("You can't divide by 0!")
❸   else:
        print(answer)
```

We ask Python to try to complete the division operation in a try block ❶, which includes only the code that might cause an error. Any code that depends on the try block succeeding is added to the else block. In this case if the division operation is successful, we use the else block to print the result ❸.

The except block tells Python how to respond when a ZeroDivisionError arises ❷. If the try block doesn't succeed because of a division by zero error, we print a friendly message telling the user how to avoid this kind of error. The program continues to run, and the user never sees a traceback:

```
Give me two numbers, and I'll divide them.
Enter 'q' to quit.

First number: 5
Second number: 0
You can't divide by 0!
```

```
First number: 5
Second number: 2
2.5

First number: q
```

The try-except-else block works like this: Python attempts to run the code in the try block. The only code that should go in a try block is code that might cause an exception to be raised. Sometimes you'll have additional code that should run only if the try block was successful; this code goes in the else block. The except block tells Python what to do in case a certain exception arises when it tries to run the code in the try block.

By anticipating likely sources of errors, you can write robust programs that continue to run even when they encounter invalid data and missing resources. Your code will be resistant to innocent user mistakes and malicious attacks.

Handling the FileNotFoundError Exception

One common issue when working with files is handling missing files. The file you're looking for might be in a different location, the filename may be misspelled, or the file may not exist at all. You can handle all of these situations in a straightforward way with a try-except block.

Let's try to read a file that doesn't exist. The following program tries to read in the contents of *Alice in Wonderland*, but I haven't saved the file *alice.txt* in the same directory as *alice.py*:

alice.py
```
filename = 'alice.txt'

with open(filename, encoding='utf-8') as f:
    contents = f.read()
```

There are two changes here. One is the use of the variable f to represent the file object, which is a common convention. The second is the use of the encoding argument. This argument is needed when your system's default encoding doesn't match the encoding of the file that's being read.

Python can't read from a missing file, so it raises an exception:

```
Traceback (most recent call last):
  File "alice.py", line 3, in <module>
    with open(filename, encoding='utf-8') as f:
FileNotFoundError: [Errno 2] No such file or directory: 'alice.txt'
```

The last line of the traceback reports a FileNotFoundError: this is the exception Python creates when it can't find the file it's trying to open.

In this example, the open() function produces the error, so to handle it, the try block will begin with the line that contains open():

```
filename = 'alice.txt'

try:
    with open(filename, encoding='utf-8') as f:
        contents = f.read()
except FileNotFoundError:
    print(f"Sorry, the file {filename} does not exist.")
```

In this example, the code in the try block produces a FileNotFoundError, so Python looks for an except block that matches that error. Python then runs the code in that block, and the result is a friendly error message instead of a traceback:

```
Sorry, the file alice.txt does not exist.
```

The program has nothing more to do if the file doesn't exist, so the error-handling code doesn't add much to this program. Let's build on this example and see how exception handling can help when you're working with more than one file.

Analyzing Text

You can analyze text files containing entire books. Many classic works of literature are available as simple text files because they are in the public domain. The texts used in this section come from Project Gutenberg (*http://gutenberg .org/*). Project Gutenberg maintains a collection of literary works that are available in the public domain, and it's a great resource if you're interested in working with literary texts in your programming projects.

Let's pull in the text of *Alice in Wonderland* and try to count the number of words in the text. We'll use the string method split(), which can build a list of words from a string. Here's what split() does with a string containing just the title "Alice in Wonderland":

```
>>> title = "Alice in Wonderland"
>>> title.split()
['Alice', 'in', 'Wonderland']
```

The split() method separates a string into parts wherever it finds a space and stores all the parts of the string in a list. The result is a list of words from the string, although some punctuation may also appear with some of the words. To count the number of words in *Alice in Wonderland*, we'll use split() on the entire text. Then we'll count the items in the list to get a rough idea of the number of words in the text:

```
filename = 'alice.txt'

try:
```

```
    with open(filename, encoding='utf-8') as f:
        contents = f.read()
except FileNotFoundError:
    print(f"Sorry, the file {filename} does not exist.")
else:
    # Count the approximate number of words in the file.
❶  words = contents.split()
❷  num_words = len(words)
❸  print(f"The file {filename} has about {num_words} words.")
```

I moved the file *alice.txt* to the correct directory, so the try block will
work this time. At ❶ we take the string contents, which now contains the
entire text of *Alice in Wonderland* as one long string, and use the split()
method to produce a list of all the words in the book. When we use len() on
this list to examine its length, we get a good approximation of the number
of words in the original string ❷. At ❸ we print a statement that reports
how many words were found in the file. This code is placed in the else block
because it will work only if the code in the try block was executed successfully. The output tells us how many words are in *alice.txt*:

```
The file alice.txt has about 29465 words.
```

The count is a little high because extra information is provided by the
publisher in the text file used here, but it's a good approximation of the
length of *Alice in Wonderland*.

Working with Multiple Files

Let's add more books to analyze. But before we do, let's move the bulk of
this program to a function called count_words(). By doing so, it will be easier
to run the analysis for multiple books:

word_count.py

```
def count_words(filename):
❶  """Count the approximate number of words in a file."""
    try:
        with open(filename, encoding='utf-8') as f:
            contents = f.read()
    except FileNotFoundError:
        print(f"Sorry, the file {filename} does not exist.")
    else:
        words = contents.split()
        num_words = len(words)
        print(f"The file {filename} has about {num_words} words.")

filename = 'alice.txt'
count_words(filename)
```

Most of this code is unchanged. We simply indented it and moved it
into the body of count_words(). It's a good habit to keep comments up to date
when you're modifying a program, so we changed the comment to a docstring and reworded it slightly ❶.

Now we can write a simple loop to count the words in any text we want to analyze. We do this by storing the names of the files we want to analyze in a list, and then we call count_words() for each file in the list. We'll try to count the words for *Alice in Wonderland*, *Siddhartha*, *Moby Dick*, and *Little Women*, which are all available in the public domain. I've intentionally left *siddhartha.txt* out of the directory containing *word_count.py*, so we can see how well our program handles a missing file:

```
def count_words(filename):
    --snip--

filenames = ['alice.txt', 'siddhartha.txt', 'moby_dick.txt', 'little_women.txt']
for filename in filenames:
    count_words(filename)
```

The missing *siddhartha.txt* file has no effect on the rest of the program's execution:

```
The file alice.txt has about 29465 words.
Sorry, the file siddhartha.txt does not exist.
The file moby_dick.txt has about 215830 words.
The file little_women.txt has about 189079 words.
```

Using the try-except block in this example provides two significant advantages. We prevent our users from seeing a traceback, and we let the program continue analyzing the texts it's able to find. If we don't catch the FileNotFoundError that *siddhartha.txt* raised, the user would see a full traceback, and the program would stop running after trying to analyze *Siddhartha*. It would never analyze *Moby Dick* or *Little Women*.

Failing Silently

In the previous example, we informed our users that one of the files was unavailable. But you don't need to report every exception you catch. Sometimes you'll want the program to fail silently when an exception occurs and continue on as if nothing happened. To make a program fail silently, you write a try block as usual, but you explicitly tell Python to do nothing in the except block. Python has a pass statement that tells it to do nothing in a block:

```
def count_words(filename):
    """Count the approximate number of words in a file."""
    try:
        --snip--
    except FileNotFoundError:
❶       pass
    else:
        --snip--

filenames = ['alice.txt', 'siddhartha.txt', 'moby_dick.txt', 'little_women.txt']
for filename in filenames:
    count_words(filename)
```

The only difference between this listing and the previous one is the pass statement at ❶. Now when a FileNotFoundError is raised, the code in the except block runs, but nothing happens. No traceback is produced, and there's no output in response to the error that was raised. Users see the word counts for each file that exists, but they don't see any indication that a file wasn't found:

```
The file alice.txt has about 29465 words.
The file moby_dick.txt has about 215830 words.
The file little_women.txt has about 189079 words.
```

The pass statement also acts as a placeholder. It's a reminder that you're choosing to do nothing at a specific point in your program's execution and that you might want to do something there later. For example, in this program we might decide to write any missing filenames to a file called *missing_files.txt*. Our users wouldn't see this file, but we'd be able to read the file and deal with any missing texts.

Deciding Which Errors to Report

How do you know when to report an error to your users and when to fail silently? If users know which texts are supposed to be analyzed, they might appreciate a message informing them why some texts were not analyzed. If users expect to see some results but don't know which books are supposed to be analyzed, they might not need to know that some texts were unavailable. Giving users information they aren't looking for can decrease the usability of your program. Python's error-handling structures give you fine-grained control over how much to share with users when things go wrong; it's up to you to decide how much information to share.

Well-written, properly tested code is not very prone to internal errors, such as syntax or logical errors. But every time your program depends on something external, such as user input, the existence of a file, or the availability of a network connection, there is a possibility of an exception being raised. A little experience will help you know where to include exception handling blocks in your program and how much to report to users about errors that arise.

TRY IT YOURSELF

10-6. Addition: One common problem when prompting for numerical input occurs when people provide text instead of numbers. When you try to convert the input to an int, you'll get a ValueError. Write a program that prompts for two numbers. Add them together and print the result. Catch the ValueError if either input value is not a number, and print a friendly error message. Test your program by entering two numbers and then by entering some text instead of a number.

(continued)

10-7. Addition Calculator: Wrap your code from Exercise 10-6 in a while loop so the user can continue entering numbers even if they make a mistake and enter text instead of a number.

10-8. Cats and Dogs: Make two files, *cats.txt* and *dogs.txt*. Store at least three names of cats in the first file and three names of dogs in the second file. Write a program that tries to read these files and print the contents of the file to the screen. Wrap your code in a try-except block to catch the FileNotFound error, and print a friendly message if a file is missing. Move one of the files to a different location on your system, and make sure the code in the except block executes properly.

10-9. Silent Cats and Dogs: Modify your except block in Exercise 10-8 to fail silently if either file is missing.

10-10. Common Words: Visit Project Gutenberg (*https://gutenberg.org/*) and find a few texts you'd like to analyze. Download the text files for these works, or copy the raw text from your browser into a text file on your computer.

You can use the count() method to find out how many times a word or phrase appears in a string. For example, the following code counts the number of times 'row' appears in a string:

```
>>> line = "Row, row, row your boat"
>>> line.count('row')
2
>>> line.lower().count('row')
3
```

Notice that converting the string to lowercase using lower() catches all appearances of the word you're looking for, regardless of how it's formatted.

Write a program that reads the files you found at Project Gutenberg and determines how many times the word 'the' appears in each text. This will be an approximation because it will also count words such as 'then' and 'there'. Try counting 'the ', with a space in the string, and see how much lower your count is.

Storing Data

Many of your programs will ask users to input certain kinds of information. You might allow users to store preferences in a game or provide data for a visualization. Whatever the focus of your program is, you'll store the information users provide in data structures such as lists and dictionaries. When users close a program, you'll almost always want to save the information they entered. A simple way to do this involves storing your data using the json module.

The json module allows you to dump simple Python data structures into a file and load the data from that file the next time the program runs. You can also use json to share data between different Python programs. Even better, the JSON data format is not specific to Python, so you can share data you store in the JSON format with people who work in many other programming languages. It's a useful and portable format, and it's easy to learn.

NOTE *The JSON (JavaScript Object Notation) format was originally developed for JavaScript. However, it has since become a common format used by many languages, including Python.*

Using json.dump() and json.load()

Let's write a short program that stores a set of numbers and another program that reads these numbers back into memory. The first program will use json.dump() to store the set of numbers, and the second program will use json.load().

The json.dump() function takes two arguments: a piece of data to store and a file object it can use to store the data. Here's how you can use json.dump() to store a list of numbers:

*number
_writer.py*

```
import json

numbers = [2, 3, 5, 7, 11, 13]

❶ filename = 'numbers.json'
❷ with open(filename, 'w') as f:
❸     json.dump(numbers, f)
```

We first import the json module and then create a list of numbers to work with. At ❶ we choose a filename in which to store the list of numbers. It's customary to use the file extension *.json* to indicate that the data in the file is stored in the JSON format. Then we open the file in write mode, which allows json to write the data to the file ❷. At ❸ we use the json.dump() function to store the list numbers in the file *numbers.json*.

This program has no output, but let's open the file *numbers.json* and look at it. The data is stored in a format that looks just like Python:

```
[2, 3, 5, 7, 11, 13]
```

Now we'll write a program that uses json.load() to read the list back into memory:

*number
_reader.py*

```
import json

❶ filename = 'numbers.json'
❷ with open(filename) as f:
❸     numbers = json.load(f)

print(numbers)
```

At ❶ we make sure to read from the same file we wrote to. This time when we open the file, we open it in read mode because Python only needs to read from the file ❷. At ❸ we use the json.load() function to load the information stored in *numbers.json*, and we assign it to the variable numbers. Finally we print the recovered list of numbers and see that it's the same list created in *number_writer.py*:

```
[2, 3, 5, 7, 11, 13]
```

This is a simple way to share data between two programs.

Saving and Reading User-Generated Data

Saving data with json is useful when you're working with user-generated data, because if you don't store your user's information somehow, you'll lose it when the program stops running. Let's look at an example where we prompt the user for their name the first time they run a program and then remember their name when they run the program again.

Let's start by storing the user's name:

remember_me.py
```
import json

❶ username = input("What is your name? ")

filename = 'username.json'
with open(filename, 'w') as f:
❷     json.dump(username, f)
❸     print(f"We'll remember you when you come back, {username}!")
```

At ❶ we prompt for a username to store. Next, we use json.dump(), passing it a username and a file object, to store the username in a file ❷. Then we print a message informing the user that we've stored their information ❸:

```
What is your name? Eric
We'll remember you when you come back, Eric!
```

Now let's write a new program that greets a user whose name has already been stored:

greet_user.py
```
import json

filename = 'username.json'

with open(filename) as f:
❶     username = json.load(f)
❷     print(f"Welcome back, {username}!")
```

At ❶ we use `json.load()` to read the information stored in *username.json* and assign it to the variable username. Now that we've recovered the username, we can welcome them back ❷:

```
Welcome back, Eric!
```

We need to combine these two programs into one file. When someone runs *remember_me.py*, we want to retrieve their username from memory if possible; therefore, we'll start with a try block that attempts to recover the username. If the file *username.json* doesn't exist, we'll have the except block prompt for a username and store it in *username.json* for next time:

remember _me.py

```
import json

# Load the username, if it has been stored previously.
#  Otherwise, prompt for the username and store it.
filename = 'username.json'
try:
❶    with open(filename) as f:
❷        username = json.load(f)
❸ except FileNotFoundError:
❹    username = input("What is your name? ")
❺    with open(filename, 'w') as f:
        json.dump(username, f)
        print(f"We'll remember you when you come back, {username}!")
else:
    print(f"Welcome back, {username}!")
```

There's no new code here; blocks of code from the last two examples are just combined into one file. At ❶ we try to open the file *username.json*. If this file exists, we read the username back into memory ❷ and print a message welcoming back the user in the else block. If this is the first time the user runs the program, *username.json* won't exist and a `FileNotFoundError` will occur ❸. Python will move on to the except block where we prompt the user to enter their username ❹. We then use `json.dump()` to store the username and print a greeting ❺.

Whichever block executes, the result is a username and an appropriate greeting. If this is the first time the program runs, this is the output:

```
What is your name? Eric
We'll remember you when you come back, Eric!
```

Otherwise:

```
Welcome back, Eric!
```

This is the output you see if the program was already run at least once.

Refactoring

Often, you'll come to a point where your code will work, but you'll recognize that you could improve the code by breaking it up into a series of functions that have specific jobs. This process is called *refactoring*. Refactoring makes your code cleaner, easier to understand, and easier to extend.

We can refactor *remember_me.py* by moving the bulk of its logic into one or more functions. The focus of *remember_me.py* is on greeting the user, so let's move all of our existing code into a function called greet_user():

remember _me.py

```
import json

def greet_user():
❶    """Greet the user by name."""
    filename = 'username.json'
    try:
        with open(filename) as f:
            username = json.load(f)
    except FileNotFoundError:
        username = input("What is your name? ")
        with open(filename, 'w') as f:
            json.dump(username, f)
            print(f"We'll remember you when you come back, {username}!")
    else:
        print(f"Welcome back, {username}!")

greet_user()
```

Because we're using a function now, we update the comments with a docstring that reflects how the program currently works ❶. This file is a little cleaner, but the function greet_user() is doing more than just greeting the user—it's also retrieving a stored username if one exists and prompting for a new username if one doesn't exist.

Let's refactor greet_user() so it's not doing so many different tasks. We'll start by moving the code for retrieving a stored username to a separate function:

```
import json

def get_stored_username():
❶    """Get stored username if available."""
    filename = 'username.json'
    try:
        with open(filename) as f:
            username = json.load(f)
    except FileNotFoundError:
❷        return None
    else:
        return username
```

```
def greet_user():
    """Greet the user by name."""
    username = get_stored_username()
❸   if username:
        print(f"Welcome back, {username}!")
    else:
        username = input("What is your name? ")
        filename = 'username.json'
        with open(filename, 'w') as f:
            json.dump(username, f)
            print(f"We'll remember you when you come back, {username}!")

greet_user()
```

The new function get_stored_username() has a clear purpose, as stated in the docstring at ❶. This function retrieves a stored username and returns the username if it finds one. If the file *username.json* doesn't exist, the function returns None ❷. This is good practice: a function should either return the value you're expecting, or it should return None. This allows us to perform a simple test with the return value of the function. At ❸ we print a welcome back message to the user if the attempt to retrieve a username was successful, and if it doesn't, we prompt for a new username.

We should factor one more block of code out of greet_user(). If the username doesn't exist, we should move the code that prompts for a new username to a function dedicated to that purpose:

```
import json

def get_stored_username():
    """Get stored username if available."""
    --snip--

def get_new_username():
    """Prompt for a new username."""
    username = input("What is your name? ")
    filename = 'username.json'
    with open(filename, 'w') as f:
        json.dump(username, f)
    return username

def greet_user():
    """Greet the user by name."""
    username = get_stored_username()
    if username:
        print(f"Welcome back, {username}!")
    else:
        username = get_new_username()
        print(f"We'll remember you when you come back, {username}!")

greet_user()
```

Each function in this final version of *remember_me.py* has a single, clear purpose. We call greet_user(), and that function prints an appropriate message: it either welcomes back an existing user or greets a new user. It does this by calling get_stored_username(), which is responsible only for retrieving a stored username if one exists. Finally, greet_user() calls get_new_username() if necessary, which is responsible only for getting a new username and storing it. This compartmentalization of work is an essential part of writing clear code that will be easy to maintain and extend.

TRY IT YOURSELF

10-11. Favorite Number: Write a program that prompts for the user's favorite number. Use json.dump() to store this number in a file. Write a separate program that reads in this value and prints the message, "I know your favorite number! It's _____."

10-12. Favorite Number Remembered: Combine the two programs from Exercise 10-11 into one file. If the number is already stored, report the favorite number to the user. If not, prompt for the user's favorite number and store it in a file. Run the program twice to see that it works.

10-13. Verify User: The final listing for *remember_me.py* assumes either that the user has already entered their username or that the program is running for the first time. We should modify it in case the current user is not the person who last used the program.

Before printing a welcome back message in greet_user(), ask the user if this is the correct username. If it's not, call get_new_username() to get the correct username.

Summary

In this chapter, you learned how to work with files. You learned to read an entire file at once and read through a file's contents one line at a time. You learned to write to a file and append text onto the end of a file. You read about exceptions and how to handle the exceptions you're likely to see in your programs. Finally, you learned how to store Python data structures so you can save information your users provide, preventing them from having to start over each time they run a program.

In Chapter 11 you'll learn efficient ways to test your code. This will help you trust that the code you develop is correct, and it will help you identify bugs that are introduced as you continue to build on the programs you've written.

11

TESTING YOUR CODE

When you write a function or a class, you can also write tests for that code. Testing proves that your code works as it's supposed to in response to all the input types it's designed to receive. When you write tests, you can be confident that your code will work correctly as more people begin to use your programs. You'll also be able to test new code as you add it to make sure your changes don't break your program's existing behavior. Every programmer makes mistakes, so every programmer must test their code often, catching problems before users encounter them.

In this chapter you'll learn to test your code using tools in Python's unittest module. You'll learn to build a test case and check that a set of inputs results in the output you want. You'll see what a passing test looks like and what a failing test looks like, and you'll learn how a failing test can help you improve your code. You'll learn to test functions and classes, and you'll start to understand how many tests to write for a project.

Testing a Function

To learn about testing, we need code to test. Here's a simple function that takes in a first and last name, and returns a neatly formatted full name:

name
_function.py

```
def get_formatted_name(first, last):
    """Generate a neatly formatted full name."""
    full_name = f"{first} {last}"
    return full_name.title()
```

The function get_formatted_name() combines the first and last name with a space in between to complete a full name, and then capitalizes and returns the full name. To check that get_formatted_name() works, let's make a program that uses this function. The program *names.py* lets users enter a first and last name, and see a neatly formatted full name:

names.py

```
from name_function import get_formatted_name

print("Enter 'q' at any time to quit.")
while True:
    first = input("\nPlease give me a first name: ")
    if first == 'q':
        break
    last = input("Please give me a last name: ")
    if last == 'q':
        break

    formatted_name = get_formatted_name(first, last)
    print(f"\tNeatly formatted name: {formatted_name}.")
```

This program imports get_formatted_name() from *name_function.py*. The user can enter a series of first and last names, and see the formatted full names that are generated:

```
Enter 'q' at any time to quit.

Please give me a first name: janis
Please give me a last name: joplin
        Neatly formatted name: Janis Joplin.

Please give me a first name: bob
Please give me a last name: dylan
        Neatly formatted name: Bob Dylan.

Please give me a first name: q
```

We can see that the names generated here are correct. But let's say we want to modify get_formatted_name() so it can also handle middle names. As we do so, we want to make sure we don't break the way the function handles names that have only a first and last name. We could test our code by running *names.py* and entering a name like Janis Joplin every time we modify get_formatted_name(), but that would become tedious. Fortunately,

Python provides an efficient way to automate the testing of a function's output. If we automate the testing of get_formatted_name(), we can always be confident that the function will work when given the kinds of names we've written tests for.

Unit Tests and Test Cases

The module unittest from the Python standard library provides tools for testing your code. A *unit test* verifies that one specific aspect of a function's behavior is correct. A *test case* is a collection of unit tests that together prove that a function behaves as it's supposed to, within the full range of situations you expect it to handle. A good test case considers all the possible kinds of input a function could receive and includes tests to represent each of these situations. A test case with *full coverage* includes a full range of unit tests covering all the possible ways you can use a function. Achieving full coverage on a large project can be daunting. It's often good enough to write tests for your code's critical behaviors and then aim for full coverage only if the project starts to see widespread use.

A Passing Test

The syntax for setting up a test case takes some getting used to, but once you've set up the test case it's straightforward to add more unit tests for your functions. To write a test case for a function, import the unittest module and the function you want to test. Then create a class that inherits from unittest.TestCase, and write a series of methods to test different aspects of your function's behavior.

Here's a test case with one method that verifies that the function get_formatted_name() works correctly when given a first and last name:

test_name
_function.py

```
import unittest
from name_function import get_formatted_name

❶ class NamesTestCase(unittest.TestCase):
      """Tests for 'name_function.py'."""

      def test_first_last_name(self):
          """Do names like 'Janis Joplin' work?"""
❷        formatted_name = get_formatted_name('janis', 'joplin')
❸        self.assertEqual(formatted_name, 'Janis Joplin')

❹ if __name__ == '__main__':
      unittest.main()
```

First, we import unittest and the function we want to test, get_formatted _name(). At ❶ we create a class called NamesTestCase, which will contain a series of unit tests for get_formatted_name(). You can name the class anything you want, but it's best to call it something related to the function you're about to test and to use the word *Test* in the class name. This class must inherit from the class unittest.TestCase so Python knows how to run the tests you write.

NamesTestCase contains a single method that tests one aspect of get_formatted_name(). We call this method test_first_last_name() because we're verifying that names with only a first and last name are formatted correctly. Any method that starts with test_ will be run automatically when we run *test_name_function.py*. Within this test method, we call the function we want to test. In this example we call get_formatted_name() with the arguments 'janis' and 'joplin', and assign the result to formatted_name ❷.

At ❸ we use one of unittest's most useful features: an *assert* method. Assert methods verify that a result you received matches the result you expected to receive. In this case, because we know get_formatted_name() is supposed to return a capitalized, properly spaced full name, we expect the value of formatted_name to be Janis Joplin. To check if this is true, we use unittest's assertEqual() method and pass it formatted_name and 'Janis Joplin'. The line

```
self.assertEqual(formatted_name, 'Janis Joplin')
```

says, "Compare the value in formatted_name to the string 'Janis Joplin'. If they are equal as expected, fine. But if they don't match, let me know!"

We're going to run this file directly, but it's important to note that many testing frameworks import your test files before running them. When a file is imported, the interpreter executes the file as it's being imported. The if block at ❹ looks at a special variable, __name__, which is set when the program is executed. If this file is being run as the main program, the value of __name__ is set to '__main__'. In this case, we call unittest.main(), which runs the test case. When a testing framework imports this file, the value of __name__ won't be '__main__' and this block will not be executed.

When we run *test_name_function.py*, we get the following output:

```
.
----------------------------------------------------------------------
Ran 1 test in 0.000s

OK
```

The dot on the first line of output tells us that a single test passed. The next line tells us that Python ran one test, and it took less than 0.001 seconds to run. The final OK tells us that all unit tests in the test case passed.

This output indicates that the function get_formatted_name() will always work for names that have a first and last name unless we modify the function. When we modify get_formatted_name(), we can run this test again. If the test case passes, we know the function will still work for names like Janis Joplin.

A Failing Test

What does a failing test look like? Let's modify get_formatted_name() so it can handle middle names, but we'll do so in a way that breaks the function for names with just a first and last name, like Janis Joplin.

Here's a new version of get_formatted_name() that requires a middle name argument:

```
def get_formatted_name(first, middle, last):
    """Generate a neatly formatted full name."""
    full_name = f"{first} {middle} {last}"
    return full_name.title()
```

This version should work for people with middle names, but when we test it, we see that we've broken the function for people with just a first and last name. This time, running the file *test_name_function.py* gives this output:

```
❶ E
================================================================
❷ ERROR: test_first_last_name (__main__.NamesTestCase)
----------------------------------------------------------------
❸ Traceback (most recent call last):
  File "test_name_function.py", line 8, in test_first_last_name
    formatted_name = get_formatted_name('janis', 'joplin')
TypeError: get_formatted_name() missing 1 required positional argument: 'last'


----------------------------------------------------------------
❹ Ran 1 test in 0.000s

❺ FAILED (errors=1)
```

There's a lot of information here because there's a lot you might need to know when a test fails. The first item in the output is a single E ❶, which tells us one unit test in the test case resulted in an error. Next, we see that test_first_last_name() in NamesTestCase caused an error ❷. Knowing which test failed is critical when your test case contains many unit tests. At ❸ we see a standard traceback, which reports that the function call get_formatted_name('janis', 'joplin') no longer works because it's missing a required positional argument.

We also see that one unit test was run ❹. Finally, we see an additional message that the overall test case failed and that one error occurred when running the test case ❺. This information appears at the end of the output so you see it right away; you don't need to scroll up through a long output listing to find out how many tests failed.

Responding to a Failed Test

What do you do when a test fails? Assuming you're checking the right conditions, a passing test means the function is behaving correctly and a failing test means there's an error in the new code you wrote. So when a test fails, don't change the test. Instead, fix the code that caused the test to fail. Examine the changes you just made to the function, and figure out how those changes broke the desired behavior.

In this case get_formatted_name() used to require only two parameters: a first name and a last name. Now it requires a first name, middle name, and last name. The addition of that mandatory middle name parameter broke the desired behavior of get_formatted_name(). The best option here is to make the middle name optional. Once we do, our test for names like Janis Joplin should pass again, and we should be able to accept middle names as well. Let's modify get_formatted_name() so middle names are optional and then run the test case again. If it passes, we'll move on to making sure the function handles middle names properly.

To make middle names optional, we move the parameter middle to the end of the parameter list in the function definition and give it an empty default value. We also add an if test that builds the full name properly, depending on whether or not a middle name is provided:

*name
_function.py*

```python
def get_formatted_name(first, last, middle=''):
    """Generate a neatly formatted full name."""
    if middle:
        full_name = f"{first} {middle} {last}"
    else:
        full_name = f"{first} {last}"
    return full_name.title()
```

In this new version of get_formatted_name(), the middle name is optional. If a middle name is passed to the function, the full name will contain a first, middle, and last name. Otherwise, the full name will consist of just a first and last name. Now the function should work for both kinds of names. To find out if the function still works for names like Janis Joplin, let's run *test_name_function.py* again:

```
.
----------------------------------------------------------------------
Ran 1 test in 0.000s

OK
```

The test case passes now. This is ideal; it means the function works for names like Janis Joplin again without us having to test the function manually. Fixing our function was easy because the failed test helped us identify the new code that broke existing behavior.

Adding New Tests

Now that we know get_formatted_name() works for simple names again, let's write a second test for people who include a middle name. We do this by adding another method to the class NamesTestCase:

*test_name
_function.py*

```python
--snip--

class NamesTestCase(unittest.TestCase):
    """Tests for 'name_function.py'."""

    def test_first_last_name(self):
        --snip--
```

```
    def test_first_last_middle_name(self):
        """Do names like 'Wolfgang Amadeus Mozart' work?"""
❶       formatted_name = get_formatted_name(
            'wolfgang', 'mozart', 'amadeus')
        self.assertEqual(formatted_name, 'Wolfgang Amadeus Mozart')

if __name__ == '__main__':
    unittest.main()
```

We name this new method test_first_last_middle_name(). The method
name must start with *test_* so the method runs automatically when we run
test_name_function.py. We name the method to make it clear which behavior
of get_formatted_name() we're testing. As a result, if the test fails, we know
right away what kinds of names are affected. It's fine to have long method
names in your TestCase classes. They need to be descriptive so you can make
sense of the output when your tests fail, and because Python calls them
automatically, you'll never have to write code that calls these methods.

To test the function, we call get_formatted_name() with a first, last, and
middle name ❶, and then we use assertEqual() to check that the returned
full name matches the full name (first, middle, and last) that we expect.
When we run *test_name_function.py* again, both tests pass:

```
..
----------------------------------------------------------------------
Ran 2 tests in 0.000s

OK
```

Great! We now know that the function still works for names like Janis
Joplin, and we can be confident that it will work for names like Wolfgang
Amadeus Mozart as well.

TRY IT YOURSELF

11-1. City, Country: Write a function that accepts two parameters: a city name
and a country name. The function should return a single string of the form
City, Country, such as Santiago, Chile. Store the function in a module called
city_functions.py.

Create a file called *test_cities.py* that tests the function you just wrote
(remember that you need to import unittest and the function you want to test).
Write a method called test_city_country() to verify that calling your function
with values such as 'santiago' and 'chile' results in the correct string. Run
test_cities.py, and make sure test_city_country() passes.

(continued)

11-2. Population: Modify your function so it requires a third parameter, population. It should now return a single string of the form *City, Country – population xxx*, such as Santiago, Chile – population 5000000. Run *test _cities.py* again. Make sure test_city_country() fails this time.

Modify the function so the population parameter is optional. Run *test _cities.py* again, and make sure test_city_country() passes again.

Write a second test called test_city_country_population() that verifies you can call your function with the values 'santiago', 'chile', and 'population=5000000'. Run *test_cities.py* again, and make sure this new test passes.

Testing a Class

In the first part of this chapter, you wrote tests for a single function. Now you'll write tests for a class. You'll use classes in many of your own programs, so it's helpful to be able to prove that your classes work correctly. If you have passing tests for a class you're working on, you can be confident that improvements you make to the class won't accidentally break its current behavior.

A Variety of Assert Methods

Python provides a number of assert methods in the unittest.TestCase class. As mentioned earlier, assert methods test whether a condition you believe is true at a specific point in your code is indeed true. If the condition is true as expected, your assumption about how that part of your program behaves is confirmed; you can be confident that no errors exist. If the condition you assume is true is actually not true, Python raises an exception.

Table 11-1 describes six commonly used assert methods. With these methods you can verify that returned values equal or don't equal expected values, that values are True or False, and that values are in or not in a given list. You can use these methods only in a class that inherits from unittest .TestCase, so let's look at how we can use one of these methods in the context of testing an actual class.

Table 11-1: Assert Methods Available from the unittest Module

Method	Use
assertEqual(a, b)	Verify that a == b
assertNotEqual(a, b)	Verify that a != b
assertTrue(x)	Verify that x is True
assertFalse(x)	Verify that x is False
assertIn(*item*, *list*)	Verify that *item* is in *list*
assertNotIn(*item*, *list*)	Verify that *item* is not in *list*

A Class to Test

Testing a class is similar to testing a function—much of your work involves testing the behavior of the methods in the class. But there are a few differences, so let's write a class to test. Consider a class that helps administer anonymous surveys:

survey.py

```
class AnonymousSurvey:
    """Collect anonymous answers to a survey question."""

❶  def __init__(self, question):
        """Store a question, and prepare to store responses."""
        self.question = question
        self.responses = []

❷  def show_question(self):
        """Show the survey question."""
        print(self.question)

❸  def store_response(self, new_response):
        """Store a single response to the survey."""
        self.responses.append(new_response)

❹  def show_results(self):
        """Show all the responses that have been given."""
        print("Survey results:")
        for response in self.responses:
            print(f"- {response}")
```

This class starts with a survey question that you provide ❶ and includes an empty list to store responses. The class has methods to print the survey question ❷, add a new response to the response list ❸, and print all the responses stored in the list ❹. To create an instance from this class, all you have to provide is a question. Once you have an instance representing a particular survey, you display the survey question with show_question(), store a response using store_response(), and show results with show_results().

To show that the AnonymousSurvey class works, let's write a program that uses the class:

*language
_survey.py*

```
from survey import AnonymousSurvey

# Define a question, and make a survey.
question = "What language did you first learn to speak?"
my_survey = AnonymousSurvey(question)

# Show the question, and store responses to the question.
my_survey.show_question()
print("Enter 'q' at any time to quit.\n")
while True:
    response = input("Language: ")
    if response == 'q':
        break
    my_survey.store_response(response)
```

```
# Show the survey results.
print("\nThank you to everyone who participated in the survey!")
my_survey.show_results()
```

This program defines a question ("What language did you first learn to speak?") and creates an AnonymousSurvey object with that question. The program calls show_question() to display the question and then prompts for responses. Each response is stored as it is received. When all responses have been entered (the user inputs q to quit), show_results() prints the survey results:

```
What language did you first learn to speak?
Enter 'q' at any time to quit.

Language: English
Language: Spanish
Language: English
Language: Mandarin
Language: q

Thank you to everyone who participated in the survey!
Survey results:
- English
- Spanish
- English
- Mandarin
```

This class works for a simple anonymous survey. But let's say we want to improve AnonymousSurvey and the module it's in, survey. We could allow each user to enter more than one response. We could write a method to list only unique responses and to report how many times each response was given. We could write another class to manage nonanonymous surveys.

Implementing such changes would risk affecting the current behavior of the class AnonymousSurvey. For example, it's possible that while trying to allow each user to enter multiple responses, we could accidentally change how single responses are handled. To ensure we don't break existing behavior as we develop this module, we can write tests for the class.

Testing the AnonymousSurvey Class

Let's write a test that verifies one aspect of the way AnonymousSurvey behaves. We'll write a test to verify that a single response to the survey question is stored properly. We'll use the assertIn() method to verify that the response is in the list of responses after it's been stored:

test _survey.py

```
import unittest
from survey import AnonymousSurvey

❶ class TestAnonymousSurvey(unittest.TestCase):
    """Tests for the class AnonymousSurvey"""
```

```
❷      def test_store_single_response(self):
           """Test that a single response is stored properly."""
           question = "What language did you first learn to speak?"
❸          my_survey = AnonymousSurvey(question)
           my_survey.store_response('English')
❹          self.assertIn('English', my_survey.responses)

   if __name__ == '__main__':
       unittest.main()
```

We start by importing the unittest module and the class we want to test, AnonymousSurvey. We call our test case TestAnonymousSurvey, which again inherits from unittest.TestCase ❶. The first test method will verify that when we store a response to the survey question, the response ends up in the survey's list of responses. A good descriptive name for this method is test_store_single_response() ❷. If this test fails, we'll know from the method name shown in the output of the failing test that there was a problem storing a single response to the survey.

To test the behavior of a class, we need to make an instance of the class. At ❸ we create an instance called my_survey with the question "What language did you first learn to speak?" We store a single response, English, using the store_response() method. Then we verify that the response was stored correctly by asserting that English is in the list my_survey.responses ❹.

When we run *test_survey.py*, the test passes:

```
.
----------------------------------------------------------------------
Ran 1 test in 0.001s

OK
```

This is good, but a survey is useful only if it generates more than one response. Let's verify that three responses can be stored correctly. To do this, we add another method to TestAnonymousSurvey:

```
import unittest
from survey import AnonymousSurvey

class TestAnonymousSurvey(unittest.TestCase):
    """Tests for the class AnonymousSurvey"""

    def test_store_single_response(self):
        --snip--

    def test_store_three_responses(self):
        """Test that three individual responses are stored properly."""
        question = "What language did you first learn to speak?"
        my_survey = AnonymousSurvey(question)
❶       responses = ['English', 'Spanish', 'Mandarin']
        for response in responses:
            my_survey.store_response(response)

❷       for response in responses:
```

```
        self.assertIn(response, my_survey.responses)

if __name__ == '__main__':
    unittest.main()
```

We call the new method test_store_three_responses(). We create a survey object just like we did in test_store_single_response(). We define a list
containing three different responses ❶, and then we call store_response()
for each of these responses. Once the responses have been stored, we write
another loop and assert that each response is now in my_survey.responses ❷.

When we run *test_survey.py* again, both tests (for a single response and
for three responses) pass:

```
..
----------------------------------------------------------------------
Ran 2 tests in 0.000s

OK
```

This works perfectly. However, these tests are a bit repetitive, so we'll
use another feature of unittest to make them more efficient.

The setUp() Method

In *test_survey.py* we created a new instance of AnonymousSurvey in each test
method, and we created new responses in each method. The unittest.TestCase
class has a setUp() method that allows you to create these objects once and
then use them in each of your test methods. When you include a setUp()
method in a TestCase class, Python runs the setUp() method before running
each method starting with *test_*. Any objects created in the setUp() method
are then available in each test method you write.

Let's use setUp() to create a survey instance and a set of responses that
can be used in test_store_single_response() and test_store_three_responses():

```
import unittest
from survey import AnonymousSurvey

class TestAnonymousSurvey(unittest.TestCase):
    """Tests for the class AnonymousSurvey."""

    def setUp(self):
        """
        Create a survey and a set of responses for use in all test methods.
        """
        question = "What language did you first learn to speak?"
❶       self.my_survey = AnonymousSurvey(question)
❷       self.responses = ['English', 'Spanish', 'Mandarin']

    def test_store_single_response(self):
        """Test that a single response is stored properly."""
        self.my_survey.store_response(self.responses[0])
        self.assertIn(self.responses[0], self.my_survey.responses)
```

```
def test_store_three_responses(self):
    """Test that three individual responses are stored properly."""
    for response in self.responses:
        self.my_survey.store_response(response)
    for response in self.responses:
        self.assertIn(response, self.my_survey.responses)

if __name__ == '__main__':
    unittest.main()
```

The method setUp() does two things: it creates a survey instance ❶, and it creates a list of responses ❷. Each of these is prefixed by self, so they can be used anywhere in the class. This makes the two test methods simpler, because neither one has to make a survey instance or a response. The method test_store_single_response() verifies that the first response in self.responses—self.responses[0]—can be stored correctly, and test_store _three_responses() verifies that all three responses in self.responses can be stored correctly.

When we run *test_survey.py* again, both tests still pass. These tests would be particularly useful when trying to expand AnonymousSurvey to handle multiple responses for each person. After modifying the code to accept multiple responses, you could run these tests and make sure you haven't affected the ability to store a single response or a series of individual responses.

When you're testing your own classes, the setUp() method can make your test methods easier to write. You make one set of instances and attributes in setUp() and then use these instances in all your test methods. This is much easier than making a new set of instances and attributes in each test method.

NOTE   *When a test case is running, Python prints one character for each unit test as it is completed. A passing test prints a dot, a test that results in an error prints an E, and a test that results in a failed assertion prints an F. This is why you'll see a different number of dots and characters on the first line of output when you run your test cases. If a test case takes a long time to run because it contains many unit tests, you can watch these results to get a sense of how many tests are passing.*

TRY IT YOURSELF

11-3. Employee: Write a class called Employee. The __init__() method should take in a first name, a last name, and an annual salary, and store each of these as attributes. Write a method called give_raise() that adds $5,000 to the annual salary by default but also accepts a different raise amount.

Write a test case for Employee. Write two test methods, test_give_default _raise() and test_give_custom_raise(). Use the setUp() method so you don't have to create a new employee instance in each test method. Run your test case, and make sure both tests pass.

Summary

In this chapter you learned to write tests for functions and classes using tools in the unittest module. You learned to write a class that inherits from unittest.TestCase, and you learned to write test methods that verify specific behaviors your functions and classes should exhibit. You learned to use the setUp() method to efficiently create instances and attributes from your classes that can be used in all the test methods for a class.

Testing is an important topic that many beginners don't learn. You don't have to write tests for all the simple projects you try as a beginner. But as soon as you start to work on projects that involve significant development effort, you should test the critical behaviors of your functions and classes. You'll be more confident that new work on your project won't break the parts that work, and this will give you the freedom to make improvements to your code. If you accidentally break existing functionality, you'll know right away, so you can still fix the problem easily. Responding to a failed test that you ran is much easier than responding to a bug report from an unhappy user.

Other programmers respect your projects more if you include some initial tests. They'll feel more comfortable experimenting with your code and be more willing to work with you on projects. If you want to contribute to a project that other programmers are working on, you'll be expected to show that your code passes existing tests and you'll usually be expected to write tests for new behavior you introduce to the project.

Play around with tests to become familiar with the process of testing your code. Write tests for the most critical behaviors of your functions and classes, but don't aim for full coverage in early projects unless you have a specific reason to do so.

PART II

PROJECTS

Congratulations! You now know enough about Python to start building interactive and meaningful projects. Creating your own projects will teach you new skills and solidify your understanding of the concepts introduced in Part I.

Part II contains three types of projects, and you can choose to do any or all of these projects in whichever order you like. Here's a brief description of each project to help you decide which to dig into first.

Alien Invasion: Making a Game with Python

In the *Alien Invasion* project (Chapters 12, 13, and 14), you'll use the Pygame package to develop a 2D game in which the aim is to shoot down a fleet of aliens as they drop down the screen in levels that increase in speed and difficulty. At the end of the project, you'll have learned skills that will enable you to develop your own 2D games in Pygame.

Data Visualization

The Data Visualization project starts in Chapter 15, in which you'll learn to generate data and create a series of functional and beautiful visualizations of that data using Matplotlib and Plotly. Chapter 16 teaches you to access data from online sources and feed it into a visualization package to create plots of weather data and a map of global earthquake activity. Finally, Chapter 17 shows you how to write a program to automatically download and visualize data. Learning to make visualizations allows you to explore the field of data mining, which is a highly sought-after skill in the world today.

Web Applications

In the Web Applications project (Chapters 18, 19, and 20), you'll use the Django package to create a simple web application that allows users to keep a journal about any number of topics they've been learning about. Users will create an account with a username and password, enter a topic, and then make entries about what they're learning. You'll also learn how to deploy your app so anyone in the world can access it.

After completing this project, you'll be able to start building your own simple web applications, and you'll be ready to delve into more thorough resources on building applications with Django.

PROJECT 1

ALIEN INVASION

12

A SHIP THAT FIRES BULLETS

Let's build a game called *Alien Invasion*!
We'll use Pygame, a collection of fun, powerful Python modules that manage graphics,
animation, and even sound, making it easier
for you to build sophisticated games. With Pygame
handling tasks like drawing images to the screen, you
can focus on the higher-level logic of game dynamics.

In this chapter, you'll set up Pygame, and then create a rocket ship that
moves right and left and fires bullets in response to player input. In the next
two chapters, you'll create a fleet of aliens to destroy, and then continue to
refine the game by setting limits on the number of ships you can use and
adding a scoreboard.

While building this game, you'll also learn how to manage large projects that span multiple files. We'll refactor a lot of code and manage file
contents to organize the project and make the code efficient.

Making games is an ideal way to have fun while learning a language. It's deeply satisfying to play a game you wrote, and writing a simple game will help you comprehend how professionals develop games. As you work through this chapter, enter and run the code to identify how each code block contributes to overall gameplay. Experiment with different values and settings to better understand how to refine interactions in your games.

NOTE   *Alien Invasion spans a number of different files, so make a new* alien_invasion *folder on your system. Be sure to save all files for the project to this folder so your* import *statements will work correctly.*

Also, if you feel comfortable using version control, you might want to use it for this project. If you haven't used version control before, see Appendix D for an overview.

Planning Your Project

When you're building a large project, it's important to prepare a plan before you begin to write code. Your plan will keep you focused and make it more likely that you'll complete the project.

Let's write a description of the general gameplay. Although the following description doesn't cover every detail of *Alien Invasion*, it provides a clear idea of how to start building the game:

> In *Alien Invasion*, the player controls a rocket ship that appears at the bottom center of the screen. The player can move the ship right and left using the arrow keys and shoot bullets using the spacebar. When the game begins, a fleet of aliens fills the sky and moves across and down the screen. The player shoots and destroys the aliens. If the player shoots all the aliens, a new fleet appears that moves faster than the previous fleet. If any alien hits the player's ship or reaches the bottom of the screen, the player loses a ship. If the player loses three ships, the game ends.

For the first development phase, we'll make a ship that can move right and left and fires bullets when the player presses the spacebar. After setting up this behavior, we can create the aliens and refine the gameplay.

Installing Pygame

Before you begin coding, install Pygame. The `pip` module helps you download and install Python packages. To install Pygame, enter the following command at a terminal prompt:

```
$ python -m pip install --user pygame
```

This command tells Python to run the `pip` module and install the `pygame` package to the current user's Python installation. If you use a command other than python to run programs or start a terminal session, such as python3, your command will look like this:

```
$ python3 -m pip install --user pygame
```

 NOTE *If this command doesn't work on macOS, try running the command again without the --user flag.*

Starting the Game Project

We'll begin building the game by creating an empty Pygame window. Later, we'll draw the game elements, such as the ship and the aliens, on this window. We'll also make our game respond to user input, set the background color, and load a ship image.

Creating a Pygame Window and Responding to User Input

We'll make an empty Pygame window by creating a class to represent the game. In your text editor, create a new file and save it as *alien_invasion.py*; then enter the following:

alien_invasion.py
```
import sys

import pygame

class AlienInvasion:
    """Overall class to manage game assets and behavior."""

    def __init__(self):
        """Initialize the game, and create game resources."""
❶       pygame.init()

❷       self.screen = pygame.display.set_mode((1200, 800))
        pygame.display.set_caption("Alien Invasion")

    def run_game(self):
        """Start the main loop for the game."""
❸       while True:
            # Watch for keyboard and mouse events.
❹           for event in pygame.event.get():
❺               if event.type == pygame.QUIT:
                    sys.exit()

            # Make the most recently drawn screen visible.
❻           pygame.display.flip()

if __name__ == '__main__':
    # Make a game instance, and run the game.
    ai = AlienInvasion()
    ai.run_game()
```

First, we import the sys and pygame modules. The pygame module contains the functionality we need to make a game. We'll use tools in the sys module to exit the game when the player quits.

Alien Invasion starts as a class called AlienInvasion. In the __init__() method, the pygame.init() function initializes the background settings that Pygame needs to work properly ❶. At ❷, we call pygame.display.set_mode() to create a display window, on which we'll draw all the game's graphical elements. The argument (1200, 800) is a tuple that defines the dimensions of the game window, which will be 1200 pixels wide by 800 pixels high. (You can adjust these values depending on your display size.) We assign this display window to the attribute self.screen, so it will be available in all methods in the class.

The object we assigned to self.screen is called a *surface*. A surface in Pygame is a part of the screen where a game element can be displayed. Each element in the game, like an alien or a ship, is its own surface. The surface returned by display.set_mode() represents the entire game window. When we activate the game's animation loop, this surface will be redrawn on every pass through the loop, so it can be updated with any changes triggered by user input.

The game is controlled by the run_game() method. This method contains a while loop ❸ that runs continually. The while loop contains an event loop and code that manages screen updates. An *event* is an action that the user performs while playing the game, such as pressing a key or moving the mouse. To make our program respond to events, we write this *event loop* to *listen* for events and perform appropriate tasks depending on the kinds of events that occur. The for loop at ❹ is an event loop.

To access the events that Pygame detects, we'll use the pygame.event .get() function. This function returns a list of events that have taken place since the last time this function was called. Any keyboard or mouse event will cause this for loop to run. Inside the loop, we'll write a series of if statements to detect and respond to specific events. For example, when the player clicks the game window's close button, a pygame.QUIT event is detected and we call sys.exit() to exit the game ❺.

The call to pygame.display.flip() at ❻ tells Pygame to make the most recently drawn screen visible. In this case, it simply draws an empty screen on each pass through the while loop, erasing the old screen so only the new screen is visible. When we move the game elements around, pygame.display .flip() continually updates the display to show the new positions of game elements and hides the old ones, creating the illusion of smooth movement.

At the end of the file, we create an instance of the game, and then call run_game(). We place run_game() in an if block that only runs if the file is called directly. When you run this *alien_invasion.py* file, you should see an empty Pygame window.

Setting the Background Color

Pygame creates a black screen by default, but that's boring. Let's set a different background color. We'll do this at the end of the __init__() method.

```
def __init__(self):
    --snip--
    pygame.display.set_caption("Alien Invasion")

    # Set the background color.
❶   self.bg_color = (230, 230, 230)

def run_game(self):
    --snip--
        for event in pygame.event.get():
            if event.type == pygame.QUIT:
                sys.exit()

        # Redraw the screen during each pass through the loop.
❷       self.screen.fill(self.bg_color)

        # Make the most recently drawn screen visible.
        pygame.display.flip()
```

Colors in Pygame are specified as RGB colors: a mix of red, green, and blue. Each color value can range from 0 to 255. The color value (255, 0, 0) is red, (0, 255, 0) is green, and (0, 0, 255) is blue. You can mix different RGB values to create up to 16 million colors. The color value (230, 230, 230) mixes equal amounts of red, blue, and green, which produces a light gray background color. We assign this color to self.bg_color ❶.

At ❷, we fill the screen with the background color using the fill() method, which acts on a surface and takes only one argument: a color.

Creating a Settings Class

Each time we introduce new functionality into the game, we'll typically create some new settings as well. Instead of adding settings throughout the code, let's write a module called settings that contains a class called Settings to store all these values in one place. This approach allows us to work with just one settings object any time we need to access an individual setting. This also makes it easier to modify the game's appearance and behavior as our project grows: to modify the game, we'll simply change some values in *settings.py*, which we'll create next, instead of searching for different settings throughout the project.

Create a new file named *settings.py* inside your *alien_invasion* folder, and add this initial Settings class:

```
class Settings:
    """A class to store all settings for Alien Invasion."""

    def __init__(self):
        """Initialize the game's settings."""
        # Screen settings
        self.screen_width = 1200
        self.screen_height = 800
        self.bg_color = (230, 230, 230)
```

To make an instance of Settings in the project and use it to access our settings, we need to modify *alien_invasion.py* as follows:

alien_invasion.py

```
--snip--
import pygame

from settings import Settings

class AlienInvasion:
    """Overall class to manage game assets and behavior."""

    def __init__(self):
        """Initialize the game, and create game resources."""
        pygame.init()
❶      self.settings = Settings()

❷      self.screen = pygame.display.set_mode(
            (self.settings.screen_width, self.settings.screen_height))
        pygame.display.set_caption("Alien Invasion")

    def run_game(self):
        --snip--
        # Redraw the screen during each pass through the loop.
❸      self.screen.fill(self.settings.bg_color)

        # Make the most recently drawn screen visible.
        pygame.display.flip()
--snip--
```

We import Settings into the main program file. Then we create an instance of Settings and assign it to self.settings ❶, after making the call to pygame.init(). When we create a screen ❷, we use the screen_width and screen_height attributes of self.settings, and then we use self.settings to access the background color when filling the screen at ❸ as well.

When you run *alien_invasion.py* now you won't yet see any changes, because all we've done is move the settings we were already using elsewhere. Now we're ready to start adding new elements to the screen.

Adding the Ship Image

Let's add the ship to our game. To draw the player's ship on the screen, we'll load an image and then use the Pygame blit() method to draw the image.

When you're choosing artwork for your games, be sure to pay attention to licensing. The safest and cheapest way to start is to use freely licensed graphics that you can use and modify, from a website like *https://pixabay.com/*.

You can use almost any type of image file in your game, but it's easiest when you use a bitmap (*.bmp*) file because Pygame loads bitmaps by default. Although you can configure Pygame to use other file types, some file types depend on certain image libraries that must be installed on your computer. Most images you'll find are in *.jpg* or *.png* formats, but you can convert them to bitmaps using tools like Photoshop, GIMP, and Paint.

Pay particular attention to the background color in your chosen image. Try to find a file with a transparent or solid background that you can replace with any background color using an image editor. Your games will look best if the image's background color matches your game's background color. Alternatively, you can match your game's background to the image's background.

For *Alien Invasion*, you can use the file *ship.bmp* (Figure 12-1), which is available in the book's resources at *https://nostarch.com/pythoncrashcourse2e/*. The file's background color matches the settings we're using in this project. Make a folder called *images* inside your main *alien_invasion* project folder. Save the file *ship.bmp* in the *images* folder.

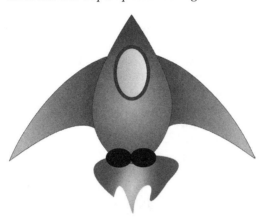

Figure 12-1: The ship for Alien Invasion

Creating the Ship Class

After choosing an image for the ship, we need to display it on the screen. To use our ship, we'll create a new ship module that will contain the class Ship. This class will manage most of the behavior of the player's ship:

ship.py
```python
import pygame

class Ship:
    """A class to manage the ship."""

    def __init__(self, ai_game):
        """Initialize the ship and set its starting position."""
❶       self.screen = ai_game.screen
❷       self.screen_rect = ai_game.screen.get_rect()

        # Load the ship image and get its rect.
❸       self.image = pygame.image.load('images/ship.bmp')
        self.rect = self.image.get_rect()
```

```
                    # Start each new ship at the bottom center of the screen.
❹            self.rect.midbottom = self.screen_rect.midbottom

❺      def blitme(self):
              """Draw the ship at its current location."""
              self.screen.blit(self.image, self.rect)
```

Pygame is efficient because it lets you treat all game elements like rect-angles (*rects*), even if they're not exactly shaped like rectangles. Treating an element as a rectangle is efficient because rectangles are simple geometric shapes. When Pygame needs to figure out whether two game elements have collided, for example, it can do this more quickly if it treats each object as a rectangle. This approach usually works well enough that no one playing the game will notice that we're not working with the exact shape of each game element. We'll treat the ship and the screen as rectangles in this class.

We import the pygame module before defining the class. The __init__() method of Ship takes two parameters: the self reference and a reference to the current instance of the AlienInvasion class. This will give Ship access to all the game resources defined in AlienInvasion. At ❶ we assign the screen to an attribute of Ship, so we can access it easily in all the methods in this class. At ❷ we access the screen's rect attribute using the get_rect() method and assign it to self.screen_rect. Doing so allows us to place the ship in the correct location on the screen.

To load the image, we call pygame.image.load() ❸ and give it the location of our ship image. This function returns a surface representing the ship, which we assign to self.image. When the image is loaded, we call get_rect() to access the ship surface's rect attribute so we can later use it to place the ship.

When you're working with a rect object, you can use the x- and y-coordinates of the top, bottom, left, and right edges of the rectangle, as well as the center, to place the object. You can set any of these values to establish the current position of the rect. When you're centering a game element, work with the center, centerx, or centery attributes of a rect. When you're working at an edge of the screen, work with the top, bottom, left, or right attributes. There are also attributes that combine these properties, such as midbottom, midtop, midleft, and midright. When you're adjusting the horizontal or vertical placement of the rect, you can just use the x and y attributes, which are the x- and y-coordinates of its top-left corner. These attributes spare you from having to do calculations that game developers formerly had to do manually, and you'll use them often.

NOTE   *In Pygame, the origin (0, 0) is at the top-left corner of the screen, and coordinates increase as you go down and to the right. On a 1200 by 800 screen, the origin is at the top-left corner, and the bottom-right corner has the coordinates (1200, 800). These coordinates refer to the game window, not the physical screen.*

We'll position the ship at the bottom center of the screen. To do so, make the value of self.rect.midbottom match the midbottom attribute of the screen's rect ❹. Pygame uses these rect attributes to position the ship image so it's centered horizontally and aligned with the bottom of the screen.

At ❺, we define the blitme() method, which draws the image to the screen at the position specified by self.rect.

Drawing the Ship to the Screen

Now let's update *alien_invasion.py* so it creates a ship and calls the ship's blitme() method:

alien_invasion.py

```
--snip--
from settings import Settings
from ship import Ship

class AlienInvasion:
    """Overall class to manage game assets and behavior."""

    def __init__(self):
        --snip--
        pygame.display.set_caption("Alien Invasion")

❶       self.ship = Ship(self)

    def run_game(self):
            --snip--
            # Redraw the screen during each pass through the loop.
            self.screen.fill(self.settings.bg_color)
❷           self.ship.blitme()

            # Make the most recently drawn screen visible.
            pygame.display.flip()
--snip--
```

We import Ship and then make an instance of Ship after the screen has been created ❶. The call to Ship() requires one argument, an instance of AlienInvasion. The self argument here refers to the current instance of AlienInvasion. This is the parameter that gives Ship access to the game's resources, such as the screen object. We assign this Ship instance to self.ship.

After filling the background, we draw the ship on the screen by calling ship.blitme(), so the ship appears on top of the background ❷.

When you run *alien_invasion.py* now, you should see an empty game screen with the rocket ship sitting at the bottom center, as shown in Figure 12-2.

Figure 12-2: Alien Invasion *with the ship at the bottom center of the screen*

Refactoring: The _check_events() and _update_screen() Methods

In large projects, you'll often refactor code you've written before adding more code. Refactoring simplifies the structure of the code you've already written, making it easier to build on. In this section, we'll break the run_game() method, which is getting lengthy, into two helper methods. A *helper method* does work inside a class but isn't meant to be called through an instance. In Python, a single leading underscore indicates a helper method.

The _check_events() Method

We'll move the code that manages events to a separate method called _check_events(). This will simplify run_game() and isolate the event management loop. Isolating the event loop allows you to manage events separately from other aspects of the game, such as updating the screen.

Here's the AlienInvasion class with the new _check_events() method, which only affects the code in run_game():

alien_invasion.py
```
    def run_game(self):
        """Start the main loop for the game."""
        while True:
❶           self._check_events()
```

```
                # Redraw the screen during each pass through the loop.
                --snip--

❷      def _check_events(self):
            """Respond to keypresses and mouse events."""
            for event in pygame.event.get():
                if event.type == pygame.QUIT:
                    sys.exit()
```

We make a new _check_events() method ❷ and move the lines that check whether the player has clicked to close the window into this new method.

To call a method from within a class, use dot notation with the variable self and the name of the method ❶. We call the method from inside the while loop in run_game().

The _update_screen() Method

To further simplify run_game(), we'll move the code for updating the screen to a separate method called _update_screen():

alien_invasion.py

```
def run_game(self):
    """Start the main loop for the game."""
    while True:
        self._check_events()
        self._update_screen()

def _check_events(self):
    --snip--

def _update_screen(self):
    """Update images on the screen, and flip to the new screen."""
    self.screen.fill(self.settings.bg_color)
    self.ship.blitme()

    pygame.display.flip()
```

We moved the code that draws the background and the ship and flips the screen to _update_screen(). Now the body of the main loop in run_game() is much simpler. It's easy to see that we're looking for new events and updating the screen on each pass through the loop.

If you've already built a number of games, you'll probably start out by breaking your code into methods like these. But if you've never tackled a project like this, you probably won't know how to structure your code. This approach of writing code that works and then restructuring it as it grows more complex gives you an idea of a realistic development process: you start out writing your code as simply as possible, and then refactor it as your project becomes more complex.

Now that we've restructured the code to make it easier to add to, we can work on the dynamic aspects of the game!

Piloting the Ship

Next, we'll give the player the ability to move the ship right and left. We'll write code that responds when the player presses the right or left arrow key. We'll focus on movement to the right first, and then we'll apply the same principles to control movement to the left. As we add this code, you'll learn how to control the movement of images on the screen and respond to user input.

Responding to a Keypress

Whenever the player presses a key, that keypress is registered in Pygame as an event. Each event is picked up by the `pygame.event.get()` method. We need to specify in our _check_events() method what kind of events we want the game to check for. Each keypress is registered as a KEYDOWN event.

When Pygame detects a KEYDOWN event, we need to check whether the key that was pressed is one that triggers a certain action. For example, if the player presses the right arrow key, we want to increase the ship's rect.x value to move the ship to the right:

alien_invasion.py

```
    def _check_events(self):
        """Respond to keypresses and mouse events."""
        for event in pygame.event.get():
            if event.type == pygame.QUIT:
                sys.exit()
❶           elif event.type == pygame.KEYDOWN:
❷               if event.key == pygame.K_RIGHT:
                    # Move the ship to the right.
❸                   self.ship.rect.x += 1
```

Inside _check_events() we add an elif block to the event loop to respond when Pygame detects a KEYDOWN event ❶. We check whether the key pressed, event.key, is the right arrow key ❷. The right arrow key is represented by pygame.K_RIGHT. If the right arrow key was pressed, we move the ship to the right by increasing the value of self.ship.rect.x by 1 ❸.

When you run *alien_invasion.py* now, the ship should move to the right one pixel every time you press the right arrow key. That's a start, but it's not an efficient way to control the ship. Let's improve this control by allowing continuous movement.

Allowing Continuous Movement

When the player holds down the right arrow key, we want the ship to continue moving right until the player releases the key. We'll have the game detect a pygame.KEYUP event so we'll know when the right arrow key is released; then we'll use the KEYDOWN and KEYUP events together with a flag called moving_right to implement continuous motion.

When the moving_right flag is False, the ship will be motionless. When the player presses the right arrow key, we'll set the flag to True, and when the player releases the key, we'll set the flag to False again.

The Ship class controls all attributes of the ship, so we'll give it an attribute called moving_right and an update() method to check the status of the moving_right flag. The update() method will change the position of the ship if the flag is set to True. We'll call this method once on each pass through the while loop to update the position of the ship.

Here are the changes to Ship:

ship.py

```
class Ship:
    """A class to manage the ship."""

    def __init__(self, ai_game):
        --snip--
        # Start each new ship at the bottom center of the screen.
        self.rect.midbottom = self.screen_rect.midbottom

        # Movement flag
❶       self.moving_right = False

❷   def update(self):
        """Update the ship's position based on the movement flag."""
        if self.moving_right:
            self.rect.x += 1

    def blitme(self):
        --snip--
```

We add a self.moving_right attribute in the __init__() method and set it to False initially ❶. Then we add update(), which moves the ship right if the flag is True ❷. The update() method will be called through an instance of Ship, so it's not considered a helper method.

Now we need to modify _check_events() so that moving_right is set to True when the right arrow key is pressed and False when the key is released:

alien_invasion.py

```
    def _check_events(self):
        """Respond to keypresses and mouse events."""
        for event in pygame.event.get():
            --snip--
            elif event.type == pygame.KEYDOWN:
                if event.key == pygame.K_RIGHT:
❶                   self.ship.moving_right = True
❷           elif event.type == pygame.KEYUP:
```

```
            if event.key == pygame.K_RIGHT:
                self.ship.moving_right = False
```

At ❶, we modify how the game responds when the player presses the right arrow key: instead of changing the ship's position directly, we merely set moving_right to True. At ❷, we add a new elif block, which responds to KEYUP events. When the player releases the right arrow key (K_RIGHT), we set moving_right to False.

Next, we modify the while loop in run_game() so it calls the ship's update() method on each pass through the loop:

alien_invasion.py

```
def run_game(self):
    """Start the main loop for the game."""
    while True:
        self._check_events()
        self.ship.update()
        self._update_screen()
```

The ship's position will be updated after we've checked for keyboard events and before we update the screen. This allows the ship's position to be updated in response to player input and ensures the updated position will be used when drawing the ship to the screen.

When you run *alien_invasion.py* and hold down the right arrow key, the ship should move continuously to the right until you release the key.

Moving Both Left and Right

Now that the ship can move continuously to the right, adding movement to the left is straightforward. Again, we'll modify the Ship class and the _check _events() method. Here are the relevant changes to __init__() and update() in Ship:

ship.py

```
def __init__(self, ai_game):
    --snip--
    # Movement flags
    self.moving_right = False
    self.moving_left = False

def update(self):
    """Update the ship's position based on movement flags."""
    if self.moving_right:
        self.rect.x += 1
    if self.moving_left:
        self.rect.x -= 1
```

In __init__(), we add a self.moving_left flag. In update(), we use two separate if blocks rather than an elif to allow the ship's rect.x value to be increased and then decreased when both arrow keys are held down. This results in the ship standing still. If we used elif for motion to the left, the right arrow key would always have priority. Doing it this way makes the movements more accurate when switching from right to left when the player might momentarily hold down both keys.

We have to make two adjustments to _check_events():

alien_invasion.py

```python
def _check_events(self):
    """Respond to keypresses and mouse events."""
    for event in pygame.event.get():
        --snip--
        elif event.type == pygame.KEYDOWN:
            if event.key == pygame.K_RIGHT:
                self.ship.moving_right = True
            elif event.key == pygame.K_LEFT:
                self.ship.moving_left = True

        elif event.type == pygame.KEYUP:
            if event.key == pygame.K_RIGHT:
                self.ship.moving_right = False
            elif event.key == pygame.K_LEFT:
                self.ship.moving_left = False
```

If a KEYDOWN event occurs for the K_LEFT key, we set moving_left to True. If a KEYUP event occurs for the K_LEFT key, we set moving_left to False. We can use elif blocks here because each event is connected to only one key. If the player presses both keys at once, two separate events will be detected.

When you run *alien_invasion.py* now, you should be able to move the ship continuously to the right and left. If you hold down both keys, the ship should stop moving.

Next, we'll further refine the ship's movement. Let's adjust the ship's speed and limit how far the ship can move so it can't disappear off the sides of the screen.

Adjusting the Ship's Speed

Currently, the ship moves one pixel per cycle through the while loop, but we can take finer control of the ship's speed by adding a ship_speed attribute to the Settings class. We'll use this attribute to determine how far to move the ship on each pass through the loop. Here's the new attribute in *settings.py*:

settings.py

```python
class Settings:
    """A class to store all settings for Alien Invasion."""

    def __init__(self):
        --snip--

        # Ship settings
        self.ship_speed = 1.5
```

We set the initial value of ship_speed to 1.5. When the ship moves now, its position is adjusted by 1.5 pixels rather than 1 pixel on each pass through the loop.

We're using decimal values for the speed setting to give us finer control of the ship's speed when we increase the tempo of the game later on. However, rect attributes such as x store only integer values, so we need to make some modifications to Ship:

ship.py

```
class Ship:
    """A class to manage the ship."""

❶    def __init__(self, ai_game):
        """Initialize the ship and set its starting position."""
        self.screen = ai_game.screen
        self.settings = ai_game.settings
        --snip--

        # Start each new ship at the bottom center of the screen.
        --snip--

        # Store a decimal value for the ship's horizontal position.
❷      self.x = float(self.rect.x)

        # Movement flags
        self.moving_right = False
        self.moving_left = False

    def update(self):
        """Update the ship's position based on movement flags."""
        # Update the ship's x value, not the rect.
        if self.moving_right:
❸          self.x += self.settings.ship_speed
        if self.moving_left:
            self.x -= self.settings.ship_speed

        # Update rect object from self.x.
❹      self.rect.x = self.x

    def blitme(self):
        --snip--
```

We create a settings attribute for Ship, so we can use it in update() ❶. Because we're adjusting the position of the ship by fractions of a pixel, we need to assign the position to a variable that can store a decimal value. You can use a decimal value to set an attribute of rect, but the rect will only keep the integer portion of that value. To keep track of the ship's position accurately, we define a new self.x attribute that can hold decimal values ❷. We use the float() function to convert the value of self.rect.x to a decimal and assign this value to self.x.

Now when we change the ship's position in update(), the value of self.x is adjusted by the amount stored in settings.ship_speed ❸. After self.x has been updated, we use the new value to update self.rect.x, which controls the position of the ship ❹. Only the integer portion of self.x will be stored in self.rect.x, but that's fine for displaying the ship.

Now we can change the value of ship_speed, and any value greater than one will make the ship move faster. This will help make the ship respond quickly enough to shoot down aliens, and it will let us change the tempo of the game as the player progresses in gameplay.

NOTE *If you're using macOS, you might notice that the ship moves very slowly, even with a high speed setting. You can remedy this problem by running the game in fullscreen mode, which we'll implement shortly.*

Limiting the Ship's Range

At this point, the ship will disappear off either edge of the screen if you hold down an arrow key long enough. Let's correct this so the ship stops moving when it reaches the screen's edge. We do this by modifying the update() method in Ship:

ship.py
```
    def update(self):
        """Update the ship's position based on movement flags."""
        # Update the ship's x value, not the rect.
❶      if self.moving_right and self.rect.right < self.screen_rect.right:
            self.x += self.settings.ship_speed
❷      if self.moving_left and self.rect.left > 0:
            self.x -= self.settings.ship_speed

        # Update rect object from self.x.
        self.rect.x = self.x
```

This code checks the position of the ship before changing the value of self.x. The code self.rect.right returns the x-coordinate of the right edge of the ship's rect. If this value is less than the value returned by self.screen _rect.right, the ship hasn't reached the right edge of the screen ❶. The same goes for the left edge: if the value of the left side of the rect is greater than zero, the ship hasn't reached the left edge of the screen ❷. This ensures the ship is within these bounds before adjusting the value of self.x.

When you run *alien_invasion.py* now, the ship should stop moving at either edge of the screen. This is pretty cool; all we've done is add a conditional test in an if statement, but it feels like the ship hits a wall or a force field at either edge of the screen!

Refactoring _check_events()

The _check_events() method will increase in length as we continue to develop the game, so let's break _check_events() into two more methods: one that handles KEYDOWN events and another that handles KEYUP events:

alien_invasion.py
```
    def _check_events(self):
        """Respond to keypresses and mouse events."""
        for event in pygame.event.get():
```

```
            if event.type == pygame.QUIT:
                sys.exit()
            elif event.type == pygame.KEYDOWN:
                self._check_keydown_events(event)
            elif event.type == pygame.KEYUP:
                self._check_keyup_events(event)

    def _check_keydown_events(self, event):
        """Respond to keypresses."""
        if event.key == pygame.K_RIGHT:
            self.ship.moving_right = True
        elif event.key == pygame.K_LEFT:
            self.ship.moving_left = True

    def _check_keyup_events(self, event):
        """Respond to key releases."""
        if event.key == pygame.K_RIGHT:
            self.ship.moving_right = False
        elif event.key == pygame.K_LEFT:
            self.ship.moving_left = False
```

We make two new helper methods: _check_keydown_events() and _check
_keyup_events(). Each needs a self parameter and an event parameter. The
bodies of these two methods are copied from _check_events(), and we've
replaced the old code with calls to the new methods. The _check_events()
method is simpler now with this cleaner code structure, which will make it
easier to develop further responses to player input.

Pressing Q to Quit

Now that we're responding to keypresses efficiently, we can add another
way to quit the game. It gets tedious to click the X at the top of the game
window to end the game every time you test a new feature, so we'll add a
keyboard shortcut to end the game when the player presses Q:

alien_invasion.py
```
    def _check_keydown_events(self, event):
        --snip--
        elif event.key == pygame.K_LEFT:
            self.ship.moving_left = True
        elif event.key == pygame.K_q:
            sys.exit()
```

In _check_keydown_events(), we add a new block that ends the game when
the player presses Q. Now, when testing, you can press Q to close the game
rather than using your cursor to close the window.

Running the Game in Fullscreen Mode

Pygame has a fullscreen mode that you might like better than running the
game in a regular window. Some games look better in fullscreen mode, and
macOS users might see better performance in fullscreen mode.

To run the game in fullscreen mode, make the following changes in
__init__():

alien_invasion.py

```
def __init__(self):
    """Initialize the game, and create game resources."""
    pygame.init()
    self.settings = Settings()

➊   self.screen = pygame.display.set_mode((0, 0), pygame.FULLSCREEN)
➋   self.settings.screen_width = self.screen.get_rect().width
    self.settings.screen_height = self.screen.get_rect().height
    pygame.display.set_caption("Alien Invasion")
```

When creating the screen surface, we pass a size of (0, 0) and the
parameter pygame.FULLSCREEN ➊. This tells Pygame to figure out a window size
that will fill the screen. Because we don't know the width and height of the
screen ahead of time, we update these settings after the screen is created ➋.
We use the width and height attributes of the screen's rect to update the
settings object.

If you like how the game looks or behaves in fullscreen mode, keep
these settings. If you liked the game better in its own window, you can
revert back to the original approach where we set a specific screen size for
the game.

NOTE *Make sure you can quit by pressing Q before running the game in fullscreen mode;
Pygame offers no default way to quit a game while in fullscreen mode.*

A Quick Recap

In the next section, we'll add the ability to shoot bullets, which involves adding a new file called *bullet.py* and making some modifications to some of the
files we're already using. Right now, we have three files containing a number of classes and methods. To be clear about how the project is organized,
let's review each of these files before adding more functionality.

alien_invasion.py

The main file, *alien_invasion.py*, contains the AlienInvasion class. This class
creates a number of important attributes used throughout the game: the
settings are assigned to settings, the main display surface is assigned to
screen, and a ship instance is created in this file as well. The main loop of
the game, a while loop, is also stored in this module. The while loop calls
_check_events(), ship.update(), and _update_screen().

The _check_events() method detects relevant events, such as keypresses and releases, and processes each of these types of events through
the methods _check_keydown_events() and _check_keyup_events(). For now,

these methods manage the ship's movement. The `AlienInvasion` class also contains `_update_screen()`, which redraws the screen on each pass through the main loop.

The *alien_invasion.py* file is the only file you need to run when you want to play *Alien Invasion*. The other files—*settings.py* and *ship.py*—contain code that is imported into this file.

settings.py

The *settings.py* file contains the `Settings` class. This class only has an `__init__()` method, which initializes attributes controlling the game's appearance and the ship's speed.

ship.py

The *ship.py* file contains the `Ship` class. The `Ship` class has an `__init__()` method, an `update()` method to manage the ship's position, and a `blitme()` method to draw the ship to the screen. The image of the ship is stored in *ship.bmp*, which is in the *images* folder.

TRY IT YOURSELF

12-3. Pygame Documentation: We're far enough into the game now that you might want to look at some of the Pygame documentation. The Pygame home page is at *https://www.pygame.org/*, and the home page for the documentation is at *https://www.pygame.org/docs/*. Just skim the documentation for now. You won't need it to complete this project, but it will help if you want to modify *Alien Invasion* or make your own game afterward.

12-4. Rocket: Make a game that begins with a rocket in the center of the screen. Allow the player to move the rocket up, down, left, or right using the four arrow keys. Make sure the rocket never moves beyond any edge of the screen.

12-5. Keys: Make a Pygame file that creates an empty screen. In the event loop, print the `event.key` attribute whenever a `pygame.KEYDOWN` event is detected. Run the program and press various keys to see how Pygame responds.

Shooting Bullets

Now let's add the ability to shoot bullets. We'll write code that fires a bullet, which is represented by a small rectangle, when the player presses the space-bar. Bullets will then travel straight up the screen until they disappear off the top of the screen.

Adding the Bullet Settings

At the end of the __init__() method, we'll update *settings.py* to include the values we'll need for a new Bullet class:

settings.py

```
def __init__(self):
    --snip--
    # Bullet settings
    self.bullet_speed = 1.0
    self.bullet_width = 3
    self.bullet_height = 15
    self.bullet_color = (60, 60, 60)
```

These settings create dark gray bullets with a width of 3 pixels and a height of 15 pixels. The bullets will travel slightly slower than the ship.

Creating the Bullet Class

Now create a *bullet.py* file to store our Bullet class. Here's the first part of *bullet.py*:

bullet.py

```
import pygame
from pygame.sprite import Sprite

class Bullet(Sprite):
    """A class to manage bullets fired from the ship"""

    def __init__(self, ai_game):
        """Create a bullet object at the ship's current position."""
        super().__init__()
        self.screen = ai_game.screen
        self.settings = ai_game.settings
        self.color = self.settings.bullet_color

        # Create a bullet rect at (0, 0) and then set correct position.
❶       self.rect = pygame.Rect(0, 0, self.settings.bullet_width,
            self.settings.bullet_height)
❷       self.rect.midtop = ai_game.ship.rect.midtop

        # Store the bullet's position as a decimal value.
❸       self.y = float(self.rect.y)
```

The Bullet class inherits from Sprite, which we import from the pygame .sprite module. When you use sprites, you can group related elements in your game and act on all the grouped elements at once. To create a bullet instance, __init__() needs the current instance of AlienInvasion, and we call super() to inherit properly from Sprite. We also set attributes for the screen and settings objects, and for the bullet's color.

At ❶, we create the bullet's rect attribute. The bullet isn't based on an image, so we have to build a rect from scratch using the pygame.Rect() class. This class requires the x- and y-coordinates of the top-left corner of the rect, and the width and height of the rect. We initialize the rect at (0, 0), but we'll move it to the correct location in the next line, because the bullet's position depends on the ship's position. We get the width and height of the bullet from the values stored in self.settings.

At ❷, we set the bullet's midtop attribute to match the ship's midtop attribute. This will make the bullet emerge from the top of the ship, making it look like the bullet is fired from the ship. We store a decimal value for the bullet's y-coordinate so we can make fine adjustments to the bullet's speed ❸.

Here's the second part of *bullet.py*, update() and draw_bullet():

<table>
<tr><td>bullet.py</td><td></td><td>

```
def update(self):
    """Move the bullet up the screen."""
    # Update the decimal position of the bullet.
    self.y -= self.settings.bullet_speed
    # Update the rect position.
    self.rect.y = self.y

def draw_bullet(self):
    """Draw the bullet to the screen."""
    pygame.draw.rect(self.screen, self.color, self.rect)
```

</td></tr>
</table>

The update() method manages the bullet's position. When a bullet is fired, it moves up the screen, which corresponds to a decreasing y-coordinate value. To update the position, we subtract the amount stored in settings .bullet_speed from self.y ❶. We then use the value of self.y to set the value of self.rect.y ❷.

The bullet_speed setting allows us to increase the speed of the bullets as the game progresses or as needed to refine the game's behavior. Once a bullet is fired, we never change the value of its x-coordinate, so it will travel vertically in a straight line even if the ship moves.

When we want to draw a bullet, we call draw_bullet(). The draw.rect() function fills the part of the screen defined by the bullet's rect with the color stored in self.color ❸.

Storing Bullets in a Group

Now that we have a Bullet class and the necessary settings defined, we can write code to fire a bullet each time the player presses the spacebar. We'll create a group in AlienInvasion to store all the live bullets so we can manage the bullets that have already been fired. This group will be an instance of the pygame.sprite.Group class, which behaves like a list with some extra functionality that's helpful when building games. We'll use this group to draw bullets to the screen on each pass through the main loop and to update each bullet's position.

We'll create the group in __init__():

alien_invasion.py

```
def __init__(self):
    --snip--
    self.ship = Ship(self)
    self.bullets = pygame.sprite.Group()
```

Then we need to update the position of the bullets on each pass through the while loop:

alien_invasion.py

```
    def run_game(self):
        """Start the main loop for the game."""
        while True:
            self._check_events()
            self.ship.update()
❶           self.bullets.update()
            self._update_screen()
```

When you call update() on a group ❶, the group automatically calls update() for each sprite in the group. The line self.bullets.update() calls bullet.update() for each bullet we place in the group bullets.

Firing Bullets

In AlienInvasion, we need to modify _check_keydown_events() to fire a bullet when the player presses the spacebar. We don't need to change _check_keyup _events() because nothing happens when the spacebar is released. We also need to modify _update_screen() to make sure each bullet is drawn to the screen before we call flip().

We know there will be a bit of work to do when we fire a bullet, so let's write a new method, _fire_bullet(), to handle this work:

alien_invasion.py

```
--snip--
from ship import Ship
❶ from bullet import Bullet

class AlienInvasion:
    --snip--
    def _check_keydown_events(self, event):
        --snip--
        elif event.key == pygame.K_q:
            sys.exit()
❷       elif event.key == pygame.K_SPACE:
            self._fire_bullet()

    def _check_keyup_events(self, event):
        --snip--

    def _fire_bullet(self):
        """Create a new bullet and add it to the bullets group."""
❸       new_bullet = Bullet(self)
❹       self.bullets.add(new_bullet)

    def _update_screen(self):
        """Update images on the screen, and flip to the new screen."""
        self.screen.fill(self.settings.bg_color)
        self.ship.blitme()
❺       for bullet in self.bullets.sprites():
            bullet.draw_bullet()
```

```
         pygame.display.flip()
--snip--
```

First, we import Bullet ❶. Then we call _fire_bullet() when the space-bar is pressed ❷. In _fire_bullet(), we make an instance of Bullet and call it new_bullet ❸. We then add it to the group bullets using the add() method ❹. The add() method is similar to append(), but it's a method that's written specifically for Pygame groups.

The bullets.sprites() method returns a list of all sprites in the group bullets. To draw all fired bullets to the screen, we loop through the sprites in bullets and call draw_bullet() on each one ❺.

When you run *alien_invasion.py* now, you should be able to move the ship right and left, and fire as many bullets as you want. The bullets travel up the screen and disappear when they reach the top, as shown in Figure 12-3. You can alter the size, color, and speed of the bullets in *settings.py*.

Figure 12-3: The ship after firing a series of bullets

Deleting Old Bullets

At the moment, the bullets disappear when they reach the top, but only because Pygame can't draw them above the top of the screen. The bullets actually continue to exist; their y-coordinate values just grow increasingly negative. This is a problem, because they continue to consume memory and processing power.

We need to get rid of these old bullets, or the game will slow down from doing so much unnecessary work. To do this, we need to detect when the bottom value of a bullet's rect has a value of 0, which indicates the bullet has passed off the top of the screen:

alien_invasion.py

```
def run_game(self):
    """Start the main loop for the game."""
    while True:
        self._check_events()
        self.ship.update()
        self.bullets.update()

        # Get rid of bullets that have disappeared.
❶      for bullet in self.bullets.copy():
❷          if bullet.rect.bottom <= 0:
❸              self.bullets.remove(bullet)
❹      print(len(self.bullets))

        self._update_screen()
```

When you use a for loop with a list (or a group in Pygame), Python expects that the list will stay the same length as long as the loop is running. Because we can't remove items from a list or group within a for loop, we have to loop over a copy of the group. We use the copy() method to set up the for loop ❶, which enables us to modify bullets inside the loop. We check each bullet to see whether it has disappeared off the top of the screen at ❷. If it has, we remove it from bullets ❸. At ❹ we insert a print() call to show how many bullets currently exist in the game and verify that they're being deleted when they reach the top of the screen.

If this code works correctly, we can watch the terminal output while firing bullets and see that the number of bullets decreases to zero after each series of bullets has cleared the top of the screen. After you run the game and verify that bullets are being deleted properly, remove the print() call. If you leave it in, the game will slow down significantly because it takes more time to write output to the terminal than it does to draw graphics to the game window.

Limiting the Number of Bullets

Many shooting games limit the number of bullets a player can have on the screen at one time; doing so encourages players to shoot accurately. We'll do the same in *Alien Invasion*.

First, store the number of bullets allowed in *settings.py*:

settings.py

```
# Bullet settings
--snip--
self.bullet_color = (60, 60, 60)
self.bullets_allowed = 3
```

This limits the player to three bullets at a time. We'll use this setting in AlienInvasion to check how many bullets exist before creating a new bullet in _fire_bullet():

alien_invasion.py

```
def _fire_bullet(self):
    """Create a new bullet and add it to the bullets group."""
    if len(self.bullets) < self.settings.bullets_allowed:
        new_bullet = Bullet(self)
        self.bullets.add(new_bullet)
```

When the player presses the spacebar, we check the length of bullets. If len(self.bullets) is less than three, we create a new bullet. But if three bullets are already active, nothing happens when the spacebar is pressed. When you run the game now, you should be able to fire bullets only in groups of three.

Creating the _update_bullets() Method

We want to keep the AlienInvasion class reasonably well organized, so now that we've written and checked the bullet management code, we can move it to a separate method. We'll create a new method called _update_bullets() and add it just before _update_screen():

alien_invasion.py

```
def _update_bullets(self):
    """Update position of bullets and get rid of old bullets."""
    # Update bullet positions.
    self.bullets.update()

    # Get rid of bullets that have disappeared.
    for bullet in self.bullets.copy():
        if bullet.rect.bottom <= 0:
            self.bullets.remove(bullet)
```

The code for _update_bullets() is cut and pasted from run_game(); all we've done here is clarify the comments.

The while loop in run_game() looks simple again:

alien_invasion.py

```
    while True:
        self._check_events()
        self.ship.update()
        self._update_bullets()
        self._update_screen()
```

Now our main loop contains only minimal code, so we can quickly read the method names and understand what's happening in the game. The main loop checks for player input, and then updates the position of the ship and any bullets that have been fired. We then use the updated positions to draw a new screen.

Run *alien_invasion.py* one more time, and make sure you can still fire bullets without errors.

Summary

In this chapter, you learned to make a plan for a game and learned the basic structure of a game written in Pygame. You learned to set a background color and store settings in a separate class where you can adjust them more easily. You saw how to draw an image to the screen and give the player control over the movement of game elements. You created elements that move on their own, like bullets flying up a screen, and deleted objects that are no longer needed. You also learned to refactor code in a project on a regular basis to facilitate ongoing development.

In Chapter 13, we'll add aliens to *Alien Invasion*. By the end of the chapter, you'll be able to shoot down aliens, hopefully before they reach your ship!

13

ALIENS!

In this chapter, we'll add aliens to *Alien Invasion.* We'll add one alien near the top of the screen and then generate a whole fleet of aliens. We'll make the fleet advance sideways and down, and we'll get rid of any aliens hit by a bullet. Finally, we'll limit the number of ships a player has and end the game when the player runs out of ships.

As you work through this chapter, you'll learn more about Pygame and about managing a large project. You'll also learn to detect collisions between game objects, like bullets and aliens. Detecting collisions helps you define interactions between elements in your games: for example, you can confine a character inside the walls of a maze or pass a ball between two characters. We'll continue to work from a plan that we revisit occasionally to maintain the focus of our code-writing sessions.

Before we start writing new code to add a fleet of aliens to the screen, let's look at the project and update our plan.

Reviewing the Project

When you're beginning a new phase of development on a large project, it's always a good idea to revisit your plan and clarify what you want to accomplish with the code you're about to write. In this chapter, we'll:

- Examine our code and determine if we need to refactor before implementing new features.
- Add a single alien to the top-left corner of the screen with appropriate spacing around it.
- Use the spacing around the first alien and the overall screen size to determine how many aliens can fit on the screen. We'll write a loop to create aliens to fill the upper portion of the screen.
- Make the fleet move sideways and down until the entire fleet is shot down, an alien hits the ship, or an alien reaches the ground. If the entire fleet is shot down, we'll create a new fleet. If an alien hits the ship or the ground, we'll destroy the ship and create a new fleet.
- Limit the number of ships the player can use, and end the game when the player has used up the allotted number of ships.

We'll refine this plan as we implement features, but this is sufficient to start with.

You should also review your existing code when you begin working on a new series of features in a project. Because each new phase typically makes a project more complex, it's best to clean up any cluttered or inefficient code. We've been refactoring as we go, so there isn't any code that we need to refactor at this point.

Creating the First Alien

Placing one alien on the screen is like placing a ship on the screen. Each alien's behavior is controlled by a class called Alien, which we'll structure like the Ship class. We'll continue using bitmap images for simplicity. You can find your own image for an alien or use the one shown in Figure 13-1, which is available in the book's resources at *https://nostarch.com/pythoncrashcourse2e/*. This image has a gray background, which matches the screen's background color. Make sure you save the image file you choose in the *images* folder.

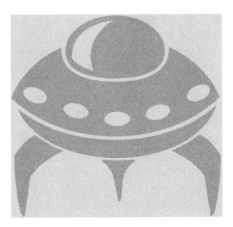

Figure 13-1: The alien we'll use to build the fleet

Creating the Alien Class

Now we'll write the Alien class and save it as *alien.py*:

alien.py
```
import pygame
from pygame.sprite import Sprite

class Alien(Sprite):
    """A class to represent a single alien in the fleet."""

    def __init__(self, ai_game):
        """Initialize the alien and set its starting position."""
        super().__init__()
        self.screen = ai_game.screen

        # Load the alien image and set its rect attribute.
        self.image = pygame.image.load('images/alien.bmp')
        self.rect = self.image.get_rect()

        # Start each new alien near the top left of the screen.
    ❶   self.rect.x = self.rect.width
        self.rect.y = self.rect.height

        # Store the alien's exact horizontal position.
    ❷   self.x = float(self.rect.x)
```

Most of this class is like the Ship class except for the aliens' placement on the screen. We initially place each alien near the top-left corner of the screen; we add a space to the left of it that's equal to the alien's width and a space above it equal to its height ❶ so it's easy to see. We're mainly concerned with the aliens' horizontal speed, so we'll track the horizontal position of each alien precisely ❷.

This `Alien` class doesn't need a method for drawing it to the screen; instead, we'll use a Pygame group method that automatically draws all the elements of a group to the screen.

Creating an Instance of the Alien

We want to create an instance of `Alien` so we can see the first alien on the screen. Because it's part of our setup work, we'll add the code for this instance at the end of the `__init__()` method in `AlienInvasion`. Eventually, we'll create an entire fleet of aliens, which will be quite a bit of work, so we'll make a new helper method called `_create_fleet()`.

The order of methods in a class doesn't matter, as long as there's some consistency to how they're placed. I'll place `_create_fleet()` just before the `_update_screen()` method, but anywhere in `AlienInvasion` will work. First, we'll import the `Alien` class.

Here are the updated `import` statements for *alien_invasion.py*:

alien_invasion.py

```
--snip--
from bullet import Bullet
from alien import Alien
```

And here's the updated `__init__()` method:

alien_invasion.py

```
def __init__(self):
    --snip--
    self.ship = Ship(self)
    self.bullets = pygame.sprite.Group()
    self.aliens = pygame.sprite.Group()

    self._create_fleet()
```

We create a group to hold the fleet of aliens, and we call `_create_fleet()`, which we're about to write.

Here's the new `_create_fleet()` method:

alien_invasion.py

```
def _create_fleet(self):
    """Create the fleet of aliens."""
    # Make an alien.
    alien = Alien(self)
    self.aliens.add(alien)
```

In this method, we're creating one instance of `Alien`, and then adding it to the group that will hold the fleet. The alien will be placed in the default upper-left area of the screen, which is perfect for the first alien.

To make the alien appear, we need to call the group's draw() method in _update_screen():

```
def _update_screen(self):
    --snip--
    for bullet in self.bullets.sprites():
        bullet.draw_bullet()
    self.aliens.draw(self.screen)

    pygame.display.flip()
```

When you call draw() on a group, Pygame draws each element in the group at the position defined by its rect attribute. The draw() method requires one argument: a surface on which to draw the elements from the group. Figure 13-2 shows the first alien on the screen.

Figure 13-2: The first alien appears.

Now that the first alien appears correctly, we'll write the code to draw an entire fleet.

Building the Alien Fleet

To draw a fleet, we need to figure out how many aliens can fit across the screen and how many rows of aliens can fit down the screen. We'll first figure out the horizontal spacing between aliens and create a row; then we'll determine the vertical spacing and create an entire fleet.

Determining How Many Aliens Fit in a Row

To figure out how many aliens fit in a row, let's look at how much horizontal space we have. The screen width is stored in `settings.screen_width`, but we need an empty margin on either side of the screen. We'll make this margin the width of one alien. Because we have two margins, the available space for aliens is the screen width minus two alien widths:

```
available_space_x = settings.screen_width - (2 * alien_width)
```

We also need to set the spacing between aliens; we'll make it one alien width. The space needed to display one alien is twice its width: one width for the alien and one width for the empty space to its right. To find the number of aliens that fit across the screen, we divide the available space by two times the width of an alien. We use *floor division* (`//`), which divides two numbers and drops any remainder, so we'll get an integer number of aliens:

```
number_aliens_x = available_space_x // (2 * alien_width)
```

We'll use these calculations when we create the fleet.

NOTE *One great aspect of calculations in programming is that you don't have to be sure your formulas are correct when you first write them. You can try them out and see if they work. At worst, you'll have a screen that's overcrowded with aliens or has too few aliens. You can then revise your calculations based on what you see on the screen.*

Creating a Row of Aliens

We're ready to generate a full row of aliens. Because our code for making a single alien works, we'll rewrite `_create_fleet()` to make a whole row of aliens:

alien_invasion.py

```
    def _create_fleet(self):
        """Create the fleet of aliens."""
        # Create an alien and find the number of aliens in a row.
        # Spacing between each alien is equal to one alien width.
❶       alien = Alien(self)
❷       alien_width = alien.rect.width
❸       available_space_x = self.settings.screen_width - (2 * alien_width)
        number_aliens_x = available_space_x // (2 * alien_width)

        # Create the first row of aliens.
❹       for alien_number in range(number_aliens_x):
            # Create an alien and place it in the row.
            alien = Alien(self)
❺           alien.x = alien_width + 2 * alien_width * alien_number
            alien.rect.x = alien.x
            self.aliens.add(alien)
```

We've already thought through most of this code. We need to know the alien's width and height to place aliens, so we create an alien at ❶ before we perform calculations. This alien won't be part of the fleet, so don't add it to the group aliens. At ❷ we get the alien's width from its rect attribute and store this value in alien_width so we don't have to keep working through the rect attribute. At ❸ we calculate the horizontal space available for aliens and the number of aliens that can fit into that space.

Next, we set up a loop that counts from 0 to the number of aliens we need to make ❹. In the main body of the loop, we create a new alien and then set its x-coordinate value to place it in the row ❺. Each alien is pushed to the right one alien width from the left margin. Next, we multiply the alien width by 2 to account for the space each alien takes up, including the empty space to its right, and we multiply this amount by the alien's position in the row. We use the alien's x attribute to set the position of its rect. Then we add each new alien to the group aliens.

When you run *Alien Invasion* now, you should see the first row of aliens appear, as in Figure 13-3.

Figure 13-3: The first row of aliens

The first row is offset to the left, which is actually good for gameplay. The reason is that we want the fleet to move right until it hits the edge of the screen, then drop down a bit, then move left, and so forth. Like the classic game *Space Invaders*, this movement is more interesting than having the fleet drop straight down. We'll continue this motion until all aliens are shot down or until an alien hits the ship or the bottom of the screen.

Depending on the screen width you've chosen, the alignment of the first row of aliens might look slightly different on your system.

Refactoring _create_fleet()

If the code we've written so far was all we need to create a fleet, we'd probably leave _create_fleet() as is. But we have more work to do, so let's clean up the method a bit. We'll add a new helper method, _create_alien(), and call it from _create_fleet():

alien_invasion.py

```
def _create_fleet(self):
    --snip--
    # Create the first row of aliens.
    for alien_number in range(number_aliens_x):
        self._create_alien(alien_number)

def _create_alien(self, alien_number):
    """Create an alien and place it in the row."""
    alien = Alien(self)
    alien_width = alien.rect.width
    alien.x = alien_width + 2 * alien_width * alien_number
    alien.rect.x = alien.x
    self.aliens.add(alien)
```

The method _create_alien() requires one parameter in addition to self: it needs the alien number that's currently being created. We use the same body we made for _create_fleet() except that we get the width of an alien inside the method instead of passing it as an argument. This refactoring will make it easier to add new rows and create an entire fleet.

Adding Rows

To finish the fleet, we'll determine the number of rows that fit on the screen and then repeat the loop for creating the aliens in one row until we have the correct number of rows. To determine the number of rows, we find the available vertical space by subtracting the alien height from the top, the ship height from the bottom, and two alien heights from the bottom of the screen:

```
available_space_y = settings.screen_height - (3 * alien_height) - ship_height
```

The result will create some empty space above the ship, so the player has some time to start shooting aliens at the beginning of each level.

Each row needs some empty space below it, which we'll make equal to the height of one alien. To find the number of rows, we divide the available space by two times the height of an alien. We use floor division because we can only make an integer number of rows. (Again, if these calculations are off, we'll see it right away and adjust our approach until we have reasonable spacing.)

```
number_rows = available_space_y // (2 * alien_height)
```

Now that we know how many rows fit in a fleet, we can repeat the code for creating a row:

alien_invasion.py

```
    def _create_fleet(self):
        --snip--
        alien = Alien(self)
❶      alien_width, alien_height = alien.rect.size
        available_space_x = self.settings.screen_width - (2 * alien_width)
        number_aliens_x = available_space_x // (2 * alien_width)

        # Determine the number of rows of aliens that fit on the screen.
        ship_height = self.ship.rect.height
❷      available_space_y = (self.settings.screen_height -
                                (3 * alien_height) - ship_height)
        number_rows = available_space_y // (2 * alien_height)

        # Create the full fleet of aliens.
❸      for row_number in range(number_rows):
            for alien_number in range(number_aliens_x):
                self._create_alien(alien_number, row_number)

    def _create_alien(self, alien_number, row_number):
        """Create an alien and place it in the row."""
        alien = Alien(self)
        alien_width, alien_height = alien.rect.size
        alien.x = alien_width + 2 * alien_width * alien_number
        alien.rect.x = alien.x
❹      alien.rect.y = alien.rect.height + 2 * alien.rect.height * row_number
        self.aliens.add(alien)
```

We need the width and height of an alien, so at ❶ we use the attribute size, which contains a tuple with the width and height of a rect object. To calculate the number of rows we can fit on the screen, we write our available _space_y calculation right after the calculation for available_space_x ❷. The calculation is wrapped in parentheses so the outcome can be split over two lines, which results in lines of 79 characters or less, as is recommended.

To create multiple rows, we use two nested loops: one outer and one inner loop ❸. The inner loop creates the aliens in one row. The outer loop counts from 0 to the number of rows we want; Python uses the code for making a single row and repeats it number_rows times.

To nest the loops, write the new for loop and indent the code you want to repeat. (Most text editors make it easy to indent and unindent blocks of code, but for help see Appendix B.) Now when we call _create_alien(), we include an argument for the row number so each row can be placed farther down the screen.

The definition of _create_alien() needs a parameter to hold the row number. Within _create_alien(), we change an alien's y-coordinate value when it's not in the first row ❹ by starting with one alien's height to create empty space at the top of the screen. Each row starts two alien heights below the previous row, so we multiply the alien height by two and then by the row number. The first row number is 0, so the vertical placement of the first row is unchanged. All subsequent rows are placed farther down the screen.

When you run the game now, you should see a full fleet of aliens, as shown in Figure 13-4.

Figure 13-4: The full fleet appears.

In the next section, we'll make the fleet move!

TRY IT YOURSELF

13-1. Stars: Find an image of a star. Make a grid of stars appear on the screen.

13-2. Better Stars: You can make a more realistic star pattern by introducing randomness when you place each star. Recall that you can get a random number like this:

```
from random import randint
random_number = randint(-10, 10)
```

This code returns a random integer between –10 and 10. Using your code in Exercise 13-1, adjust each star's position by a random amount.

Making the Fleet Move

Now let's make the fleet of aliens move to the right across the screen until it hits the edge, and then make it drop a set amount and move in the other direction. We'll continue this movement until all aliens have been shot down, one collides with the ship, or one reaches the bottom of the screen. Let's begin by making the fleet move to the right.

Moving the Aliens Right

To move the aliens, we'll use an update() method in *alien.py*, which we'll call for each alien in the group of aliens. First, add a setting to control the speed of each alien:

settings.py
```
def __init__(self):
    --snip--
    # Alien settings
    self.alien_speed = 1.0
```

Then use this setting to implement update():

alien.py
```
def __init__(self, ai_game):
    """Initialize the alien and set its starting position."""
    super().__init__()
    self.screen = ai_game.screen
    self.settings = ai_game.settings
    --snip--

def update(self):
    """Move the alien to the right."""
❶  self.x += self.settings.alien_speed
❷  self.rect.x = self.x
```

We create a settings parameter in __init__() so we can access the alien's speed in update(). Each time we update an alien's position, we move it to the right by the amount stored in alien_speed. We track the alien's exact position with the self.x attribute, which can hold decimal values ❶. We then use the value of self.x to update the position of the alien's rect ❷.

In the main while loop, we already have calls to update the ship and bullet positions. Now we'll add a call to update the position of each alien as well:

alien_invasion.py
```
while True:
    self._check_events()
    self.ship.update()
    self._update_bullets()
    self._update_aliens()
    self._update_screen()
```

We're about to write some code to manage the movement of the fleet, so we create a new method called _update_aliens(). We set the aliens' positions to update after the bullets have been updated, because we'll soon be checking to see whether any bullets hit any aliens.

Where you place this method in the module is not critical. But to keep the code organized, I'll place it just after _update_bullets() to match the order of method calls in the while loop. Here's the first version of _update_aliens():

alien_invasion.py

```
def _update_aliens(self):
    """Update the positions of all aliens in the fleet."""
    self.aliens.update()
```

We use the update() method on the aliens group, which calls each alien's update() method. When you run *Alien Invasion* now, you should see the fleet move right and disappear off the side of the screen.

Creating Settings for Fleet Direction

Now we'll create the settings that will make the fleet move down the screen and to the left when it hits the right edge of the screen. Here's how to implement this behavior:

settings.py

```
# Alien settings
self.alien_speed = 1.0
self.fleet_drop_speed = 10
# fleet_direction of 1 represents right; -1 represents left.
self.fleet_direction = 1
```

The setting fleet_drop_speed controls how quickly the fleet drops down the screen each time an alien reaches either edge. It's helpful to separate this speed from the aliens' horizontal speed so you can adjust the two speeds independently.

To implement the setting fleet_direction, we could use a text value, such as 'left' or 'right', but we'd end up with if-elif statements testing for the fleet direction. Instead, because we have only two directions to deal with, let's use the values 1 and –1, and switch between them each time the fleet changes direction. (Using numbers also makes sense because moving right involves adding to each alien's x-coordinate value, and moving left involves subtracting from each alien's x-coordinate value.)

Checking Whether an Alien Has Hit the Edge

We need a method to check whether an alien is at either edge, and we need to modify update() to allow each alien to move in the appropriate direction. This code is part of the Alien class:

alien.py

```
def check_edges(self):
    """Return True if alien is at edge of screen."""
    screen_rect = self.screen.get_rect()
```

```
❶        if self.rect.right >= screen_rect.right or self.rect.left <= 0:
             return True

     def update(self):
         """Move the alien right or left."""
❷        self.x += (self.settings.alien_speed *
                        self.settings.fleet_direction)
         self.rect.x = self.x
```

We can call the new method check_edges() on any alien to see whether it's at the left or right edge. The alien is at the right edge if the right attribute of its rect is greater than or equal to the right attribute of the screen's rect. It's at the left edge if its left value is less than or equal to 0 ❶.

We modify the method update() to allow motion to the left or right by multiplying the alien's speed by the value of fleet_direction ❷. If fleet _direction is 1, the value of alien_speed will be added to the alien's current position, moving the alien to the right; if fleet_direction is –1, the value will be subtracted from the alien's position, moving the alien to the left.

Dropping the Fleet and Changing Direction

When an alien reaches the edge, the entire fleet needs to drop down and change direction. Therefore, we need to add some code to AlienInvasion because that's where we'll check whether any aliens are at the left or right edge. We'll make this happen by writing the methods _check_fleet_edges() and _change_fleet_direction(), and then modifying _update_aliens(). I'll put these new methods after _create_alien(), but again the placement of these methods in the class isn't critical.

alien_invasion.py

```
     def _check_fleet_edges(self):
         """Respond appropriately if any aliens have reached an edge."""
❶        for alien in self.aliens.sprites():
             if alien.check_edges():
❷                self._change_fleet_direction()
                 break

     def _change_fleet_direction(self):
         """Drop the entire fleet and change the fleet's direction."""
         for alien in self.aliens.sprites():
❸            alien.rect.y += self.settings.fleet_drop_speed
         self.settings.fleet_direction *= -1
```

In _check_fleet_edges(), we loop through the fleet and call check_edges() on each alien ❶. If check_edges() returns True, we know an alien is at an edge and the whole fleet needs to change direction; so we call _change_fleet _direction() and break out of the loop ❷. In _change_fleet_direction(), we loop through all the aliens and drop each one using the setting fleet_drop _speed ❸; then we change the value of fleet_direction by multiplying its current value by –1. The line that changes the fleet's direction isn't part of the for loop. We want to change each alien's vertical position, but we only want to change the direction of the fleet once.

Here are the changes to _update_aliens():

alien_invasion.py

```
def _update_aliens(self):
    """
    Check if the fleet is at an edge,
      then update the positions of all aliens in the fleet.
    """
    self._check_fleet_edges()
    self.aliens.update()
```

We've modified the method by calling _check_fleet_edges() before updating each alien's position.

When you run the game now, the fleet should move back and forth between the edges of the screen and drop down every time it hits an edge. Now we can start shooting down aliens and watch for any aliens that hit the ship or reach the bottom of the screen.

TRY IT YOURSELF

13-3. Raindrops: Find an image of a raindrop and create a grid of raindrops. Make the raindrops fall toward the bottom of the screen until they disappear.

13-4. Steady Rain: Modify your code in Exercise 13-3 so when a row of raindrops disappears off the bottom of the screen, a new row appears at the top of the screen and begins to fall.

Shooting Aliens

We've built our ship and a fleet of aliens, but when the bullets reach the aliens, they simply pass through because we aren't checking for collisions. In game programming, *collisions* happen when game elements overlap. To make the bullets shoot down aliens, we'll use the method sprite.groupcollide() to look for collisions between members of two groups.

Detecting Bullet Collisions

We want to know right away when a bullet hits an alien so we can make an alien disappear as soon as it's hit. To do this, we'll look for collisions immediately after updating the position of all the bullets.

The sprite.groupcollide() function compares the rects of each element in one group with the rects of each element in another group. In this case, it compares each bullet's rect with each alien's rect and returns a dictionary containing the bullets and aliens that have collided. Each key in the dictionary will be a bullet, and the corresponding value will be the alien that was hit. (We'll also use this dictionary when we implement a scoring system in Chapter 14.)

Add the following code to the end of _update_bullets() to check for collisions between bullets and aliens:

alien_invasion.py

```
def _update_bullets(self):
    """Update position of bullets and get rid of old bullets."""
    --snip--

    # Check for any bullets that have hit aliens.
    #   If so, get rid of the bullet and the alien.
    collisions = pygame.sprite.groupcollide(
            self.bullets, self.aliens, True, True)
```

The new code we added compares the positions of all the bullets in self.bullets and all the aliens in self.aliens, and identifies any that overlap. Whenever the rects of a bullet and alien overlap, groupcollide() adds a key-value pair to the dictionary it returns. The two True arguments tell Pygame to delete the bullets and aliens that have collided. (To make a high-powered bullet that can travel to the top of the screen, destroying every alien in its path, you could set the first Boolean argument to False and keep the second Boolean argument set to True. The aliens hit would disappear, but all bullets would stay active until they disappeared off the top of the screen.)

When you run *Alien Invasion* now, aliens you hit should disappear. Figure 13-5 shows a fleet that has been partially shot down.

Figure 13-5: We can shoot aliens!

Making Larger Bullets for Testing

You can test many features of the game simply by running the game. But some features are tedious to test in the normal version of the game. For example, it's a lot of work to shoot down every alien on the screen multiple times to test whether your code responds to an empty fleet correctly.

To test particular features, you can change certain game settings to focus on a particular area. For example, you might shrink the screen so there are fewer aliens to shoot down or increase the bullet speed and give yourself lots of bullets at once.

My favorite change for testing *Alien Invasion* is to use really wide bullets that remain active even after they've hit an alien (see Figure 13-6). Try setting `bullet_width` to 300, or even 3000, to see how quickly you can shoot down the fleet!

Figure 13-6: Extra-powerful bullets make some aspects of the game easier to test.

Changes like these will help you test the game more efficiently and possibly spark ideas for giving players bonus powers. Just remember to restore the settings to normal when you're finished testing a feature.

Repopulating the Fleet

One key feature of *Alien Invasion* is that the aliens are relentless: every time the fleet is destroyed, a new fleet should appear.

To make a new fleet of aliens appear after a fleet has been destroyed, we first check whether the `aliens` group is empty. If it is, we make a call to `_create_fleet()`. We'll perform this check at the end of `_update_bullets()`, because that's where individual aliens are destroyed.

```
def _update_bullets(self):
    --snip--
❶    if not self.aliens:
        # Destroy existing bullets and create new fleet.
❷        self.bullets.empty()
        self._create_fleet()
```

At ❶, we check whether the aliens group is empty. An empty group evaluates to False, so this is a simple way to check whether the group is empty. If it is, we get rid of any existing bullets by using the empty() method, which removes all the remaining sprites from a group ❷. We also call _create _fleet(), which fills the screen with aliens again.

Now a new fleet appears as soon as you destroy the current fleet.

Speeding Up the Bullets

If you've tried firing at the aliens in the game's current state, you might find that the bullets aren't traveling at the best speed for gameplay. They might be a little slow on your system or way too fast. At this point, you can modify the settings to make the gameplay interesting and enjoyable on your system.

We modify the speed of the bullets by adjusting the value of bullet_speed in *settings.py*. On my system, I'll adjust the value of bullet_speed to 1.5, so the bullets travel a little faster:

```
# Bullet settings
self.bullet_speed = 1.5
self.bullet_width = 3
--snip--
```

The best value for this setting depends on your system's speed, so find a value that works for you. You can adjust other settings as well.

Refactoring _update_bullets()

Let's refactor _update_bullets() so it's not doing so many different tasks. We'll move the code for dealing with bullet and alien collisions to a separate method:

```
def _update_bullets(self):
    --snip--
    # Get rid of bullets that have disappeared.
    for bullet in self.bullets.copy():
        if bullet.rect.bottom <= 0:
            self.bullets.remove(bullet)

    self._check_bullet_alien_collisions()

def _check_bullet_alien_collisions(self):
    """Respond to bullet-alien collisions."""
    # Remove any bullets and aliens that have collided.
```

```
collisions = pygame.sprite.groupcollide(
        self.bullets, self.aliens, True, True)

if not self.aliens:
    # Destroy existing bullets and create new fleet.
    self.bullets.empty()
    self._create_fleet()
```

We've created a new method, _check_bullet_alien_collisions(), to look for collisions between bullets and aliens, and to respond appropriately if the entire fleet has been destroyed. Doing so keeps _update_bullets() from growing too long and simplifies further development.

TRY IT YOURSELF

13-5. Sideways Shooter Part 2: We've come a long way since Exercise 12-6, Sideways Shooter. For this exercise, try to develop Sideways Shooter to the same point we've brought *Alien Invasion* to. Add a fleet of aliens, and make them move sideways toward the ship. Or, write code that places aliens at random positions along the right side of the screen and then sends them toward the ship. Also, write code that makes the aliens disappear when they're hit.

Ending the Game

What's the fun and challenge in a game if you can't lose? If the player doesn't shoot down the fleet quickly enough, we'll have the aliens destroy the ship when they make contact. At the same time, we'll limit the number of ships a player can use, and we'll destroy the ship when an alien reaches the bottom of the screen. The game will end when the player has used up all their ships.

Detecting Alien and Ship Collisions

We'll start by checking for collisions between aliens and the ship so we can respond appropriately when an alien hits it. We'll check for alien and ship collisions immediately after updating the position of each alien in AlienInvasion:

alien_invasion.py
```
def _update_aliens(self):
    --snip--
    self.aliens.update()

    # Look for alien-ship collisions.
❶   if pygame.sprite.spritecollideany(self.ship, self.aliens):
❷       print("Ship hit!!!")
```

The `spritecollideany()` function takes two arguments: a sprite and a group. The function looks for any member of the group that has collided with the sprite and stops looping through the group as soon as it finds one member that has collided with the sprite. Here, it loops through the group aliens and returns the first alien it finds that has collided with ship.

If no collisions occur, `spritecollideany()` returns None and the `if` block at ❶ won't execute. If it finds an alien that has collided with the ship, it returns that alien and the `if` block executes: it prints *Ship hit!!!* ❷. When an alien hits the ship, we'll need to do a number of tasks: we'll need to delete all remaining aliens and bullets, recenter the ship, and create a new fleet. Before we write code to do all this, we need to know that our approach for detecting alien and ship collisions works correctly. Writing a `print()` call is a simple way to ensure we're detecting these collisions properly.

Now when you run *Alien Invasion,* the message *Ship hit!!!* should appear in the terminal whenever an alien runs into the ship. When you're testing this feature, set `alien_drop_speed` to a higher value, such as 50 or 100, so the aliens reach your ship faster.

Responding to Alien and Ship Collisions

Now we need to figure out exactly what will happen when an alien collides with the ship. Instead of destroying the ship instance and creating a new one, we'll count how many times the ship has been hit by tracking statistics for the game. Tracking statistics will also be useful for scoring.

Let's write a new class, GameStats, to track game statistics, and save it as *game_stats.py*:

game_stats.py
```
class GameStats:
    """Track statistics for Alien Invasion."""

    def __init__(self, ai_game):
        """Initialize statistics."""
        self.settings = ai_game.settings
        self.reset_stats()

    def reset_stats(self):
        """Initialize statistics that can change during the game."""
        self.ships_left = self.settings.ship_limit
```

We'll make one GameStats instance for the entire time *Alien Invasion* is running. But we'll need to reset some statistics each time the player starts a new game. To do this, we'll initialize most of the statistics in the reset _stats() method instead of directly in __init__(). We'll call this method from __init__() so the statistics are set properly when the GameStats instance is first created ❶. But we'll also be able to call reset_stats() any time the player starts a new game.

Right now we have only one statistic, `ships_left`, the value of which will change throughout the game. The number of ships the player starts with should be stored in *settings.py* as `ship_limit`:

settings.py
```
# Ship settings
self.ship_speed = 1.5
self.ship_limit = 3
```

We also need to make a few changes in *alien_invasion.py* to create an instance of GameStats. First, we'll update the import statements at the top of the file:

alien_invasion.py
```
import sys
from time import sleep

import pygame

from settings import Settings
from game_stats import GameStats
from ship import Ship
--snip--
```

We import the `sleep()` function from the `time` module in the Python standard library so we can pause the game for a moment when the ship is hit. We also import GameStats.

We'll create an instance of GameStats in __init__():

alien_invasion.py
```
def __init__(self):
    --snip--
    self.screen = pygame.display.set_mode(
        (self.settings.screen_width, self.settings.screen_height))
    pygame.display.set_caption("Alien Invasion")

    # Create an instance to store game statistics.
    self.stats = GameStats(self)

    self.ship = Ship(self)
    --snip--
```

We make the instance after creating the game window but before defining other game elements, such as the ship.

When an alien hits the ship, we'll subtract one from the number of ships left, destroy all existing aliens and bullets, create a new fleet, and reposition the ship in the middle of the screen. We'll also pause the game for a moment so the player can notice the collision and regroup before a new fleet appears.

Let's put most of this code in a new method called _ship_hit(). We'll call this method from _update_aliens() when an alien hits the ship:

alien_invasion.py
```
def _ship_hit(self):
    """Respond to the ship being hit by an alien."""
```

```
      # Decrement ships_left.
❶     self.stats.ships_left -= 1

      # Get rid of any remaining aliens and bullets.
❷     self.aliens.empty()
      self.bullets.empty()

      # Create a new fleet and center the ship.
❸     self._create_fleet()
      self.ship.center_ship()

      # Pause.
❹     sleep(0.5)
```

The new method _ship_hit() coordinates the response when an alien
hits a ship. Inside _ship_hit(), the number of ships left is reduced by 1 at ❶,
after which we empty the groups aliens and bullets ❷.

Next, we create a new fleet and center the ship ❸. (We'll add the
method center_ship() to Ship in a moment.) Then we add a pause after the
updates have been made to all the game elements but before any changes
have been drawn to the screen, so the player can see that their ship has
been hit ❹. The sleep() call pauses program execution for half a second,
long enough for the player to see that the alien has hit the ship. When the
sleep() function ends, code execution moves on to the _update_screen()
method, which draws the new fleet to the screen.

In _update_aliens(), we replace the print() call with a call to _ship_hit()
when an alien hits the ship:

alien_invasion.py
```
def _update_aliens(self):
    --snip--
    if pygame.sprite.spritecollideany(self.ship, self.aliens):
        self._ship_hit()
```

Here's the new method center_ship(); add it to the end of *ship.py*:

ship.py
```
def center_ship(self):
    """Center the ship on the screen."""
    self.rect.midbottom = self.screen_rect.midbottom
    self.x = float(self.rect.x)
```

We center the ship the same way we did in __init__(). After centering
it, we reset the self.x attribute, which allows us to track the ship's exact
position.

NOTE *Notice that we never make more than one ship; we make only one ship instance for the
whole game and recenter it whenever the ship has been hit. The statistic ships_left
will tell us when the player has run out of ships.*

Run the game, shoot a few aliens, and let an alien hit the ship. The
game should pause, and a new fleet should appear with the ship centered
at the bottom of the screen again.

Aliens that Reach the Bottom of the Screen

If an alien reaches the bottom of the screen, we'll have the game respond the same way it does when an alien hits the ship. To check when this happens, add a new method in *alien_invasion.py*:

alien_invasion.py

```
def _check_aliens_bottom(self):
    """Check if any aliens have reached the bottom of the screen."""
    screen_rect = self.screen.get_rect()
    for alien in self.aliens.sprites():
❶       if alien.rect.bottom >= screen_rect.bottom:
            # Treat this the same as if the ship got hit.
            self._ship_hit()
            break
```

The method _check_aliens_bottom() checks whether any aliens have reached the bottom of the screen. An alien reaches the bottom when its rect.bottom value is greater than or equal to the screen's rect.bottom attribute ❶. If an alien reaches the bottom, we call _ship_hit(). If one alien hits the bottom, there's no need to check the rest, so we break out of the loop after calling _ship_hit().

We'll call this method from _update_aliens():

alien_invasion.py

```
def _update_aliens(self):
    --snip--
    # Look for alien-ship collisions.
    if pygame.sprite.spritecollideany(self.ship, self.aliens):
        self._ship_hit()

    # Look for aliens hitting the bottom of the screen.
    self._check_aliens_bottom()
```

We call _check_aliens_bottom() after updating the positions of all the aliens and after looking for alien and ship collisions ❷. Now a new fleet will appear every time the ship is hit by an alien or an alien reaches the bottom of the screen.

Game Over!

Alien Invasion feels more complete now, but the game never ends. The value of ships_left just grows increasingly negative. Let's add a game_active flag as an attribute to GameStats to end the game when the player runs out of ships. We'll set this flag at the end of the __init__() method in GameStats:

game_stats.py

```
def __init__(self, ai_game):
    --snip--
    # Start Alien Invasion in an active state.
    self.game_active = True
```

Now we add code to _ship_hit() that sets game_active to False when the player has used up all their ships:

alien_invasion.py

```
def _ship_hit(self):
    """Respond to ship being hit by alien."""
    if self.stats.ships_left > 0:
        # Decrement ships_left.
        self.stats.ships_left -= 1
        --snip--
        # Pause.
        sleep(0.5)
    else:
        self.stats.game_active = False
```

Most of _ship_hit() is unchanged. We've moved all the existing code into an if block, which tests to make sure the player has at least one ship remaining. If so, we create a new fleet, pause, and move on. If the player has no ships left, we set game_active to False.

Identifying When Parts of the Game Should Run

We need to identify the parts of the game that should always run and the parts that should run only when the game is active:

alien_invasion.py

```
def run_game(self):
    """Start the main loop for the game."""
    while True:
        self._check_events()

        if self.stats.game_active:
            self.ship.update()
            self._update_bullets()
            self._update_aliens()

        self._update_screen()
```

In the main loop, we always need to call _check_events(), even if the game is inactive. For example, we still need to know if the user presses Q to quit the game or clicks the button to close the window. We also continue updating the screen so we can make changes to the screen while waiting to see whether the player chooses to start a new game. The rest of the function calls only need to happen when the game is active, because when the game is inactive, we don't need to update the positions of game elements.

Now when you play *Alien Invasion*, the game should freeze when you've used up all your ships.

Summary

In this chapter, you learned how to add a large number of identical elements to a game by creating a fleet of aliens. You used nested loops to create a grid of elements, and you made a large set of game elements move by calling each element's update() method. You learned to control the direction of objects on the screen and to respond to specific situations, such as when the fleet reaches the edge of the screen. You detected and responded to collisions when bullets hit aliens and aliens hit the ship. You also learned how to track statistics in a game and use a game_active flag to determine when the game is over.

In the next and final chapter of this project, we'll add a Play button so the player can choose when to start their first game and whether to play again when the game ends. We'll speed up the game each time the player shoots down the entire fleet, and we'll add a scoring system. The final result will be a fully playable game!

14

SCORING

In this chapter, we'll finish the *Alien Invasion* game. We'll add a Play button to start a game on demand or to restart a game once it ends. We'll also change the game so it speeds up when the player moves up a level, and implement a scoring system. By the end of the chapter, you'll know enough to start writing games that increase in difficulty as a player progresses and show scores.

Adding the Play Button

In this section, we'll add a Play button that appears before a game begins and reappears when the game ends so the player can play again.

Right now the game begins as soon as you run *alien_invasion.py*. Let's start the game in an inactive state and then prompt the player to click a Play button to begin. To do this, modify the __init__() method of GameStats:

game_stats.py
```
def __init__(self, ai_game):
    """Initialize statistics."""
    self.settings = ai_game.settings
    self.reset_stats()

    # Start game in an inactive state.
    self.game_active = False
```

Now the game should start in an inactive state with no way for the player to start it until we make a Play button.

Creating a Button Class

Because Pygame doesn't have a built-in method for making buttons, we'll write a Button class to create a filled rectangle with a label. You can use this code to make any button in a game. Here's the first part of the Button class; save it as *button.py*:

button.py
```
import pygame.font

class Button:

❶    def __init__(self, ai_game, msg):
        """Initialize button attributes."""
        self.screen = ai_game.screen
        self.screen_rect = self.screen.get_rect()

        # Set the dimensions and properties of the button.
❷        self.width, self.height = 200, 50
        self.button_color = (0, 255, 0)
        self.text_color = (255, 255, 255)
❸        self.font = pygame.font.SysFont(None, 48)

        # Build the button's rect object and center it.
❹        self.rect = pygame.Rect(0, 0, self.width, self.height)
        self.rect.center = self.screen_rect.center

        # The button message needs to be prepped only once.
❺        self._prep_msg(msg)
```

First, we import the pygame.font module, which lets Pygame render text to the screen. The __init__() method takes the parameters self, the ai_game object, and msg, which contains the button's text ❶. We set the button dimensions at ❷, and then set button_color to color the button's rect object bright green and set text_color to render the text in white.

At ❸, we prepare a font attribute for rendering text. The None argument tells Pygame to use the default font, and 48 specifies the size of the text. To center the button on the screen, we create a rect for the button ❹ and set its center attribute to match that of the screen.

Pygame works with text by rendering the string you want to display as an image. At ❺, we call _prep_msg() to handle this rendering.

Here's the code for _prep_msg():

button.py

```
    def _prep_msg(self, msg):
        """Turn msg into a rendered image and center text on the button."""
❶      self.msg_image = self.font.render(msg, True, self.text_color,
            self.button_color)
❷      self.msg_image_rect = self.msg_image.get_rect()
        self.msg_image_rect.center = self.rect.center
```

The _prep_msg() method needs a self parameter and the text to be rendered as an image (msg). The call to font.render() turns the text stored in msg into an image, which we then store in self.msg_image ❶. The font.render() method also takes a Boolean value to turn antialiasing on or off (antialiasing makes the edges of the text smoother). The remaining arguments are the specified font color and background color. We set antialiasing to True and set the text background to the same color as the button. (If you don't include a background color, Pygame will try to render the font with a transparent background.)

At ❷, we center the text image on the button by creating a rect from the image and setting its center attribute to match that of the button.

Finally, we create a draw_button() method that we can call to display the button onscreen:

button.py

```
    def draw_button(self):
        # Draw blank button and then draw message.
        self.screen.fill(self.button_color, self.rect)
        self.screen.blit(self.msg_image, self.msg_image_rect)
```

We call screen.fill() to draw the rectangular portion of the button. Then we call screen.blit() to draw the text image to the screen, passing it an image and the rect object associated with the image. This completes the Button class.

Drawing the Button to the Screen

We'll use the Button class to create a Play button in AlienInvasion. First, we'll update the import statements:

alien_invasion.py

```
--snip--
from game_stats import GameStats
from button import Button
```

Because we need only one Play button, we'll create the button in the __init__() method of AlienInvasion. We can place this code at the very end of __init__():

```
def __init__(self):
    --snip--
    self._create_fleet()

    # Make the Play button.
    self.play_button = Button(self, "Play")
```

This code creates an instance of Button with the label *Play*, but it doesn't draw the button to the screen. We'll call the button's draw_button() method in _update_screen():

```
def _update_screen(self):
    --snip--
    self.aliens.draw(self.screen)

    # Draw the play button if the game is inactive.
    if not self.stats.game_active:
        self.play_button.draw_button()

    pygame.display.flip()
```

To make the Play button visible above all other elements on the screen, we draw it after all the other elements have been drawn but before flipping to a new screen. We include it in an if block, so the button only appears when the game is inactive.

Now when you run *Alien Invasion*, you should see a Play button in the center of the screen, as shown in Figure 14-1.

Figure 14-1: A Play button appears when the game is inactive.

Starting the Game

To start a new game when the player clicks Play, add the following `elif` block to the end of `_check_events()` to monitor mouse events over the button:

alien_invasion.py

```
def _check_events(self):
    """Respond to keypresses and mouse events."""
    for event in pygame.event.get():
        if event.type == pygame.QUIT:
            --snip--
❶       elif event.type == pygame.MOUSEBUTTONDOWN:
❷           mouse_pos = pygame.mouse.get_pos()
❸           self._check_play_button(mouse_pos)
```

Pygame detects a MOUSEBUTTONDOWN event when the player clicks anywhere on the screen ❶, but we want to restrict our game to respond to mouse clicks only on the Play button. To accomplish this, we use pygame.mouse.get_pos(), which returns a tuple containing the mouse cursor's x- and y-coordinates when the mouse button is clicked ❷. We send these values to the new method _check_play_button() ❸.

Here's _check_play_button(), which I chose to place after _check_events():

alien_invasion.py

```
def _check_play_button(self, mouse_pos):
    """Start a new game when the player clicks Play."""
❶   if self.play_button.rect.collidepoint(mouse_pos):
        self.stats.game_active = True
```

We use the rect method collidepoint() to check whether the point of the mouse click overlaps the region defined by the Play button's rect ❶. If so, we set game_active to True, and the game begins!

At this point, you should be able to start and play a full game. When the game ends, the value of game_active should become False and the Play button should reappear.

Resetting the Game

The Play button code we just wrote works the first time the player clicks Play. But it doesn't work after the first game ends, because the conditions that caused the game to end haven't been reset.

To reset the game each time the player clicks Play, we need to reset the game statistics, clear out the old aliens and bullets, build a new fleet, and center the ship, as shown here:

alien_invasion.py

```
def _check_play_button(self, mouse_pos):
    """Start a new game when the player clicks Play."""
    if self.play_button.rect.collidepoint(mouse_pos):
        # Reset the game statistics.
❶       self.stats.reset_stats()
        self.stats.game_active = True

        # Get rid of any remaining aliens and bullets.
❷       self.aliens.empty()
```

```
                    self.bullets.empty()

                    # Create a new fleet and center the ship.
❸                   self._create_fleet()
                    self.ship.center_ship()
```

At ❶, we reset the game statistics, which gives the player three new ships. Then we set game_active to True so the game will begin as soon as the code in this function finishes running. We empty the aliens and bullets groups ❷, and then create a new fleet and center the ship ❸.

Now the game will reset properly each time you click Play, allowing you to play it as many times as you want!

Deactivating the Play Button

One issue with our Play button is that the button region on the screen will continue to respond to clicks even when the Play button isn't visible. If you click the Play button area by accident after a game begins, the game will restart!

To fix this, set the game to start only when game_active is False:

alien_invasion.py

```
        def _check_play_button(self, mouse_pos):
            """Start a new game when the player clicks Play."""
❶           button_clicked = self.play_button.rect.collidepoint(mouse_pos)
❷           if button_clicked and not self.stats.game_active:
                # Reset the game statistics.
                self.stats.reset_stats()
                --snip--
```

The flag button_clicked stores a True or False value ❶, and the game will restart only if Play is clicked *and* the game is not currently active ❷. To test this behavior, start a new game and repeatedly click where the Play button should be. If everything works as expected, clicking the Play button area should have no effect on the gameplay.

Hiding the Mouse Cursor

We want the mouse cursor to be visible to begin play, but once play begins, it just gets in the way. To fix this, we'll make it invisible when the game becomes active. We can do this at the end of the if block in _check_play_button():

alien_invasion.py

```
        def _check_play_button(self, mouse_pos):
            """Start a new game when the player clicks Play."""
            button_clicked = self.play_button.rect.collidepoint(mouse_pos)
            if button_clicked and not self.stats.game_active:
                --snip--
                # Hide the mouse cursor.
                pygame.mouse.set_visible(False)
```

Passing `False` to `set_visible()` tells Pygame to hide the cursor when the mouse is over the game window.

We'll make the cursor reappear once the game ends so the player can click Play again to begin a new game. Here's the code to do that:

alien_invasion.py

```python
def _ship_hit(self):
    """Respond to ship being hit by alien."""
    if self.stats.ships_left > 0:
        --snip--
    else:
        self.stats.game_active = False
        pygame.mouse.set_visible(True)
```

We make the cursor visible again as soon as the game becomes inactive, which happens in `_ship_hit()`. Attention to details like this makes your game more professional looking and allows the player to focus on playing rather than figuring out the user interface.

TRY IT YOURSELF

14-1. Press P to Play: Because *Alien Invasion* uses keyboard input to control the ship, it would be useful to start the game with a keypress. Add code that lets the player press P to start. It might help to move some code from _check _play_button() to a _start_game() method that can be called from _check_play _button() *and* _check_keydown_events().

14-2. Target Practice: Create a rectangle at the right edge of the screen that moves up and down at a steady rate. Then have a ship appear on the left side of the screen that the player can move up and down while firing bullets at the moving, rectangular target. Add a Play button that starts the game, and when the player misses the target three times, end the game and make the Play button reappear. Let the player restart the game with this Play button.

Leveling Up

In our current game, once a player shoots down the entire alien fleet, the player reaches a new level, but the game difficulty doesn't change. Let's liven things up a bit and make the game more challenging by increasing the game's speed each time a player clears the screen.

Modifying the Speed Settings

We'll first reorganize the Settings class to group the game settings into static and changing ones. We'll also make sure that settings that change

during the game reset when we start a new game. Here's the __init__()
method for *settings.py*:

```
def __init__(self):
    """Initialize the game's static settings."""
    # Screen settings
    self.screen_width = 1200
    self.screen_height = 800
    self.bg_color = (230, 230, 230)

    # Ship settings
    self.ship_limit = 3

    # Bullet settings
    self.bullet_width = 3
    self.bullet_height = 15
    self.bullet_color = 60, 60, 60
    self.bullets_allowed = 3

    # Alien settings
    self.fleet_drop_speed = 10

    # How quickly the game speeds up
❶   self.speedup_scale = 1.1

❷   self.initialize_dynamic_settings()
```

We continue to initialize those settings that stay constant in the __init__()
method. At ❶, we add a speedup_scale setting to control how quickly the game
speeds up: a value of 2 will double the game speed every time the player
reaches a new level; a value of 1 will keep the speed constant. A value like
1.1 should increase the speed enough to make the game challenging but not
impossible. Finally, we call the initialize_dynamic_settings() method to initialize the values for attributes that need to change throughout the game ❷.

Here's the code for initialize_dynamic_settings():

```
def initialize_dynamic_settings(self):
    """Initialize settings that change throughout the game."""
    self.ship_speed = 1.5
    self.bullet_speed = 3.0
    self.alien_speed = 1.0

    # fleet_direction of 1 represents right; -1 represents left.
    self.fleet_direction = 1
```

This method sets the initial values for the ship, bullet, and alien
speeds. We'll increase these speeds as the player progresses in the game
and reset them each time the player starts a new game. We include fleet
_direction in this method so the aliens always move right at the beginning
of a new game. We don't need to increase the value of fleet_drop_speed,
because when the aliens move faster across the screen, they'll also come
down the screen faster.

To increase the speeds of the ship, bullets, and aliens each time the player reaches a new level, we'll write a new method called `increase_speed()`:

settings.py

```
def increase_speed(self):
    """Increase speed settings."""
    self.ship_speed *= self.speedup_scale
    self.bullet_speed *= self.speedup_scale
    self.alien_speed *= self.speedup_scale
```

To increase the speed of these game elements, we multiply each speed setting by the value of `speedup_scale`.

We increase the game's tempo by calling `increase_speed()` in `_check_bullet_alien_collisions()` when the last alien in a fleet has been shot down:

alien_invasion.py

```
def _check_bullet_alien_collisions(self):
    --snip--
    if not self.aliens:
        # Destroy existing bullets and create new fleet.
        self.bullets.empty()
        self._create_fleet()
        self.settings.increase_speed()
```

Changing the values of the speed settings `ship_speed`, `alien_speed`, and `bullet_speed` is enough to speed up the entire game!

Resetting the Speed

Now we need to return any changed settings to their initial values each time the player starts a new game; otherwise, each new game would start with the increased speed settings of the previous game:

alien_invasion.py

```
def _check_play_button(self, mouse_pos):
    """Start a new game when the player clicks Play."""
    button_clicked = self.play_button.rect.collidepoint(mouse_pos)
    if button_clicked and not self.stats.game_active:
        # Reset the game settings.
        self.settings.initialize_dynamic_settings()
        --snip--
```

Playing *Alien Invasion* should be more fun and challenging now. Each time you clear the screen, the game should speed up and become slightly more difficult. If the game becomes too difficult too quickly, decrease the value of `settings.speedup_scale`. Or if the game isn't challenging enough, increase the value slightly. Find a sweet spot by ramping up the difficulty in a reasonable amount of time. The first couple of screens should be easy, the next few challenging but doable, and subsequent screens almost impossibly difficult.

Scoring

Let's implement a scoring system to track the game's score in real time and display the high score, level, and number of ships remaining.

The score is a game statistic, so we'll add a score attribute to GameStats:

game_stats.py
```
class GameStats:
    --snip--
    def reset_stats(self):
        """Initialize statistics that can change during the game."""
        self.ships_left = self.ai_settings.ship_limit
        self.score = 0
```

To reset the score each time a new game starts, we initialize score in reset_stats() rather than __init__().

Displaying the Score

To display the score on the screen, we first create a new class, Scoreboard. For now, this class will just display the current score, but eventually we'll use it to report the high score, level, and number of ships remaining as well. Here's the first part of the class; save it as *scoreboard.py*:

scoreboard.py
```
import pygame.font

class Scoreboard:
    """A class to report scoring information."""

❶   def __init__(self, ai_game):
        """Initialize scorekeeping attributes."""
        self.screen = ai_game.screen
        self.screen_rect = self.screen.get_rect()
        self.settings = ai_game.settings
        self.stats = ai_game.stats

        # Font settings for scoring information.
❷       self.text_color = (30, 30, 30)
❸       self.font = pygame.font.SysFont(None, 48)
```

```
                              # Prepare the initial score image.
❹                             self.prep_score()
```

Because Scoreboard writes text to the screen, we begin by importing the pygame.font module. Next, we give __init__() the ai_game parameter so it can access the settings, screen, and stats objects, which it will need to report the values we're tracking ❶. Then we set a text color ❷ and instantiate a font object ❸.

To turn the text to be displayed into an image, we call prep_score() ❹, which we define here:

scoreboard.py
```
              def prep_score(self):
                  """Turn the score into a rendered image."""
❶                 score_str = str(self.stats.score)
❷                 self.score_image = self.font.render(score_str, True,
                          self.text_color, self.settings.bg_color)

                  # Display the score at the top right of the screen.
❸                 self.score_rect = self.score_image.get_rect()
❹                 self.score_rect.right = self.screen_rect.right - 20
❺                 self.score_rect.top = 20
```

In prep_score(), we turn the numerical value stats.score into a string ❶, and then pass this string to render(), which creates the image ❷. To display the score clearly onscreen, we pass the screen's background color and the text color to render().

We'll position the score in the upper-right corner of the screen and have it expand to the left as the score increases and the width of the number grows. To make sure the score always lines up with the right side of the screen, we create a rect called score_rect ❸ and set its right edge 20 pixels from the right edge of the screen ❹. We then place the top edge 20 pixels down from the top of the screen ❺.

Then we create a show_score() method to display the rendered score image:

scoreboard.py
```
              def show_score(self):
                  """Draw score to the screen."""
                  self.screen.blit(self.score_image, self.score_rect)
```

This method draws the score image onscreen at the location score_rect specifies.

Making a Scoreboard

To display the score, we'll create a Scoreboard instance in AlienInvasion. First, let's update the import statements:

alien_invasion.py
```
--snip--
from game_stats import GameStats
from scoreboard import Scoreboard
--snip--
```

Next, we make an instance of Scoreboard in __init__():

alien_invasion.py

```
def __init__(self):
    --snip--
    pygame.display.set_caption("Alien Invasion")

    # Create an instance to store game statistics,
    #   and create a scoreboard.
    self.stats = GameStats(self)
    self.sb = Scoreboard(self)
    --snip--
```

Then we draw the scoreboard onscreen in _update_screen():

alien_invasion.py

```
def _update_screen(self):
    --snip--
    self.aliens.draw(self.screen)

    # Draw the score information.
    self.sb.show_score()

    # Draw the play button if the game is inactive.
    --snip--
```

We call show_score() just before we draw the Play button.

When you run *Alien Invasion* now, a 0 should appear at the top right of the screen. (At this point, we just want to make sure the score appears in the right place before developing the scoring system further.) Figure 14-2 shows the score as it appears before the game starts.

Figure 14-2: The score appears at the top-right corner of the screen.

Next, we'll assign point values to each alien!

Updating the Score as Aliens Are Shot Down

To write a live score onscreen, we update the value of stats.score whenever an alien is hit, and then call prep_score() to update the score image. But first, let's determine how many points a player gets each time they shoot down an alien:

settings.py

```
def initialize_dynamic_settings(self):
    --snip--

    # Scoring
    self.alien_points = 50
```

We'll increase each alien's point value as the game progresses. To make sure this point value is reset each time a new game starts, we set the value in initialize_dynamic_settings().

Let's update the score each time an alien is shot down in _check_bullet _alien_collisions():

alien_invasion.py

```
def _check_bullet_alien_collisions(self):
    """Respond to bullet-alien collisions."""
    # Remove any bullets and aliens that have collided.
    collisions = pygame.sprite.groupcollide(
            self.bullets, self.aliens, True, True)

    if collisions:
        self.stats.score += self.settings.alien_points
        self.sb.prep_score()
    --snip--
```

When a bullet hits an alien, Pygame returns a collisions dictionary. We check whether the dictionary exists, and if it does, the alien's value is added to the score. We then call prep_score() to create a new image for the updated score.

Now when you play *Alien Invasion*, you should be able to rack up points!

Resetting the Score

Right now, we're only prepping a new score *after* an alien has been hit, which works for most of the game. But we still see the old score when a new game starts until the first alien is hit in the new game.

We can fix this by prepping the score when starting a new game:

alien_invasion.py

```
def _check_play_button(self, mouse_pos):
    --snip--
    if button_clicked and not self.stats.game_active:
        --snip--
        # Reset the game statistics.
        self.stats.reset_stats()
```

```
                self.stats.game_active = True
                self.sb.prep_score()
                --snip--
```

We call prep_score() after resetting the game stats when starting a new game. This preps the scoreboard with a 0 score.

Making Sure to Score All Hits

As currently written, our code could miss scoring for some aliens. For example, if two bullets collide with aliens during the same pass through the loop or if we make an extra-wide bullet to hit multiple aliens, the player will only receive points for hitting one of the aliens. To fix this, let's refine the way that bullet and alien collisions are detected.

In _check_bullet_alien_collisions(), any bullet that collides with an alien becomes a key in the collisions dictionary. The value associated with each bullet is a list of aliens it has collided with. We loop through the values in the collisions dictionary to make sure we award points for each alien hit:

alien_invasion.py

```
    def _check_bullet_alien_collisions(self):
        --snip--
        if collisions:
❶           for aliens in collisions.values():
                self.stats.score += self.settings.alien_points * len(aliens)
            self.sb.prep_score()
        --snip--
```

If the collisions dictionary has been defined, we loop through all values in the dictionary. Remember that each value is a list of aliens hit by a single bullet. We multiply the value of each alien by the number of aliens in each list and add this amount to the current score. To test this, change the width of a bullet to 300 pixels and verify that you receive points for each alien you hit with your extra-wide bullets; then return the bullet width to its normal value.

Increasing Point Values

Because the game gets more difficult each time a player reaches a new level, aliens in later levels should be worth more points. To implement this functionality, we'll add code to increase the point value when the game's speed increases:

settings.py

```
class Settings:
    """A class to store all settings for Alien Invasion."""

    def __init__(self):
        --snip--
        # How quickly the game speeds up
        self.speedup_scale = 1.1
```

```
         # How quickly the alien point values increase
❶        self.score_scale = 1.5

         self.initialize_dynamic_settings()

     def initialize_dynamic_settings(self):
         --snip--

     def increase_speed(self):
         """Increase speed settings and alien point values."""
         self.ship_speed *= self.speedup_scale
         self.bullet_speed *= self.speedup_scale
         self.alien_speed *= self.speedup_scale

❷        self.alien_points = int(self.alien_points * self.score_scale)
```

We define a rate at which points increase, which we call score_scale ❶. A small increase in speed (1.1) makes the game more challenging quickly. But to see a more notable difference in scoring, we need to change the alien point value by a larger amount (1.5). Now when we increase the game's speed, we also increase the point value of each hit ❷. We use the int() function to increase the point value by whole integers.

To see the value of each alien, add a print() call to the increase_speed() method in Settings:

settings.py

```
     def increase_speed(self):
         --snip--
         self.alien_points = int(self.alien_points * self.score_scale)
         print(self.alien_points)
```

The new point value should appear in the terminal every time you reach a new level.

NOTE   *Be sure to remove the print() call after verifying that the point value is increasing, or it might affect your game's performance and distract the player.*

Rounding the Score

Most arcade-style shooting games report scores as multiples of 10, so let's follow that lead with our scores. Also, let's format the score to include comma separators in large numbers. We'll make this change in Scoreboard:

scoreboard.py

```
     def prep_score(self):
         """Turn the score into a rendered image."""
❶        rounded_score = round(self.stats.score, -1)
❷        score_str = "{:,}".format(rounded_score)
         self.score_image = self.font.render(score_str, True,
                 self.text_color, self.settings.bg_color)
         --snip--
```

The round() function normally rounds a decimal number to a set number of decimal places given as the second argument. However, when you pass a negative number as the second argument, round() will round the value to the nearest 10, 100, 1000, and so on. The code at ❶ tells Python to round the value of stats.score to the nearest 10 and store it in rounded_score.

At ❷, a string formatting directive tells Python to insert commas into numbers when converting a numerical value to a string: for example, to output 1,000,000 instead of 1000000. Now when you run the game, you should see a neatly formatted, rounded score even when you rack up lots of points, as shown in Figure 14-3.

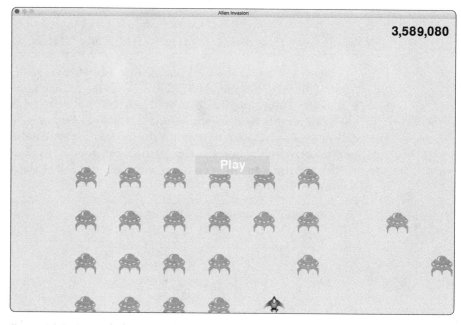

Figure 14-3: A rounded score with comma separators

High Scores

Every player wants to beat a game's high score, so let's track and report high scores to give players something to work toward. We'll store high scores in GameStats:

game_stats.py

```
def __init__(self, ai_game):
    --snip--
    # High score should never be reset.
    self.high_score = 0
```

Because the high score should never be reset, we initialize high_score in __init__() rather than in reset_stats().

Next, we'll modify Scoreboard to display the high score. Let's start with the __init__() method:

scoreboard.py
```
def __init__(self, ai_game):
    --snip--
    # Prepare the initial score images.
    self.prep_score()
❶  self.prep_high_score()
```

The high score will be displayed separately from the score, so we need a new method, prep_high_score(), to prepare the high score image ❶.

Here's the prep_high_score() method:

scoreboard.py
```
def prep_high_score(self):
    """Turn the high score into a rendered image."""
❶  high_score = round(self.stats.high_score, -1)
    high_score_str = "{:,}".format(high_score)
❷  self.high_score_image = self.font.render(high_score_str, True,
            self.text_color, self.settings.bg_color)

    # Center the high score at the top of the screen.
    self.high_score_rect = self.high_score_image.get_rect()
❸  self.high_score_rect.centerx = self.screen_rect.centerx
❹  self.high_score_rect.top = self.score_rect.top
```

We round the high score to the nearest 10 and format it with commas ❶. We then generate an image from the high score ❷, center the high score rect horizontally ❸, and set its top attribute to match the top of the score image ❹.

The show_score() method now draws the current score at the top right and the high score at the top center of the screen:

scoreboard.py
```
def show_score(self):
    """Draw score to the screen."""
    self.screen.blit(self.score_image, self.score_rect)
    self.screen.blit(self.high_score_image, self.high_score_rect)
```

To check for high scores, we'll write a new method, check_high_score(), in Scoreboard:

scoreboard.py
```
def check_high_score(self):
    """Check to see if there's a new high score."""
    if self.stats.score > self.stats.high_score:
        self.stats.high_score = self.stats.score
        self.prep_high_score()
```

The method check_high_score() checks the current score against the high score. If the current score is greater, we update the value of high_score and call prep_high_score() to update the high score's image.

We need to call check_high_score() each time an alien is hit after updating the score in _check_bullet_alien_collisions():

alien_invasion.py

```
def _check_bullet_alien_collisions(self):
    --snip--
    if collisions:
        for aliens in collisions.values():
            self.stats.score += self.settings.alien_points * len(aliens)
        self.sb.prep_score()
        self.sb.check_high_score()
    --snip--
```

We call check_high_score() when the collisions dictionary is present, and we do so after updating the score for all the aliens that have been hit.

The first time you play *Alien Invasion*, your score will be the high score, so it will be displayed as the current score and the high score. But when you start a second game, your high score should appear in the middle and your current score at the right, as shown in Figure 14-4.

Figure 14-4: The high score is shown at the top center of the screen.

Displaying the Level

To display the player's level in the game, we first need an attribute in GameStats representing the current level. To reset the level at the start of each new game, initialize it in reset_stats():

game_stats.py

```
def reset_stats(self):
    """Initialize statistics that can change during the game."""
    self.ships_left = self.settings.ship_limit
```

```
self.score = 0
self.level = 1
```

To have Scoreboard display the current level, we call a new method, prep _level(), from __init__():

scoreboard.py

```
def __init__(self, ai_game):
    --snip--
    self.prep_high_score()
    self.prep_level()
```

Here's prep_level():

scoreboard.py

```
    def prep_level(self):
        """Turn the level into a rendered image."""
        level_str = str(self.stats.level)
❶       self.level_image = self.font.render(level_str, True,
                self.text_color, self.settings.bg_color)

        # Position the level below the score.
        self.level_rect = self.level_image.get_rect()
❷       self.level_rect.right = self.score_rect.right
❸       self.level_rect.top = self.score_rect.bottom + 10
```

The prep_level() method creates an image from the value stored in stats.level ❶ and sets the image's right attribute to match the score's right attribute ❷. It then sets the top attribute 10 pixels beneath the bottom of the score image to leave space between the score and the level ❸.

We also need to update show_score():

scoreboard.py

```
    def show_score(self):
        """Draw scores and level to the screen."""
        self.screen.blit(self.score_image, self.score_rect)
        self.screen.blit(self.high_score_image, self.high_score_rect)
        self.screen.blit(self.level_image, self.level_rect)
```

This new line draws the level image to the screen.

We'll increment stats.level and update the level image in _check_bullet _alien_collisions():

alien_invasion.py

```
    def _check_bullet_alien_collisions(self):
        --snip--
        if not self.aliens:
            # Destroy existing bullets and create new fleet.
            self.bullets.empty()
            self._create_fleet()
            self.settings.increase_speed()

            # Increase level.
            self.stats.level += 1
            self.sb.prep_level()
```

If a fleet is destroyed, we increment the value of stats.level and call
prep_level() to make sure the new level displays correctly.

To ensure the level image updates properly at the start of a new game,
we also call prep_level() when the player clicks the Play button:

```
def _check_play_button(self, mouse_pos):
    --snip--
    if button_clicked and not self.stats.game_active:
        --snip--
        self.sb.prep_score()
        self.sb.prep_level()
        --snip--
```

We call prep_level() right after calling prep_score().

Now you'll see how many levels you've completed, as shown in
Figure 14-5.

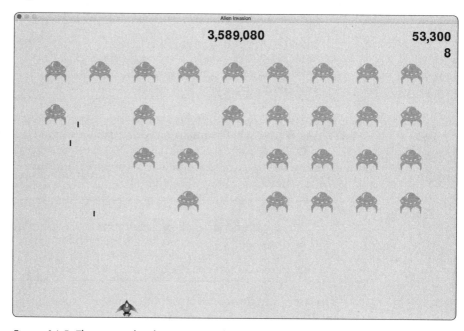

Figure 14-5: The current level appears just below the current score.

NOTE   *In some classic games, the scores have labels, such as Score, High Score, and Level.
We've omitted these labels because the meaning of each number becomes clear once
you've played the game. To include these labels, add them to the score strings just
before the calls to font.render() in Scoreboard.*

Displaying the Number of Ships

Finally, let's display the number of ships the player has left, but this time,
let's use a graphic. To do so, we'll draw ships in the upper-left corner of

the screen to represent how many ships are left, just as many classic arcade games do.

First, we need to make Ship inherit from Sprite so we can create a group of ships:

ship.py

```
import pygame
from pygame.sprite import Sprite

❶ class Ship(Sprite):
      """A class to manage the ship."""

      def __init__(self, ai_game):
          """Initialize the ship and set its starting position."""
❷         super().__init__()
          --snip--
```

Here we import Sprite, make sure Ship inherits from Sprite ❶, and call super() at the beginning of __init__() ❷.

Next, we need to modify Scoreboard to create a group of ships we can display. Here are the import statements for Scoreboard:

scoreboard.py

```
import pygame.font
from pygame.sprite import Group

from ship import Ship
```

Because we're making a group of ships, we import the Group and Ship classes.

Here's __init__():

scoreboard.py

```
def __init__(self, ai_game):
    """Initialize scorekeeping attributes."""
    self.ai_game = ai_game
    self.screen = ai_game.screen
    --snip--
    self.prep_level()
    self.prep_ships()
```

We assign the game instance to an attribute, because we'll need it to create some ships. We call prep_ships() after the call to prep_level().

Here's prep_ships():

scoreboard.py

```
  def prep_ships(self):
      """Show how many ships are left."""
❶     self.ships = Group()
❷     for ship_number in range(self.stats.ships_left):
          ship = Ship(self.ai_game)
❸         ship.rect.x = 10 + ship_number * ship.rect.width
❹         ship.rect.y = 10
❺         self.ships.add(ship)
```

The prep_ships() method creates an empty group, self.ships, to hold the ship instances ❶. To fill this group, a loop runs once for every ship the player has left ❷. Inside the loop, we create a new ship and set each ship's x-coordinate value so the ships appear next to each other with a 10-pixel margin on the left side of the group of ships ❸. We set the y-coordinate value 10 pixels down from the top of the screen so the ships appear in the upper-left corner of the screen ❹. Then we add each new ship to the group ships ❺.

Now we need to draw the ships to the screen:

scoreboard.py

```
def show_score(self):
    """Draw scores, level, and ships to the screen."""
    self.screen.blit(self.score_image, self.score_rect)
    self.screen.blit(self.high_score_image, self.high_score_rect)
    self.screen.blit(self.level_image, self.level_rect)
    self.ships.draw(self.screen)
```

To display the ships on the screen, we call draw() on the group, and Pygame draws each ship.

To show the player how many ships they have to start with, we call prep_ships() when a new game starts. We do this in _check_play_button() in AlienInvasion:

alien_invasion.py

```
def _check_play_button(self, mouse_pos):
    --snip--
    if button_clicked and not self.stats.game_active:
        --snip--
        self.sb.prep_score()
        self.sb.prep_level()
        self.sb.prep_ships()
        --snip--
```

We also call prep_ships() when a ship is hit to update the display of ship images when the player loses a ship:

alien_invasion.py

```
def _ship_hit(self):
    """Respond to ship being hit by alien."""
    if self.stats.ships_left > 0:
        # Decrement ships_left, and update scoreboard.
        self.stats.ships_left -= 1
        self.sb.prep_ships()
        --snip--
```

We call prep_ships() after decreasing the value of ships_left, so the correct number of ships displays each time a ship is destroyed.

Figure 14-6 shows the complete scoring system with the remaining ships displayed at the top left of the screen.

Figure 14-6: The complete scoring system for Alien Invasion

TRY IT YOURSELF

14-5. All-Time High Score: The high score is reset every time a player closes and restarts *Alien Invasion*. Fix this by writing the high score to a file before calling sys.exit() and reading in the high score when initializing its value in GameStats.

14-6. Refactoring: Look for methods that are doing more than one task, and refactor them to organize your code and make it efficient. For example, move some of the code in _check_bullet_alien_collisions(), which starts a new level when the fleet of aliens has been destroyed, to a function called start_new _level(). Also, move the four separate method calls in the __init__() method in Scoreboard to a method called prep_images() to shorten __init__(). The prep_images() method could also help simplify _check_play_button() or start _game() if you've already refactored _check_play_button().

NOTE   *Before attempting to refactor the project, see Appendix D to learn how to restore the project to a working state if you introduce bugs while refactoring.*

(continued)

14-7. Expanding the Game: Think of a way to expand *Alien Invasion*. For example, you could program the aliens to shoot bullets down at the ship or add shields for your ship to hide behind, which can be destroyed by bullets from either side. Or use something like the `pygame.mixer` module to add sound effects, such as explosions and shooting sounds.

14-8. Sideways Shooter, Final Version: Continue developing Sideways Shooter, using everything we've done in this project. Add a Play button, make the game speed up at appropriate points, and develop a scoring system. Be sure to refactor your code as you work, and look for opportunities to customize the game beyond what was shown in this chapter.

Summary

In this chapter, you learned how to implement a Play button to start a new game, detect mouse events, and hide the cursor in active games. You can use what you've learned to create other buttons in your games, like a Help button to display instructions on how to play. You also learned how to modify the speed of a game as it progresses, implement a progressive scoring system, and display information in textual and nontextual ways.

PROJECT 2

DATA VISUALIZATION

15

GENERATING DATA

Data visualization involves exploring data through visual representations. It's closely associated with *data analysis,* which uses code to explore the patterns and connections in a data set. A data set can be made up of a small list of numbers that fits in one line of code or it can be many gigabytes of data.

Making beautiful data representations is about more than pretty pictures. When a representation of a data set is simple and visually appealing, its meaning becomes clear to viewers. People will see patterns and significance in your data sets that they never knew existed.

Fortunately, you don't need a supercomputer to visualize complex data. With Python's efficiency, you can quickly explore data sets made of millions of individual data points on just a laptop. Also, the data points don't have to be numbers. With the basics you learned in the first part of this book, you can analyze nonnumerical data as well.

People use Python for data-intensive work in genetics, climate research, political and economic analysis, and much more. Data scientists have written an impressive array of visualization and analysis tools in Python, many of which are available to you as well. One of the most popular tools is Matplotlib, a mathematical plotting library. We'll use Matplotlib to make simple plots, such as line graphs and scatter plots. Then we'll create a more interesting data set based on the concept of a random walk—a visualization generated from a series of random decisions.

We'll also use a package called Plotly, which creates visualizations that work well on digital devices. Plotly generates visualizations that automatically resize to fit a variety of display devices. These visualizations can also include a number of interactive features, such as emphasizing particular aspects of the data set when users hover over different parts of the visualization. We'll use Plotly to analyze the results of rolling dice.

Installing Matplotlib

To use Matplotlib for your initial set of visualizations, you'll need to install it using pip, a module that downloads and installs Python packages. Enter the following command at a terminal prompt:

```
$ python -m pip install --user matplotlib
```

This command tells Python to run the pip module and install the matplotlib package to the current user's Python installation. If you use a command other than python on your system to run programs or start a terminal session, such as python3, your command will look like this:

```
$ python3 -m pip install --user matplotlib
```

NOTE   *If this command doesn't work on macOS, try running the command again without the --user flag.*

To see the kinds of visualizations you can make with Matplotlib, visit the sample gallery at *https://matplotlib.org/gallery/*. When you click a visualization in the gallery, you'll see the code used to generate the plot.

Plotting a Simple Line Graph

Let's plot a simple line graph using Matplotlib, and then customize it to create a more informative data visualization. We'll use the square number sequence 1, 4, 9, 16, 25 as the data for the graph.

Just provide Matplotlib with the numbers, as shown here, and Matplotlib should do the rest:

```
import matplotlib.pyplot as plt

squares = [1, 4, 9, 16, 25]
```

```
❶ fig, ax = plt.subplots()
  ax.plot(squares)

  plt.show()
```

We first import the `pyplot` module using the alias `plt` so we don't have to type `pyplot` repeatedly. (You'll see this convention often in online examples, so we'll do the same here.) The `pyplot` module contains a number of functions that generate charts and plots.

We create a list called `squares` to hold the data that we'll plot. Then we follow another common Matplotlib convention by calling the `subplots()` function ❶. This function can generate one or more plots in the same figure. The variable `fig` represents the entire figure or collection of plots that are generated. The variable `ax` represents a single plot in the figure and is the variable we'll use most of the time.

We then use the `plot()` method, which will try to plot the data it's given in a meaningful way. The function `plt.show()` opens Matplotlib's viewer and displays the plot, as shown in Figure 15-1. The viewer allows you to zoom and navigate the plot, and when you click the disk icon, you can save any plot images you like.

Figure 15-1: One of the simplest plots you can make in Matplotlib

Changing the Label Type and Line Thickness

Although the plot in Figure 15-1 shows that the numbers are increasing, the label type is too small and the line is a little thin to read easily. Fortunately, Matplotlib allows you to adjust every feature of a visualization.

We'll use a few of the available customizations to improve this plot's readability, as shown here:

mpl_squares.py

```
import matplotlib.pyplot as plt

squares = [1, 4, 9, 16, 25]

fig, ax = plt.subplots()
❶ ax.plot(squares, linewidth=3)

# Set chart title and label axes.
❷ ax.set_title("Square Numbers", fontsize=24)
❸ ax.set_xlabel("Value", fontsize=14)
  ax.set_ylabel("Square of Value", fontsize=14)

# Set size of tick labels.
❹ ax.tick_params(axis='both', labelsize=14)

plt.show()
```

The linewidth parameter at ❶ controls the thickness of the line that plot() generates. The set_title() method at ❷ sets a title for the chart. The fontsize parameters, which appear repeatedly throughout the code, control the size of the text in various elements on the chart.

The set_xlabel() and set_ylabel() methods allow you to set a title for each of the axes ❸, and the method tick_params() styles the tick marks ❹. The arguments shown here affect the tick marks on both the x- and y-axes (axis='both') and set the font size of the tick mark labels to 14 (labelsize=14).

As you can see in Figure 15-2, the resulting chart is much easier to read. The label type is bigger, and the line graph is thicker. It's often worth experimenting with these values to get an idea of what will look best in the resulting graph.

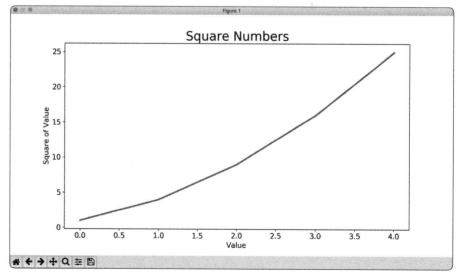

Figure 15-2: The chart is much easier to read now.

Correcting the Plot

But now that we can read the chart better, we see that the data is not plotted correctly. Notice at the end of the graph that the square of 4.0 is shown as 25! Let's fix that.

When you give plot() a sequence of numbers, it assumes the first data point corresponds to an x-coordinate value of 0, but our first point corresponds to an x-value of 1. We can override the default behavior by giving plot() the input and output values used to calculate the squares:

mpl_squares.py

```
import matplotlib.pyplot as plt

input_values = [1, 2, 3, 4, 5]
squares = [1, 4, 9, 16, 25]

fig, ax = plt.subplots()
ax.plot(input_values, squares, linewidth=3)

# Set chart title and label axes.
--snip--
```

Now plot() will graph the data correctly because we've provided the input and output values, so it doesn't have to assume how the output numbers were generated. The resulting plot, shown in Figure 15-3, is correct.

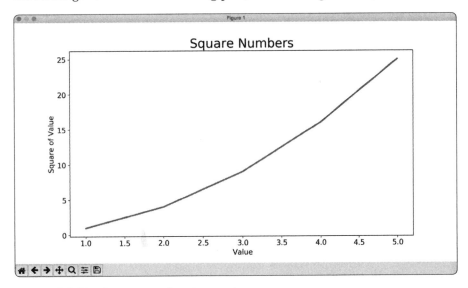

Figure 15-3: The data is now plotted correctly.

You can specify numerous arguments when using plot() and use a number of functions to customize your plots. We'll continue to explore these customization functions as we work with more interesting data sets throughout this chapter.

Using Built-in Styles

Matplotlib has a number of predefined styles available, with good starting settings for background colors, gridlines, line widths, fonts, font sizes, and more that will make your visualizations appealing without requiring much customization. To see the styles available on your system, run the following lines in a terminal session:

```
>>> import matplotlib.pyplot as plt
>>> plt.style.available
['seaborn-dark', 'seaborn-darkgrid', 'seaborn-ticks', 'fivethirtyeight',
--snip--
```

To use any of these styles, add one line of code before starting to generate the plot:

mpl_squares.py
```
import matplotlib.pyplot as plt

input_values = [1, 2, 3, 4, 5]
squares = [1, 4, 9, 16, 25]

plt.style.use('seaborn')
fig, ax = plt.subplots()
--snip--
```

This code generates the plot shown in Figure 15-4. A wide variety of styles is available; play around with these styles to find some that you like.

Figure 15-4: The built-in seaborn style

Plotting and Styling Individual Points with scatter()

Sometimes, it's useful to plot and style individual points based on certain characteristics. For example, you might plot small values in one color and larger values in a different color. You could also plot a large data set with one set of styling options and then emphasize individual points by replotting them with different options.

To plot a single point, use the scatter() method. Pass the single (*x*, *y*) values of the point of interest to scatter() to plot those values:

scatter_squares.py
```
import matplotlib.pyplot as plt

plt.style.use('seaborn')
fig, ax = plt.subplots()
ax.scatter(2, 4)

plt.show()
```

Let's style the output to make it more interesting. We'll add a title, label the axes, and make sure all the text is large enough to read:

```
import matplotlib.pyplot as plt

plt.style.use('seaborn')
fig, ax = plt.subplots()
❶ ax.scatter(2, 4, s=200)

# Set chart title and label axes.
ax.set_title("Square Numbers", fontsize=24)
ax.set_xlabel("Value", fontsize=14)
ax.set_ylabel("Square of Value", fontsize=14)

# Set size of tick labels.
ax.tick_params(axis='both', which='major', labelsize=14)

plt.show()
```

At ❶ we call scatter() and use the s argument to set the size of the dots used to draw the graph. When you run *scatter_squares.py* now, you should see a single point in the middle of the chart, as shown in Figure 15-5.

Figure 15-5: Plotting a single point

Plotting a Series of Points with scatter()

To plot a series of points, we can pass scatter() separate lists of x- and y-values, like this:

scatter_squares.py

```
import matplotlib.pyplot as plt

x_values = [1, 2, 3, 4, 5]
y_values = [1, 4, 9, 16, 25]

plt.style.use('seaborn')
fig, ax = plt.subplots()
ax.scatter(x_values, y_values, s=100)

# Set chart title and label axes.
--snip--
```

The x_values list contains the numbers to be squared, and y_values contains the square of each number. When these lists are passed to scatter(), Matplotlib reads one value from each list as it plots each point. The points to be plotted are (1, 1), (2, 4), (3, 9), (4, 16), and (5, 25); Figure 15-6 shows the result.

Figure 15-6: A scatter plot with multiple points

Calculating Data Automatically

Writing lists by hand can be inefficient, especially when we have many points. Rather than passing our points in a list, let's use a loop in Python to do the calculations for us.

Here's how this would look with 1000 points:

scatter_squares.py
```
import matplotlib.pyplot as plt

❶ x_values = range(1, 1001)
   y_values = [x**2 for x in x_values]

   plt.style.use('seaborn')
   fig, ax = plt.subplots()
❷ ax.scatter(x_values, y_values, s=10)

   # Set chart title and label axes.
   --snip--

   # Set the range for each axis.
❸ ax.axis([0, 1100, 0, 1100000])

   plt.show()
```

We start with a range of x-values containing the numbers 1 through 1000 ❶. Next, a list comprehension generates the y-values by looping through the x-values (for x in x_values), squaring each number (x**2) and storing the results in y_values. We then pass the input and output lists to scatter() ❷. Because this is a large data set, we use a smaller point size.

At ❸ we use the axis() method to specify the range of each axis. The axis() method requires four values: the minimum and maximum values for the x-axis and the y-axis. Here, we run the x-axis from 0 to 1100 and the y-axis from 0 to 1,100,000. Figure 15-7 shows the result.

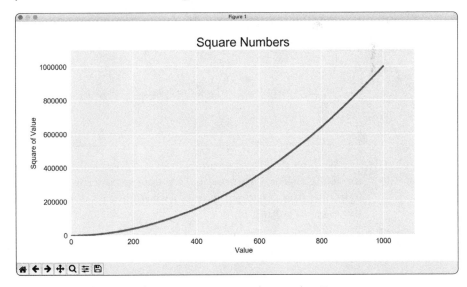

Figure 15-7: Python can plot 1000 points as easily as it plots 5 points.

Defining Custom Colors

To change the color of the points, pass c to scatter() with the name of a color to use in quotation marks, as shown here:

```
ax.scatter(x_values, y_values, c='red', s=10)
```

You can also define custom colors using the RGB color model. To define a color, pass the c argument a tuple with three decimal values (one each for red, green, and blue in that order), using values between 0 and 1. For example, the following line creates a plot with light-green dots:

```
ax.scatter(x_values, y_values, c=(0, 0.8, 0), s=10)
```

Values closer to 0 produce dark colors, and values closer to 1 produce lighter colors.

Using a Colormap

A *colormap* is a series of colors in a gradient that moves from a starting to an ending color. You use colormaps in visualizations to emphasize a pattern in the data. For example, you might make low values a light color and high values a darker color.

The pyplot module includes a set of built-in colormaps. To use one of these colormaps, you need to specify how pyplot should assign a color to each point in the data set. Here's how to assign each point a color based on its y-value:

scatter_squares.py
```
import matplotlib.pyplot as plt

x_values = range(1, 1001)
y_values = [x**2 for x in x_values]

ax.scatter(x_values, y_values, c=y_values, cmap=plt.cm.Blues, s=10)

# Set chart title and label axes.
--snip--
```

We pass the list of y-values to c, and then tell pyplot which colormap to use using the cmap argument. This code colors the points with lower y-values light blue and colors the points with higher y-values dark blue. Figure 15-8 shows the resulting plot.

NOTE   *You can see all the colormaps available in* pyplot *at* https://matplotlib.org/; *go to* ***Examples***, *scroll down to* ***Color***, *and click* ***Colormap reference***.

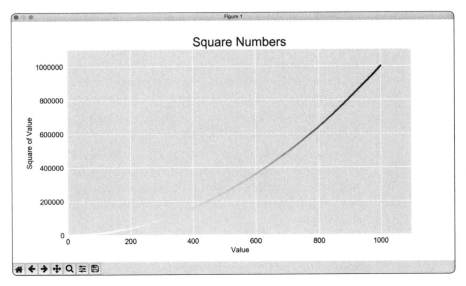

Figure 15-8: A plot using the Blues colormap

Saving Your Plots Automatically

If you want your program to automatically save the plot to a file, you can replace the call to plt.show() with a call to plt.savefig():

```
plt.savefig('squares_plot.png', bbox_inches='tight')
```

The first argument is a filename for the plot image, which will be saved in the same directory as *scatter_squares.py*. The second argument trims extra whitespace from the plot. If you want the extra whitespace around the plot, just omit this argument.

TRY IT YOURSELF

15-1. Cubes: A number raised to the third power is a *cube*. Plot the first five cubic numbers, and then plot the first 5000 cubic numbers.

15-2. Colored Cubes: Apply a colormap to your cubes plot.

Random Walks

In this section, we'll use Python to generate data for a random walk, and then use Matplotlib to create a visually appealing representation of that data. A *random walk* is a path that has no clear direction but is determined by a series of random decisions, each of which is left entirely to chance. You might imagine a random walk as the path a confused ant would take if it took every step in a random direction.

Random walks have practical applications in nature, physics, biology, chemistry, and economics. For example, a pollen grain floating on a drop of water moves across the surface of the water because it's constantly pushed around by water molecules. Molecular motion in a water drop is random, so the path a pollen grain traces on the surface is a random walk. The code we'll write next models many real-world situations.

Creating the RandomWalk() Class

To create a random walk, we'll create a RandomWalk class, which will make random decisions about which direction the walk should take. The class needs three attributes: one variable to store the number of points in the walk and two lists to store the x- and y-coordinate values of each point in the walk.

We'll only need two methods for the RandomWalk class: the __init__() method and fill_walk(), which will calculate the points in the walk. Let's start with __init__() as shown here:

random_walk.py ❶
```
from random import choice

class RandomWalk:
    """A class to generate random walks."""
```

❷
```
    def __init__(self, num_points=5000):
        """Initialize attributes of a walk."""
        self.num_points = num_points
```

❸
```
        # All walks start at (0, 0).
        self.x_values = [0]
        self.y_values = [0]
```

To make random decisions, we'll store possible moves in a list and use the choice() function, from the random module, to decide which move to make each time a step is taken ❶. We then set the default number of points in a walk to 5000, which is large enough to generate some interesting patterns but small enough to generate walks quickly ❷. Then at ❸ we make two lists to hold the x- and y-values, and we start each walk at the point (0, 0).

Choosing Directions

We'll use the fill_walk() method, as shown here, to fill our walk with points and determine the direction of each step. Add this method to *random_walk.py*:

random_walk.py
```
    def fill_walk(self):
        """Calculate all the points in the walk."""
```

❶
```
        # Keep taking steps until the walk reaches the desired length.
        while len(self.x_values) < self.num_points:
```

❷
```
            # Decide which direction to go and how far to go in that direction.
            x_direction = choice([1, -1])
```

```
    ❸   x_distance = choice([0, 1, 2, 3, 4])
        x_step = x_direction * x_distance

        y_direction = choice([1, -1])
        y_distance = choice([0, 1, 2, 3, 4])
    ❹   y_step = y_direction * y_distance

        # Reject moves that go nowhere.
    ❺   if x_step == 0 and y_step == 0:
            continue

        # Calculate the new position.
    ❻   x = self.x_values[-1] + x_step
        y = self.y_values[-1] + y_step

        self.x_values.append(x)
        self.y_values.append(y)
```

At ❶ we set up a loop that runs until the walk is filled with the correct number of points. The main part of the fill_walk() method tells Python how to simulate four random decisions: will the walk go right or left? How far will it go in that direction? Will it go up or down? How far will it go in that direction?

We use choice([1, -1]) to choose a value for x_direction, which returns either 1 for right movement or –1 for left ❷. Next, choice([0, 1, 2, 3, 4]) tells Python how far to move in that direction (x_distance) by randomly selecting an integer between 0 and 4. (The inclusion of a 0 allows us to take steps along the y-axis as well as steps that have movement along both axes.)

At ❸ and ❹ we determine the length of each step in the *x* and *y* directions by multiplying the direction of movement by the distance chosen. A positive result for x_step means move right, a negative result means move left, and 0 means move vertically. A positive result for y_step means move up, negative means move down, and 0 means move horizontally. If the value of both x_step and y_step are 0, the walk doesn't go anywhere, so we continue the loop to ignore this move ❺.

To get the next x-value for the walk, we add the value in x_step to the last value stored in x_values ❻ and do the same for the y-values. When we have these values, we append them to x_values and y_values.

Plotting the Random Walk

Here's the code to plot all the points in the walk:

rw_visual.py
```
import matplotlib.pyplot as plt

from random_walk import RandomWalk

# Make a random walk.
❶ rw = RandomWalk()
rw.fill_walk()
```

```
# Plot the points in the walk.
plt.style.use('classic')
fig, ax = plt.subplots()
❷ ax.scatter(rw.x_values, rw.y_values, s=15)
plt.show()
```

We begin by importing pyplot and RandomWalk. We then create a random walk and store it in rw ❶, making sure to call fill_walk(). At ❷ we feed the walk's x- and y-values to scatter() and choose an appropriate dot size. Figure 15-9 shows the resulting plot with 5000 points. (The images in this section omit Matplotlib's viewer, but you'll continue to see it when you run *rw_visual.py*.)

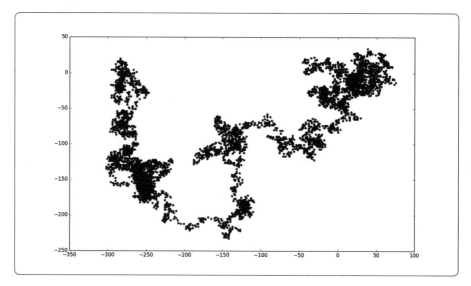

Figure 15-9: A random walk with 5000 points

Generating Multiple Random Walks

Every random walk is different, and it's fun to explore the various patterns that can be generated. One way to use the preceding code to make multiple walks without having to run the program several times is to wrap it in a while loop, like this:

rw_visual.py
```
import matplotlib.pyplot as plt

from random_walk import RandomWalk

# Keep making new walks, as long as the program is active.
while True:
    # Make a random walk.
    rw = RandomWalk()
    rw.fill_walk()

    # Plot the points in the walk.
    plt.style.use('classic')
```

```
fig, ax = plt.subplots()
ax.scatter(rw.x_values, rw.y_values, s=15)
plt.show()

keep_running = input("Make another walk? (y/n): ")
if keep_running == 'n':
    break
```

This code generates a random walk, displays it in Matplotlib's viewer, and pauses with the viewer open. When you close the viewer, you'll be asked whether you want to generate another walk. Press **y** to generate walks that stay near the starting point, that wander off mostly in one direction, that have thin sections connecting larger groups of points, and so on. When you want to end the program, press **n**.

Styling the Walk

In this section, we'll customize our plots to emphasize the important characteristics of each walk and deemphasize distracting elements. To do so, we identify the characteristics we want to emphasize, such as where the walk began, where it ended, and the path taken. Next, we identify the characteristics to deemphasize, such as tick marks and labels. The result should be a simple visual representation that clearly communicates the path taken in each random walk.

Coloring the Points

We'll use a colormap to show the order of the points in the walk, and then remove the black outline from each dot so the color of the dots will be clearer. To color the points according to their position in the walk, we pass the c argument a list containing the position of each point. Because the points are plotted in order, the list just contains the numbers from 0 to 4999, as shown here:

rw_visual.py
```
--snip--
while True:
    # Make a random walk.
    rw = RandomWalk()
    rw.fill_walk()

    # Plot the points in the walk.
    plt.style.use('classic')
    fig, ax = plt.subplots()
❶   point_numbers = range(rw.num_points)
    ax.scatter(rw.x_values, rw.y_values, c=point_numbers, cmap=plt.cm.Blues,
        edgecolors='none', s=15)
    plt.show()

    keep_running = input("Make another walk? (y/n): ")
    --snip--
```

At ❶ we use range() to generate a list of numbers equal to the number of points in the walk. Then we store them in the list point_numbers, which we'll use to set the color of each point in the walk. We pass point_numbers to the c argument, use the Blues colormap, and then pass edgecolors='none' to get rid of the black outline around each point. The result is a plot of the walk that varies from light to dark blue along a gradient, as shown in Figure 15-10.

Figure 15-10: A random walk colored with the Blues colormap

Plotting the Starting and Ending Points

In addition to coloring points to show their position along the walk, it would be useful to see where each walk begins and ends. To do so, we can plot the first and last points individually after the main series has been plotted. We'll make the end points larger and color them differently to make them stand out, as shown here:

rw_visual.py
```
--snip--
while True:
    --snip--
    ax.scatter(rw.x_values, rw.y_values, c=point_numbers, cmap=plt.cm.Blues,
        edgecolors='none', s=15)

    # Emphasize the first and last points.
    ax.scatter(0, 0, c='green', edgecolors='none', s=100)
    ax.scatter(rw.x_values[-1], rw.y_values[-1], c='red', edgecolors='none',
        s=100)

    plt.show()
    --snip--
```

To show the starting point, we plot point (0, 0) in green in a larger size
(s=100) than the rest of the points. To mark the end point, we plot the last
x- and y-value in the walk in red with a size of 100. Make sure you insert this
code just before the call to plt.show() so the starting and ending points are
drawn on top of all the other points.

When you run this code, you should be able to spot exactly where each
walk begins and ends. (If these end points don't stand out clearly, adjust
their color and size until they do.)

Cleaning Up the Axes

Let's remove the axes in this plot so they don't distract from the path of
each walk. To turn off the axes, use this code:

rw_visual.py

```
--snip--
while True:
    --snip--
    ax.scatter(rw.x_values[-1], rw.y_values[-1], c='red', edgecolors='none',
        s=100)

    # Remove the axes.
❶   ax.get_xaxis().set_visible(False)
    ax.get_yaxis().set_visible(False)

    plt.show()
    --snip--
```

To modify the axes, we use the ax.get_xaxis() and ax.get_yaxis() methods ❶ to set the visibility of each axis to False. As you continue to work with
visualizations, you'll frequently see this chaining of methods.

Run *rw_visual.py* now; you should see a series of plots with no axes.

Adding Plot Points

Let's increase the number of points to give us more data to work with.
To do so, we increase the value of num_points when we make a RandomWalk
instance and adjust the size of each dot when drawing the plot, as shown
here:

rw_visual.py

```
--snip--
while True:
    # Make a random walk.
    rw = RandomWalk(50_000)
    rw.fill_walk()

    # Plot the points in the walk.
    plt.style.use('classic')
    fig, ax = plt.subplots()
    point_numbers = range(rw.num_points)
    ax.scatter(rw.x_values, rw.y_values, c=point_numbers, cmap=plt.cm.Blues,
        edgecolor='none', s=1)
    --snip--
```

This example creates a random walk with 50,000 points (to mirror real-world data) and plots each point at size s=1. The resulting walk is wispy and cloud-like, as shown in Figure 15-11. As you can see, we've created a piece of art from a simple scatter plot!

Experiment with this code to see how much you can increase the number of points in a walk before your system starts to slow down significantly or the plot loses its visual appeal.

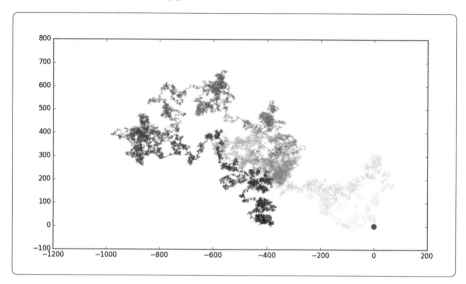

Figure 15-11: A walk with 50,000 points

Altering the Size to Fill the Screen

A visualization is much more effective at communicating patterns in data if it fits nicely on the screen. To make the plotting window better fit your screen, adjust the size of Matplotlib's output, like this:

rw_visual.py

```
--snip--
while True:
    # Make a random walk.
    rw = RandomWalk(50_000)
    rw.fill_walk()

    # Plot the points in the walk.
    plt.style.use('classic')
    fig, ax = plt.subplots(figsize=(15, 9))
    --snip--
```

When creating the plot, you can pass a figsize argument to set the size of the figure. The figsize parameter takes a tuple, which tells Matplotlib the dimensions of the plotting window in inches.

Matplotlib assumes that your screen resolution is 100 pixels per inch; if this code doesn't give you an accurate plot size, adjust the numbers as necessary. Or, if you know your system's resolution, pass `plt.subplots()` the resolution using the `dpi` parameter to set a plot size that makes effective use of the space available on your screen, as shown here:

```
fig, ax = plt.subplots(figsize=(10, 6), dpi=128)
```

TRY IT YOURSELF

15-3. Molecular Motion: Modify *rw_visual.py* by replacing `ax.scatter()` with `ax.plot()`. To simulate the path of a pollen grain on the surface of a drop of water, pass in the `rw.x_values` and `rw.y_values`, and include a `linewidth` argument. Use 5000 instead of 50,000 points.

15-4. Modified Random Walks: In the `RandomWalk` class, `x_step` and `y_step` are generated from the same set of conditions. The direction is chosen randomly from the list `[1, -1]` and the distance from the list `[0, 1, 2, 3, 4]`. Modify the values in these lists to see what happens to the overall shape of your walks. Try a longer list of choices for the distance, such as 0 through 8, or remove the −1 from the *x* or *y* direction list.

15-5. Refactoring: The `fill_walk()` method is lengthy. Create a new method called `get_step()` to determine the direction and distance for each step, and then calculate the step. You should end up with two calls to `get_step()` in `fill_walk()`:

```
x_step = self.get_step()
y_step = self.get_step()
```

This refactoring should reduce the size of `fill_walk()` and make the method easier to read and understand.

Rolling Dice with Plotly

In this section, we'll use the Python package Plotly to produce interactive visualizations. Plotly is particularly useful when you're creating visualizations that will be displayed in a browser, because the visualizations will scale automatically to fit the viewer's screen. Visualizations that Plotly generates are also interactive; when the user hovers over certain elements on the screen, information about that element is highlighted.

In this project, we'll analyze the results of rolling dice. When you roll one regular, six-sided die, you have an equal chance of rolling any of the numbers from 1 through 6. However, when you use two dice, you're more likely to roll certain numbers rather than others. We'll try to determine which numbers are most likely to occur by generating a data set that represents rolling dice. Then we'll plot the results of a large number of rolls to determine which results are more likely than others.

The study of rolling dice is often used in mathematics to explain various types of data analysis. But it also has real-world applications in casinos and other gambling scenarios, as well as in the way games like Monopoly and many role-playing games are played.

Installing Plotly

Install Plotly using pip, just as you did for Matplotlib:

```
$ python -m pip install --user plotly
```

If you used **python3** or something else when installing Matplotlib, make sure you use the same command here.

To see what kind of visualizations are possible with Plotly, visit the gallery of chart types at *https://plot.ly/python/*. Each example includes source code, so you can see how Plotly generates the visualizations.

Creating the Die Class

We'll create the following Die class to simulate the roll of one die:

die.py
```
from random import randint

class Die:
    """A class representing a single die."""

❶    def __init__(self, num_sides=6):
        """Assume a six-sided die."""
        self.num_sides = num_sides

    def roll(self):
        """Return a random value between 1 and number of sides."""
❷        return randint(1, self.num_sides)
```

The __init__() method takes one optional argument. With the Die class, when an instance of our die is created, the number of sides will always be six if no argument is included. If an argument *is* included, that value will set the number of sides on the die ❶. (Dice are named for their number of sides: a six-sided die is a D6, an eight-sided die is a D8, and so on.)

The roll() method uses the randint() function to return a random number between 1 and the number of sides ❷. This function can return the starting value (1), the ending value (num_sides), or any integer between the two.

Rolling the Die

Before creating a visualization based on the Die class, let's roll a D6, print the results, and check that the results look reasonable:

die_visual.py

```
from die import Die

# Create a D6.
❶ die = Die()

# Make some rolls, and store results in a list.
results = []
❷ for roll_num in range(100):
      result = die.roll()
      results.append(result)

print(results)
```

At ❶ we create an instance of Die with the default six sides. At ❷ we roll the die 100 times and store the results of each roll in the list results. Here's a sample set of results:

```
[4, 6, 5, 6, 1, 5, 6, 3, 5, 3, 5, 3, 2, 2, 1, 3, 1, 5, 3, 6, 3, 6, 5, 4,
 1, 1, 4, 2, 3, 6, 4, 2, 6, 4, 1, 3, 2, 5, 6, 3, 6, 2, 1, 1, 3, 4, 1, 4,
 3, 5, 1, 4, 5, 5, 2, 3, 3, 1, 2, 3, 5, 6, 2, 5, 6, 1, 3, 2, 1, 1, 1, 6,
 5, 5, 2, 2, 6, 4, 1, 4, 5, 1, 1, 1, 4, 5, 3, 3, 1, 3, 5, 4, 5, 6, 5, 4,
 1, 5, 1, 2]
```

A quick scan of these results shows that the Die class seems to be working. We see the values 1 and 6, so we know the smallest and largest possible values are being returned, and because we don't see 0 or 7, we know all the results are in the appropriate range. We also see each number from 1 through 6, which indicates that all possible outcomes are represented. Let's determine exactly how many times each number appears.

Analyzing the Results

We'll analyze the results of rolling one D6 by counting how many times we roll each number:

die_visual.py

```
--snip--
# Make some rolls, and store results in a list.
results = []
❶ for roll_num in range(1000):
      result = die.roll()
      results.append(result)

# Analyze the results.
frequencies = []
❷ for value in range(1, die.num_sides+1):
❸     frequency = results.count(value)
```

❹   `frequencies.append(frequency)`

```
print(frequencies)
```

Because we're no longer printing the results, we can increase the number of simulated rolls to 1000 ❶. To analyze the rolls, we create the empty list frequencies to store the number of times each value is rolled. We loop through the possible values (1 through 6 in this case) at ❷, count how many times each number appears in results ❸, and then append this value to the frequencies list ❹. We then print this list before making a visualization:

```
[155, 167, 168, 170, 159, 181]
```

These results look reasonable: we see six frequencies, one for each possible number when you roll a D6, and we see that no frequency is significantly higher than any other. Now let's visualize these results.

Making a Histogram

With a list of frequencies, we can make a *histogram* of the results. A histogram is a bar chart showing how often certain results occur. Here's the code to create the histogram:

die_visual.py
```
from plotly.graph_objs import Bar, Layout
from plotly import offline

from die import Die
--snip--

# Analyze the results.
frequencies = []
for value in range(1, die.num_sides+1):
    frequency = results.count(value)
    frequencies.append(frequency)

# Visualize the results.
```
❶ `x_values = list(range(1, die.num_sides+1))`
❷ `data = [Bar(x=x_values, y=frequencies)]`

❸ `x_axis_config = {'title': 'Result'}`
  `y_axis_config = {'title': 'Frequency of Result'}`
❹ `my_layout = Layout(title='Results of rolling one D6 1000 times',`
  `        xaxis=x_axis_config, yaxis=y_axis_config)`
❺ `offline.plot({'data': data, 'layout': my_layout}, filename='d6.html')`

To make a histogram, we need a bar for each of the possible results. We store these in a list called x_values, which starts at 1 and ends at the number of sides on the die ❶. Plotly doesn't accept the results of the range() function directly, so we need to convert the range to a list explicitly using the list() function. The Plotly class Bar() represents a data set that will be formatted as a bar chart ❷. This class needs a list of x-values, and a list of y-values. The class must be wrapped in square brackets, because a data set can have multiple elements.

Each axis can be configured in a number of ways, and each configuration option is stored as an entry in a dictionary. At this point, we're just setting the title of each axis ❸. The Layout() class returns an object that specifies the layout and configuration of the graph as a whole ❹. Here we set the title of the graph and pass the x- and y-axis configuration dictionaries as well.

To generate the plot, we call the offline.plot() function ❺. This function needs a dictionary containing the data and layout objects, and it also accepts a name for the file where the graph will be saved. We store the output in a file called *d6.html*.

When you run the program *die_visual.py*, a browser will probably open showing the file *d6.html*. If this doesn't happen automatically, open a new tab in any web browser, and then open the file *d6.html* (in the folder where you saved *die_visual.py*). You should see a chart that looks like the one in Figure 15-12. (I've modified this chart slightly for printing; by default, Plotly generates charts with smaller text than what you see here.)

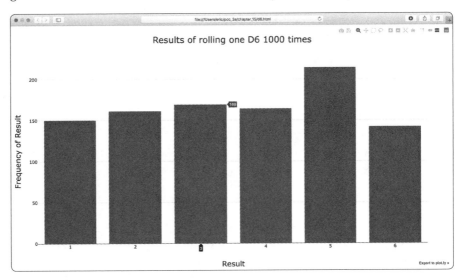

Figure 15-12: A simple bar chart created with Plotly

Notice that Plotly has made the chart interactive: hover your cursor over any bar in the chart, and you'll see the associated data. This feature is particularly useful when you're plotting multiple data sets on the same chart. Also notice the icons in the upper right, which allow you to pan and zoom the visualization, and save your visualization as an image.

Rolling Two Dice

Rolling two dice results in larger numbers and a different distribution of results. Let's modify our code to create two D6 dice to simulate the way we roll a pair of dice. Each time we roll the pair, we'll add the two numbers (one from each die) and store the sum in results. Save a copy of *die_visual.py* as *dice_visual.py*, and make the following changes:

dice_visual.py

```
from plotly.graph_objs import Bar, Layout
from plotly import offline

from die import Die

# Create two D6 dice.
die_1 = Die()
die_2 = Die()

# Make some rolls, and store results in a list.
results = []
for roll_num in range(1000):
❶    result = die_1.roll() + die_2.roll()
     results.append(result)

# Analyze the results.
frequencies = []
❷ max_result = die_1.num_sides + die_2.num_sides
❸ for value in range(2, max_result+1):
     frequency = results.count(value)
     frequencies.append(frequency)

# Visualize the results.
x_values = list(range(2, max_result+1))
data = [Bar(x=x_values, y=frequencies)]

❹ x_axis_config = {'title': 'Result', 'dtick': 1}
y_axis_config = {'title': 'Frequency of Result'}
my_layout = Layout(title='Results of rolling two D6 dice 1000 times',
        xaxis=x_axis_config, yaxis=y_axis_config)
offline.plot({'data': data, 'layout': my_layout}, filename='d6_d6.html')
```

After creating two instances of Die, we roll the dice and calculate the sum of the two dice for each roll ❶. The largest possible result (12) is the sum of the largest number on both dice, which we store in max_result ❷. The smallest possible result (2) is the sum of the smallest number on both dice. When we analyze the results, we count the number of results for each value between 2 and max_result ❸. (We could have used range(2, 13), but this would work only for two D6 dice. When modeling real-world situations, it's best to write code that can easily model a variety of situations. This code allows us to simulate rolling a pair of dice with any number of sides.)

When creating the chart, we include the dtick key in the x_axis_config dictionary ❹. This setting controls the spacing between tick marks on the x-axis. Now that we have more bars on the histogram, Plotly's default settings will only label some of the bars. The `'dtick': 1` setting tells Plotly to label every tick mark. We also update the title of the chart and change the output filename as well.

After running this code, you should see a chart that looks like the one in Figure 15-13.

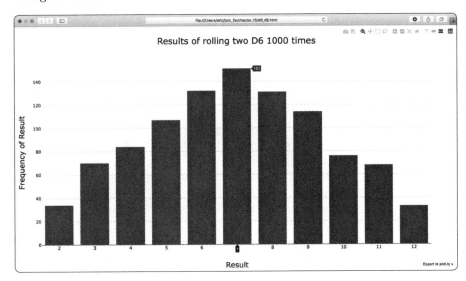

Figure 15-13: Simulated results of rolling two six-sided dice 1000 times

This graph shows the approximate results you're likely to get when you roll a pair of D6 dice. As you can see, you're least likely to roll a 2 or a 12 and most likely to roll a 7. This happens because there are six ways to roll a 7, namely: 1 and 6, 2 and 5, 3 and 4, 4 and 3, 5 and 2, or 6 and 1.

Rolling Dice of Different Sizes

Let's create a six-sided die and a ten-sided die, and see what happens when we roll them 50,000 times:

dice_visual.py

```
from plotly.graph_objs import Bar, Layout
from plotly import offline

from die import Die

# Create a D6 and a D10.
die_1 = Die()
➊ die_2 = Die(10)

# Make some rolls, and store results in a list.
results = []
for roll_num in range(50_000):
    result = die_1.roll() + die_2.roll()
    results.append(result)
```

```
# Analyze the results.
--snip--

# Visualize the results.
x_values = list(range(2, max_result+1))
data = [Bar(x=x_values, y=frequencies)]

x_axis_config = {'title': 'Result', 'dtick': 1}
y_axis_config = {'title': 'Frequency of Result'}
```
❷ `my_layout = Layout(title='Results of rolling a D6 and a D10 50000 times',`
```
        xaxis=x_axis_config, yaxis=y_axis_config)
offline.plot({'data': data, 'layout': my_layout}, filename='d6_d10.html')
```

To make a D10, we pass the argument 10 when creating the second Die instance ❶ and change the first loop to simulate 50,000 rolls instead of 1000. We change the title of the graph and update the output filename as well ❷.

Figure 15-14 shows the resulting chart. Instead of one most likely result, there are five. This happens because there's still only one way to roll the smallest value (1 and 1) and the largest value (6 and 10), but the smaller die limits the number of ways you can generate the middle numbers: there are six ways to roll a 7, 8, 9, 10, and 11. Therefore, these are the most common results, and you're equally likely to roll any one of these numbers.

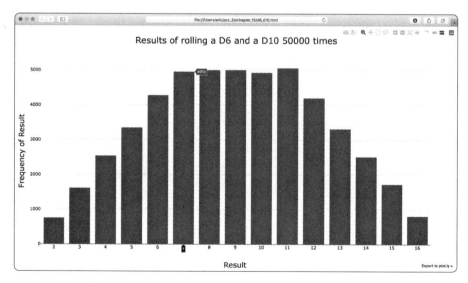

Figure 15-14: The results of rolling a six-sided die and a ten-sided die 50,000 times

Our ability to use Plotly to model the rolling of dice gives us considerable freedom in exploring this phenomenon. In just minutes you can simulate a tremendous number of rolls using a large variety of dice.

15-6. Two D8s: Create a simulation showing what happens when you roll two eight-sided dice 1000 times. Try to picture what you think the visualization will look like before you run the simulation; then see if your intuition was correct. Gradually increase the number of rolls until you start to see the limits of your system's capabilities.

15-7. Three Dice: When you roll three D6 dice, the smallest number you can roll is 3 and the largest number is 18. Create a visualization that shows what happens when you roll three D6 dice.

15-8. Multiplication: When you roll two dice, you usually add the two numbers together to get the result. Create a visualization that shows what happens if you multiply these numbers instead.

15-9. Die Comprehensions: For clarity, the listings in this section use the long form of for loops. If you're comfortable using list comprehensions, try writing a comprehension for one or both of the loops in each of these programs.

15-10. Practicing with Both Libraries: Try using Matplotlib to make a die-rolling visualization, and use Plotly to make the visualization for a random walk. (You'll need to consult the documentation for each library to complete this exercise.)

Summary

In this chapter, you learned to generate data sets and create visualizations of that data. You created simple plots with Matplotlib and used a scatter plot to explore random walks. You also created a histogram with Plotly and used a histogram to explore the results of rolling dice of different sizes.

Generating your own data sets with code is an interesting and powerful way to model and explore a wide variety of real-world situations. As you continue to work through the data visualization projects that follow, keep an eye out for situations you might be able to model with code. Look at the visualizations you see in news media, and see if you can identify those that were generated using methods similar to the ones you're learning in these projects.

In Chapter 16, you'll download data from online sources and continue to use Matplotlib and Plotly to explore that data.

16

DOWNLOADING DATA

In this chapter, you'll download data sets from online sources and create working visualizations of that data. You can find an incredible variety of data online, much of which hasn't been examined thoroughly. The ability to analyze this data allows you to discover patterns and connections that no one else has found.

We'll access and visualize data stored in two common data formats, CSV and JSON. We'll use Python's csv module to process weather data stored in the CSV (comma-separated values) format and analyze high and low temperatures over time in two different locations. We'll then use Matplotlib to generate a chart based on our downloaded data to display variations in temperature in two dissimilar environments: Sitka, Alaska, and Death Valley, California. Later in the chapter, we'll use the json module to access earthquake data stored in the JSON format and use Plotly to draw a world map showing the locations and magnitudes of recent earthquakes.

By the end of this chapter, you'll be prepared to work with different types and data set formats, and you'll have a deeper understanding of how to build complex visualizations. Being able to access and visualize online data of different types and formats is essential to working with a wide variety of real-world data sets.

The CSV File Format

One simple way to store data in a text file is to write the data as a series of values separated by commas, which is called *comma-separated values.* The resulting files are called *CSV* files. For example, here's a chunk of weather data in CSV format:

```
"USW00025333","SITKA AIRPORT, AK US","2018-01-01","0.45",,"48","38"
```

This is an excerpt of some weather data from January 1, 2018 in Sitka, Alaska. It includes the day's high and low temperatures, as well as a number of other measurements from that day. CSV files can be tricky for humans to read, but they're easy for programs to process and extract values from, which speeds up the data analysis process.

We'll begin with a small set of CSV-formatted weather data recorded in Sitka, which is available in the book's resources at *https://nostarch.com /pythoncrashcourse2e/.* Make a folder called *data* inside the folder where you're saving this chapter's programs. Copy the file *sitka_weather_07-2018 _simple.csv* into this new folder. (After you download the book's resources, you'll have all the files you need for this project.)

NOTE *The weather data in this project was originally downloaded from* https://ncdc .noaa.gov/cdo-web/.

Parsing the CSV File Headers

Python's csv module in the standard library parses the lines in a CSV file and allows us to quickly extract the values we're interested in. Let's start by examining the first line of the file, which contains a series of headers for the data. These headers tell us what kind of information the data holds:

sitka_highs.py
```
import csv

filename = 'data/sitka_weather_07-2018_simple.csv'
❶ with open(filename) as f:
❷     reader = csv.reader(f)
❸     header_row = next(reader)
       print(header_row)
```

After importing the csv module, we assign the name of the file we're working with to filename. We then open the file and assign the resulting file object to f ❶. Next, we call `csv.reader()` and pass it the file object as an argument to create a reader object associated with that file ❷. We assign the reader object to `reader`.

The `csv` module contains a `next()` function, which returns the next line in the file when passed the reader object. In the preceding listing, we call `next()` only once so we get the first line of the file, which contains the file headers ❸. We store the data that's returned in `header_row`. As you can see, `header_row` contains meaningful, weather-related headers that tell us what information each line of data holds:

```
['STATION', 'NAME', 'DATE', 'PRCP', 'TAVG', 'TMAX', 'TMIN']
```

The reader object processes the first line of comma-separated values in the file and stores each as an item in a list. The header `STATION` represents the code for the weather station that recorded this data. The position of this header tells us that the first value in each line will be the weather station code. The `NAME` header indicates that the second value in each line is the name of the weather station that made the recording. The rest of the headers specify what kinds of information were recorded in each reading. The data we're most interested in for now are the date, the high temperature (`TMAX`), and the low temperature (`TMIN`). This is a simple data set that contains only precipitation and temperature-related data. When you download your own weather data, you can choose to include a number of other measurements relating to wind speed, direction, and more detailed precipitation data.

Printing the Headers and Their Positions

To make it easier to understand the file header data, we print each header and its position in the list:

sitka_highs.py

```
--snip--
with open(filename) as f:
    reader = csv.reader(f)
    header_row = next(reader)

❶   for index, column_header in enumerate(header_row):
        print(index, column_header)
```

The `enumerate()` function returns both the index of each item and the value of each item as you loop through a list ❶. (Note that we've removed the line `print(header_row)` in favor of this more detailed version.)

Here's the output showing the index of each header:

```
0 STATION
1 NAME
2 DATE
3 PRCP
4 TAVG
5 TMAX
6 TMIN
```

Here we see that the dates and their high temperatures are stored in columns 2 and 5. To explore this data, we'll process each row of data in *sitka_weather_07-2018_simple.csv* and extract the values with the indexes 2 and 5.

Extracting and Reading Data

Now that we know which columns of data we need, let's read in some of that data. First, we'll read in the high temperature for each day:

sitka_highs.py
```
--snip--
with open(filename) as f:
    reader = csv.reader(f)
    header_row = next(reader)

    # Get high temperatures from this file.
❶   highs = []
❷   for row in reader:
❸       high = int(row[5])
        highs.append(high)

print(highs)
```

We make an empty list called highs ❶ and then loop through the remaining rows in the file ❷. The reader object continues from where it left off in the CSV file and automatically returns each line following its current position. Because we've already read the header row, the loop will begin at the second line where the actual data begins. On each pass through the loop, we pull the data from index 5, which corresponds to the header TMAX, and assign it to the variable high ❸. We use the int() function to convert the data, which is stored as a string, to a numerical format so we can use it. We then append this value to highs.

The following listing shows the data now stored in highs:

```
[62, 58, 70, 70, 67, 59, 58, 62, 66, 59, 56, 63, 65, 58, 56, 59, 64, 60, 60,
 61, 65, 65, 63, 59, 64, 65, 68, 66, 64, 67, 65]
```

We've extracted the high temperature for each date and stored each value in a list. Now let's create a visualization of this data.

Plotting Data in a Temperature Chart

To visualize the temperature data we have, we'll first create a simple plot of the daily highs using Matplotlib, as shown here:

sitka_highs.py
```
import csv

import matplotlib.pyplot as plt

filename = 'data/sitka_weather_07-2018_simple.csv'
with open(filename) as f:
    --snip--
```

```
# Plot the high temperatures.
plt.style.use('seaborn')
fig, ax = plt.subplots()
❶ ax.plot(highs, c='red')

# Format plot.
❷ ax.set_title("Daily high temperatures, July 2018", fontsize=24)
❸ ax.set_xlabel('', fontsize=16)
ax.set_ylabel("Temperature (F)", fontsize=16)
ax.tick_params(axis='both', which='major', labelsize=16)

plt.show()
```

We pass the list of highs to plot() and pass c='red' to plot the points in red ❶. (We'll plot the highs in red and the lows in blue.) We then specify a few other formatting details, such as the title, font size, and labels ❷, which you should recognize from Chapter 15. Because we have yet to add the dates, we won't label the x-axis, but ax.set_xlabel() does modify the font size to make the default labels more readable ❸. Figure 16-1 shows the resulting plot: a simple line graph of the high temperatures for July 2018 in Sitka, Alaska.

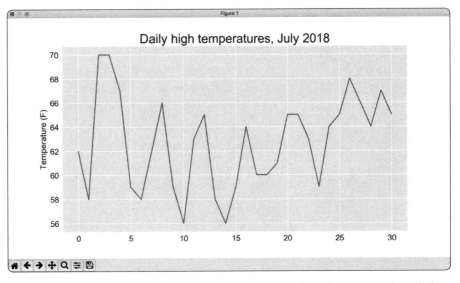

Figure 16-1: A line graph showing daily high temperatures for July 2018 in Sitka, Alaska

The datetime Module

Let's add dates to our graph to make it more useful. The first date from the weather data file is in the second row of the file:

```
"USW00025333","SITKA AIRPORT, AK US","2018-07-01","0.25",,"62","50"
```

The data will be read in as a string, so we need a way to convert the string "2018-07-01" to an object representing this date. We can construct an object representing July 1, 2018 using the `strptime()` method from the datetime module. Let's see how `strptime()` works in a terminal session:

```
>>> from datetime import datetime
>>> first_date = datetime.strptime('2018-07-01', '%Y-%m-%d')
>>> print(first_date)
2018-07-01 00:00:00
```

We first import the `datetime` class from the `datetime` module. Then we call the method `strptime()` using the string containing the date we want to work with as its first argument. The second argument tells Python how the date is formatted. In this example, Python interprets '%Y-' to mean the part of the string before the first dash is a four-digit year; '%m-' means the part of the string before the second dash is a number representing the month; and '%d' means the last part of the string is the day of the month, from 1 to 31.

The `strptime()` method can take a variety of arguments to determine how to interpret the date. Table 16-1 shows some of these arguments.

Table 16-1: Date and Time Formatting Arguments from the datetime Module

Argument	Meaning
%A	Weekday name, such as *Monday*
%B	Month name, such as *January*
%m	Month, as a number (01 to 12)
%d	Day of the month, as a number (01 to 31)
%Y	Four-digit year, such as 2019
%y	Two-digit year, such as 19
%H	Hour, in 24-hour format (00 to 23)
%I	Hour, in 12-hour format (01 to 12)
%p	AM or PM
%M	Minutes (00 to 59)
%S	Seconds (00 to 61)

Plotting Dates

Now we can improve our temperature data plot by extracting dates for the daily highs and passing those highs and dates to `plot()`, as shown here:

sitka_highs.py

```
import csv
from datetime import datetime

import matplotlib.pyplot as plt

filename = 'data/sitka_weather_07-2018_simple.csv'
```

```
with open(filename) as f:
    reader = csv.reader(f)
    header_row = next(reader)

    # Get dates and high temperatures from this file.
❶   dates, highs = [], []
    for row in reader:
❷       current_date = datetime.strptime(row[2], '%Y-%m-%d')
        high = int(row[5])
        dates.append(current_date)
        highs.append(high)

# Plot the high temperatures.
plt.style.use('seaborn')
fig, ax = plt.subplots()
❸ ax.plot(dates, highs, c='red')

# Format plot.
ax.set_title("Daily high temperatures, July 2018", fontsize=24)
ax.set_xlabel('', fontsize=16)
❹ fig.autofmt_xdate()
ax.set_ylabel("Temperature (F)", fontsize=16)
ax.tick_params(axis='both', which='major', labelsize=16)

plt.show()
```

We create two empty lists to store the dates and high temperatures from the file ❶. We then convert the data containing the date information (row[2]) to a datetime object ❷ and append it to dates. We pass the dates and the high temperature values to plot() ❸. The call to fig.autofmt_xdate() ❹ draws the date labels diagonally to prevent them from overlapping. Figure 16-2 shows the improved graph.

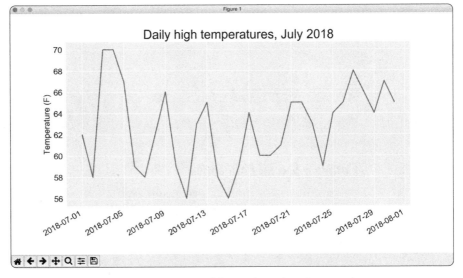

Figure 16-2: The graph is more meaningful now that it has dates on the x-axis.

Plotting a Longer Timeframe

With our graph set up, let's add more data to get a more complete picture of the weather in Sitka. Copy the file *sitka_weather_2018_simple.csv*, which contains a full year's worth of weather data for Sitka, to the folder where you're storing the data for this chapter's programs.

Now we can generate a graph for the entire year's weather:

sitka_highs.py

```
--snip--
❶ filename = 'data/sitka_weather_2018_simple.csv'
with open(filename) as f:
--snip--
# Format plot.
❷ ax.set_title("Daily high temperatures - 2018", fontsize=24)
ax.set_xlabel('', fontsize=16)
--snip--
```

We modify the filename to use the new data file *sitka_weather_2018_simple.csv* ❶, and we update the title of our plot to reflect the change in its content ❷. Figure 16-3 shows the resulting plot.

Figure 16-3: A year's worth of data

Plotting a Second Data Series

We can make our informative graph even more useful by including the low temperatures. We need to extract the low temperatures from the data file and then add them to our graph, as shown here:

sitka_highs _lows.py

```
--snip--
filename = 'sitka_weather_2018_simple.csv'
```

```
with open(filename) as f:
    reader = csv.reader(f)
    header_row = next(reader)

    # Get dates, and high and low temperatures from this file.
❶  dates, highs, lows = [], [], []
    for row in reader:
        current_date = datetime.strptime(row[2], '%Y-%m-%d')
        high = int(row[5])
❷      low = int(row[6])
        dates.append(current_date)
        highs.append(high)
        lows.append(low)

# Plot the high and low temperatures.
plt.style.use('seaborn')
fig, ax = plt.subplots()
ax.plot(dates, highs, c='red')
❸ ax.plot(dates, lows, c='blue')

# Format plot.
❹ ax.set_title("Daily high and low temperatures - 2018", fontsize=24)
--snip--
```

At ❶ we add the empty list lows to hold low temperatures, and then extract and store the low temperature for each date from the seventh position in each row (row[6]) ❷. At ❸ we add a call to plot() for the low temperatures and color these values blue. Finally, we update the title ❹. Figure 16-4 shows the resulting chart.

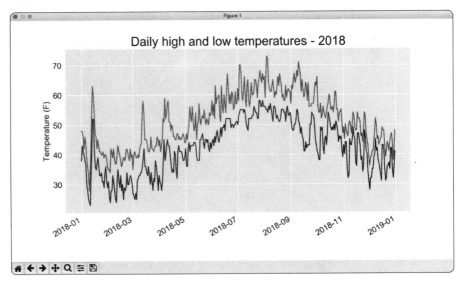

Figure 16-4: Two data series on the same plot

Shading an Area in the Chart

Having added two data series, we can now examine the range of temperatures for each day. Let's add a finishing touch to the graph by using shading to show the range between each day's high and low temperatures. To do so, we'll use the fill_between() method, which takes a series of x-values and two series of y-values, and fills the space between the two y-value series:

sitka_highs_lows.py

```
--snip--
# Plot the high and low temperatures.
plt.style.use('seaborn')
fig, ax = plt.subplots()
❶ ax.plot(dates, highs, c='red', alpha=0.5)
ax.plot(dates, lows, c='blue', alpha=0.5)
❷ ax.fill_between(dates, highs, lows, facecolor='blue', alpha=0.1)
--snip--
```

The alpha argument at ❶ controls a color's transparency. An alpha value of 0 is completely transparent, and 1 (the default) is completely opaque. By setting alpha to 0.5, we make the red and blue plot lines appear lighter.

At ❷ we pass fill_between() the list dates for the x-values and then the two y-value series highs and lows. The facecolor argument determines the color of the shaded region; we give it a low alpha value of 0.1 so the filled region connects the two data series without distracting from the information they represent. Figure 16-5 shows the plot with the shaded region between the highs and lows.

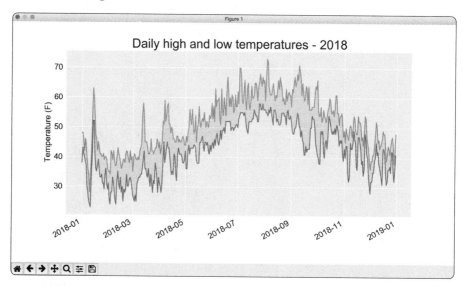

Figure 16-5: The region between the two data sets is shaded.

The shading helps make the range between the two data sets immediately apparent.

Error Checking

We should be able to run the *sitka_highs_lows.py* code using data for any location. But some weather stations collect different data than others, and some occasionally malfunction and fail to collect some of the data they're supposed to. Missing data can result in exceptions that crash our programs unless we handle them properly.

For example, let's see what happens when we attempt to generate a temperature plot for Death Valley, California. Copy the file *death_valley_2018 _simple.csv* to the folder where you're storing the data for this chapter's programs.

First, let's run the code to see the headers that are included in this data file:

death_valley
_highs_lows.py

```python
import csv

filename = 'data/death_valley_2018_simple.csv'
with open(filename) as f:
    reader = csv.reader(f)
    header_row = next(reader)

    for index, column_header in enumerate(header_row):
        print(index, column_header)
```

Here's the output:

```
0 STATION
1 NAME
2 DATE
3 PRCP
4 TMAX
5 TMIN
6 TOBS
```

The date is in the same position at index 2. But the high and low temperatures are at indexes 4 and 5, so we'd need to change the indexes in our code to reflect these new positions. Instead of including an average temperature reading for the day, this station includes TOBS, a reading for a specific observation time.

I removed one of the temperature readings from this file to show what happens when some data is missing from a file. Change *sitka_highs_lows.py* to generate a graph for Death Valley using the indexes we just noted, and see what happens:

death_valley
_highs_lows.py

```python
--snip--
filename = 'data/death_valley_2018_simple.csv'
with open(filename) as f:
    --snip--
    # Get dates, and high and low temperatures from this file.
    dates, highs, lows = [], [], []
    for row in reader:
        current_date = datetime.strptime(row[2], '%Y-%m-%d')
```

```
❶        high = int(row[4])
         low = int(row[5])
         dates.append(current_date)
--snip--
```

At ❶ we update the indexes to correspond to this file's `TMAX` and `TMIN` positions.

When we run the program, we get an error, as shown in the last line in the following output:

```
Traceback (most recent call last):
  File "death_valley_highs_lows.py", line 15, in <module>
    high = int(row[4])
ValueError: invalid literal for int() with base 10: ''
```

The traceback tells us that Python can't process the high temperature for one of the dates because it can't turn an empty string (`''`) into an integer. Rather than look through the data and finding out which reading is missing, we'll just handle cases of missing data directly.

We'll run error-checking code when the values are being read from the CSV file to handle exceptions that might arise. Here's how that works:

death_valley _highs_lows.py

```
--snip--
filename = 'data/death_valley_2018_simple.csv'
with open(filename) as f:
    --snip--
    for row in reader:
            current_date = datetime.strptime(row[2], '%Y-%m-%d')
❶          try:
                high = int(row[4])
                low = int(row[5])
            except ValueError:
❷              print(f"Missing data for {current_date}")
❸          else:
                dates.append(current_date)
                highs.append(high)
                lows.append(low)

# Plot the high and low temperatures.
--snip--

# Format plot.
❹ title = "Daily high and low temperatures - 2018\nDeath Valley, CA"
ax.set_title(title, fontsize=20)
ax.set_xlabel('', fontsize=16)
--snip--
```

Each time we examine a row, we try to extract the date and the high and low temperature ❶. If any data is missing, Python will raise a `ValueError` and we handle it by printing an error message that includes the date of the missing data ❷. After printing the error, the loop will continue processing the next row. If all data for a date is retrieved without error, the else block will run and the data will be appended to the appropriate lists ❸. Because we're plotting information for a new location, we update the title to include the location on the plot, and we use a smaller font size to accommodate the longer title ❹.

When you run *death_valley_highs_lows.py* now, you'll see that only one date had missing data:

```
Missing data for 2018-02-18 00:00:00
```

Because the error is handled appropriately, our code is able to generate a plot, which skips over the missing data. Figure 16-6 shows the resulting plot.

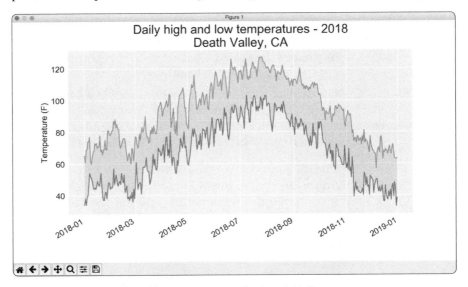

Figure 16-6: Daily high and low temperatures for Death Valley

Comparing this graph to the Sitka graph, we can see that Death Valley is warmer overall than southeast Alaska, as we expect. Also, the range of temperatures each day is greater in the desert. The height of the shaded region makes this clear.

Many data sets you work with will have missing, improperly formatted, or incorrect data. You can use the tools you learned in the first half of this book to handle these situations. Here we used a try-except-else block to handle missing data. Sometimes you'll use continue to skip over some data or use remove() or del to eliminate some data after it's been extracted. Use any approach that works, as long as the result is a meaningful, accurate visualization.

Downloading Your Own Data

If you want to download your own weather data, follow these steps:

1. Visit the NOAA Climate Data Online site at *https://www.ncdc.noaa.gov /cdo-web/*. In the *Discover Data By* section, click **Search Tool**. In the *Select a Dataset* box, choose **Daily Summaries**.

2. Select a date range, and in the *Search For* section, choose **ZIP Codes**. Enter the ZIP Code you're interested in, and click **Search**.

3. On the next page, you'll see a map and some information about the area you're focusing on. Below the location name, click **View Full Details**, or click the map and then click **Full Details**.

4. Scroll down and click **Station List** to see the weather stations that are available in this area. Choose one of the stations, and click **Add to Cart**. This data is free, even though the site uses a shopping cart icon. In the upper-right corner, click the cart.

5. In *Select the Output*, choose **Custom GHCN-Daily CSV**. Make sure the date range is correct, and click **Continue**.

6. On the next page, you can select the kinds of data you want. You can download one kind of data, for example, focusing on air temperature, or you can download all the data available from this station. Make your choices, and then click **Continue**.

7. On the last page, you'll see a summary of your order. Enter your email address, and click **Submit Order**. You'll receive a confirmation that your order was received, and in a few minutes you should receive another email with a link to download your data.

The data you download will be structured just like the data we worked with in this section. It might have different headers than those you saw in this section. But if you follow the same steps we used here, you should be able to generate visualizations of the data you're interested in.

TRY IT YOURSELF

16-1. Sitka Rainfall: Sitka is in a temperate rainforest, so it gets a fair amount of rainfall. In the data file *sitka_weather_2018_simple.csv* is a header called PRCP, which represents daily rainfall amounts. Make a visualization focusing on the data in this column. You can repeat the exercise for Death Valley if you're curious how little rainfall occurs in a desert.

16-2. Sitka–Death Valley Comparison: The temperature scales on the Sitka and Death Valley graphs reflect the different data ranges. To accurately compare the temperature range in Sitka to that of Death Valley, you need identical scales on the y-axis. Change the settings for the y-axis on one or both of the charts in Figures 16-5 and 16-6. Then make a direct comparison between temperature ranges in Sitka and Death Valley (or any two places you want to compare).

16-3. San Francisco: Are temperatures in San Francisco more like temperatures in Sitka or temperatures in Death Valley? Download some data for San Francisco, and generate a high-low temperature plot for San Francisco to make a comparison.

Mapping Global Data Sets: JSON Format

In this section, you'll download a data set representing all the earthquakes that have occurred in the world during the previous month. Then you'll make a map showing the location of these earthquakes and how significant each one was. Because the data is stored in the JSON format, we'll work with it using the json module. Using Plotly's beginner-friendly mapping tool for location-based data, you'll create visualizations that clearly show the global distribution of earthquakes.

Downloading Earthquake Data

Copy the file *eq_1_day_m1.json* to the folder where you're storing the data for this chapter's programs. Earthquakes are categorized by their magni-tude on the Richter scale. This file includes data for all earthquakes with a magnitude M1 or greater that took place in the last 24 hours (at the time of this writing). This data comes from one of the United States Geological Survey's earthquake data feeds, which you can find at *https://earthquake.usgs .gov/earthquakes/feed/*.

Examining JSON Data

When you open *eq_1_day_m1.json*, you'll see that it's very dense and hard to read:

```
{"type":"FeatureCollection","metadata":{"generated":1550361461000,...
{"type":"Feature","properties":{"mag":1.2,"place":"11km NNE of Nor...
{"type":"Feature","properties":{"mag":4.3,"place":"69km NNW of Ayn...
{"type":"Feature","properties":{"mag":3.6,"place":"126km SSE of Co...
{"type":"Feature","properties":{"mag":2.1,"place":"21km NNW of Teh...
{"type":"Feature","properties":{"mag":4,"place":"57km SSW of Kakto...
--snip--
```

This file is formatted more for machines than it is for humans. But we can see that the file contains some dictionaries, as well as informa-tion that we're interested in, such as earthquake magnitudes and locations.

The json module provides a variety of tools for exploring and working with JSON data. Some of these tools will help us reformat the file so we can look at the raw data more easily before we begin to work with it programmatically.

Let's start by loading the data and displaying it in a format that's easier to read. This is a long data file, so instead of printing it, we'll rewrite the data to a new file. Then we can open that file and scroll back and forth easily through the data:

*eq_explore
_data.py*

```
import json

# Explore the structure of the data.
filename = 'data/eq_data_1_day_m1.json'
with open(filename) as f:
❶     all_eq_data = json.load(f)

❷ readable_file = 'data/readable_eq_data.json'
with open(readable_file, 'w') as f:
❸     json.dump(all_eq_data, f, indent=4)
```

We first import the json module to load the data properly from the file, and then store the entire set of data in all_eq_data ❶. The json.load() function converts the data into a format Python can work with: in this case, a giant dictionary. At ❷ we create a file to write this same data into a more readable format. The json.dump() function takes a JSON data object and a file object, and writes the data to that file ❸. The indent=4 argument tells dump() to format the data using indentation that matches the data's structure.

When you look in your *data* directory and open the file *readable_eq_data .json*, here's the first part of what you'll see:

*readable_eq
_data.json*

```
{
      "type": "FeatureCollection",
❶     "metadata": {
          "generated": 1550361461000,
          "url": "https://earthquake.usgs.gov/earthquakes/.../1.0_day.geojson",
          "title": "USGS Magnitude 1.0+ Earthquakes, Past Day",
          "status": 200,
          "api": "1.7.0",
          "count": 158
      },
❷     "features": [
      --snip--
```

The first part of the file includes a section with the key "metadata". This tells us when the data file was generated and where we can find the data online. It also gives us a human-readable title and the number of earthquakes included in this file. In this 24-hour period, 158 earthquakes were recorded.

This *geoJSON* file has a structure that's helpful for location-based data. The information is stored in a list associated with the key "features" ❷. Because this file contains earthquake data, the data is in list form where every item in the list corresponds to a single earthquake. This structure might look confusing, but it's quite powerful. It allows geologists to store as much information as they need to in a dictionary about each earthquake, and then stuff all those dictionaries into one big list.

Let's look at a dictionary representing a single earthquake:

readable_eq
_data.json

```
--snip--
    {
        "type": "Feature",
❶       "properties": {
            "mag": 0.96,
            --snip--
❷           "title": "M 1.0 - 8km NE of Aguanga, CA"
        },
❸       "geometry": {
            "type": "Point",
            "coordinates": [
❹               -116.7941667,
❺               33.4863333,
                3.22
            ]
        },
        "id": "ci37532978"
    },
```

The key "properties" contains a lot of information about each earthquake ❶. We're mainly interested in the magnitude of each quake, which is associated with the key "mag". We're also interested in the title of each earthquake, which provides a nice summary of its magnitude and location ❷.

The key "geometry" helps us understand where the earthquake occurred ❸. We'll need this information to map each event. We can find the longitude ❹ and the latitude ❺ for each earthquake in a list associated with the key "coordinates".

This file contains way more nesting than we'd use in the code we write, so if it looks confusing, don't worry: Python will handle most of the complexity. We'll only be working with one or two nesting levels at a time. We'll start by pulling out a dictionary for each earthquake that was recorded in the 24-hour time period.

NOTE *When we talk about locations, we often say the location's latitude first, followed by the longitude. This convention probably arose because humans discovered latitude long before we developed the concept of longitude. However, many geospatial frameworks list the longitude first and then the latitude, because this corresponds to the (x, y) convention we use in mathematical representations. The geoJSON format follows the (longitude, latitude) convention, and if you use a different framework it's important to learn what convention that framework follows.*

Making a List of All Earthquakes

First, we'll make a list that contains all the information about every earthquake that occurred.

*eq_explore
_data.py*

```
import json

# Explore the structure of the data.
filename = 'data/eq_data_1_day_m1.json'
with open(filename) as f:
    all_eq_data = json.load(f)

all_eq_dicts = all_eq_data['features']
print(len(all_eq_dicts))
```

We take the data associated with the key 'features' and store it in all_eq _dicts. We know this file contains records about 158 earthquakes, and the output verifies that we've captured all of the earthquakes in the file:

```
158
```

Notice how short this code is. The neatly formatted file *readable_eq_data .json* has over 6,000 lines. But in just a few lines, we can read through all that data and store it in a Python list. Next, we'll pull the magnitudes from each earthquake.

Extracting Magnitudes

Using the list containing data about each earthquake, we can loop through that list and extract any information we want. Now we'll pull the magnitude of each earthquake:

*eq_explore
_data.py*

```
--snip--
all_eq_dicts = all_eq_data['features']

❶ mags = []
for eq_dict in all_eq_dicts:
❷     mag = eq_dict['properties']['mag']
    mags.append(mag)

print(mags[:10])
```

We make an empty list to store the magnitudes, and then loop through the dictionary all_eq_dicts ❶. Inside this loop, each earthquake is represented by the dictionary eq_dict. Each earthquake's magnitude is stored in the 'properties' section of this dictionary under the key 'mag' ❷. We store each magnitude in the variable mag, and then append it to the list mags.

We print the first 10 magnitudes, so we can see whether we're getting the correct data:

```
[0.96, 1.2, 4.3, 3.6, 2.1, 4, 1.06, 2.3, 4.9, 1.8]
```

Next, we'll pull the location data for each earthquake, and then we can make a map of the earthquakes.

Extracting Location Data

The location data is stored under the key "geometry". Inside the geometry dictionary is a "coordinates" key, and the first two values in this list are the longitude and latitude. Here's how we'll pull this data:

eq_explore
_data.py
```
--snip--
all_eq_dicts = all_eq_data['features']

mags, lons, lats = [], [], []
for eq_dict in all_eq_dicts:
    mag = eq_dict['properties']['mag']
❶   lon = eq_dict['geometry']['coordinates'][0]
    lat = eq_dict['geometry']['coordinates'][1]
    mags.append(mag)
    lons.append(lon)
    lats.append(lat)

print(mags[:10])
print(lons[:5])
print(lats[:5])
```

We make empty lists for the longitudes and latitudes. The code eq_dict ['geometry'] accesses the dictionary representing the geometry element of the earthquake ❶. The second key, 'coordinates', pulls the list of values associated with 'coordinates'. Finally, the 0 index asks for the first value in the list of coordinates, which corresponds to an earthquake's longitude.

When we print the first five longitudes and latitudes, the output shows that we're pulling the correct data:

```
[0.96, 1.2, 4.3, 3.6, 2.1, 4, 1.06, 2.3, 4.9, 1.8]
[-116.7941667, -148.9865, -74.2343, -161.6801, -118.5316667]
[33.4863333, 64.6673, -12.1025, 54.2232, 35.3098333]
```

With this data, we can move on to mapping each earthquake.

Building a World Map

With the information we've pulled so far, we can build a simple world map. Although it won't look presentable yet, we want to make sure the information is displayed correctly before focusing on style and presentation issues. Here's the initial map:

eq_world_map.py
```
import json

❶ from plotly.graph_objs import Scattergeo, Layout
from plotly import offline

--snip--
```

```
for eq_dict in all_eq_dicts:
    --snip--

    # Map the earthquakes.
❷ data = [Scattergeo(lon=lons, lat=lats)]
❸ my_layout = Layout(title='Global Earthquakes')

❹ fig = {'data': data, 'layout': my_layout}
  offline.plot(fig, filename='global_earthquakes.html')
```

We import the Scattergeo chart type and the Layout class, and then import the offline module to render the map ❶. As we did when making a bar chart, we define a list called data. We create the Scattergeo object inside this list ❷, because you can plot more than one data set on any visualization you make. A Scattergeo chart type allows you to overlay a scatter plot of geographic data on a map. In the simplest use of this chart type, you only need to provide a list of longitudes and a list of latitudes.

We give the chart an appropriate title ❸ and create a dictionary called fig that contains the data and the layout ❹. Finally, we pass fig to the plot() function along with a descriptive filename for the output. When you run this file, you should see a map that looks like the one in Figure 16-7. Earthquakes usually occur near plate boundaries, which matches what we see in the chart.

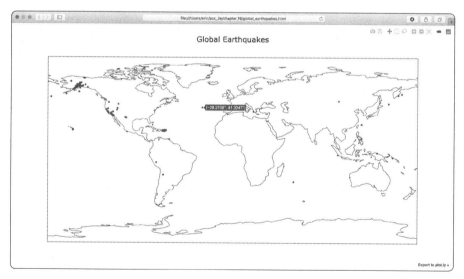

Figure 16-7: A simple map showing where all the earthquakes in the last 24 hours occurred

We can do a lot of modifications to make this map more meaningful and easier to read, so let's make some of these changes.

A Different Way of Specifying Chart Data

Before we configure the chart, let's look at a slightly different way to specify the data for a Plotly chart. In the current chart, the data list is defined in one line:

```python
data = [Scattergeo(lon=lons, lat=lats)]
```

This is one of the simplest ways to define the data for a chart in Plotly. But it's not the best way when you want to customize the presentation. Here's an equivalent way to define the data for the current chart:

```python
data = [{
    'type': 'scattergeo',
    'lon': lons,
    'lat': lats,
}]
```

In this approach, all the information about the data is structured as key-value pairs in a dictionary. If you put this code into *eq_plot.py*, you'll see the same chart we just generated. This format allows us to specify customizations more easily than the previous format.

Customizing Marker Size

When we're figuring out how to improve the map's styling, we should focus on aspects of the data that we want to communicate more clearly. The current map shows the location of each earthquake, but it doesn't communicate the severity of any earthquake. We want viewers to immediately see where the most significant earthquakes occur in the world.

To do this, we'll change the size of markers depending on the magnitude of each earthquake:

eq_world_map.py
```python
import json
--snip--
# Map the earthquakes.
data = [{
    'type': 'scattergeo',
    'lon': lons,
    'lat': lats,
❶    'marker': {
❷        'size': [5*mag for mag in mags],
    },
}]
my_layout = Layout(title='Global Earthquakes')
--snip--
```

Plotly offers a huge variety of customizations you can make to a data series, each of which can be expressed as a key-value pair. Here we're using the key 'marker' to specify how big each marker on the map should be ❶. We use a nested dictionary as the value associated with 'marker', because you can specify a number of settings for all the markers in a series.

We want the size to correspond to the magnitude of each earthquake. But if we just pass in the mags list, the markers would be too small to easily see the size differences. We need to multiply the magnitude by a scale factor to get an appropriate marker size. On my screen, a value of 5 works well; a slightly smaller or larger value might work better for your map. We use a list comprehension, which generates an appropriate marker size for each value in the mags list ❷.

When you run this code, you should see a map that looks like the one in Figure 16-8. This is a much better map, but we can still do more.

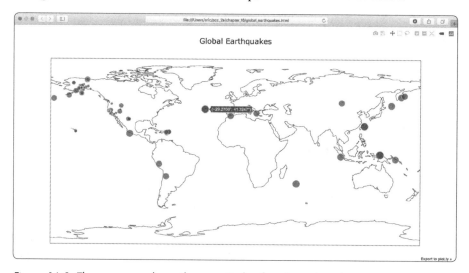

Figure 16-8: The map now shows the magnitude of each earthquake.

Customizing Marker Colors

We can also customize each marker's color to provide some classification to the severity of each earthquake. We'll use Plotly's colorscales to do this. Before you make these changes, copy the file *eq_data_30_day_m1.json* to your data directory. This file includes earthquake data for a 30-day period, and the map will be much more interesting to look at using this larger data set.

Here's how to use a colorscale to represent the magnitude of each earthquake:

eq_world_map.py

```
--snip--
❶ filename = 'data/eq_data_30_day_m1.json'
--snip--
# Map the earthquakes.
data = [{
    --snip--
```

```
        'marker': {
            'size': [5*mag for mag in mags],
❷          'color': mags,
❸          'colorscale': 'Viridis',
❹          'reversescale': True,
❺          'colorbar': {'title': 'Magnitude'},
        },
}]
--snip--
```

Be sure to update the filename so you're using the 30-day data set ❶. All the significant changes here occur in the 'marker' dictionary, because we're only modifying the markers' appearance. The 'color' setting tells Plotly what values it should use to determine where each marker falls on the colorscale ❷. We use the mags list to determine the color that's used. The 'colorscale' setting tells Plotly which range of colors to use: 'Viridis' is a colorscale that ranges from dark blue to bright yellow and works well for this data set ❸. We set 'reversescale' to True, because we want to use bright yellow for the lowest values and dark blue for the most severe earthquakes ❹. The 'colorbar' setting allows us to control the appearance of the colorscale shown on the side of the map. Here we title the colorscale 'Magnitude' to make it clear what the colors represent ❹.

When you run the program now, you'll see a much nicer-looking map. In Figure 16-9, the colorscale shows the severity of individual earthquakes. Plotting this many earthquakes really makes it clear where the tectonic plate boundaries are!

Figure 16-9: In 30 days' worth of earthquakes, color and size are used to represent the magnitude of each earthquake.

Other Colorscales

You can also choose from a number of other colorscales. To see the available colorscales, save the following short program as *show_color_scales.py*:

show_color_scales.py

```
from plotly import colors

for key in colors.PLOTLY_SCALES.keys():
    print(key)
```

Plotly stores the colorscales in the colors module. The colorscales are defined in the dictionary PLOTLY_SCALES, and the names of the colorscales serve as the keys in the dictionary. Here's the output showing all the available colorscales:

```
Greys
YlGnBu
Greens
--snip--
Viridis
```

Feel free to try out these colorscales; remember that you can reverse any of these scales using the reversescale setting.

NOTE   *If you print the PLOTLY_SCALES dictionary, you can see how colorscales are defined. Every scale has a beginning color and an end color, and some scales have one or more intermediate colors defined as well. Plotly interpolates shades between each of these defined colors.*

Adding Hover Text

To finish this map, we'll add some informative text that appears when you hover over the marker representing an earthquake. In addition to showing the longitude and latitude, which appear by default, we'll show the magnitude and provide a description of the approximate location as well.

To make this change, we need to pull a little more data from the file and add it to the dictionary in data as well:

eq_world_map.py
```
--snip--
➊ mags, lons, lats, hover_texts = [], [], [], []
  for eq_dict in all_eq_dicts:
      --snip--
      lat = eq_dict['geometry']['coordinates'][1]
➋     title = eq_dict['properties']['title']
      mags.append(mag)
      lons.append(lon)
      lats.append(lat)
      hover_texts.append(title)
  --snip--
```

```
# Map the earthquakes.
data = [{
    'type': 'scattergeo',
    'lon': lons,
    'lat': lats,
❸    'text': hover_texts,
    'marker': {
        --snip--
    },
}]
--snip--
```

We first make a list called hover_texts to store the label we'll use for each marker ❶. The "title" section of the earthquake data contains a descriptive name of the magnitude and location of each earthquake in addition to its longitude and latitude. At ❷ we pull this information and assign it to the variable title, and then append it to the list hover_texts.

When we include the key 'text' in the data object, Plotly uses this value as a label for each marker when the viewer hovers over the marker. When we pass a list that matches the number of markers, Plotly pulls an individual label for each marker it generates ❸. When you run this program, you should be able to hover over any marker, see a description of where that earthquake took place, and read its exact magnitude.

This is impressive! In approximately 40 lines of code, we've created a visually appealing and meaningful map of global earthquake activity that also illustrates the geological structure of the planet. Plotly offers a wide range of ways you can customize the appearance and behavior of your visualizations. Using Plotly's many options, you can make charts and maps that show exactly what you want them to.

TRY IT YOURSELF

16-6. Refactoring: The loop that pulls data from all_eq_dicts uses variables for the magnitude, longitude, latitude, and title of each earthquake before appending these values to their appropriate lists. This approach was chosen for clarity in how to pull data from a JSON file, but it's not necessary in your code. Instead of using these temporary variables, pull each value from eq_dict and append it to the appropriate list in one line. Doing so should shorten the body of this loop to just four lines.

16-7. Automated Title: In this section, we specified the title manually when defining my_layout, which means we have to remember to update the title every time the source file changes. Instead, you can use the title for the data set in the metadata part of the JSON file. Pull this value, assign it to a variable, and use this for the title of the map when you're defining my_layout.

(continued)

16-8. Recent Earthquakes: You can find data files containing information about the most recent earthquakes over 1-hour, 1-day, 7-day, and 30-day periods online. Go to *https://earthquake.usgs.gov/earthquakes/feed/v1.0/geojson.php* and you'll see a list of links to data sets for various time periods, focusing on earthquakes of different magnitudes. Download one of these data sets, and create a visualization of the most recent earthquake activity.

16-9. World Fires: In the resources for this chapter, you'll find a file called *world_fires_1_day.csv*. This file contains information about fires burning in different locations around the globe, including the latitude and longitude, and the brightness of each fire. Using the data processing work from the first part of this chapter and the mapping work from this section, make a map that shows which parts of the world are affected by fires.

You can download more recent versions of this data at *https://earthdata.nasa.gov/earth-observation-data/near-real-time/firms/active-fire-data/*. You can find links to the data in CSV format in the *TXT* section.

Summary

In this chapter, you learned to work with real-world data sets. You processed CSV and JSON files, and extracted the data you want to focus on. Using historical weather data, you learned more about working with Matplotlib, including how to use the datetime module and how to plot multiple data series on one chart. You plotted geographical data on a world map in Plotly and styled Plotly maps and charts as well.

As you gain experience working with CSV and JSON files, you'll be able to process almost any data you want to analyze. You can download most online data sets in either or both of these formats. By working with these formats, you'll be able to learn how to work with other data formats more easily as well.

In the next chapter, you'll write programs that automatically gather their own data from online sources, and then you'll create visualizations of that data. These are fun skills to have if you want to program as a hobby and critical skills if you're interested in programming professionally.

17

WORKING WITH APIs

In this chapter, you'll learn how to write a
self-contained program that generates a visualization based on data that it retrieves. Your
program will use a web *application programming
interface (API)* to automatically request specific information from a website—rather than entire pages—and
then use that information to generate a visualization. Because programs
written like this will always use current data to generate a visualization,
even when that data might be rapidly changing, it will always be up to date.

Using a Web API

A web API is a part of a website designed to interact with programs. Those
programs use very specific URLs to request certain information. This kind
of request is called an *API call*. The requested data will be returned in an

easily processed format, such as JSON or CSV. Most apps that rely on external data sources, such as apps that integrate with social media sites, rely on API calls.

Git and GitHub

We'll base our visualization on information from GitHub, a site that allows programmers to collaborate on coding projects. We'll use GitHub's API to request information about Python projects on the site, and then generate an interactive visualization of the relative popularity of these projects using Plotly.

GitHub (*https://github.com/*) takes its name from Git, a distributed version control system. Git helps people manage their work on a project, so changes made by one person won't interfere with changes other people are making. When you implement a new feature in a project, Git tracks the changes you make to each file. When your new code works, you *commit* the changes you've made, and Git records the new state of your project. If you make a mistake and want to revert your changes, you can easily return to any previously working state. (To learn more about version control using Git, see Appendix D.) Projects on GitHub are stored in *repositories*, which contain everything associated with the project: its code, information on its collaborators, any issues or bug reports, and so on.

When users on GitHub like a project, they can "star" it to show their support and keep track of projects they might want to use. In this chapter, we'll write a program to automatically download information about the most-starred Python projects on GitHub, and then we'll create an informative visualization of these projects.

Requesting Data Using an API Call

GitHub's API lets you request a wide range of information through API calls. To see what an API call looks like, enter the following into your browser's address bar and press ENTER:

```
https://api.github.com/search/repositories?q=language:python&sort=stars
```

This call returns the number of Python projects currently hosted on GitHub, as well as information about the most popular Python repositories. Let's examine the call. The first part, `https://api.github.com/`, directs the request to the part of GitHub that responds to API calls. The next part, `search/repositories`, tells the API to conduct a search through all repositories on GitHub.

The question mark after `repositories` signals that we're about to pass an argument. The q stands for *query*, and the equal sign (=) lets us begin specifying a query (q=). By using `language:python`, we indicate that we want information only on repositories that have Python as the primary language. The final part, `&sort=stars`, sorts the projects by the number of stars they've been given.

The following snippet shows the first few lines of the response.

```
{
❶    "total_count": 3494012,
❷    "incomplete_results": false,
❸    "items": [
        {
          "id": 21289110,
          "node_id": "MDEwOlJlcG9zaXRvcnkyMTI4OTExMA==",
          "name": "awesome-python",
          "full_name": "vinta/awesome-python",
          --snip--
```

You can see from the response that this URL is not primarily intended to be entered by humans, because it's in a format that's meant to be processed by a program. GitHub found 3,494,012 Python projects as of this writing ❶. Because the value for "incomplete_results" is false, we know that the request was successful (it's not incomplete) ❷. If GitHub had been unable to fully process the API request, it would have returned true here. The "items" returned are displayed in the list that follows, which contains details about the most popular Python projects on GitHub ❸.

Installing Requests

The Requests package allows a Python program to easily request information from a website and examine the response. Use pip to install Requests:

```
$ python -m pip install --user requests
```

This line tells Python to run the pip module and install the Requests package to the current user's Python installation. If you use **python3** or a different command when running programs or installing packages, make sure you use the same command here.

NOTE *If this command doesn't work on macOS, try running the command again without the --user flag.*

Processing an API Response

Now we'll begin to write a program to automatically issue an API call and process the results by identifying the most starred Python projects on GitHub:

python_repos.py ❶ import requests

```
    # Make an API call and store the response.
❷   url = 'https://api.github.com/search/repositories?q=language:python&sort=stars'
❸   headers = {'Accept': 'application/vnd.github.v3+json'}
❹   r = requests.get(url, headers=headers)
❺   print(f"Status code: {r.status_code}")
```

```
                 # Store API response in a variable.
❻ response_dict = r.json()

                 # Process results.
                 print(response_dict.keys())
```

At ❶ we import the requests module. At ❷ we store the URL of the API call in the url variable. GitHub is currently on the third version of its API, so we define headers for the API call ❸ that ask explicitly to use this version of the API. Then we use requests to make the call to the API ❹.

We call get() and pass it the URL and the header that we defined, and we assign the response object to the variable r. The response object has an attribute called status_code, which tells us whether the request was successful. (A status code of 200 indicates a successful response.) At ❺ we print the value of status_code so we can make sure the call went through successfully.

The API returns the information in JSON format, so we use the json() method to convert the information to a Python dictionary ❻. We store the resulting dictionary in response_dict.

Finally, we print the keys from response_dict and see this output:

```
Status code: 200
dict_keys(['total_count', 'incomplete_results', 'items'])
```

Because the status code is 200, we know that the request was successful. The response dictionary contains only three keys: 'total_count', 'incomplete _results', and 'items'. Let's take a look inside the response dictionary.

NOTE   *Simple calls like this should return a complete set of results, so it's safe to ignore the value associated with* 'incomplete_results'. *But when you're making more complex API calls, your program should check this value.*

Working with the Response Dictionary

With the information from the API call stored as a dictionary, we can work with the data stored there. Let's generate some output that summarizes the information. This is a good way to make sure we received the information we expected and to start examining the information we're interested in:

python_repos.py
```
import requests

# Make an API call and store the response.
--snip--

# Store API response in a variable.
response_dict = r.json()
❶ print(f"Total repositories: {response_dict['total_count']}")

# Explore information about the repositories.
❷ repo_dicts = response_dict['items']
print(f"Repositories returned: {len(repo_dicts)}")
```

```
# Examine the first repository.
```
❸ `repo_dict = repo_dicts[0]`
❹ `print(f"\nKeys: {len(repo_dict)}")`
❺ `for key in sorted(repo_dict.keys()):`
  `    print(key)`

At ❶ we print the value associated with `'total_count'`, which represents the total number of Python repositories on GitHub.

The value associated with `'items'` is a list containing a number of dictionaries, each of which contains data about an individual Python repository. At ❷ we store this list of dictionaries in `repo_dicts`. We then print the length of `repo_dicts` to see how many repositories we have information for.

To look closer at the information returned about each repository, we pull out the first item from `repo_dicts` and store it in `repo_dict` ❸. We then print the number of keys in the dictionary to see how much information we have ❹. At ❺ we print all the dictionary's keys to see what kind of information is included.

The results give us a clearer picture of the actual data:

```
Status code: 200
Total repositories: 3494030
Repositories returned: 30
```

❶ `Keys: 73`
`archive_url`
`archived`
`assignees_url`
`--snip--`
`url`
`watchers`
`watchers_count`

GitHub's API returns a lot of information about each repository: there are 73 keys in `repo_dict` ❶. When you look through these keys, you'll get a sense of the kind of information you can extract about a project. (The only way to know what information is available through an API is to read the documentation or to examine the information through code, as we're doing here.)

Let's pull out the values for some of the keys in `repo_dict`:

python_repos.py
```
--snip--
# Explore information about the repositories.
repo_dicts = response_dict['items']
print(f"Repositories returned: {len(repo_dicts)}")

# Examine the first repository.
repo_dict = repo_dicts[0]

print("\nSelected information about first repository:")
```
❶ `print(f"Name: {repo_dict['name']}")`
❷ `print(f"Owner: {repo_dict['owner']['login']}")`
❸ `print(f"Stars: {repo_dict['stargazers_count']}")`
`print(f"Repository: {repo_dict['html_url']}")`

```
❹ print(f"Created: {repo_dict['created_at']}")
❺ print(f"Updated: {repo_dict['updated_at']}")
  print(f"Description: {repo_dict['description']}")
```

Here, we print the values for a number of keys from the first repository's dictionary. At ❶ we print the name of the project. An entire dictionary represents the project's owner, so at ❷ we use the key owner to access the
dictionary representing the owner, and then use the key login to get the
owner's login name. At ❸ we print how many stars the project has earned
and the URL for the project's GitHub repository. We then show when it was
created ❹ and when it was last updated ❺. Finally, we print the repository's
description; the output should look something like this:

```
Status code: 200
Total repositories: 3494032
Repositories returned: 30

Selected information about first repository:
Name: awesome-python
Owner: vinta
Stars: 61549
Repository: https://github.com/vinta/awesome-python
Created: 2014-06-27T21:00:06Z
Updated: 2019-02-17T04:30:00Z
Description: A curated list of awesome Python frameworks, libraries, software
    and resources
```

We can see that the most-starred Python project on GitHub as of this
writing is *awesome-python*, its owner is user *vinta*, and it has been starred
by more than 60,000 GitHub users. We can see the URL for the project's
repository, its creation date of June 2014, and that it was updated recently.
Additionally, the description tells us that awesome-python contains a list of
popular Python resources.

Summarizing the Top Repositories

When we make a visualization for this data, we'll want to include more than
one repository. Let's write a loop to print selected information about each
repository the API call returns so we can include them all in the visualization:

python_repos.py
```
--snip--
# Explore information about the repositories.
repo_dicts = response_dict['items']
print(f"Repositories returned: {len(repo_dicts)}")

❶ print("\nSelected information about each repository:")
❷ for repo_dict in repo_dicts:
      print(f"\nName: {repo_dict['name']}")
      print(f"Owner: {repo_dict['owner']['login']}")
      print(f"Stars: {repo_dict['stargazers_count']}")
      print(f"Repository: {repo_dict['html_url']}")
      print(f"Description: {repo_dict['description']}")
```

We print an introductory message at ❶. At ❷ we loop through all the dictionaries in repo_dicts. Inside the loop, we print the name of each project, its owner, how many stars it has, its URL on GitHub, and the project's description, as shown here:

```
Status code: 200
Total repositories: 3494040
Repositories returned: 30

Selected information about each repository:

Name: awesome-python
Owner: vinta
Stars: 61549
Repository: https://github.com/vinta/awesome-python
Description: A curated list of awesome Python frameworks, libraries, software
  and resources

Name: system-design-primer
Owner: donnemartin
Stars: 57256
Repository: https://github.com/donnemartin/system-design-primer
Description: Learn how to design large-scale systems. Prep for the system
  design interview.  Includes Anki flashcards.
--snip--

Name: python-patterns
Owner: faif
Stars: 19058
Repository: https://github.com/faif/python-patterns
Description: A collection of design patterns/idioms in Python
```

Some interesting projects appear in these results, and it might be worth looking at a few. But don't spend too much time, because shortly we'll create a visualization that will make the results much easier to read.

Monitoring API Rate Limits

Most APIs are rate limited, which means there's a limit to how many requests you can make in a certain amount of time. To see if you're approaching GitHub's limits, enter *https://api.github.com/rate_limit* into a web browser. You should see a response that begins like this:

```
{
  "resources": {
    "core": {
      "limit": 60,
      "remaining": 58,
      "reset": 1550385312
    },
❶   "search": {
❷     "limit": 10,
❸     "remaining": 8,
```

```
❹        "reset": 1550381772
       },
       --snip--
```

The information we're interested in is the rate limit for the search API ❶. We see at ❷ that the limit is 10 requests per minute and that we have 8 requests remaining for the current minute ❸. The reset value represents the time in *Unix* or *epoch time* (the number of seconds since midnight on January 1, 1970) when our quota will reset ❹. If you reach your quota, you'll get a short response that lets you know you've reached the API limit. If you reach the limit, just wait until your quota resets.

NOTE *Many APIs require you to register and obtain an API key to make API calls. As of this writing, GitHub has no such requirement, but if you obtain an API key, your limits will be much higher.*

Visualizing Repositories Using Plotly

Let's make a visualization using the data we have now to show the relative popularity of Python projects on GitHub. We'll make an interactive bar chart: the height of each bar will represent the number of stars the project has acquired, and you can click the bar's label to go to that project's home on GitHub. Save a copy of the program we've been working on as *python _repos_visual.py*, and then modify it so it reads as follows:

python_repos _visual.py

```python
import requests

❶ from plotly.graph_objs import Bar
from plotly import offline

❷ # Make an API call and store the response.
url = 'https://api.github.com/search/repositories?q=language:python&sort=stars'
headers = {'Accept': 'application/vnd.github.v3+json'}
r = requests.get(url, headers=headers)
print(f"Status code: {r.status_code}")

# Process results.
response_dict = r.json()
repo_dicts = response_dict['items']
❸ repo_names, stars = [], []
for repo_dict in repo_dicts:
    repo_names.append(repo_dict['name'])
    stars.append(repo_dict['stargazers_count'])

# Make visualization.
❹ data = [{
    'type': 'bar',
    'x': repo_names,
    'y': stars,
}]
```

```
❺ my_layout = {
        'title': 'Most-Starred Python Projects on GitHub',
        'xaxis': {'title': 'Repository'},
        'yaxis': {'title': 'Stars'},
    }

    fig = {'data': data, 'layout': my_layout}
    offline.plot(fig, filename='python_repos.html')
```

We import the Bar class and the offline module from plotly ❶. We don't
need to import the Layout class because we'll use the dictionary approach
to define the layout, just as we did for the data list in the earthquake mapping project in Chapter 16. We continue to print the status of the API call
response so we'll know if there is a problem ❷. We also remove some of
the code that processes the API response, because we're no longer in the
exploratory phase; we know we have the data we want.

We then create two empty lists ❸ to store the data we'll include in the
initial chart. We'll need the name of each project to label the bars, and the
number of stars to determine the height of the bars. In the loop, we append
the name of each project and the number of stars it has to these lists.

Next, we define the data list ❹. This contains a dictionary, like we used
in Chapter 16, which defines the type of the plot and provides the data for
the x- and y-values. The x-values are the names of the projects, and the y-
values are the number of stars each project has been given.

At ❺ we define the layout for this chart using the dictionary approach.
Instead of making an instance of the Layout class, we build a dictionary with
the layout specifications we want to use. We set a title for the overall chart,
and we define a label for each axis.

Figure 17-1 shows the resulting chart. We can see that the first few projects are significantly more popular than the rest, but all of them are important projects in the Python ecosystem.

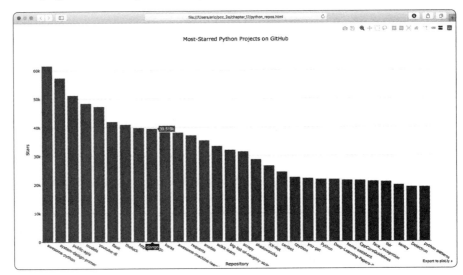

Figure 17-1: The most-starred Python projects on GitHub

Refining Plotly Charts

Let's refine the chart's styling. As you saw in Chapter 16, you can include all the styling directives as key-value pairs in the data and my_layout dictionaries.

Changes to the data object affect the bars. Here's a modified version of the data object for our chart that gives us a specific color and a clear border for each bar:

*python_repos
_visual.py*

```
--snip--
data = [{
    'type': 'bar',
    'x': repo_names,
    'y': stars,
    'marker': {
        'color': 'rgb(60, 100, 150)',
        'line': {'width': 1.5, 'color': 'rgb(25, 25, 25)'}
    },
    'opacity': 0.6,
}]
--snip--
```

The marker settings shown here affect the design of the bars. We set a custom blue color for the bars and specify that they'll be outlined with a dark gray line that's 1.5 pixels wide. We also set the opacity of the bars to 0.6 to soften the appearance of the chart a little.

Next, we'll modify my_layout:

*python_repos
_visual.py*

```
  --snip--
  my_layout = {
      'title': 'Most-Starred Python Projects on GitHub',
❶     'titlefont': {'size': 28},
❷     'xaxis': {
          'title': 'Repository',
          'titlefont': {'size': 24},
          'tickfont': {'size': 14},
      },
❸     'yaxis': {
          'title': 'Stars',
          'titlefont': {'size': 24},
          'tickfont': {'size': 14},
      },
  }
  --snip--
```

We use the 'titlefont' key to define the font size of the overall chart title ❶. Within the 'xaxis' dictionary, we add settings to control the font size of the x-axis title ('titlefont') and also of the tick labels ('tickfont') ❷. Because these are individual nested dictionaries, you can include keys for the color and font family of the axis titles and tick labels. At ❸ we define similar settings for the y-axis.

Figure 17-2 shows the restyled chart.

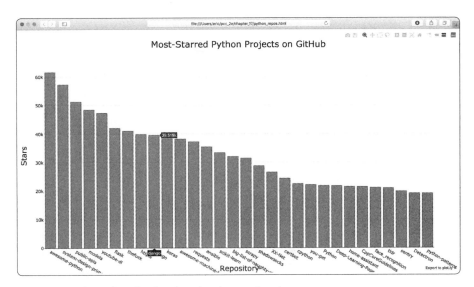

Figure 17-2: The styling for the chart has been refined.

Adding Custom Tooltips

In Plotly, you can hover the cursor over an individual bar to show the information that the bar represents. This is commonly called a *tooltip*, and in this case, it currently shows the number of stars a project has. Let's create a custom tooltip to show each project's description as well as the project's owner.

We need to pull some additional data to generate the tooltips and modify the data object:

python_repos
_visual.py

```
--snip--
# Process results.
response_dict = r.json()
repo_dicts = response_dict['items']
❶ repo_names, stars, labels = [], [], []
for repo_dict in repo_dicts:
    repo_names.append(repo_dict['name'])
    stars.append(repo_dict['stargazers_count'])

❷    owner = repo_dict['owner']['login']
    description = repo_dict['description']
❸    label = f"{owner}<br />{description}"
    labels.append(label)


# Make visualization.
data = [{
    'type': 'bar',
    'x': repo_names,
    'y': stars,
❹    'hovertext': labels,
    'marker': {
```

```
            'color': 'rgb(60, 100, 150)',
            'line': {'width': 1.5, 'color': 'rgb(25, 25, 25)'}
        },
        'opacity': 0.6,
}]
--snip--
```

We first define a new empty list, labels, to hold the text we want to display for each project ❶. In the loop where we process the data, we pull the owner and the description for each project ❷. Plotly allows you to use HTML code within text elements, so we generate a string for the label with a line break (<br />) between the project owner's username and the description ❸. We then store this label in the list labels.

In the data dictionary, we add an entry with the key 'hovertext' and assign it the list we just created ❹. As Plotly creates each bar, it will pull labels from this list and only display them when the viewer hovers over a bar.

Figure 17-3 shows the resulting chart.

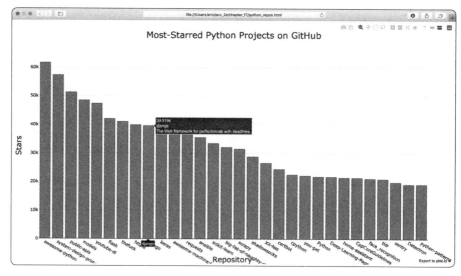

Figure 17-3: Hovering over a bar shows the project's owner and description.

Adding Clickable Links to Our Graph

Because Plotly allows you to use HTML on text elements, we can easily add links to a chart. Let's use the x-axis labels as a way to let the viewer visit any project's home page on GitHub. We need to pull the URLs from the data and use them when generating the x-axis labels:

python_repos
_visual.py

```
--snip--
# Process results.
response_dict = r.json()
repo_dicts = response_dict['items']
```

```
❶ repo_links, stars, labels = [], [], []
  for repo_dict in repo_dicts:
      repo_name = repo_dict['name']
❷     repo_url = repo_dict['html_url']
❸     repo_link = f"<a href='{repo_url}'>{repo_name}</a>"
      repo_links.append(repo_link)

      stars.append(repo_dict['stargazers_count'])
      --snip--

  # Make visualization.
  data = [{
      'type': 'bar',
❹     'x': repo_links,
      'y': stars,
      --snip--
  }]
  --snip--
```

We update the name of the list we're creating from `repo_names` to `repo
_links` to more accurately communicate the kind of information we're put-
ting together for the chart ❶. We then pull the URL for the project from
`repo_dict` and assign it to the temporary variable `repo_url` ❷. At ❸ we generate a link to the project. We use the HTML anchor tag, which has the form
`<a href='URL'>link text</a>`, to generate the link. We then append this link
to the list `repo_links`.

At ❹ we use this list for the x-values in the chart. The result looks the
same as before, but now the viewer can click any of the project names at
the bottom of the chart to visit that project's home page on GitHub. Now
we have an interactive, informative visualization of data retrieved through
an API!

More About Plotly and the GitHub API

To read more about working with Plotly charts, there are two good places
to start. You can find the *Plotly User Guide in Python* at *https://plot.ly/python
/user-guide/*. This resource gives you a better understanding of how Plotly
uses your data to construct a visualization and why it approaches defining
data visualizations in this way.

The *python figure reference* at *https://plot.ly/python/reference/* lists all the settings you can use to configure Plotly visualizations. All the possible chart
types are listed as well as all the attributes you can set for every configuration option.

For more about the GitHub API, refer to its documentation at *https://
developer.github.com/v3/*. Here you'll learn how to pull a wide variety of specific information from GitHub. If you have a GitHub account, you can work
with your own data as well as the publicly available data for other users'
repositories.

The Hacker News API

To explore how to use API calls on other sites, let's take a quick look at Hacker News (*http://news.ycombinator.com/*). On Hacker News, people share articles about programming and technology, and engage in lively discussions about those articles. The Hacker News API provides access to data about all submissions and comments on the site, and you can use the API without having to register for a key.

The following call returns information about the current top article as of this writing:

```
https://hacker-news.firebaseio.com/v0/item/19155826.json
```

When you enter this URL in a browser, you'll see that the text on the page is enclosed by braces, meaning it's a dictionary. But the response is difficult to examine without some better formatting. Let's run this URL through the json.dump() method, like we did in the earthquake project in Chapter 16, so we can explore the kind of information that's returned about an article:

hn_article.py
```python
import requests
import json

# Make an API call, and store the response.
url = 'https://hacker-news.firebaseio.com/v0/item/19155826.json'
r = requests.get(url)
print(f"Status code: {r.status_code}")

# Explore the structure of the data.
response_dict = r.json()
readable_file = 'data/readable_hn_data.json'
with open(readable_file, 'w') as f:
    json.dump(response_dict, f, indent=4)
```

Everything in this program should look familiar, because we've used it all in the previous two chapters. The output is a dictionary of information about the article with the ID 19155826:

readable_hn
_data.json
```
{
      "by": "jimktrains2",
❶     "descendants": 220,
      "id": 19155826,
❷     "kids": [
          19156572,
          19158857,
          --snip--
      ],
      "score": 722,
      "time": 1550085414,
❸     "title": "Nasa's Mars Rover Opportunity Concludes a 15-Year Mission",
      "type": "story",
❹     "url": "https://www.nytimes.com/.../mars-opportunity-rover-dead.html"
}
```

The dictionary contains a number of keys we can work with. The key 'descendants' tells us the number of comments the article has received ❶. The key 'kids' provides the IDs of all comments made directly in response to this submission ❷. Each of these comments might have comments of their own as well, so the number of descendants a submission has is usually greater than its number of kids. We can see the title of the article being discussed ❸, and a URL for the article that's being discussed as well ❹.

The following URL returns a simple list of all the IDs of the current top articles on Hacker News:

```
https://hacker-news.firebaseio.com/v0/topstories.json
```

We can use this call to find out which articles are on the home page right now, and then generate a series of API calls similar to the one we just examined. With this approach, we can print a summary of all the articles on the front page of Hacker News at the moment:

hn_submissions.py

```
from operator import itemgetter

import requests

# Make an API call and store the response.
❶ url = 'https://hacker-news.firebaseio.com/v0/topstories.json'
r = requests.get(url)
print(f"Status code: {r.status_code}")

# Process information about each submission.
❷ submission_ids = r.json()
❸ submission_dicts = []
for submission_id in submission_ids[:30]:
    # Make a separate API call for each submission.
❹    url = f"https://hacker-news.firebaseio.com/v0/item/{submission_id}.json"
    r = requests.get(url)
    print(f"id: {submission_id}\tstatus: {r.status_code}")
    response_dict = r.json()

    # Build a dictionary for each article.
❺    submission_dict = {
        'title': response_dict['title'],
        'hn_link': f"http://news.ycombinator.com/item?id={submission_id}",
        'comments': response_dict['descendants'],
    }
❻    submission_dicts.append(submission_dict)

❼ submission_dicts = sorted(submission_dicts, key=itemgetter('comments'),
                            reverse=True)

❽ for submission_dict in submission_dicts:
    print(f"\nTitle: {submission_dict['title']}")
    print(f"Discussion link: {submission_dict['hn_link']}")
    print(f"Comments: {submission_dict['comments']}")
```

First, we make an API call, and then print the status of the response ❶. This API call returns a list containing the IDs of up to the 500 most popular articles on Hacker News at the time the call is issued. We then convert the response object to a Python list at ❷, which we store in submission_ids. We'll use these IDs to build a set of dictionaries that each store information about one of the current submissions.

We set up an empty list called submission_dicts at ❸ to store these dictionaries. We then loop through the IDs of the top 30 submissions. We make a new API call for each submission by generating a URL that includes the current value of submission_id ❹. We print the status of each request along with its ID, so we can see whether it's successful.

At ❺ we create a dictionary for the submission currently being processed, where we store the title of the submission, a link to the discussion page for that item, and the number of comments the article has received so far. Then we append each submission_dict to the list submission_dicts ❻.

Each submission on Hacker News is ranked according to an overall score based on a number of factors including how many times it's been voted up, how many comments it's received, and how recent the submission is. We want to sort the list of dictionaries by the number of comments. To do this, we use a function called itemgetter() ❼, which comes from the operator module. We pass this function the key 'comments', and it pulls the value associated with that key from each dictionary in the list. The sorted() function then uses this value as its basis for sorting the list. We sort the list in reverse order to place the most-commented stories first.

Once the list is sorted, we loop through the list at ❽ and print out three pieces of information about each of the top submissions: the title, a link to the discussion page, and the number of comments the submission currently has:

```
Status code: 200
id: 19155826    status: 200
id: 19180181    status: 200
id: 19181473    status: 200
--snip--

Title: Nasa's Mars Rover Opportunity Concludes a 15-Year Mission
Discussion link: http://news.ycombinator.com/item?id=19155826
Comments: 220

Title: Ask HN: Is it practical to create a software-controlled model rocket?
Discussion link: http://news.ycombinator.com/item?id=19180181
Comments: 72

Title: Making My Own USB Keyboard from Scratch
Discussion link: http://news.ycombinator.com/item?id=19181473
Comments: 62
--snip--
```

You would use a similar process to access and analyze information with any API. With this data, you could make a visualization showing which submissions have inspired the most active recent discussions. This is also the basis for apps that provide a customized reading experience for sites like Hacker News. To learn more about what kind of information you can access through the Hacker News API, visit the documentation page at *https://github .com/HackerNews/API/*.

TRY IT YOURSELF

17-1. Other Languages: Modify the API call in *python_repos.py* so it generates a chart showing the most popular projects in other languages. Try languages such as *JavaScript, Ruby, C, Java, Perl, Haskell,* and *Go.*

17-2. Active Discussions: Using the data from *hn_submissions.py,* make a bar chart showing the most active discussions currently happening on Hacker News. The height of each bar should correspond to the number of comments each submission has. The label for each bar should include the submission's title and should act as a link to the discussion page for that submission.

17-3. Testing python_repos.py: In *python_repos.py,* we printed the value of status_code to make sure the API call was successful. Write a program called *test_python_repos.py* that uses unittest to assert that the value of status_code is 200. Figure out some other assertions you can make—for example, that the number of items returned is expected and that the total number of repositories is greater than a certain amount.

17-4. Further Exploration: Visit the documentation for Plotly and either the GitHub API or the Hacker News API. Use some of the information you find there to either customize the style of the plots we've already made or pull some different information and create your own visualizations.

Summary

In this chapter, you learned how to use APIs to write self-contained programs that automatically gather the data they need and use that data to create a visualization. You used the GitHub API to explore the most-starred Python projects on GitHub, and you also looked briefly at the Hacker News API. You learned how to use the Requests package to automatically issue an API call to GitHub and how to process the results of that call. Some Plotly settings were also introduced that further customize the appearance of the charts you generate.

In the next chapter, you'll use Django to build a web application as your final project.

PROJECT 3

WEB APPLICATIONS

18

GETTING STARTED WITH DJANGO

Behind the scenes, today's websites are rich applications that act like fully developed desktop applications. Python has a great set of tools called Django for building web applications. Django is a *web framework*—a set of tools designed to help you build interactive websites. In this chapter, you'll learn how to use Django (*https://djangoproject.com/*) to build a project called Learning Log—an online journal system that lets you keep track of information you've learned about particular topics.

We'll write a specification for this project, and then we'll define models for the data the app will work with. We'll use Django's admin system to enter some initial data, and then you'll learn to write views and templates so Django can build the site's pages.

Django can respond to page requests and make it easier to read and write to a database, manage users, and much more. In Chapters 19 and 20, you'll refine the Learning Log project and then deploy it to a live server so you (and your friends) can use it.

Setting Up a Project

When beginning a project, you first need to describe the project in a specification, or *spec*. Then you'll set up a virtual environment in which to build the project.

Writing a Spec

A full spec details the project goals, describes the project's functionality, and discusses its appearance and user interface. Like any good project or business plan, a spec should keep you focused and help keep your project on track. We won't write a full project spec here, but we'll lay out a few clear goals to keep the development process focused. Here's the spec we'll use:

> We'll write a web app called Learning Log that allows users to log the topics they're interested in and to make journal entries as they learn about each topic. The Learning Log home page will describe the site and invite users to either register or log in. Once logged in, a user can create new topics, add new entries, and read and edit existing entries.

When you learn about a new topic, keeping a journal of what you've learned can be helpful in tracking and revisiting information. A good app makes this process efficient.

Creating a Virtual Environment

To work with Django, we'll first set up a virtual environment. A *virtual environment* is a place on your system where you can install packages and isolate them from all other Python packages. Separating one project's libraries from other projects is beneficial and will be necessary when we deploy Learning Log to a server in Chapter 20.

Create a new directory for your project called *learning_log*, switch to that directory in a terminal, and enter the following code to create a virtual environment:

```
learning_log$ python -m venv ll_env
learning_log$
```

Here we're running the venv virtual environment module and using it to create a virtual environment named *ll_env* (note that this is *ll_env* with two lowercase *L*s, not two ones). If you use a command such as `python3` when running programs or installing packages, make sure to use that command here.

Activating the Virtual Environment

Now we need to activate the virtual environment using the following command:

```
learning_log$ source ll_env/bin/activate
❶ (ll_env)learning_log$
```

This command runs the script *activate* in *ll_env/bin*. When the environment is active, you'll see the name of the environment in parentheses, as shown at ❶; then you can install packages to the environment and use packages that have already been installed. Packages you install in *ll_env* will be available only while the environment is active.

NOTE *If you're using Windows, use the command* `ll_env\Scripts\activate` *(without the word* `source`*) to activate the virtual environment. If you're using PowerShell, you might need to capitalize* `Activate`*.*

To stop using a virtual environment, enter **deactivate**:

```
(ll_env)learning_log$ deactivate
learning_log$
```

The environment will also become inactive when you close the terminal it's running in.

Installing Django

Once the virtual environment is activated, enter the following to install Django:

```
(ll_env)learning_log$ pip install django
Collecting django
--snip--
Installing collected packages: pytz, django
Successfully installed django-2.2.0 pytz-2018.9 sqlparse-0.2.4
(ll_env)learning_log$
```

Because we're working in a virtual environment, which is its own self-contained environment, this command is the same on all systems. There's no need to use the `--user` flag, and there's no need to use longer commands, such as `python -m pip install` *package_name*.

Keep in mind that Django will be available only when the *ll_env* environment is active.

NOTE *Django releases a new version about every eight months, so you may see a newer version when you install Django. This project will most likely work as it's written here, even on newer versions of Django. If you want to make sure to use the same version of Django you see here, use the command* `pip install django==2.2.*`*. This will install the latest release of Django 2.2. If you have any issues related to the version you're using, see the online resources for the book at* https://nostarch.com/pythoncrashcourse2e/.

Creating a Project in Django

Without leaving the active virtual environment (remember to look for *ll_env* in parentheses in the terminal prompt), enter the following commands to create a new project:

```
❶ (ll_env)learning_log$ django-admin startproject learning_log .
❷ (ll_env)learning_log$ ls
  learning_log ll_env manage.py
❸ (ll_env)learning_log$ ls learning_log
  __init__.py  settings.py  urls.py  wsgi.py
```

The command at ❶ tells Django to set up a new project called *learning _log*. The dot at the end of the command creates the new project with a directory structure that will make it easy to deploy the app to a server when we're finished developing it.

NOTE *Don't forget this dot, or you might run into some configuration issues when you deploy the app. If you forget the dot, delete the files and folders that were created (except* ll_env*), and run the command again.*

Running the ls command (dir on Windows) ❷ shows that Django has created a new directory called *learning_log*. It also created a *manage.py* file, which is a short program that takes in commands and feeds them to the relevant part of Django to run them. We'll use these commands to manage tasks, such as working with databases and running servers.

The *learning_log* directory contains four files ❸; the most important are *settings.py*, *urls.py*, and *wsgi.py*. The *settings.py* file controls how Django interacts with your system and manages your project. We'll modify a few of these settings and add some settings of our own as the project evolves. The *urls.py* file tells Django which pages to build in response to browser requests. The *wsgi.py* file helps Django serve the files it creates. The filename is an acronym for *web server gateway interface*.

Creating the Database

Django stores most of the information for a project in a database, so next we need to create a database that Django can work with. Enter the following command (still in an active environment):

```
  (ll_env)learning_log$ python manage.py migrate
❶ Operations to perform:
    Apply all migrations: admin, auth, contenttypes, sessions
  Running migrations:
    Applying contenttypes.0001_initial... OK
    Applying auth.0001_initial... OK
    --snip--
    Applying sessions.0001_initial... OK
❷ (ll_env)learning_log$ ls
  db.sqlite3  learning_log  ll_env  manage.py
```

Any time we modify a database, we say we're *migrating* the database. Issuing the migrate command for the first time tells Django to make sure the database matches the current state of the project. The first time we run this command in a new project using SQLite (more about SQLite in a moment), Django will create a new database for us. At ❶, Django reports that it will prepare the database to store information it needs to handle administrative and authentication tasks.

Running the ls command shows that Django created another file called *db.sqlite3* ❷. SQLite is a database that runs off a single file; it's ideal for writing simple apps because you won't have to pay much attention to managing the database.

NOTE *In an active virtual environment, use the command* python *to run* manage.py *commands, even if you use something different, like* python3, *to run other programs. In a virtual environment, the command* python *refers to the version of Python that created the virtual environment.*

Viewing the Project

Let's make sure that Django has set up the project properly. Enter the runserver command as follows to view the project in its current state:

```
(ll_env)learning_log$ python manage.py runserver
Watchman unavailable: pywatchman not installed.
Watching for file changes with StatReloader
Performing system checks...
```

❶ System check identified no issues (0 silenced).
  February 18, 2019 - 16:26:07
❷ Django version 2.2.0, using settings 'learning_log.settings'
❸ Starting development server at http://127.0.0.1:8000/
  Quit the server with CONTROL-C.

Django should start a server called the *development server*, so you can view the project on your system to see how well it works. When you request a page by entering a URL in a browser, the Django server responds to that request by building the appropriate page and sending it to the browser.

At ❶, Django checks to make sure the project is set up properly; at ❷ it reports the version of Django in use and the name of the settings file in use; and at ❸ it reports the URL where the project is being served. The URL *http://127.0.0.1:8000/* indicates that the project is listening for requests on port 8000 on your computer, which is called a localhost. The term *localhost* refers to a server that only processes requests on your system; it doesn't allow anyone else to see the pages you're developing.

Open a web browser and enter the URL *http://localhost:8000/*, or *http://127.0.0.1:8000/* if the first one doesn't work. You should see something like Figure 18-1, a page that Django creates to let you know all is working properly so far. Keep the server running for now, but when you want to stop the server, press CTRL-C in the terminal where the runserver command was issued.

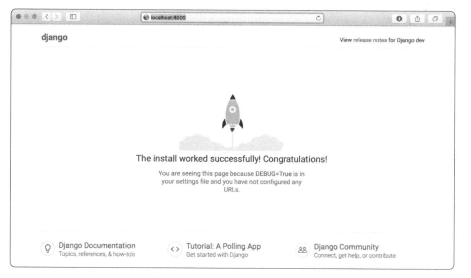

Figure 18-1: Everything is working so far.

NOTE *If you receive the error message* That port is already in use, *tell Django to use a different port by entering* `python manage.py runserver 8001`, *and then cycle through higher numbers until you find an open port.*

TRY IT YOURSELF

18-1. New Projects: To get a better idea of what Django does, build a couple of empty projects and look at what Django creates. Make a new folder with a simple name, like *snap_gram* or *insta_chat* (outside of your *learning_log* directory), navigate to that folder in a terminal, and create a virtual environment. Install Django and run the command `django-admin.py startproject snap_gram .` (make sure you include the dot at the end of the command).

Look at the files and folders this command creates, and compare them to Learning Log. Do this a few times until you're familiar with what Django creates when starting a new project. Then delete the project directories if you wish.

Starting an App

A Django *project* is organized as a group of individual *apps* that work together to make the project work as a whole. For now, we'll create just one app to do most of our project's work. We'll add another app in Chapter 19 to manage user accounts.

You should leave the development server running in the terminal window you opened earlier. Open a new terminal window (or tab), and navigate to the directory that contains *manage.py*. Activate the virtual environment, and then run the startapp command:

```
learning_log$ source ll_env/bin/activate
(ll_env)learning_log$ python manage.py startapp learning_logs
❶ (ll_env)learning_log$ ls
db.sqlite3  learning_log  learning_logs  ll_env  manage.py
❷ (ll_env)learning_log$ ls learning_logs/
__init__.py  admin.py  apps.py  migrations  models.py  tests.py  views.py
```

The command startapp *appname* tells Django to create the infrastructure needed to build an app. When you look in the project directory now, you'll see a new folder called *learning_logs* ❶. Open that folder to see what Django has created ❷. The most important files are *models.py*, *admin.py*, and *views.py*. We'll use *models.py* to define the data we want to manage in our app. We'll look at *admin.py* and *views.py* a little later.

Defining Models

Let's think about our data for a moment. Each user will need to create a number of topics in their learning log. Each entry they make will be tied to a topic, and these entries will be displayed as text. We'll also need to store the timestamp of each entry, so we can show users when they made each entry.

Open the file *models.py*, and look at its existing content:

models.py
```
from django.db import models

# Create your models here.
```

A module called models is being imported for us, and we're being invited to create models of our own. A *model* tells Django how to work with the data that will be stored in the app. Code-wise, a model is just a class; it has attributes and methods, just like every class we've discussed. Here's the model for the topics users will store:

```
from django.db import models

class Topic(models.Model):
    """A topic the user is learning about."""
❶    text = models.CharField(max_length=200)
❷    date_added = models.DateTimeField(auto_now_add=True)

❸    def __str__(self):
        """Return a string representation of the model."""
        return self.text
```

We've created a class called `Topic`, which inherits from `Model`—a parent class included in Django that defines a model's basic functionality. We add two attributes to the `Topic` class: text and date_added.

The text attribute is a `CharField`—a piece of data that's made up of characters, or text ❶. You use `CharField` when you want to store a small amount of text, such as a name, a title, or a city. When we define a `CharField` attribute, we have to tell Django how much space it should reserve in the database. Here we give it a `max_length` of 200 characters, which should be enough to hold most topic names.

The date_added attribute is a `DateTimeField`—a piece of data that will record a date and time ❷. We pass the argument auto_now_add=True, which tells Django to automatically set this attribute to the current date and time whenever the user creates a new topic.

NOTE *To see the different kinds of fields you can use in a model, see the* Django Model Field Reference *at* https://docs.djangoproject.com/en/2.2/ref/models /fields/. *You won't need all the information right now, but it will be extremely useful when you're developing your own apps.*

We tell Django which attribute to use by default when it displays information about a topic. Django calls a __str__() method to display a simple representation of a model. Here we've written a __str__() method that returns the string stored in the text attribute ❸.

Activating Models

To use our models, we have to tell Django to include our app in the overall project. Open *settings.py* (in the *learning_log/learning_log* directory); you'll see a section that tells Django which apps are installed and work together in the project:

settings.py
```
--snip--
INSTALLED_APPS = [
    'django.contrib.admin',
    'django.contrib.auth',
    'django.contrib.contenttypes',
    'django.contrib.sessions',
    'django.contrib.messages',
    'django.contrib.staticfiles',
]
--snip--
```

Add our app to this list by modifying `INSTALLED_APPS` so it looks like this:

```
--snip--
INSTALLED_APPS = [
    # My apps
    'learning_logs',

    # Default django apps.
    'django.contrib.admin',
```

```
--snip--
]
--snip--
```

Grouping apps together in a project helps to keep track of them as the project grows to include more apps. Here we start a section called *My apps*, which includes only `learning_logs` for now. It's important to place your own apps before the default apps in case you need to override any behavior of the default apps with your own custom behavior.

Next, we need to tell Django to modify the database so it can store information related to the model `Topic`. From the terminal, run the following command:

```
(ll_env)learning_log$ python manage.py makemigrations learning_logs
Migrations for 'learning_logs':
  learning_logs/migrations/0001_initial.py
    - Create model Topic
(ll_env)learning_log$
```

The command `makemigrations` tells Django to figure out how to modify the database so it can store the data associated with any new models we've defined. The output here shows that Django has created a migration file called *0001_initial.py*. This migration will create a table for the model `Topic` in the database.

Now we'll apply this migration and have Django modify the database for us:

```
(ll_env)learning_log$ python manage.py migrate
Operations to perform:
  Apply all migrations: admin, auth, contenttypes, learning_logs, sessions
Running migrations:
❶  Applying learning_logs.0001_initial... OK
```

Most of the output from this command is identical to the first time we issued the `migrate` command. The line we need to check appears at ❶, where Django confirms that the migration for `learning_logs` worked `OK`.

Whenever we want to modify the data that Learning Log manages, we'll follow these three steps: modify *models.py*, call makemigrations on `learning_logs`, and tell Django to migrate the project.

The Django Admin Site

Django makes it easy to work with your models through the *admin site*. Only the site's administrators use the admin site, not general users. In this section, we'll set up the admin site and use it to add some topics through the `Topic` model.

Setting Up a Superuser

Django allows you to create a *superuser*, a user who has all privileges available on the site. A user's *privileges* control the actions that user can take.

The most restrictive privilege settings allow a user to only read public information on the site. Registered users typically have the privilege of reading their own private data and some selected information available only to members. To effectively administer a web application, the site owner usually needs access to all information stored on the site. A good administrator is careful with their users' sensitive information, because users put a lot of trust into the apps they access.

To create a superuser in Django, enter the following command and respond to the prompts:

```
(ll_env)learning_log$ python manage.py createsuperuser
❶ Username (leave blank to use 'eric'): ll_admin
❷ Email address:
❸ Password:
Password (again):
Superuser created successfully.
(ll_env)learning_log$
```

When you issue the command createsuperuser, Django prompts you to enter a username for the superuser ❶. Here I'm using *ll_admin*, but you can enter any username you want. You can enter an email address if you want or just leave this field blank ❷. You'll need to enter your password twice ❸.

NOTE *Some sensitive information can be hidden from a site's administrators. For example, Django doesn't store the password you enter; instead, it stores a string derived from the password, called a* hash. *Each time you enter your password, Django hashes your entry and compares it to the stored hash. If the two hashes match, you're authenticated. By requiring hashes to match, if an attacker gains access to a site's database, they'll be able to read its stored hashes but not the passwords. When a site is set up properly, it's almost impossible to get the original passwords from the hashes.*

Registering a Model with the Admin Site

Django includes some models in the admin site automatically, such as User and Group, but the models we create need to be added manually.

When we started the learning_logs app, Django created an *admin.py* file in the same directory as *models.py*. Open the *admin.py* file:

admin.py
```
from django.contrib import admin

# Register your models here.
```

To register Topic with the admin site, enter the following:

```
from django.contrib import admin

❶ from .models import Topic

❷ admin.site.register(Topic)
```

This code first imports the model we want to register, Topic ❶. The dot in front of models tells Django to look for *models.py* in the same directory as *admin.py*. The code admin.site.register() tells Django to manage our model through the admin site ❷.

Now use the superuser account to access the admin site. Go to *http://localhost:8000/admin/*, and enter the username and password for the superuser you just created. You should see a screen like the one in Figure 18-2. This page allows you to add new users and groups, and change existing ones. You can also work with data related to the Topic model that we just defined.

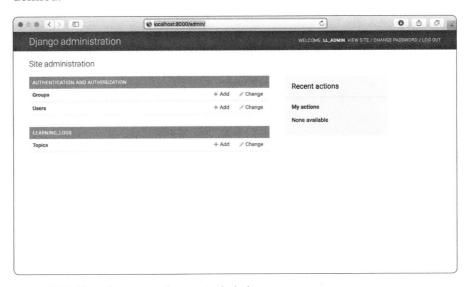

Figure 18-2: The admin site with Topic included

NOTE   *If you see a message in your browser that the web page is not available, make sure you still have the Django server running in a terminal window. If you don't, activate a virtual environment and reissue the command python manage.py runserver. If you're having trouble viewing your project at any point in the development process, closing any open terminals and reissuing the runserver command is a good first troubleshooting step.*

Adding Topics

Now that Topic has been registered with the admin site, let's add our first topic. Click **Topics** to go to the Topics page, which is mostly empty, because we have no topics to manage yet. Click **Add Topic**, and a form for adding a new topic appears. Enter **Chess** in the first box and click **Save**. You'll be sent back to the Topics admin page, and you'll see the topic you just created.

Let's create a second topic so we'll have more data to work with. Click **Add Topic** again, and enter **Rock Climbing**. Click **Save**, and you'll be sent back to the main Topics page again. Now you'll see Chess and Rock Climbing listed.

Defining the Entry Model

For a user to record what they've been learning about chess and rock climbing, we need to define a model for the kinds of entries users can make in their learning logs. Each entry needs to be associated with a particular topic. This relationship is called a *many-to-one relationship*, meaning many entries can be associated with one topic.

Here's the code for the Entry model. Place it in your *models.py* file:

models.py

```
from django.db import models

class Topic(models.Model):
    --snip--

❶ class Entry(models.Model):
      """Something specific learned about a topic."""
❷     topic = models.ForeignKey(Topic, on_delete=models.CASCADE)
❸     text = models.TextField()
      date_added = models.DateTimeField(auto_now_add=True)

❹     class Meta:
          verbose_name_plural = 'entries'

      def __str__(self):
          """Return a string representation of the model."""
❺         return f"{self.text[:50]}..."
```

The Entry class inherits from Django's base Model class, just as Topic did ❶. The first attribute, topic, is a ForeignKey instance ❷. A *foreign key* is a database term; it's a reference to another record in the database. This is the code that connects each entry to a specific topic. Each topic is assigned a key, or ID, when it's created. When Django needs to establish a connection between two pieces of data, it uses the key associated with each piece of information. We'll use these connections shortly to retrieve all the entries associated with a certain topic. The on_delete=models.CASCADE argument tells Django that when a topic is deleted, all the entries associated with that topic should be deleted as well. This is known as a *cascading delete*.

Next is an attribute called text, which is an instance of TextField ❸. This kind of field doesn't need a size limit, because we don't want to limit the size of individual entries. The date_added attribute allows us to present entries in the order they were created and to place a timestamp next to each entry.

At ❹ we nest the Meta class inside our Entry class. The Meta class holds extra information for managing a model; here, it allows us to set a special attribute telling Django to use *Entries* when it needs to refer to more than one entry. Without this, Django would refer to multiple entries as *Entrys*.

The __str__() method tells Django which information to show when it refers to individual entries. Because an entry can be a long body of text, we tell Django to show just the first 50 characters of text ❺. We also add an ellipsis to clarify that we're not always displaying the entire entry.

Migrating the Entry Model

Because we've added a new model, we need to migrate the database again. This process will become quite familiar: you modify *models.py*, run the command python manage.py makemigrations *app_name*, and then run the command python manage.py migrate.

Migrate the database and check the output by entering the following commands:

```
(ll_env)learning_log$ python manage.py makemigrations learning_logs
Migrations for 'learning_logs':
❶   learning_logs/migrations/0002_entry.py
      - Create model Entry
(ll_env)learning_log$ python manage.py migrate
Operations to perform:
--snip--
❷   Applying learning_logs.0002_entry... OK
```

A new migration called *0002_entry.py* is generated, which tells Django how to modify the database to store information related to the model Entry ❶. When we issue the migrate command, we see that Django applied this migration, and everything was okay ❷.

Registering Entry with the Admin Site

We also need to register the Entry model. Here's what *admin.py* should look like now:

admin.py
```
from django.contrib import admin

from .models import Topic, Entry

admin.site.register(Topic)
admin.site.register(Entry)
```

Go back to *http://localhost/admin/*, and you should see *Entries* listed under *Learning_Logs*. Click the **Add** link for Entries, or click **Entries**, and then choose **Add entry**. You should see a drop-down list to select the topic you're creating an entry for and a text box for adding an entry. Select **Chess** from the drop-down list, and add an entry. Here's the first entry I made:

> The opening is the first part of the game, roughly the first ten moves or so. In the opening, it's a good idea to do three things—bring out your bishops and knights, try to control the center of the board, and castle your king.

> Of course, these are just guidelines. It will be important to learn when to follow these guidelines and when to disregard these suggestions.

When you click **Save**, you'll be brought back to the main admin page for entries. Here, you'll see the benefit of using text[:50] as the string representation for each entry; it's much easier to work with multiple entries in the admin interface if you see only the first part of an entry rather than the entire text of each entry.

Make a second entry for Chess and one entry for Rock Climbing so we have some initial data. Here's a second entry for Chess:

> In the opening phase of the game, it's important to bring out your bishops and knights. These pieces are powerful and maneuverable enough to play a significant role in the beginning moves of a game.

And here's a first entry for Rock Climbing:

> One of the most important concepts in climbing is to keep your weight on your feet as much as possible. There's a myth that climbers can hang all day on their arms. In reality, good climbers have practiced specific ways of keeping their weight over their feet whenever possible.

These three entries will give us something to work with as we continue to develop Learning Log.

The Django Shell

With some data entered, we can examine that data programmatically through an interactive terminal session. This interactive environment is called the Django *shell*, and it's a great environment for testing and troubleshooting your project. Here's an example of an interactive shell session:

```
(ll_env)learning_log$ python manage.py shell
❶ >>> from learning_logs.models import Topic
>>> Topic.objects.all()
<QuerySet [<Topic: Chess>, <Topic: Rock Climbing>]>
```

The command python manage.py shell, run in an active virtual environment, launches a Python interpreter that you can use to explore the data stored in your project's database. Here, we import the model Topic from the learning_logs.models module ❶. We then use the method Topic.objects.all() to get all the instances of the model Topic; the list that's returned is called a *queryset*.

We can loop over a queryset just as we'd loop over a list. Here's how you can see the ID that's been assigned to each topic object:

```
>>> topics = Topic.objects.all()
>>> for topic in topics:
...     print(topic.id, topic)
```

```
...
1 Chess
2 Rock Climbing
```

We store the queryset in `topics`, and then print each topic's `id` attribute and the string representation of each topic. We can see that Chess has an ID of 1, and Rock Climbing has an ID of 2.

If you know the ID of a particular object, you can use the method `Topic.objects.get()` to retrieve that object and examine any attribute the object has. Let's look at the `text` and `date_added` values for Chess:

```
>>> t = Topic.objects.get(id=1)
>>> t.text
'Chess'
>>> t.date_added
datetime.datetime(2019, 2, 19, 1, 55, 31, 98500, tzinfo=<UTC>)
```

We can also look at the entries related to a certain topic. Earlier we defined the `topic` attribute for the `Entry` model. This was a `ForeignKey`, a connection between each entry and a topic. Django can use this connection to get every entry related to a certain topic, like this:

```
❶ >>> t.entry_set.all()
<QuerySet [<Entry: The opening is the first part of the game, roughly...>,
<Entry:
In the opening phase of the game, it's important t...>]>
```

To get data through a foreign key relationship, you use the lowercase name of the related model followed by an underscore and the word set ❶. For example, say you have the models `Pizza` and `Topping`, and `Topping` is related to `Pizza` through a foreign key. If your object is called `my_pizza`, representing a single pizza, you can get all of the pizza's toppings using the code `my_pizza.topping_set.all()`.

We'll use this kind of syntax when we begin to code the pages users can request. The shell is very useful for making sure your code retrieves the data you want it to. If your code works as you expect it to in the shell, you can expect it to work properly in the files within your project. If your code generates errors or doesn't retrieve the data you expect it to, it's much easier to troubleshoot your code in the simple shell environment than within the files that generate web pages. We won't refer to the shell much, but you should continue using it to practice working with Django's syntax for accessing the data stored in the project.

NOTE *Each time you modify your models, you'll need to restart the shell to see the effects of those changes. To exit a shell session, press CTRL-D; on Windows, press CTRL-Z and then press ENTER.*

18-2. Short Entries: The __str__() method in the Entry model currently appends an ellipsis to every instance of Entry when Django shows it in the admin site or the shell. Add an if statement to the __str__() method that adds an ellipsis only if the entry is longer than 50 characters. Use the admin site to add an entry that's fewer than 50 characters in length, and check that it doesn't have an ellipsis when viewed.

18-3. The Django API: When you write code to access the data in your project, you're writing a *query*. Skim through the documentation for querying your data at *https://docs.djangoproject.com/en/2.2/topics/db/queries/*. Much of what you see will look new to you, but it will be very useful as you start to work on your own projects.

18-4. Pizzeria: Start a new project called pizzeria with an app called pizzas. Define a model Pizza with a field called name, which will hold name values, such as Hawaiian and Meat Lovers. Define a model called Topping with fields called pizza and name. The pizza field should be a foreign key to Pizza, and name should be able to hold values such as pineapple, Canadian bacon, and sausage.

Register both models with the admin site, and use the site to enter some pizza names and toppings. Use the shell to explore the data you entered.

Making Pages: The Learning Log Home Page

Making web pages with Django consists of three stages: defining URLs, writing views, and writing templates. You can do these in any order, but in this project we'll always start by defining the URL pattern. A URL pattern describes the way the URL is laid out. It also tells Django what to look for when matching a browser request with a site URL so it knows which page to return.

Each URL then maps to a particular *view*—the view function retrieves and processes the data needed for that page. The view function often renders the page using a *template*, which contains the overall structure of the page. To see how this works, let's make the home page for Learning Log. We'll define the URL for the home page, write its view function, and create a simple template.

Because all we're doing is making sure Learning Log works as it's supposed to, we'll make a simple page for now. A functioning web app is fun to style when it's complete; an app that looks good but doesn't work well is pointless. For now, the home page will display only a title and a brief description.

Mapping a URL

Users request pages by entering URLs into a browser and clicking links, so we'll need to decide what URLs are needed. The home page URL is first: it's the base URL people use to access the project. At the moment the base URL, *http://localhost:8000/*, returns the default Django site that lets us know the project was set up correctly. We'll change this by mapping the base URL to Learning Log's home page.

In the main *learning_log* project folder, open the file *urls.py*. Here's the code you should see:

urls.py
```
❶ from django.contrib import admin
   from django.urls import path

❷ urlpatterns = [
❸     path('admin/', admin.site.urls),
   ]
```

The first two lines import a module and a function to manage URLs for the admin site ❶. The body of the file defines the urlpatterns variable ❷. In this *urls.py* file, which represents the project as a whole, the urlpatterns variable includes sets of URLs from the apps in the project. The code at ❸ includes the module admin.site.urls, which defines all the URLs that can be requested from the admin site.

We need to include the URLs for learning_logs, so add the following:

```
   from django.contrib import admin
   from django.urls import path, include

   urlpatterns = [
       path('admin/', admin.site.urls),
❶     path('', include('learning_logs.urls')),
   ]
```

We've added a line to include the module learning_logs.urls at ❶.

The default *urls.py* is in the *learning_log* folder; now we need to make a second *urls.py* file in the *learning_logs* folder. Create a new Python file and save it as *urls.py* in *learning_logs*, and enter this code into it:

urls.py
```
❶ """Defines URL patterns for learning_logs."""

❷ from django.urls import path

❸ from . import views

❹ app_name = 'learning_logs'
❺ urlpatterns = [
       # Home page
❻     path('', views.index, name='index'),
   ]
```

To make it clear which *urls.py* we're working in, we add a docstring at the beginning of the file ❶. We then import the path function, which is needed when mapping URLs to views ❷. We also import the views module ❸; the dot tells Python to import the *views.py* module from the same directory as the current *urls.py* module. The variable app_name helps Django distinguish this *urls.py* file from files of the same name in other apps within the project ❹. The variable urlpatterns in this module is a list of individual pages that can be requested from the learning_logs app ❺.

The actual URL pattern is a call to the path() function, which takes three arguments ❻. The first argument is a string that helps Django route the current request properly. Django receives the requested URL and tries to route the request to a view. It does this by searching all the URL patterns we've defined to find one that matches the current request. Django ignores the base URL for the project (*http://localhost:8000/*), so the empty string ('') matches the base URL. Any other URL won't match this pattern, and Django will return an error page if the URL requested doesn't match any existing URL patterns.

The second argument in path() ❻ specifies which function to call in *views.py*. When a requested URL matches the pattern we're defining, Django calls the index() function from *views.py* (we'll write this view function in the next section). The third argument provides the name index for this URL pattern so we can refer to it in other code sections. Whenever we want to provide a link to the home page, we'll use this name instead of writing out a URL.

Writing a View

A view function takes in information from a request, prepares the data needed to generate a page, and then sends the data back to the browser, often by using a template that defines what the page will look like.

The file *views.py* in *learning_logs* was generated automatically when we ran the command python manage.py startapp. Here's what's in *views.py* right now:

views.py

```
from django.shortcuts import render

# Create your views here.
```

Currently, this file just imports the render() function, which renders the response based on the data provided by views. Open the views file and add the following code for the home page:

```
from django.shortcuts import render

def index(request):
    """The home page for Learning Log."""
    return render(request, 'learning_logs/index.html')
```

When a URL request matches the pattern we just defined, Django looks for a function called index() in the *views.py* file. Django then passes the request object to this view function. In this case, we don't need to process any data for the page, so the only code in the function is a call to render(). The render() function here passes two arguments—the original request object and a template it can use to build the page. Let's write this template.

Writing a Template

The template defines what the page should look like, and Django fills in the relevant data each time the page is requested. A template allows you to access any data provided by the view. Because our view for the home page provided no data, this template is fairly simple.

Inside the *learning_logs* folder, make a new folder called *templates*. Inside the *templates* folder, make another folder called *learning_logs*. This might seem a little redundant (we have a folder named *learning_logs* inside a folder named *templates* inside a folder named *learning_logs*), but it sets up a structure that Django can interpret unambiguously, even in the context of a large project containing many individual apps. Inside the inner *learning_logs* folder, make a new file called *index.html*. The path to the file will be *learning_log/learning_logs/templates/learning_logs/index.html*. Enter the following code into that file:

index.html
```
<p>Learning Log</p>

<p>Learning Log helps you keep track of your learning, for any topic you're
learning about.</p>
```

This is a very simple file. If you're not familiar with HTML, the `<p></p>` tags signify paragraphs. The `<p>` tag opens a paragraph, and the `</p>` tag closes a paragraph. We have two paragraphs: the first acts as a title, and the second describes what users can do with Learning Log.

Now when you request the project's base URL, *http://localhost:8000/*, you should see the page we just built instead of the default Django page. Django will take the requested URL, and that URL will match the pattern ''; then Django will call the function views.index(), which will render the page using the template contained in *index.html*. Figure 18-3 shows the resulting page.

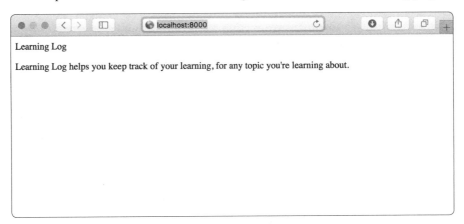

Figure 18-3: The home page for Learning Log

Although it might seem like a complicated process for creating one page, this separation between URLs, views, and templates works quite well. It allows you to think about each aspect of a project separately. In larger projects, it allows individuals working on the project to focus on the areas in which they're strongest. For example, a database specialist can focus on the models, a programmer can focus on the view code, and a web designer can focus on the templates.

NOTE *You might see the following error message:*

```
ModuleNotFoundError: No module named 'learning_logs.urls'
```

If you do, stop the development server by pressing CTRL-C in the terminal window where you issued the runserver command. Then reissue the command python manage .py runserver. You should be able to see the home page. Any time you run into an error like this, try stopping and restarting the server.

TRY IT YOURSELF

18-5. Meal Planner: Consider an app that helps people plan their meals through-out the week. Make a new folder called *meal_planner,* and start a new Django project inside this folder. Then make a new app called meal_plans. Make a simple home page for this project.

18-6. Pizzeria Home Page: Add a home page to the Pizzeria project you started in Exercise 18-4 (page 394).

Building Additional Pages

Now that we've established a routine for building a page, we can start to build out the Learning Log project. We'll build two pages that display data: a page that lists all topics and a page that shows all the entries for a particular topic. For each page, we'll specify a URL pattern, write a view function, and write a template. But before we do this, we'll create a base template that all templates in the project can inherit from.

Template Inheritance

When building a website, some elements will always need to be repeated on each page. Rather than writing these elements directly into each page, you can write a base template containing the repeated elements and then have each page inherit from the base. This approach lets you focus on developing the unique aspects of each page and makes it much easier to change the overall look and feel of the project.

The Parent Template

We'll create a template called *base.html* in the same directory as *index.html*. This file will contain elements common to all pages; every other template will inherit from *base.html*. The only element we want to repeat on each page right now is the title at the top. Because we'll include this template on every page, let's make the title a link to the home page:

base.html

```
    <p>
❶   <a href="{% url 'learning_logs:index' %}">Learning Log</a>
    </p>

❷ {% block content %}{% endblock content %}
```

The first part of this file creates a paragraph containing the name of the project, which also acts as a home page link. To generate a link, we use a *template tag*, which is indicated by braces and percent signs {% %}. A template tag generates information to be displayed on a page. Our template tag {% url 'learning_logs:index' %} generates a URL matching the URL pattern defined in *learning_logs/urls.py* with the name 'index' ❶. In this example, learning_logs is the *namespace* and index is a uniquely named URL pattern in that namespace. The namespace comes from the value we assigned to app_name in the *learning_logs/urls.py* file.

In a simple HTML page, a link is surrounded by the *anchor* tag <a>:

```
<a href="link_url">link text</a>
```

Having the template tag generate the URL for us makes it much easier to keep our links up to date. We only need to change the URL pattern in *urls.py*, and Django will automatically insert the updated URL the next time the page is requested. Every page in our project will inherit from *base.html*, so from now on, every page will have a link back to the home page.

At ❷ we insert a pair of block tags. This block, named content, is a placeholder; the child template will define the kind of information that goes in the content block.

A child template doesn't have to define every block from its parent, so you can reserve space in parent templates for as many blocks as you like; the child template uses only as many as it requires.

NOTE *In Python code, we almost always use four spaces when we indent. Template files tend to have more levels of nesting than Python files, so it's common to use only two spaces for each indentation level. You just need to ensure that you're consistent.*

The Child Template

Now we need to rewrite *index.html* to inherit from *base.html*. Add the following code to *index.html*:

index.html

```
❶ {% extends "learning_logs/base.html" %}

❷ {% block content %}
```

```
        <p>Learning Log helps you keep track of your learning, for any topic you're
        learning about.</p>
❸ {% endblock content %}
```

If you compare this to the original *index.html*, you can see that we've replaced the Learning Log title with the code for inheriting from a parent template ❶. A child template must have an {% extends %} tag on the first line to tell Django which parent template to inherit from. The file *base.html* is part of learning_logs, so we include *learning_logs* in the path to the parent template. This line pulls in everything contained in the *base.html* template and allows *index.html* to define what goes in the space reserved by the content block.

We define the content block at ❷ by inserting a {% block %} tag with the name content. Everything that we aren't inheriting from the parent template goes inside the content block. Here, that's the paragraph describing the Learning Log project. At ❸ we indicate that we're finished defining the content by using an {% endblock content %} tag. The {% endblock %} tag doesn't require a name, but if a template grows to contain multiple blocks, it can be helpful to know exactly which block is ending.

You can start to see the benefit of template inheritance: in a child template, we only need to include content that's unique to that page. This not only simplifies each template, but also makes it much easier to modify the site. To modify an element common to many pages, you only need to modify the parent template. Your changes are then carried over to every page that inherits from that template. In a project that includes tens or hundreds of pages, this structure can make it much easier and faster to improve your site.

NOTE *In a large project, it's common to have one parent template called* base.html *for the entire site and parent templates for each major section of the site. All the section templates inherit from* base.html, *and each page in the site inherits from a section template. This way you can easily modify the look and feel of the site as a whole, any section in the site, or any individual page. This configuration provides a very efficient way to work, and it encourages you to steadily update your site over time.*

The Topics Page

Now that we have an efficient approach to building pages, we can focus on our next two pages: the general topics page and the page to display entries for a single topic. The topics page will show all topics that users have created, and it's the first page that will involve working with data.

The Topics URL Pattern

First, we define the URL for the topics page. It's common to choose a simple URL fragment that reflects the kind of information presented on the page.

We'll use the word *topics*, so the URL *http://localhost:8000/topics/* will return this page. Here's how we modify *learning_logs/urls.py*:

urls.py
```
"""Defines URL patterns for learning_logs."""
--snip--
urlpatterns = [
    # Home page.
    path('', views.index, name='index'),
    # Page that shows all topics.
❶  path('topics/', views.topics, name='topics'),
]
```

We've simply added topics/ into the string argument used for the home page URL ❶. When Django examines a requested URL, this pattern will match any URL that has the base URL followed by *topics*. You can include or omit a forward slash at the end, but there can't be anything else after the word *topics*, or the pattern won't match. Any request with a URL that matches this pattern will then be passed to the function topics() in *views.py*.

The Topics View

The topics() function needs to retrieve some data from the database and send it to the template. Here's what we need to add to *views.py*:

views.py
```
    from django.shortcuts import render

❶  from .models import Topic

    def index(request):
        --snip--

❷  def topics(request):
        """Show all topics."""
❸      topics = Topic.objects.order_by('date_added')
❹      context = {'topics': topics}
❺      return render(request, 'learning_logs/topics.html', context)
```

We first import the model associated with the data we need ❶. The topics() function needs one parameter: the request object Django received from the server ❷. At ❸ we query the database by asking for the Topic objects, sorted by the date_added attribute. We store the resulting queryset in topics.

At ❹ we define a context that we'll send to the template. A *context* is a dictionary in which the keys are names we'll use in the template to access the data, and the values are the data we need to send to the template. In this case, there's one key-value pair, which contains the set of topics we'll display on the page. When building a page that uses data, we pass the context variable to render() as well as the request object and the path to the template ❺.

The Topics Template

The template for the topics page receives the context dictionary, so the template can use the data that topics() provides. Make a file called *topics.html* in the same directory as *index.html*. Here's how we can display the topics in the template:

topics.html

```
{% extends "learning_logs/base.html" %}

{% block content %}

  <p>Topics</p>
❶  <ul>
❷    {% for topic in topics %}
❸      <li>{{ topic }}</li>
❹    {% empty %}
        <li>No topics have been added yet.</li>
❺    {% endfor %}
❻  </ul>

{% endblock content %}
```

We use the {% extends %} tag to inherit from *base.html*, just as the index template does, and then open a content block. The body of this page contains a bulleted list of the topics that have been entered. In standard HTML, a bulleted list is called an *unordered list* and is indicated by the tags <ul></ul>. We begin the bulleted list of topics at ❶.

At ❷ we have another template tag equivalent to a for loop, which loops through the list topics from the context dictionary. The code used in templates differs from Python in some important ways. Python uses indentation to indicate which lines of a for statement are part of a loop. In a template, every for loop needs an explicit {% endfor %} tag indicating where the end of the loop occurs. So in a template, you'll see loops written like this:

```
{% for item in list %}
    do something with each item
{% endfor %}
```

Inside the loop, we want to turn each topic into an item in the bulleted list. To print a variable in a template, wrap the variable name in double braces. The braces won't appear on the page; they just indicate to Django that we're using a template variable. So the code {{ topic }} at ❸ will be replaced by the value of topic on each pass through the loop. The HTML tag <li></li> indicates a *list item*. Anything between these tags, inside a pair of <ul></ul> tags, will appear as a bulleted item in the list.

At ❹ we use the {% empty %} template tag, which tells Django what to do if there are no items in the list. In this case, we print a message informing the user that no topics have been added yet. The last two lines close out the for loop ❺ and then close out the bulleted list ❻.

Now we need to modify the base template to include a link to the topics page. Add the following code to *base.html*:

base.html

```
<p>
❶  <a href="{% url 'learning_logs:index' %}">Learning Log</a> -
❷  <a href="{% url 'learning_logs:topics' %}">Topics</a>
</p>

{% block content %}{% endblock content %}
```

We add a dash after the link to the home page ❶, and then add a link to the topics page using the {% url %} template tag again ❷. This line tells Django to generate a link matching the URL pattern with the name 'topics' in *learning_logs/urls.py*.

Now when you refresh the home page in your browser, you'll see a *Topics* link. When you click the link, you'll see a page that looks similar to Figure 18-4.

Figure 18-4: The topics page

Individual Topic Pages

Next, we need to create a page that can focus on a single topic, showing the topic name and all the entries for that topic. We'll again define a new URL pattern, write a view, and create a template. We'll also modify the topics page so each item in the bulleted list links to its corresponding topic page.

The Topic URL Pattern

The URL pattern for the topic page is a little different than the prior URL patterns because it will use the topic's id attribute to indicate which topic was requested. For example, if the user wants to see the detail page for the Chess topic, where the id is 1, the URL will be *http://localhost:8000/topics/1/*.

Here's a pattern to match this URL, which you should place in *learning _logs/urls.py*:

```
--snip--
urlpatterns = [
    --snip--
    # Detail page for a single topic.
    path('topics/<int:topic_id>/', views.topic, name='topic'),
]
```

Let's examine the string 'topics/<int:topic_id>/' in this URL pattern. The first part of the string tells Django to look for URLs that have the word *topics* after the base URL. The second part of the string, /<int:topic_id>/, matches an integer between two forward slashes and stores the integer value in an argument called topic_id.

When Django finds a URL that matches this pattern, it calls the view function topic() with the value stored in topic_id as an argument. We'll use the value of topic_id to get the correct topic inside the function.

The Topic View

The topic() function needs to get the topic and all associated entries from the database, as shown here:

```
  --snip--
❶ def topic(request, topic_id):
      """Show a single topic and all its entries."""
❷     topic = Topic.objects.get(id=topic_id)
❸     entries = topic.entry_set.order_by('-date_added')
❹     context = {'topic': topic, 'entries': entries}
❺     return render(request, 'learning_logs/topic.html', context)
```

This is the first view function that requires a parameter other than the request object. The function accepts the value captured by the expression /<int:topic_id>/ and stores it in topic_id ❶. At ❷ we use get() to retrieve the topic, just as we did in the Django shell. At ❸ we get the entries associated with this topic, and we order them according to date_added. The minus sign in front of date_added sorts the results in reverse order, which will display the most recent entries first. We store the topic and entries in the context dictionary ❹ and send context to the template *topic.html* ❺.

NOTE   *The code phrases at ❷ and ❸ are called* queries, *because they query the database for specific information. When you're writing queries like these in your own projects, it's helpful to try them out in the Django shell first. You'll get much quicker feedback in the shell than you will by writing a view and template, and then checking the results in a browser.*

The Topic Template

The template needs to display the name of the topic and the entries. We also need to inform the user if no entries have been made yet for this topic.

```
{% extends 'learning_logs/base.html' %}

{% block content %}
```

❶ `<p>Topic: {{ topic }}</p>`

```
    <p>Entries:</p>
```
❷ `<ul>`
❸ `{% for entry in entries %}`
```
        <li>
```
❹ `            <p>{{ entry.date_added|date:'M d, Y H:i' }}</p>`
❺ `            <p>{{ entry.text|linebreaks }}</p>`
```
        </li>
```
❻ `    {% empty %}`
```
        <li>There are no entries for this topic yet.</li>
    {% endfor %}
    </ul>

{% endblock content %}
```

We extend *base.html*, as we do for all pages in the project. Next, we show the topic that's currently being displayed ❶, which is stored in the template variable {{ topic }}. The variable topic is available because it's included in the context dictionary. We then start a bulleted list to show each of the entries ❷ and loop through them as we did the topics earlier ❸.

Each bullet lists two pieces of information: the timestamp and the full text of each entry. For the timestamp ❹, we display the value of the attribute date_added. In Django templates, a vertical line (|) represents a template *filter*—a function that modifies the value in a template variable. The filter date:'M d, Y H:i' displays timestamps in the format *January 1, 2018 23:00*. The next line displays the full value of text rather than just the first 50 characters from entry. The filter linebreaks ❺ ensures that long text entries include line breaks in a format understood by browsers rather than showing a block of uninterrupted text. At ❻ we use the {% empty %} template tag to print a message informing the user that no entries have been made.

Links from the Topics Page

Before we look at the topic page in a browser, we need to modify the topics template so each topic links to the appropriate page. Here's the change you need to make to *topics.html*:

```
--snip--
    {% for topic in topics %}
        <li>
          <a href="{% url 'learning_logs:topic' topic.id %}">{{ topic }}</a>
        </li>
    {% empty %}
--snip--
```

We use the URL template tag to generate the proper link, based on the URL pattern in learning_logs with the name 'topic'. This URL pattern requires a topic_id argument, so we add the attribute topic.id to the URL template tag. Now each topic in the list of topics is a link to a topic page, such as *http://localhost:8000/topics/1/*.

When you refresh the topics page and click a topic, you should see a page that looks like Figure 18-5.

NOTE *There's a subtle but important difference between topic.id and topic_id. The expression topic.id examines a topic and retrieves the value of the corresponding ID. The variable topic_id is a reference to that ID in the code. If you run into errors when working with IDs, make sure you're using these expressions in the appropriate ways.*

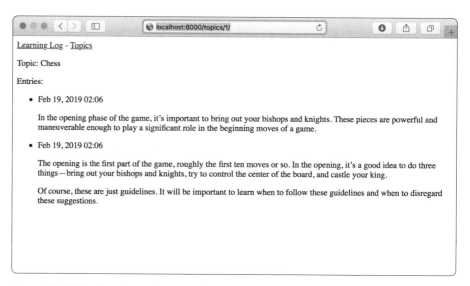

Figure 18-5: The detail page for a single topic, showing all entries for a topic

TRY IT YOURSELF

18-7. Template Documentation: Skim the Django template documentation at *https://docs.djangoproject.com/en/2.2/ref/templates/*. You can refer back to it when you're working on your own projects.

18-8. Pizzeria Pages: Add a page to the Pizzeria project from Exercise 18-6 (page 398) that shows the names of available pizzas. Then link each pizza name to a page displaying the pizza's toppings. Make sure you use template inheritance to build your pages efficiently.

Summary

In this chapter, you learned how to build simple web applications using the Django framework. You wrote a brief project specification, installed Django to a virtual environment, set up a project, and checked that the project was set up correctly. You set up an app and defined models to represent the data for your app. You learned about databases and how Django helps you migrate your database after you make a change to your models. You created a superuser for the admin site, and you used the admin site to enter some initial data.

You also explored the Django shell, which allows you to work with your project's data in a terminal session. You learned to define URLs, create view functions, and write templates to make pages for your site. You also used template inheritance to simplify the structure of individual templates and make it easier to modify the site as the project evolves.

In Chapter 19, you'll make intuitive, user-friendly pages that allow users to add new topics and entries and edit existing entries without going through the admin site. You'll also add a user registration system, allowing users to create an account and make their own learning log. This is the heart of a web app—the ability to create something that any number of users can interact with.

19

USER ACCOUNTS

At the heart of a web application is the ability for any user, anywhere in the world, to register an account with your app and start using it. In this chapter, you'll build forms so users can add their own topics and entries, and edit existing entries. You'll also learn how Django guards against common attacks to form-based pages so you don't have to spend much time thinking about securing your apps.

You'll also implement a user authentication system. You'll build a registration page for users to create accounts, and then restrict access to certain pages to logged-in users only. Then you'll modify some of the view functions so users can only see their own data. You'll learn to keep your users' data safe and secure.

Allowing Users to Enter Data

Before we build an authentication system for creating accounts, we'll first add some pages that allow users to enter their own data. We'll give users the ability to add a new topic, add a new entry, and edit their previous entries.

Currently, only a superuser can enter data through the admin site. We don't want users to interact with the admin site, so we'll use Django's form-building tools to build pages that allow users to enter data.

Adding New Topics

Let's start by allowing users to add a new topic. Adding a form-based page works in much the same way as the pages we've already built: we define a URL, write a view function, and write a template. The one major difference is the addition of a new module called *forms.py*, which will contain the forms.

The Topic ModelForm

Any page that lets a user enter and submit information on a web page is a *form*, even if it doesn't look like one. When users enter information, we need to *validate* that the information provided is the right kind of data and is not malicious, such as code to interrupt our server. We then need to process and save valid information to the appropriate place in the database. Django automates much of this work.

The simplest way to build a form in Django is to use a *ModelForm*, which uses the information from the models we defined in Chapter 18 to automatically build a form. Write your first form in the file *forms.py*, which you should create in the same directory as *models.py*:

forms.py
```
from django import forms

from .models import Topic

❶ class TopicForm(forms.ModelForm):
      class Meta:
❷         model = Topic
❸         fields = ['text']
❹         labels = {'text': ''}
```

We first import the forms module and the model we'll work with, called Topic. At ❶ we define a class called TopicForm, which inherits from forms .ModelForm.

The simplest version of a ModelForm consists of a nested Meta class telling Django which model to base the form on and which fields to include in the form. At ❷ we build a form from the Topic model and include only the text field ❸. The code at ❹ tells Django not to generate a label for the text field.

The new_topic URL

The URL for a new page should be short and descriptive. When the user wants to add a new topic, we'll send them to *http://localhost:8000/new_topic/*. Here's the URL pattern for the new_topic page, which you add to *learning_logs/urls.py*:

urls.py
```
--snip--
urlpatterns = [
    --snip--
    # Page for adding a new topic
    path('new_topic/', views.new_topic, name='new_topic'),
]
```

This URL pattern sends requests to the view function new_topic(), which we'll write next.

The new_topic() View Function

The new_topic() function needs to handle two different situations: initial requests for the new_topic page (in which case it should show a blank form) and the processing of any data submitted in the form. After data from a submitted form is processed, it needs to redirect the user back to the topics page:

views.py
```
from django.shortcuts import render, redirect

from .models import Topic
from .forms import TopicForm

--snip--
def new_topic(request):
    """Add a new topic."""
❶    if request.method != 'POST':
        # No data submitted; create a blank form.
❷        form = TopicForm()
    else:
        # POST data submitted; process data.
❸        form = TopicForm(data=request.POST)
❹        if form.is_valid():
❺            form.save()
❻            return redirect('learning_logs:topics')

    # Display a blank or invalid form.
❼    context = {'form': form}
    return render(request, 'learning_logs/new_topic.html', context)
```

We import the function redirect, which we'll use to redirect the user back to the topics page after they submit their topic. The redirect() function takes in the name of a view and redirects the user to that view. We also import the form we just wrote, TopicForm.

GET and POST Requests

The two main types of request you'll use when building web apps are GET requests and POST requests. You use *GET* requests for pages that only read data from the server. You usually use *POST* requests when the user needs to submit information through a form. We'll be specifying the POST method for processing all of our forms. (A few other kinds of requests exist, but we won't use them in this project.)

The new_topic() function takes in the request object as a parameter. When the user initially requests this page, their browser will send a GET request. Once the user has filled out and submitted the form, their browser will submit a POST request. Depending on the request, we'll know whether the user is requesting a blank form (a GET request) or asking us to process a completed form (a POST request).

The test at ❶ determines whether the request method is GET or POST. If the request method isn't POST, the request is probably GET, so we need to return a blank form (if it's another kind of request, it's still safe to return a blank form). We make an instance of TopicForm ❷, assign it to the variable form, and send the form to the template in the context dictionary ❼. Because we included no arguments when instantiating TopicForm, Django creates a blank form that the user can fill out.

If the request method is POST, the else block runs and processes the data submitted in the form. We make an instance of TopicForm ❸ and pass it the data entered by the user, stored in request.POST. The form object that's returned contains the information submitted by the user.

We can't save the submitted information in the database until we've checked that it's valid ❹. The is_valid() method checks that all required fields have been filled in (all fields in a form are required by default) and that the data entered matches the field types expected—for example, that the length of text is less than 200 characters, as we specified in *models.py* in Chapter 18. This automatic validation saves us a lot of work. If everything is valid, we can call save() ❺, which writes the data from the form to the database.

Once we've saved the data, we can leave this page. We use redirect() to redirect the user's browser to the topics page, where the user should see the topic they just entered in the list of topics.

The context variable is defined at the end of the view function, and the page is rendered using the template *new_topic.html*, which we'll create next. This code is placed outside of any if block; it will run if a blank form was created, and it will run if a submitted form is determined to be invalid. An invalid form will include some default error messages to help the user submit acceptable data.

The new_topic Template

Now we'll make a new template called *new_topic.html* to display the form we just created.

```
{% extends "learning_logs/base.html" %}

{% block content %}
  <p>Add a new topic:</p>
```
❶ `<form action="{% url 'learning_logs:new_topic' %}" method='post'>`
❷ `{% csrf_token %}`
❸ `{{ form.as_p }}`
❹ `<button name="submit">Add topic</button>`
```
  </form>

{% endblock content %}
```

This template extends *base.html*, so it has the same base structure as the rest of the pages in Learning Log. At ❶ we define an HTML form. The action argument tells the browser where to send the data submitted in the form; in this case, we send it back to the view function new_topic(). The method argument tells the browser to submit the data as a POST request.

Django uses the template tag {% csrf_token %} ❷ to prevent attackers from using the form to gain unauthorized access to the server (this kind of attack is called a *cross-site request forgery*). At ❸ we display the form; here you see how simple Django can make certain tasks, such as displaying a form. We only need to include the template variable {{ form.as_p }} for Django to create all the fields necessary to display the form automatically. The as_p modifier tells Django to render all the form elements in paragraph format, as a simple way to display the form neatly.

Django doesn't create a submit button for forms, so we define one at ❹.

Linking to the new_topic Page

Next, we include a link to the new_topic page on the topics page:

```
{% extends "learning_logs/base.html" %}

{% block content %}

  <p>Topics</p>

  <ul>
    --snip--
  </ul>

  <a href="{% url 'learning_logs:new_topic' %}">Add a new topic</a>

{% endblock content %}
```

Place the link after the list of existing topics. Figure 19-1 shows the resulting form. Use the form to add a few new topics of your own.

Figure 19-1: The page for adding a new topic

Adding New Entries

Now that the user can add a new topic, they'll want to add new entries too. We'll again define a URL, write a view function and a template, and link to the page. But first, we'll add another class to *forms.py*.

The Entry ModelForm

We need to create a form associated with the Entry model but this time with a bit more customization than TopicForm:

forms.py
```
from django import forms

from .models import Topic, Entry

class TopicForm(forms.ModelForm):
    --snip--

class EntryForm(forms.ModelForm):
    class Meta:
        model = Entry
        fields = ['text']
❶        labels = {'text': ''}
❷        widgets = {'text': forms.Textarea(attrs={'cols': 80})}
```

We update the import statement to include Entry as well as Topic. We make a new class called EntryForm that inherits from forms.ModelForm. The EntryForm class has a nested Meta class listing the model it's based on and the field to include in the form. We again give the field 'text' a blank label ❶.

At ❷ we include the widgets attribute. A *widget* is an HTML form element, such as a single-line text box, multi-line text area, or drop-down list. By including the widgets attribute, you can override Django's default widget choices. By telling Django to use a forms.Textarea element, we're customizing the input widget for the field 'text' so the text area will be 80 columns wide instead of the default 40. This gives users enough room to write a meaningful entry.

The new_entry URL

New entries must be associated with a particular topic, so we need to include a topic_id argument in the URL for adding a new entry. Here's the URL, which you add to *learning_logs/urls.py*:

urls.py
```
--snip--
urlpatterns = [
    --snip--
    # Page for adding a new entry
    path('new_entry/<int:topic_id>/', views.new_entry, name='new_entry'),
]
```

This URL pattern matches any URL with the form http://localhost: 8000/new_entry/*id*/, where *id* is a number matching the topic ID. The code `<int:topic_id>` captures a numerical value and assigns it to the variable topic_id. When a URL matching this pattern is requested, Django sends the request and the topic's ID to the new_entry() view function.

The new_entry() View Function

The view function for new_entry is much like the function for adding a new topic. Add the following code to your *views.py* file:

views.py
```
from django.shortcuts import render, redirect

from .models import Topic
from .forms import TopicForm, EntryForm

--snip--
def new_entry(request, topic_id):
    """Add a new entry for a particular topic."""
❶  topic = Topic.objects.get(id=topic_id)

❷  if request.method != 'POST':
        # No data submitted; create a blank form.
❸      form = EntryForm()
    else:
        # POST data submitted; process data.
❹      form = EntryForm(data=request.POST)
        if form.is_valid():
❺          new_entry = form.save(commit=False)
❻          new_entry.topic = topic
            new_entry.save()
❼          return redirect('learning_logs:topic', topic_id=topic_id)

    # Display a blank or invalid form.
    context = {'topic': topic, 'form': form}
    return render(request, 'learning_logs/new_entry.html', context)
```

We update the `import` statement to include the `EntryForm` we just made. The definition of `new_entry()` has a `topic_id` parameter to store the value it receives from the URL. We'll need the topic to render the page and process the form's data, so we use `topic_id` to get the correct topic object at ❶.

At ❷ we check whether the request method is POST or GET. The `if` block executes if it's a GET request, and we create a blank instance of `EntryForm` ❸.

If the request method is POST, we process the data by making an instance of `EntryForm`, populated with the POST data from the `request` object ❹. We then check whether the form is valid. If it is, we need to set the entry object's `topic` attribute before saving it to the database. When we call `save()`, we include the argument `commit=False` ❺ to tell Django to create a new entry object and assign it to `new_entry` without saving it to the database yet. We set the `topic` attribute of `new_entry` to the topic we pulled from the database at the beginning of the function ❻. Then we call `save()` with no arguments, saving the entry to the database with the correct associated topic.

The `redirect()` call at ❼ requires two arguments—the name of the view we want to redirect to and the argument that view function requires. Here, we're redirecting to `topic()`, which needs the argument `topic_id`. This view then renders the topic page that the user made an entry for, and they should see their new entry in the list of entries.

At the end of the function, we create a context dictionary and render the page using the *new_entry.html* template. This code will execute for a blank form or for a submitted form that is evaluated as invalid.

The new_entry Template

As you can see in the following code, the template for `new_entry` is similar to the template for `new_topic`:

new_entry.html

```
{% extends "learning_logs/base.html" %}

{% block content %}

❶  <p><a href="{% url 'learning_logs:topic' topic.id %}">{{ topic }}</a></p>

    <p>Add a new entry:</p>
❷  <form action="{% url 'learning_logs:new_entry' topic.id %}" method='post'>
      {% csrf_token %}
      {{ form.as_p }}
      <button name='submit'>Add entry</button>
    </form>

{% endblock content %}
```

We show the topic at the top of the page ❶, so the user can see which topic they're adding an entry to. The topic also acts as a link back to the main page for that topic.

The form's action argument includes the topic_id value in the URL, so the view function can associate the new entry with the correct topic ❷. Other than that, this template looks just like *new_topic.html.*

Linking to the new_entry Page

Next, we need to include a link to the new_entry page from each topic page in the topic template:

topic.html

```
{% extends "learning_logs/base.html" %}

{% block content %}

  <p>Topic: {{ topic }}</p>

  <p>Entries:</p>
  <p>
    <a href="{% url 'learning_logs:new_entry' topic.id %}">Add new entry</a>
  </p>

  <ul>
  --snip--
  </ul>

{% endblock content %}
```

We place the link to add entries just before showing the entries, because adding a new entry will be the most common action on this page. Figure 19-2 shows the new_entry page. Now users can add new topics and as many entries as they want for each topic. Try out the new_entry page by adding a few entries to some of the topics you've created.

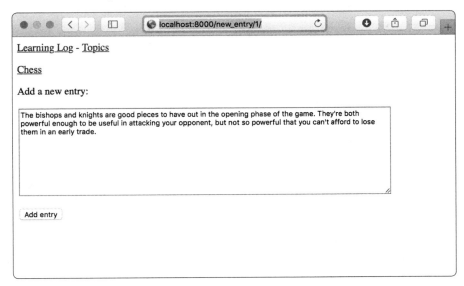

Figure 19-2: The new_entry page

Editing Entries

Now we'll make a page so users can edit the entries they've added.

The edit_entry URL

The URL for the page needs to pass the ID of the entry to be edited. Here's *learning_logs/urls.py*:

urls.py
```
--snip--
urlpatterns = [
    --snip--
    # Page for editing an entry.
    path('edit_entry/<int:entry_id>/', views.edit_entry, name='edit_entry'),
]
```

The ID passed in the URL (for example, *http://localhost:8000/edit _entry/1/)* is stored in the parameter entry_id. The URL pattern sends requests that match this format to the view function edit_entry().

The edit_entry() View Function

When the edit_entry page receives a GET request, the edit_entry() function returns a form for editing the entry. When the page receives a POST request with revised entry text, it saves the modified text into the database:

views.py
```
from django.shortcuts import render, redirect

from .models import Topic, Entry
from .forms import TopicForm, EntryForm
--snip--

def edit_entry(request, entry_id):
    """Edit an existing entry."""
❶   entry = Entry.objects.get(id=entry_id)
    topic = entry.topic

    if request.method != 'POST':
        # Initial request; pre-fill form with the current entry.
❷       form = EntryForm(instance=entry)
    else:
        # POST data submitted; process data.
❸       form = EntryForm(instance=entry, data=request.POST)
        if form.is_valid():
❹           form.save()
❺           return redirect('learning_logs:topic', topic_id=topic.id)

    context = {'entry': entry, 'topic': topic, 'form': form}
    return render(request, 'learning_logs/edit_entry.html', context)
```

We first import the Entry model. At ❶ we get the entry object that the user wants to edit and the topic associated with this entry. In the if block, which runs for a GET request, we make an instance of EntryForm with the argument instance=entry ❷. This argument tells Django to create the form prefilled with information from the existing entry object. The user will see their existing data and be able to edit that data.

When processing a POST request, we pass the instance=entry argument and the data=request.POST argument ❸. These arguments tell Django to create a form instance based on the information associated with the existing entry object, updated with any relevant data from request.POST. We then check whether the form is valid; if it is, we call save() with no arguments because the entry is already associated with the correct topic ❹. We then redirect to the topic page, where the user should see the updated version of the entry they edited ❺.

If we're showing an initial form for editing the entry or if the submitted form is invalid, we create the context dictionary and render the page using the *edit_entry.html* template.

The edit_entry Template

Next, we create an *edit_entry.html* template, which is similar to *new_entry.html*:

edit_entry.html
```
{% extends "learning_logs/base.html" %}

{% block content %}

  <p><a href="{% url 'learning_logs:topic' topic.id %}">{{ topic }}</a></p>

  <p>Edit entry:</p>

❶ <form action="{% url 'learning_logs:edit_entry' entry.id %}" method='post'>
    {% csrf_token %}
    {{ form.as_p }}
❷   <button name="submit">Save changes</button>
  </form>

{% endblock content %}
```

At ❶ the action argument sends the form back to the edit_entry() function for processing. We include the entry ID as an argument in the {% url %} tag, so the view function can modify the correct entry object. We label the submit button as *Save changes* to remind the user they're saving edits, not creating a new entry ❷.

Linking to the edit_entry Page

Now we need to include a link to the edit_entry page for each entry on the topic page:

topic.html

```
--snip--
  {% for entry in entries %}
    <li>
      <p>{{ entry.date_added|date:'M d, Y H:i' }}</p>
      <p>{{ entry.text|linebreaks }}</p>
      <p>
        <a href="{% url 'learning_logs:edit_entry' entry.id %}">Edit entry</a>
      </p>
    </li>
--snip--
```

We include the edit link after each entry's date and text has been displayed. We use the {% url %} template tag to determine the URL for the named URL pattern edit_entry, along with the ID attribute of the current entry in the loop (entry.id). The link text *Edit entry* appears after each entry on the page. Figure 19-3 shows what the topic page looks like with these links.

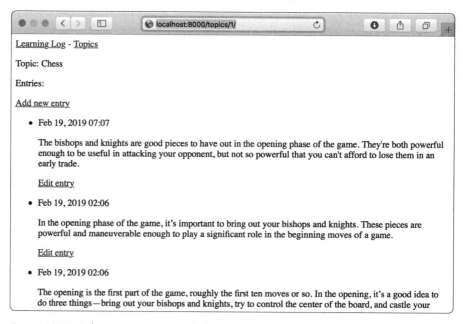

Figure 19-3: Each entry now has a link for editing that entry.

Learning Log now has most of the functionality it needs. Users can add topics and entries, and read through any set of entries they want. In the next section, we'll implement a user registration system so anyone can make an account with Learning Log and create their own set of topics and entries.

19-1. Blog: Start a new Django project called *Blog*. Create an app called *blogs* in the project and a model called BlogPost. The model should have fields like title, text, and date_added. Create a superuser for the project, and use the admin site to make a couple of short posts. Make a home page that shows all posts in chronological order.

Create a form for making new posts and another for editing existing posts. Fill in your forms to make sure they work.

Setting Up User Accounts

In this section, we'll set up a user registration and authorization system so people can register an account and log in and out. We'll create a new app to contain all the functionality related to working with users. We'll use the default user authentication system included with Django to do as much of the work as possible. We'll also modify the Topic model slightly so every topic belongs to a certain user.

The users App

We'll start by creating a new app called users, using the startapp command:

```
(ll_env)learning_log$ python manage.py startapp users
(ll_env)learning_log$ ls
❶ db.sqlite3  learning_log  learning_logs  ll_env  manage.py  users
(ll_env)learning_log$ ls users
❷ __init__.py admin.py apps.py migrations models.py tests.py views.py
```

This command makes a new directory called *users* ❶ with a structure identical to the learning_logs app ❷.

Adding users to settings.py

We need to add our new app to INSTALLED_APPS in *settings.py*, like so:

settings.py
```
--snip--
INSTALLED_APPS = [
    # My apps
    'learning_logs',
    'users',

    # Default django apps.
    --snip--
]
--snip--
```

Now Django will include the users app in the overall project.

Including the URLs from users

Next, we need to modify the root *urls.py* so it includes the URLs we'll write for the users app:

urls.py
```
from django.contrib import admin
from django.urls import path, include

urlpatterns = [
    path('admin/', admin.site.urls),
    path('users/', include('users.urls')),
    path('', include('learning_logs.urls')),
]
```

We add a line to include the file *urls.py* from users. This line will match any URL that starts with the word *users*, such as *http://localhost:8000/users /login/*.

The Login Page

We'll first implement a login page. We'll use the default `login` view Django provides, so the URL pattern for this app looks a little different. Make a new *urls.py* file in the directory *learning_log/users/*, and add the following to it:

urls.py
```
"""Defines URL patterns for users"""

from django.urls import path, include

❶ app_name = 'users'
urlpatterns = [
      # Include default auth urls.
❷     path('', include('django.contrib.auth.urls')),
  ]
```

We import the `path` function, and then import the `include` function so we can include some default authentication URLs that Django has defined. These default URLs include named URL patterns, such as `'login'` and `'logout'`. We set the variable `app_name` to `'users'` so Django can distinguish these URLs from URLs belonging to other apps ❶. Even default URLs provided by Django, when included in the users app's *urls.py* file, will be accessible through the users namespace.

The login page's pattern matches the URL *http://localhost:8000/users /login/* ❷. When Django reads this URL, the word *users* tells Django to look in *users/urls.py*, and *login* tells it to send requests to Django's default `login` view.

The login Template

When the user requests the login page, Django will use a default view function, but we still need to provide a template for the page. The default authentication views look for templates inside a folder called *registration*, so we'll need to make that folder. Inside the *learning_log/users/* directory, make a directory called *templates*; inside that, make another directory called *registration*. Here's the *login.html* template, which you should save in *learning_log /users/templates/registration*:

login.html

```
{% extends "learning_logs/base.html" %}

{% block content %}
```
❶
```
    {% if form.errors %}
      <p>Your username and password didn't match. Please try again.</p>
    {% endif %}
```
❷
```
    <form method="post" action="{% url 'users:login' %}">
      {% csrf_token %}
```
❸
```
      {{ form.as_p }}
```
❹
```
      <button name="submit">Log in</button>
```
❺
```
      <input type="hidden" name="next"
        value="{% url 'learning_logs:index' %}" />
    </form>

{% endblock content %}
```

This template extends *base.html* to ensure that the login page will have the same look and feel as the rest of the site. Note that a template in one app can inherit from a template in another app.

If the form's errors attribute is set, we display an error message ❶, reporting that the username and password combination don't match anything stored in the database.

We want the login view to process the form, so we set the action argument as the URL of the login page ❷. The login view sends a form to the template, and it's up to us to display the form ❸ and add a submit button ❹. At ❺ we include a hidden form element, 'next'; the value argument tells Django where to redirect the user after they've logged in successfully. In this case, we send the user back to the home page.

Linking to the Login Page

Let's add the login link to *base.html* so it appears on every page. We don't want the link to display when the user is already logged in, so we nest it inside an {% if %} tag:

base.html

```
<p>
  <a href="{% url 'learning_logs:index' %}">Learning Log</a> -
  <a href="{% url 'learning_logs:topics' %}">Topics</a> -
```
❶
```
  {% if user.is_authenticated %}
```
❷
```
    Hello, {{ user.username }}.
  {% else %}
```
❸
```
    <a href="{% url 'users:login' %}">Log in</a>
  {% endif %}
```

```
</p>

{% block content %}{% endblock content %}
```

In Django's authentication system, every template has a user variable available, which always has an is_authenticated attribute set: the attribute is True if the user is logged in and False if they aren't. This attribute allows you to display one message to authenticated users and another to unauthenticated users.

Here we display a greeting to users currently logged in ❶. Authenticated users have an additional username attribute set, which we use to personalize the greeting and remind the user they're logged in ❷. At ❸ we display a link to the login page for users who haven't been authenticated.

Using the Login Page

We've already set up a user account, so let's log in to see if the page works. Go to *http://localhost:8000/admin/*. If you're still logged in as an admin, look for a logout link in the header and click it.

When you're logged out, go to *http://localhost:8000/users/login/*. You should see a login page similar to the one shown in Figure 19-4. Enter the username and password you set up earlier, and you should be brought back to the index page. The header on the home page should display a greeting personalized with your username.

Figure 19-4: The login page

Logging Out

Now we need to provide a way for users to log out. We'll put a link in *base .html* that logs out users; when they click this link, they'll go to a page confirming that they've been logged out.

Adding a Logout Link to base.html

We'll add the link for logging out to *base.html* so it's available on every page. We'll include it in the {% if user.is_authenticated %} portion so only users who are already logged in can see it:

base.html
```
--snip--
  {% if user.is_authenticated %}
    Hello, {{ user.username }}.
    <a href="{% url 'users:logout' %}">Log out</a>
  {% else %}
    --snip--
```

The default named URL pattern for logging out is simply 'logout'.

The Logout Confirmation Page

Users will want to know that they've successfully logged out, so the default logout view renders the page using the template *logged_out.html*, which we'll create now. Here's a simple page confirming that the user has been logged out. Save this file in *templates/registration*, the same place where you saved *login.html*:

logged_out.html
```
{% extends "learning_logs/base.html" %}

{% block content %}
  <p>You have been logged out. Thank you for visiting!</p>
{% endblock content %}
```

We don't need anything else on this page, because *base.html* provides links back to the home page and the login page if the user wants to go back to either page.

Figure 19-5 shows the logged out page as it appears to a user who has just clicked the *Log out* link. The styling is minimal because we're focusing on building a site that works properly. When the required set of features works, we'll style the site to look more professional.

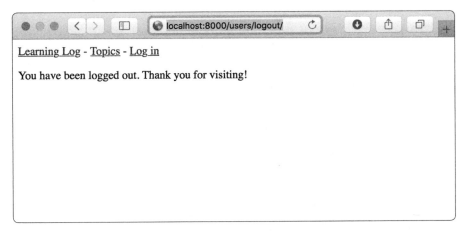

Figure 19-5: The logged out page confirms that a user has successfully logged out.

The Registration Page

Next, we'll build a page so new users can register. We'll use Django's default UserCreationForm but write our own view function and template.

The register URL

The following code provides the URL pattern for the registration page, again in *users/urls.py*:

urls.py
```
"""Defines URL patterns for users"""

from django.urls import path, include

from . import views

app_name = 'users'
urlpatterns = [
    # Include default auth urls.
    path('', include('django.contrib.auth.urls')),
    # Registration page.
    path('register/', views.register, name='register'),
]
```

We import the views module from users, which we need because we're writing our own view for the registration page. The pattern for the registration page matches the URL *http://localhost:8000/users/register/* and sends requests to the register() function we're about to write.

The register() View Function

The register() view function needs to display a blank registration form when the registration page is first requested and then process completed registration forms when they're submitted. When a registration is successful, the function also needs to log in the new user. Add the following code to *users/views.py*:

views.py
```
from django.shortcuts import render, redirect
from django.contrib.auth import login
from django.contrib.auth.forms import UserCreationForm

def register(request):
    """Register a new user."""
    if request.method != 'POST':
        # Display blank registration form.
❶      form = UserCreationForm()
    else:
        # Process completed form.
❷      form = UserCreationForm(data=request.POST)

❸      if form.is_valid():
❹          new_user = form.save()
            # Log the user in and then redirect to home page.
```

```
❺            login(request, new_user)
❻            return redirect('learning_logs:index')

    # Display a blank or invalid form.
    context = {'form': form}
    return render(request, 'registration/register.html', context)
```

We import the render() and redirect() functions. Then we import the login() function to log the user in if their registration information is correct. We also import the default UserCreationForm. In the register() function, we check whether or not we're responding to a POST request. If we're not, we make an instance of UserCreationForm with no initial data ❶.

If we're responding to a POST request, we make an instance of UserCreationForm based on the submitted data ❷. We check that the data is valid ❸—in this case, that the username has the appropriate characters, the passwords match, and the user isn't trying to do anything malicious in their submission.

If the submitted data is valid, we call the form's save() method to save the username and the hash of the password to the database ❹. The save() method returns the newly created user object, which we assign to new_user. When the user's information is saved, we log them in by calling the login() function with the request and new_user objects ❺, which creates a valid session for the new user. Finally, we redirect the user to the home page ❻, where a personalized greeting in the header tells them their registration was successful.

At the end of the function we render the page, which will either be a blank form or a submitted form that is invalid.

The register Template

Now create a template for the registration page, which will be similar to the login page. Be sure to save it in the same directory as *login.html*:

register.html
```
{% extends "learning_logs/base.html" %}

{% block content %}

  <form method="post" action="{% url 'users:register' %}">
    {% csrf_token %}
    {{ form.as_p }}

    <button name="submit">Register</button>
    <input type="hidden" name="next" value="{% url 'learning_logs:index' %}" />
  </form>

{% endblock content %}
```

We use the as_p method again so Django will display all the fields in the form appropriately, including any error messages if the form isn't filled out correctly.

Linking to the Registration Page

Next, we'll add the code to show the registration page link to any user who isn't currently logged in:

```
--snip--
  {% if user.is_authenticated %}
    Hello, {{ user.username }}.
    <a href="{% url 'users:logout' %}">Log out</a>
  {% else %}
    <a href="{% url 'users:register' %}">Register</a> -
    <a href="{% url 'users:login' %}">Log in</a>
  {% endif %}
--snip--
```

Now users who are logged in see a personalized greeting and a logout link. Users who aren't logged in see a registration page link and a login link. Try out the registration page by making several user accounts with different usernames.

In the next section, we'll restrict some of the pages so they're available only to registered users, and we'll make sure every topic belongs to a specific user.

NOTE *The registration system we've set up allows anyone to make any number of accounts for Learning Log. But some systems require users to confirm their identity by sending a confirmation email the user must reply to. By doing so, the system generates fewer spam accounts than the simple system we're using here. However, when you're learning to build apps, it's perfectly appropriate to practice with a simple user registration system like the one we're using.*

TRY IT YOURSELF

19-2. Blog Accounts: Add a user authentication and registration system to the Blog project you started in Exercise 19-1 (page 421). Make sure logged-in users see their username somewhere on the screen and unregistered users see a link to the registration page.

Allowing Users to Own Their Data

Users should be able to enter data exclusive to them, so we'll create a system to figure out which data belongs to which user. Then we'll restrict access to certain pages so users can work with only their own data.

We'll modify the Topic model so every topic belongs to a specific user. This will also take care of entries, because every entry belongs to a specific topic. We'll start by restricting access to certain pages.

Restricting Access with @login_required

Django makes it easy to restrict access to certain pages to logged-in users through the @login_required decorator. A *decorator* is a directive placed just before a function definition that Python applies to the function before it runs, to alter how the function code behaves. Let's look at an example.

Restricting Access to the Topics Page

Each topic will be owned by a user, so only registered users can request the topics page. Add the following code to *learning_logs/views.py*:

views.py
```
from django.shortcuts import render, redirect
from django.contrib.auth.decorators import login_required

from .models import Topic, Entry
--snip--

@login_required
def topics(request):
    """Show all topics."""
    --snip--
```

We first import the login_required() function. We apply login_required() as a decorator to the topics() view function by prepending login_required with the @ symbol. As a result, Python knows to run the code in login_required() before the code in topics().

The code in login_required() checks whether a user is logged in, and Django runs the code in topics() only if they are. If the user isn't logged in, they're redirected to the login page.

To make this redirect work, we need to modify *settings.py* so Django knows where to find the login page. Add the following at the very end of *settings.py*:

settings.py
```
--snip--

# My settings
LOGIN_URL = 'users:login'
```

Now when an unauthenticated user requests a page protected by the @login_required decorator, Django will send the user to the URL defined by LOGIN_URL in *settings.py*.

You can test this setting by logging out of any user accounts and going to the home page. Click the **Topics** link, which should redirect you to the login page. Then log in to any of your accounts, and from the home page click the **Topics** link again. You should be able to access the topics page.

Restricting Access Throughout Learning Log

Django makes it easy to restrict access to pages, but you have to decide which pages to protect. It's best to think about which pages need to be unrestricted first, and then restrict all the other pages in the project. You can easily correct overrestricting access, and it's less dangerous than leaving sensitive pages unrestricted.

In Learning Log, we'll keep the home page and the registration page unrestricted. We'll restrict access to every other page.

Here's *learning_logs/views.py* with @login_required decorators applied to every view except index():

views.py

```
--snip--
@login_required
def topics(request):
    --snip--

@login_required
def topic(request, topic_id):
    --snip--

@login_required
def new_topic(request):
    --snip--

@login_required
def new_entry(request, topic_id):
    --snip--

@login_required
def edit_entry(request, entry_id):
    --snip--
```

Try accessing each of these pages while logged out: you'll be redirected back to the login page. You'll also be unable to click links to pages such as new_topic. But if you enter the URL *http://localhost:8000/new_topic/,* you'll be redirected to the login page. You should restrict access to any URL that's publicly accessible and relates to private user data.

Connecting Data to Certain Users

Next, we need to connect the data to the user who submitted it. We need to connect only the data highest in the hierarchy to a user, and the lower-level data will follow. For example, in Learning Log, topics are the highest level of data in the app, and all entries are connected to a topic. As long as each topic belongs to a specific user, we can trace the ownership of each entry in the database.

We'll modify the Topic model by adding a foreign key relationship to a user. We'll then have to migrate the database. Finally, we'll modify some of the views so they only show the data associated with the currently logged in user.

Modifying the Topic Model

The modification to *models.py* is just two lines:

models.py
```
from django.db import models
from django.contrib.auth.models import User

class Topic(models.Model):
    """A topic the user is learning about."""
    text = models.CharField(max_length=200)
    date_added = models.DateTimeField(auto_now_add=True)
    owner = models.ForeignKey(User, on_delete=models.CASCADE)

    def __str__(self):
        """Return a string representation of the model."""
        return self.text

class Entry(models.Model):
    --snip--
```

We import the User model from django.contrib.auth. Then we add an owner field to Topic, which establishes a foreign key relationship to the User model. If a user is deleted, all the topics associated with that user will be deleted as well.

Identifying Existing Users

When we migrate the database, Django will modify the database so it can store a connection between each topic and a user. To make the migration, Django needs to know which user to associate with each existing topic. The simplest approach is to start by giving all existing topics to one user—for example, the superuser. But first we need to know that user's ID.

Let's look at the IDs of all users created so far. Start a Django shell session and issue the following commands:

```
(ll_env)learning_log$ python manage.py shell
❶ >>> from django.contrib.auth.models import User
❷ >>> User.objects.all()
<QuerySet [<User: ll_admin>, <User: eric>, <User: willie>]>
❸ >>> for user in User.objects.all():
...     print(user.username, user.id)
...
ll_admin 1
eric 2
willie 3
>>>
```

At ❶ we import the User model into the shell session. We then look at all the users that have been created so far ❷. The output shows three users: *ll_admin, eric,* and *willie.*

At ❸ we loop through the list of users and print each user's username and ID. When Django asks which user to associate the existing topics with, we'll use one of these ID values.

Migrating the Database

Now that we know the IDs, we can migrate the database. When we do this, Python will ask us to connect the Topic model to a particular owner temporarily or to add a default to our *models.py* file to tell it what to do. Choose option 1:

```
❶ (ll_env)learning_log$ python manage.py makemigrations learning_logs
❷ You are trying to add a non-nullable field 'owner' to topic without a default;
  we can't do that (the database needs something to populate existing rows).
❸ Please select a fix:
   1) Provide a one-off default now (will be set on all existing rows with a
      null value for this column)
   2) Quit, and let me add a default in models.py
❹ Select an option: 1
❺ Please enter the default value now, as valid Python
  The datetime and django.utils.timezone modules are available, so you can do
  e.g. timezone.now
  Type 'exit' to exit this prompt
❻ >>> 1
  Migrations for 'learning_logs':
    learning_logs/migrations/0003_topic_owner.py
  - Add field owner to topic
  (ll_env)learning_log$
```

We start by issuing the makemigrations command ❶. In the output at ❷, Django indicates that we're trying to add a required (non-nullable) field to an existing model (topic) with no default value specified. Django gives us two options at ❸: we can provide a default right now, or we can quit and add a default value in *models.py*. At ❹ we've chosen the first option. Django then asks us to enter the default value ❺.

To associate all existing topics with the original admin user, *ll_admin*, I entered the user ID of 1 at ❻. You can use the ID of any user you've created; it doesn't have to be a superuser. Django then migrates the database using this value and generates the migration file *0003_topic_owner.py*, which adds the field owner to the Topic model.

Now we can execute the migration. Enter the following in an active virtual environment:

```
(ll_env)learning_log$ python manage.py migrate
Operations to perform:
  Apply all migrations: admin, auth, contenttypes, learning_logs, sessions
Running migrations:
❶   Applying learning_logs.0003_topic_owner... OK
(ll_env)learning_log$
```

Django applies the new migration, and the result is OK ❶.

We can verify that the migration worked as expected in the shell session, like this:

```
❶ >>> from learning_logs.models import Topic
❷ >>> for topic in Topic.objects.all():
...     print(topic, topic.owner)
...
Chess ll_admin
Rock Climbing ll_admin
>>>
```

We import Topic from learning_logs.models ❶, and then loop through all existing topics, printing each topic and the user it belongs to ❷. You can see that each topic now belongs to the user *ll_admin*. (If you get an error when you run this code, try exiting the shell and starting a new shell.)

NOTE   *You can simply reset the database instead of migrating, but that will lose all existing data. It's good practice to learn how to migrate a database while maintaining the integrity of users' data. If you do want to start with a fresh database, issue the command python manage.py flush to rebuild the database structure. You'll have to create a new superuser, and all of your data will be gone.*

Restricting Topics Access to Appropriate Users

Currently, if you're logged in, you'll be able to see all the topics, no matter which user you're logged in as. We'll change that by showing users only the topics that belong to them.

Make the following change to the topics() function in *views.py*:

views.py
```
--snip--
@login_required
def topics(request):
    """Show all topics."""
    topics = Topic.objects.filter(owner=request.user).order_by('date_added')
    context = {'topics': topics}
    return render(request, 'learning_logs/topics.html', context)
--snip--
```

When a user is logged in, the request object has a request.user attribute set that stores information about the user. The query Topic.objects .filter(owner=request.user) tells Django to retrieve only the Topic objects from the database whose owner attribute matches the current user. Because we're not changing how the topics are displayed, we don't need to change the template for the topics page at all.

To see if this works, log in as the user you connected all existing topics to, and go to the topics page. You should see all the topics. Now log out, and log back in as a different user. The topics page should list no topics.

Protecting a User's Topics

We haven't restricted access to the topic pages yet, so any registered user could try a bunch of URLs, like *http://localhost:8000/topics/1/*, and retrieve topic pages that happen to match.

Try it yourself. While logged in as the user that owns all topics, copy the URL or note the ID in the URL of a topic, and then log out and log back in as a different user. Enter that topic's URL. You should be able to read the entries, even though you're logged in as a different user.

We'll fix this now by performing a check before retrieving the requested entries in the topic() view function:

views.py

```
from django.shortcuts import render, redirect
from django.contrib.auth.decorators import login_required
❶ from django.http import Http404

--snip--
@login_required
def topic(request, topic_id):
    """Show a single topic and all its entries."""
    topic = Topic.objects.get(id=topic_id)
    # Make sure the topic belongs to the current user.
❷  if topic.owner != request.user:
        raise Http404

    entries = topic.entry_set.order_by('-date_added')
    context = {'topic': topic, 'entries': entries}
    return render(request, 'learning_logs/topic.html', context)
--snip--
```

A 404 response is a standard error response that's returned when a requested resource doesn't exist on a server. Here we import the Http404 exception ❶, which we'll raise if the user requests a topic they shouldn't see. After receiving a topic request, we make sure the topic's user matches the currently logged in user before rendering the page. If the current user doesn't own the requested topic, we raise the Http404 exception ❷, and Django returns a 404 error page.

Now if you try to view another user's topic entries, you'll see a *Page Not Found* message from Django. In Chapter 20, we'll configure the project so users will see a proper error page.

Protecting the edit_entry Page

The edit_entry pages have URLs in the form http://localhost:8000/edit_entry /*entry_id*/, where the *entry_id* is a number. Let's protect this page so no one can use the URL to gain access to someone else's entries:

views.py

```
--snip--
@login_required
def edit_entry(request, entry_id):
    """Edit an existing entry."""
    entry = Entry.objects.get(id=entry_id)
```

```
topic = entry.topic
if topic.owner != request.user:
    raise Http404

if request.method != 'POST':
    --snip--
```

We retrieve the entry and the topic associated with this entry. We then check whether the owner of the topic matches the currently logged in user; if they don't match, we raise an Http404 exception.

Associating New Topics with the Current User

Currently, our page for adding new topics is broken, because it doesn't associate new topics with any particular user. If you try adding a new topic, you'll see the error message IntegrityError along with NOT NULL constraint failed: learning_logs_topic.owner_id. Django's saying you can't create a new topic without specifying a value for the topic's owner field.

There's a straightforward fix for this problem, because we have access to the current user through the request object. Add the following code, which associates the new topic with the current user:

views.py
```
--snip--
@login_required
def new_topic(request):
    """Add a new topic."""
    if request.method != 'POST':
        # No data submitted; create a blank form.
        form = TopicForm()
    else:
        # POST data submitted; process data.
        form = TopicForm(data=request.POST)
        if form.is_valid():
❶          new_topic = form.save(commit=False)
❷          new_topic.owner = request.user
❸          new_topic.save()
            return redirect('learning_logs:topics')

    # Display a blank or invalid form.
    context = {'form': form}
    return render(request, 'learning_logs/new_topic.html', context)
    --snip--
```

When we first call form.save(), we pass the commit=False argument because we need to modify the new topic before saving it to the database ❶. We then set the new topic's owner attribute to the current user ❷. Finally, we call save() on the topic instance just defined ❸. Now the topic has all the required data and will save successfully.

You should be able to add as many new topics as you want for as many different users as you want. Each user will have access only to their own data, whether they're viewing data, entering new data, or modifying old data.

Summary

In this chapter, you learned to use forms to allow users to add new topics and entries, and edit existing entries. You then learned how to implement user accounts. You allowed existing users to log in and out, and used Django's default UserCreationForm to let people create new accounts.

After building a simple user authentication and registration system, you restricted access to logged-in users for certain pages using the @login_required decorator. You then attributed data to specific users through a foreign key relationship. You also learned to migrate the database when the migration requires you to specify some default data.

Finally, you learned how to make sure a user can only see data that belongs to them by modifying the view functions. You retrieved appropriate data using the filter() method and compared the owner of the requested data to the currently logged in user.

It might not always be immediately obvious what data you should make available and what data you should protect, but this skill will come with practice. The decisions we've made in this chapter to secure our users' data also illustrate why working with others is a good idea when building a project: having someone else look over your project makes it more likely that you'll spot vulnerable areas.

You now have a fully functioning project running on your local machine. In the final chapter, you'll style Learning Log to make it visually appealing, and you'll deploy the project to a server so anyone with internet access can register and make an account.

20

STYLING AND DEPLOYING AN APP

Learning Log is fully functional now, but it has no styling and runs only on your local machine. In this chapter, you'll style the project in a simple but professional manner and then deploy it to a live server so anyone in the world can make an account and use it.

For the styling we'll use the Bootstrap library, a collection of tools for styling web applications so they look professional on all modern devices, from a large flat-screen monitor to a smartphone. To do this, we'll use the django-bootstrap4 app, which will also give you practice using apps made by other Django developers.

We'll deploy Learning Log using Heroku, a site that lets you push your project to one of its servers, making it available to anyone with an internet connection. We'll also start using a version control system called Git to track changes to the project.

When you're finished with Learning Log, you'll be able to develop simple web applications, make them look good, and deploy them to a live server. You'll also be able to use more advanced learning resources as you develop your skills.

Styling Learning Log

We've purposely ignored styling until now to focus on Learning Log's functionality first. This is a good way to approach development, because an app is useful only if it works. Of course, once it's working, appearance is critical so people will want to use it.

In this section, I'll introduce the django-bootstrap4 app and show you how to integrate it into a project to make it ready for live deployment.

The django-bootstrap4 App

We'll use django-bootstrap4 to integrate Bootstrap into our project. This app downloads the required Bootstrap files, places them in an appropriate location in your project, and makes the styling directives available in your project's templates.

To install django-bootstrap4, issue the following command in an active virtual environment:

```
(ll_env)learning_log$ pip install django-bootstrap4
--snip--
Successfully installed django-bootstrap4-0.0.7
```

Next, we need to add the following code to include django-bootstrap4 in INSTALLED_APPS in *settings.py*:

settings.py
```
--snip--
INSTALLED_APPS = [
    # My apps.
    'learning_logs',
    'users',

    # Third party apps.
    'bootstrap4',

    # Default django apps.
    'django.contrib.admin',
    --snip--
```

Start a new section called *Third party apps* for apps created by other developers and add 'bootstrap4' to this section. Make sure you place this section after # My apps but before the section containing Django's default apps.

Using Bootstrap to Style Learning Log

Bootstrap is a large collection of styling tools. It also has a number of templates you can apply to your project to create an overall style. It's much easier to use these templates than it is to use individual styling tools. To see the templates Bootstrap offers, go to *https://getbootstrap.com/*, click **Examples**, and look for the *Navbars* section. We'll use the *Navbar static* template, which provides a simple top navigation bar and a container for the page's content.

Figure 20-1 shows what the home page will look like after we apply Bootstrap's template to *base.html* and modify *index.html* slightly.

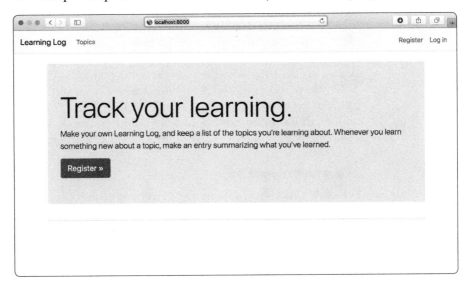

Figure 20-1: The Learning Log home page using Bootstrap

Modifying base.html

We need to modify the *base.html* template to accommodate the Bootstrap template. I'll introduce the new *base.html* in parts.

Defining the HTML Headers

The first change we'll make to *base.html* defines the HTML headers in the file, so whenever a Learning Log page is open, the browser title bar displays the site name. We'll also add some requirements for using Bootstrap in our templates. Delete everything in *base.html* and replace it with the following code:

base.html

```
❶ {% load bootstrap4 %}

❷ <!doctype html>
❸ <html lang="en">
❹ <head>
    <meta charset="utf-8">
    <meta name="viewport" content="width=device-width, initial-scale=1,
      shrink-to-fit=no">
❺   <title>Learning Log</title>

❻   {% bootstrap_css %}
    {% bootstrap_javascript jquery='full' %}

❼ </head>
```

At ❶ we load the collection of template tags available in django-bootstrap4. Next, we declare this file as an HTML document ❷ written in English ❸. An HTML file is divided into two main parts, the *head* and the *body*—the head of the file begins at ❹. The head of an HTML file doesn't contain any content: it just tells the browser what it needs to know to display the page correctly. At ❺ we include a title element for the page, which will display in the browser's title bar whenever Learning Log is open.

At ❻ we use one of django-bootstrap4's custom template tags, which tells Django to include all the Bootstrap style files. The tag that follows enables all the interactive behavior you might use on a page, such as collapsible navigation bars. At ❼ is the closing </head> tag.

Defining the Navigation Bar

The code that defines the navigation bar at the top of the page is fairly long, because it has to work well on narrow phone screens and wide desktop monitors. We'll work through the navigation bar in sections.

Here's the first part of the navigation bar:

base.html

```
--snip--
  </head>
❶ <body>

❷   <nav class="navbar navbar-expand-md navbar-light bg-light mb-4 border">

❸     <a class="navbar-brand" href="{% url 'learning_logs:index'%}">
        Learning Log</a>

❹     <button class="navbar-toggler" type="button" data-toggle="collapse"
          data-target="#navbarCollapse" aria-controls="navbarCollapse"
          aria-expanded="false" aria-label="Toggle navigation">
        <span class="navbar-toggler-icon"></span></button>
```

The first element is the opening <body> tag ❶. The *body* of an HTML file contains the content users will see on a page. At ❷ is a <nav> element that indicates the page's navigation links section. Everything contained in this element is styled according to the Bootstrap style rules defined by the selectors navbar, navbar-expand-md, and the rest that you see here. A *selector* determines which elements on a page a certain style rule applies to. The navbar-light and bg-light selectors style the navigation bar with a light-themed background. The mb in mb-4 is short for *margin-bottom*; this selector ensures that a little space appears between the navigation bar and the rest of the page. The border selector provides a thin border around the light background to set it off a little from the rest of the page.

At ❸ we set the project's name to appear at the far left of the navigation bar and make it a link to the home page; it will appear on every page in the project. The navbar-brand selector styles this link so it stands out from the rest of the links and is a way of branding the site.

At ❹ the template defines a button that appears if the browser window is too narrow to display the whole navigation bar horizontally. When the user clicks the button, the navigation elements will appear in a drop-down list. The collapse reference causes the navigation bar to collapse when the user shrinks the browser window or when the site is displayed on mobile devices with small screens.

Here's the next section of code that defines the navigation bar:

base.html

```
      --snip--
      <span class="navbar-toggler-icon"></span></button>
❶   <div class="collapse navbar-collapse" id="navbarCollapse">
❷     <ul class="navbar-nav mr-auto">
❸       <li class="nav-item">
          <a class="nav-link" href="{% url 'learning_logs:topics'%}">
              Topics</a></li>
      </ul>
```

At ❶ we open a new section of the navigation bar. The term *div* is short for division; you build a web page by dividing it into sections and defining style and behavior rules that apply to that section. Any styling or behavior rules that are defined in an opening div tag affect everything you see until the next closing div tag, which is written as </div>. This is the beginning of the part of the navigation bar that will be collapsed on narrow screens and windows.

At ❷ we define a new set of links. Bootstrap defines navigation elements as items in an unordered list with style rules that make it look nothing like a list. Every link or element you need on the bar can be included as an item in one of these lists. Here, the only item in the list is our link to the Topics page ❸.

Here's the next part of the navigation bar:

base.html

```
            --snip--
      </ul>
❶   <ul class="navbar-nav ml-auto">
❷     {% if user.is_authenticated %}
        <li class="nav-item">
❸         <span class="navbar-text">Hello, {{ user.username }}.</span>
        </li>
        <li class="nav-item">
          <a class="nav-link" href="{% url 'users:logout' %}">Log out</a>
        </li>
      {% else %}
        <li class="nav-item">
          <a class="nav-link" href="{% url 'users:register' %}">Register</a>
        </li>
        <li class="nav-item">
          <a class="nav-link" href="{% url 'users:login' %}">Log in</a></li>
      {% endif %}
      </ul>
❹   </div>

    </nav>
```

At ❶ we begin a new set of links by using another opening <ul> tag. You can have as many groups of links as you need on a page. This will be the group of links related to login and registration that appears on the right side of the navigation bar. The selector ml-auto is short for *margin-left-automatic*: this selector examines the other elements in the navigation bar and works out a left margin that pushes this group of links to the right side of the screen.

The if block at ❷ is the same conditional block we used earlier to display appropriate messages to users depending on whether or not they're logged in. The block is a little longer now because some styling rules are inside the conditional tags. At ❸ is a <span> element. The *span element* styles pieces of text, or elements of a page, that are part of a longer line. Whereas div elements create their own division in a page, span elements are continuous within a larger section. This can be confusing at first, because many pages have deeply nested div elements. Here, we're using the span element to style informational text on the navigation bar, such as the logged-in user's name. We want this information to appear different from a link, so users aren't tempted to click these elements.

At ❹ we close the div element that contains the parts of the navigation bar that will collapse on narrow screens, and at the end of this section we close the navigation bar overall. If you wanted to add more links to the navigation bar, you'd add another <li> item to any of the <ul> groups that we've defined in the navigation bar by using identical styling directives as what you've seen here.

There's still a bit more we need to add to *base.html*. We need to define two blocks that the individual pages can use to place the content specific to those pages.

Defining the Main Part of the Page

The rest of *base.html* contains the main part of the page:

base.html

```
    --snip--
    </nav>

❶  <main role="main" class="container">
❷    <div class="pb-2 mb-2 border-bottom">
        {% block page_header %}{% endblock page_header %}
      </div>
❸    <div>
        {% block content %}{% endblock content %}
      </div>
    </main>

  </body>

</html>
```

At ❶ we open a <main> tag. The *main* element is used for the most significant part of the body of a page. Here we assign the bootstrap selector container, which is a simple way to group elements on a page. We'll place two div elements in this container.

The first div element ❷ contains a page_header block. We'll use this block to title most pages. To make this section stand out from the rest of the page, we place some padding below the header. *Padding* refers to space between an element's content and its border. The selector pb-2 is a bootstrap directive that provides a moderate amount of padding at the bottom of the styled element. A *margin* is the space between an element's border and other elements on the page. We want a border only on the bottom of the page, so we use the selector border-bottom, which provides a thin border at the bottom of the page_header block.

At ❸ we define one more div element, which contains the block content. We don't apply any specific style to this block, so we can style the content of any page as we see fit for that page. We end the *base.html* file with closing tags for the main, body, and html elements.

When you load Learning Log's home page in a browser, you should see a professional-looking navigation bar that matches the one shown in Figure 20-1. Try resizing the window so it's very narrow; a button should replace the navigation bar. Click the button, and all the links should appear in a drop-down list.

Styling the Home Page Using a Jumbotron

To update the home page, we'll use a Bootstrap element called a *jumbotron*, which is a large box that stands out from the rest of the page and can contain anything you want. Typically, it's used on home pages to hold a brief description of the overall project and a call to action that invites the viewer to get involved.

Here's the revised *index.html* file:

index.html
```
{% extends "learning_logs/base.html" %}

❶ {% block page_header %}
❷   <div class="jumbotron">
❸     <h1 class="display-3">Track your learning.</h1>

❹     <p class="lead">Make your own Learning Log, and keep a list of the
          topics you're learning about. Whenever you learn something new
          about a topic, make an entry summarizing what you've learned.</p>

❺     <a class="btn btn-lg btn-primary" href="{% url 'users:register' %}"
          role="button">Register &raquo;</a>
    </div>
❻ {% endblock page_header %}
```

At ❶ we tell Django that we're about to define what goes in the page_header block. A jumbotron is just a div element with a set of styling directives applied to it ❷. The jumbotron selector applies this group of styling directives from the Bootstrap library to this element.

Inside the jumbotron are three elements. The first is a short message, *Track your learning*, that gives first-time visitors a sense of what Learning Log does. The h1 class is a first-level header, and the display-3 selector adds a thinner and taller look to this particular header ❸. At ❹ we include a longer message that provides more information about what the user can do with their learning log.

Rather than just using a text link, we create a button at ❺ that invites users to register their Learning Log account. This is the same link as in the header, but the button stands out on the page and shows the viewer what they need to do to start using the project. The selectors you see here style this as a large button that represents a call to action. The code » is an *HTML entity* that looks like two right angle brackets combined (>>). At ❻ we close the page_header block. We aren't adding any more content to this page, so we don't need to define the content block on this page.

The index page now looks like Figure 20-1 and is a significant improvement over our unstyled project.

Styling the Login Page

We've refined the overall appearance of the login page but not the login form yet. Let's make the form look consistent with the rest of the page by modifying the *login.html* file:

login.html

```
{% extends "learning_logs/base.html" %}
❶ {% load bootstrap4 %}

❷ {% block page_header %}
    <h2>Log in to your account.</h2>
   {% endblock page_header %}

   {% block content %}
❸    <form method="post" action="{% url 'users:login' %}" class="form">
       {% csrf_token %}
❹      {% bootstrap_form form %}
❺      {% buttons %}
         <button name="submit" class="btn btn-primary">Log in</button>
       {% endbuttons %}

       <input type="hidden" name="next"
         value="{% url 'learning_logs:index' %}" />
     </form>

   {% endblock content %}
```

At ❶ we load the bootstrap4 template tags into this template. At ❷ we define the page_header block, which tells the user what the page is for. Notice that we've removed the {% if form.errors %} block from the template; django-bootstrap4 manages form errors automatically.

At ❸ we add a class="form" attribute, and then we use the template tag {% bootstrap_form %} when we display the form ❹; this replaces the {{ form .as_p }} tag we were using in Chapter 19. The {% bootstrap_form %} template tag inserts Bootstrap style rules into the form's individual elements as the form is rendered. At ❺ we open a bootstrap4 template tag {% buttons %}, which adds Bootstrap styling to buttons.

Figure 20-2 shows the login form now. The page is much cleaner and has consistent styling and a clear purpose. Try logging in with an incorrect username or password; you'll see that even the error messages are styled consistently and integrate well with the overall site.

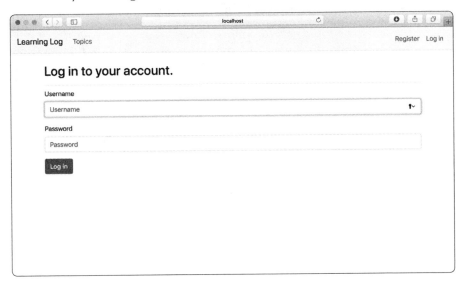

Figure 20-2: The login page styled with Bootstrap

Styling the Topics Page

Let's make sure the pages for viewing information are styled appropriately as well, starting with the topics page:

topics.html

```
{% extends "learning_logs/base.html" %}

❶ {% block page_header %}
    <h1>Topics</h1>
  {% endblock page_header %}

  {% block content %}
    <ul>
      {% for topic in topics %}
❷        <li><h3>
          <a href="{% url 'learning_logs:topic' topic.id %}">{{ topic }}</a>
        </h3></li>
      {% empty %}
        <li><h3>No topics have been added yet.</h3></li>
      {% endfor %}
    </ul>

❸    <h3><a href="{% url 'learning_logs:new_topic' %}">Add a new topic</a></h3>
  {% endblock content %}
```

We don't need the {% load bootstrap4 %} tag, because we're not using any custom bootstrap4 template tags in this file. We move the heading *Topics* into the page_header block and give it a header styling instead of using the simple paragraph tag ❶. We style each topic as an <h3> element to make them a little larger on the page ❷ and do the same for the link to add a new topic ❸.

Styling the Entries on the Topic Page

The topic page has more content than most pages, so it needs a bit more work. We'll use Bootstrap's card component to make each entry stand out. A *card* is a div with a set of flexible, predefined styles that's perfect for displaying a topic's entries:

topic.html

```
{% extends 'learning_logs/base.html' %}

❶ {% block page_header %}
    <h3>{{ topic }}</h3>
  {% endblock page_header %}

  {% block content %}
    <p>
      <a href="{% url 'learning_logs:new_entry' topic.id %}">Add new entry</a>
    </p>

    {% for entry in entries %}
❷    <div class="card mb-3">
❸      <h4 class="card-header">
         {{ entry.date_added|date:'M d, Y H:i' }}
❹        <small><a href="{% url 'learning_logs:edit_entry' entry.id %}">
             edit entry</a></small>
       </h4>
❺      <div class="card-body">
         {{ entry.text|linebreaks }}
       </div>
     </div>
    {% empty %}
      <p>There are no entries for this topic yet.</p>
    {% endfor %}

  {% endblock content %}
```

We first place the topic in the page_header block ❶. Then we delete the unordered list structure previously used in this template. Instead of making each entry a list item, we create a div element with the selector card at ❷. This card has two nested elements: one to hold the timestamp and the link to edit the entry, and another to hold the body of the entry.

The first element in the card is a header, which is an <h4> element with the selector card-header ❸. This card header contains the date the entry was made and a link to edit the entry. The <small> tag around the edit_entry link makes it appear a little smaller than the timestamp ❹. The second element is a div with the selector card-body ❺, which places the text of the entry in a simple box on the card. Notice that the Django code for including the information on the page hasn't changed; only the elements that affect the appearance of the page have changed.

Figure 20-3 shows the topic page with its new look. Learning Log's functionality hasn't changed, but it looks more professional and inviting to users now.

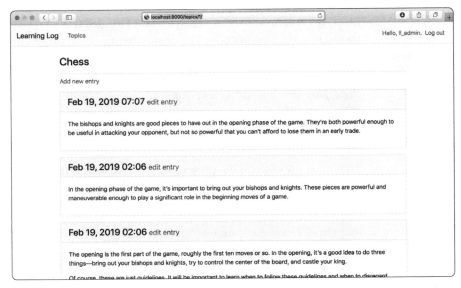

Figure 20-3: The topic page with Bootstrap styling

NOTE *If you want to use a different Bootstrap template, follow a similar process to what we've done so far in this chapter. Copy the template you want to use into* base.html, *and modify the elements that contain actual content so the template displays your project's information. Then use Bootstrap's individual styling tools to style the content on each page.*

TRY IT YOURSELF

20-1. Other Forms: We applied Bootstrap's styles to the login page. Make similar changes to the rest of the form-based pages including new_topic, new_entry, edit_entry, and register.

20-2. Stylish Blog: Use Bootstrap to style the Blog project you created in Chapter 19.

Deploying Learning Log

Now that we have a professional-looking project, let's deploy it to a live server so anyone with an internet connection can use it. We'll use Heroku, a web-based platform that allows you to manage the deployment of web applications. We'll get Learning Log up and running on Heroku.

Making a Heroku Account

To make an account, go to *https://heroku.com/* and click one of the signup links. It's free to make an account, and Heroku has a free tier that allows you to test your projects in live deployment before properly deploying them.

NOTE *Heroku's free tier has limits, such as the number of apps you can deploy and how often people can visit your app. But these limits are generous enough to let you practice deploying apps without any cost.*

Installing the Heroku CLI

To deploy and manage a project on Heroku's servers, you'll need the tools available in the Heroku Command Line Interface (CLI). To install the latest version of the Heroku CLI, visit *https://devcenter.heroku.com/articles/heroku-cli/* and follow the instructions for your operating system. The instructions will include either a one-line terminal command or an installer you can download and run.

Installing Required Packages

You'll also need to install three packages that help serve Django projects on a live server. In an active virtual environment, issue the following commands:

```
(ll_env)learning_log$ pip install psycopg2==2.7.*
(ll_env)learning_log$ pip install django-heroku
(ll_env)learning_log$ pip install gunicorn
```

The psycopg2 package is required to manage the database that Heroku uses. The django-heroku package handles almost the entire configuration our app needs to run properly on Heroku servers. This includes managing the database and storing static files in a place where they can be served properly. *Static files* contain style rules and JavaScript files. The gunicorn package provides a server capable of serving apps in a live environment.

Creating a requirements.txt File

Heroku needs to know which packages our project depends on, so we'll use pip to generate a file listing them. Again, from an active virtual environment, issue the following command:

```
(ll_env)learning_log$ pip freeze > requirements.txt
```

The freeze command tells pip to write the names of all the packages currently installed in the project into the file *requirements.txt*. Open this file to see the packages and version numbers installed in your project:

requirements.txt
```
dj-database-url==0.5.0
Django==2.2.0
django-bootstrap4==0.0.7
django-heroku==0.3.1
gunicorn==19.9.0
psycopg2==2.7.7
pytz==2018.9
sqlparse==0.2.4
whitenoise==4.1.2
```

Learning Log already depends on eight different packages with specific version numbers, so it requires a specific environment to run properly. (We installed four of these packages manually, and four of them were installed automatically as dependencies of these packages.)

When we deploy Learning Log, Heroku will install all the packages listed in *requirements.txt*, creating an environment with the same packages we're using locally. For this reason, we can be confident the deployed project will behave the same as it does on our local system. This is a huge advantage as you start to build and maintain various projects on your system.

NOTE *If a package is listed on your system but the version number differs from what's shown here, keep the version you have on your system.*

Specifying the Python Runtime

Unless you specify a Python version, Heroku will use its current default version of Python. Let's make sure Heroku uses the same version of Python we're using. In an active virtual environment, issue the command python --version:

```
(ll_env)learning_log$ python --version
Python 3.7.2
```

In this example I'm running Python 3.7.2. Make a new file called *runtime.txt* in the same directory as *manage.py*, and enter the following:

runtime.txt
```
python-3.7.2
```

This file should contain one line with your Python version specified in the format shown; make sure you enter python in lowercase, followed by a hyphen, followed by the three-part version number.

NOTE *If you get an error reporting that the Python runtime you requested isn't available, go to* https://devcenter.heroku.com/categories/language-support/ *and look for a link to* Specifying a Python Runtime. *Scan through the article to find the available runtimes, and use the one that most closely matches your Python version.*

Modifying settings.py for Heroku

Now we need to add a section at the end of *settings.py* to define some specific settings for the Heroku environment:

settings.py
```
--snip--
# My settings
LOGIN_URL = 'users:login'

# Heroku settings.
import django_heroku
django_heroku.settings(locals())
```

Here we import the django_heroku module and call the settings() function. This function modifies some settings that need specific values for the Heroku environment.

Making a Procfile to Start Processes

A *Procfile* tells Heroku which processes to start to properly serve the project. Save this one-line file as *Procfile*, with an uppercase *P* and no file extension, in the same directory as *manage.py*.

Here's the line that goes in *Procfile*:

Procfile
```
web: gunicorn learning_log.wsgi --log-file -
```

This line tells Heroku to use gunicorn as a server and to use the settings in *learning_log/wsgi.py* to launch the app. The log-file flag tells Heroku the kinds of events to log.

Using Git to Track the Project's Files

As discussed in Chapter 17, Git is a version control program that allows you to take a snapshot of the code in your project each time you implement a new feature successfully. If anything goes wrong, you can easily return to the last working snapshot of your project; for example, if you accidentally introduce a bug while working on a new feature. Each snapshot is called a *commit*.

Using Git, you can try implementing new features without worrying about breaking your project. When you're deploying to a live server, you need to make sure you're deploying a working version of your project. To read more about Git and version control, see Appendix D.

Installing Git

Git may already be installed on your system. To find out if Git is already installed, open a new terminal window and issue the command git --version:

```
(ll_env)learning_log$ git --version
git version 2.17.0
```

If you get an error message for some reason, see the installation instructions for Git in Appendix D.

Configuring Git

Git keeps track of who makes changes to a project, even when only one person is working on the project. To do this, Git needs to know your username and email. You must provide your username, but you can make up an email for your practice projects:

```
(ll_env)learning_log$ git config --global user.name "ehmatthes"
(ll_env)learning_log$ git config --global user.email "eric@example.com"
```

If you forget this step, Git will prompt you for this information when you make your first commit.

Ignoring Files

We don't need Git to track every file in the project, so we'll tell it to ignore some files. Create a file called *.gitignore* in the folder that contains *manage.py*. Notice that this filename begins with a dot and has no file extension. Here's the code that goes in *.gitignore*:

.gitignore
```
ll_env/
__pycache__/
*.sqlite3
```

We tell Git to ignore the entire *ll_env* directory, because we can re-create it automatically at any time. We also don't track the *__pycache__* directory, which contains the *.pyc* files that are created automatically when Django runs the *.py* files. We don't track changes to the local database, because it's a bad habit: if you're ever using SQLite on a server, you might accidentally overwrite the live database with your local test database when you push the project to the server. The asterisk in `*.sqlite3` tells Git to ignore any file that ends with the extension *.sqlite3*.

NOTE *If you're using macOS, add .DS_Store to your .gitignore file. This is a file that stores information about folder settings on macOS, and it has nothing to do with this project.*

Making Hidden Files Visible

Most operating systems hide files and folders that begin with a dot, such as *.gitignore*. When you open a file browser or try to open a file from an application such as Sublime Text, you won't see these kinds of files by default. But as a programmer, you'll need to see them. Here's how to view hidden files, depending on your operating system:

- On Windows, open Windows Explorer, and then open a folder such as *Desktop*. Click the **View** tab, and make sure **File name extensions** and **Hidden items** are checked.

- On macOS, you can press ⌘-SHIFT-. (dot) in any file browser window to see hidden files and folders.

- On Linux systems such as Ubuntu, you can press CTRL-H in any file browser to display hidden files and folders. To make this setting permanent, open a file browser such as Nautilus and click the options tab (indicated by three lines). Select the **Show Hidden Files** checkbox.

Committing the Project

We need to initialize a Git repository for Learning Log, add all the necessary files to the repository, and commit the initial state of the project. Here's how to do that:

```
❶ (ll_env)learning_log$ git init
  Initialized empty Git repository in /home/ehmatthes/pcc/learning_log/.git/
❷ (ll_env)learning_log$ git add .
❸ (ll_env)learning_log$ git commit -am "Ready for deployment to heroku."
  [master (root-commit) 79fef72] Ready for deployment to heroku.
   45 files changed, 712 insertions(+)
   create mode 100644 .gitignore
   create mode 100644 Procfile
   --snip--
   create mode 100644 users/views.py
❹ (ll_env)learning_log$ git status
  On branch master
  nothing to commit, working tree clean
  (ll_env)learning_log$
```

At ❶ we issue the git init command to initialize an empty repository in the directory containing Learning Log. At ❷ we use the git add . command, which adds all the files that aren't being ignored to the repository. (Don't forget the dot.) At ❸ we issue the command git commit -am *commit message*: the -a flag tells Git to include all changed files in this commit, and the -m flag tells Git to record a log message.

Issuing the git status command ❹ indicates that we're on the *master* branch and that our working tree is *clean*. This is the status you'll want to see any time you push your project to Heroku.

Pushing to Heroku

We're finally ready to push the project to Heroku. In an active virtual environment, issue the following commands:

```
❶ (ll_env)learning_log$ heroku login
  heroku: Press any key to open up the browser to login or q to exit:
  Logging in... done
  Logged in as eric@example.com
❷ (ll_env)learning_log$ heroku create
  Creating app... done, ● secret-lowlands-82594
  https://secret-lowlands-82594.herokuapp.com/ |
      https://git.heroku.com/secret-lowlands-82594.git
```

```
❸ (ll_env)learning_log$ git push heroku master
  --snip--
  remote: -----> Launching...
  remote:        Released v5
❹ remote:        https://secret-lowlands-82594.herokuapp.com/ deployed to Heroku
  remote: Verifying deploy... done.
  To https://git.heroku.com/secret-lowlands-82594.git
   * [new branch]      master -> master
  (ll_env)learning_log$
```

First you issue the heroku login command, which will take you to a page in your browser where you can log in to your Heroku account ❶. Then you tell Heroku to build an empty project ❷. Heroku generates a name made up of two words and a number; you can change this later on. Next, we issue the command git push heroku master ❸, which tells Git to push the master branch of the project to the repository Heroku just created. Then Heroku builds the project on its servers using these files. At ❹ is the URL we'll use to access the live project, which we can change along with the project name.

When you've issued these commands, the project is deployed but not fully configured. To check that the server process started correctly, use the heroku ps command:

```
  (ll_env)learning_log$ heroku ps
❶ Free dyno hours quota remaining this month: 450h 44m (81%)
  Free dyno usage for this app: 0h 0m (0%)
  For more information on dyno sleeping and how to upgrade, see:
  https://devcenter.heroku.com/articles/dyno-sleeping
❷ === web (Free): gunicorn learning_log.wsgi --log-file - (1)
  web.1: up 2019/02/19 23:40:12 -0900 (~ 10m ago)
  (ll_env)learning_log$
```

The output shows how much more time the project can be active in the next month ❶. At the time of this writing, Heroku allows free deployments to be active for up to 550 hours in a month. If a project exceeds this limit, a standard server error page will display; we'll customize this error page shortly. At ❷ we see that the process defined in *Procfile* has been started.

Now we can open the app in a browser using the command heroku open:

```
  (ll_env)learning_log$ heroku open
  (ll_env)learning_log$
```

This command spares you from opening a browser and entering the URL Heroku showed you, but that's another way to open the site. You should see the home page for Learning Log, styled correctly. However, you can't use the app yet because we haven't set up the database.

NOTE *Heroku's deployment process changes from time to time. If you have any unresolvable issues, look at Heroku's documentation for help. Go to* https://devcenter.heroku .com/, *click* **Python**, *and look for a link to* Get Started with Python *or* Deploying Python and Django Apps on Heroku. *If you don't understand what you see there, check out the suggestions in Appendix C.*

Setting Up the Database on Heroku

We need to run migrate once to set up the live database and apply all the migrations we generated during development. You can run Django and Python commands on a Heroku project using the command heroku run. Here's how to run migrate on the Heroku deployment:

```
❶ (ll_env)learning_log$ heroku run python manage.py migrate
❷ Running 'python manage.py migrate' on ● secret-lowlands-82594... up, run.3060
   --snip--
❸ Running migrations:
   --snip--
   Applying learning_logs.0001_initial... OK
   Applying learning_logs.0002_entry... OK
   Applying learning_logs.0003_topic_owner... OK
   Applying sessions.0001_initial... OK
(ll_env)learning_log$
```

We first issue the command heroku run python manage.py migrate ❶. Heroku then creates a terminal session to run the migrate command ❷. At ❸ Django applies the default migrations and the migrations we generated during the development of Learning Log.

Now when you visit your deployed app, you should be able to use it just as you did on your local system. But you won't see any of the data you entered on your local deployment, including your superuser account, because we didn't copy the data to the live server. This is normal practice: you don't usually copy local data to a live deployment because the local data is usually test data.

You can share your Heroku link to let anyone use your version of Learning Log. In the next section, we'll complete a few more tasks to finish the deployment process and set you up to continue developing Learning Log.

Refining the Heroku Deployment

Now we'll refine the deployment by creating a superuser, just as we did locally. We'll also make the project more secure by changing the setting DEBUG to False, so users won't see any extra information in error messages that they could use to attack the server.

Creating a Superuser on Heroku

You've already seen that we can run one-off commands using the heroku run command. But you can also run commands by opening a Bash terminal session while connected to the Heroku server using the command heroku run bash. Bash is the language that runs in many Linux terminals. We'll use the Bash terminal session to create a superuser so we can access the admin site on the live app:

```
(ll_env)learning_log$ heroku run bash
Running 'bash' on ● secret-lowlands-82594... up, run.9858
❶ ~ $ ls
learning_log learning_logs manage.py Procfile requirements.txt runtime.txt
```

```
        staticfiles users
❶ ~ $ python manage.py createsuperuser
   Username (leave blank to use ' u47318'): ll_admin
   Email address:
   Password:
   Password (again):
   Superuser created successfully.
❸ ~ $ exit
   exit
   (ll_env)learning_log$
```

At ❶ we run ls to see which files and directories exist on the server, which should be the same files we have on our local system. You can navigate this filesystem like any other.

NOTE   *Windows users will use the same commands shown here (such as ls instead of dir), because you're running a Linux terminal through a remote connection.*

At ❷ we run the command to create a superuser, which outputs the same prompts we saw on our local system when we created a superuser in Chapter 18. When you're finished creating the superuser in this terminal session, run the **exit** command to return to your local system's terminal session ❸.

Now you can add */admin/* to the end of the URL for the live app and log in to the admin site. For me, the URL is *https://secret-lowlands-82594 .herokuapp.com/admin/*.

If others have already started using your project, be aware that you'll have access to all of their data! Don't take this lightly, and users will continue to trust you with their data.

Creating a User-Friendly URL on Heroku

Most likely, you'll want your URL to be friendlier and more memorable than *https://secret-lowlands-82594.herokuapp.com/*. You can rename the app using a single command:

```
(ll_env)learning_log$ heroku apps:rename learning-log
Renaming secret-lowlands-82594 to learning-log-2e... done
https://learning-log.herokuapp.com/ | https://git.heroku.com/learning-log.git
Git remote heroku updated
 ●  Don't forget to update git remotes for all other local checkouts of the app.
(ll_env)learning_log$
```

You can use letters, numbers, and dashes when naming your app, and call it whatever you want, as long as no one else has claimed the name. This deployment now lives at *https://learning-log.herokuapp.com/*. The project is no longer available at the previous URL; the apps:rename command completely moves the project to the new URL.

When you deploy your project using Heroku's free service, Heroku puts your deployment to sleep if it hasn't received any requests after a certain amount of time or if it's been too active for the free tier. The first time a user accesses the site after it's been sleeping, it will take longer to load, but the server will respond to subsequent requests more quickly. This is how Heroku can afford to offer free deployments.

Securing the Live Project

One glaring security issue exists in the way our project is currently deployed: the setting DEBUG=True in *settings.py*, which provides debug messages when errors occur. Django's error pages give you vital debugging information when you're developing a project; however, they give way too much information to attackers if you leave them enabled on a live server.

We'll control whether debugging information is shown on the live site by setting an environment variable. *Environment variables* are values set in a specific environment. This is one of the ways sensitive information is stored on a server, keeping it separate from the rest of the project's code.

Let's modify *settings.py* so it looks for an environment variable when the project is running on Heroku:

settings.py

```
--snip--
# Heroku settings.
import django_heroku
django_heroku.settings(locals())

if os.environ.get('DEBUG') == 'TRUE':
    DEBUG = True
elif os.environ.get('DEBUG') == 'FALSE':
    DEBUG = False
```

The method os.environ.get() reads the value associated with a specific environment variable in any environment where the project is running. If the variable we're asking for is set, the method returns its value; if it's not set, the method returns None. Using environment variables to store Boolean values can be confusing. In most cases, environment variables are stored as strings, and you have to be careful about this. Consider this snippet from a simple Python terminal session:

```
>>> bool('False')
True
```

The Boolean value of the string 'False' is True, because any non-empty string evaluates to True. So we'll use the strings 'TRUE' and 'FALSE', in all capitals, to be clear that we're not storing Python's actual True and False Boolean values. When Django reads in the environment variable with the key 'DEBUG' on Heroku, we'll set DEBUG to True if the value is 'TRUE' and False if the value is 'FALSE'.

Committing and Pushing Changes

Now we need to commit the changes made to *settings.py* to the Git repository, and then push the changes to Heroku. Here's a terminal session showing this process:

```
❶ (ll_env)learning_log$ git commit -am "Set DEBUG based on environment variables."
  [master 3427244] Set DEBUG based on environment variables.
   1 file changed, 4 insertions(+)
❷ (ll_env)learning_log$ git status
  On branch master
  nothing to commit, working tree clean
  (ll_env)learning_log$
```

We issue the git commit command with a short but descriptive commit message ❶. Remember that the -am flag makes sure Git commits all the files that have changed and records the log message. Git recognizes that one file has changed and commits this change to the repository.

At ❷ the status shows that we're working on the master branch of the repository and that there are now no new changes to commit. It's essential that you check the status for this message before pushing to Heroku. If you don't see this message, some changes haven't been committed, and those changes won't be pushed to the server. You can try issuing the commit command again, but if you're not sure how to resolve the issue, read through Appendix D to better understand how to work with Git.

Now let's push the updated repository to Heroku:

```
(ll_env)learning_log$ git push heroku master
remote: Building source:
remote:
remote: -----> Python app detected
remote: -----> Installing requirements with pip
--snip--
remote: -----> Launching...
remote:        Released v6
remote:        https://learning-log.herokuapp.com/ deployed to Heroku
remote:
remote: Verifying deploy... done.
To https://git.heroku.com/learning-log.git
   144f020..d5075a1  master -> master
(ll_env)learning_log$
```

Heroku recognizes that the repository has been updated, and it rebuilds the project to make sure all the changes have been taken into account. It doesn't rebuild the database, so we won't have to run migrate for this update.

Setting Environment Variables on Heroku

Now we can set the value we want for DEBUG in *settings.py* through Heroku. The command heroku config:set sets an environment variable for us:

```
(ll_env)learning_log$ heroku config:set DEBUG=FALSE
Setting DEBUG and restarting ● learning-log... done, v7
DEBUG: FALSE
(ll_env)learning_log$
```

Whenever you set an environment variable on Heroku, it automatically restarts the project so the environment variable can take effect.

To check that the deployment is more secure now, enter your project's URL with a path we haven't defined. For example, try to visit *http://learning -log.herokuapp.com/letmein/*. You should see a generic error page on your live deployment that doesn't give away any specific information about the project. If you try the same request on the local version of Learning Log at *http:// localhost:8000/letmein/*, you should see the full Django error page. The result is perfect: you'll see informative error messages when you're developing the project further on your own system. But users on the live site won't see critical information about the project's code.

If you're just deploying an app and you're troubleshooting the initial deployment, you can run heroku config:set DEBUG='TRUE' and temporarily see a full error report on the live site. Just make sure you reset the value to 'FALSE' once you've finished troubleshooting. Also, be careful not to do this once users are regularly accessing your site.

Creating Custom Error Pages

In Chapter 19, we configured Learning Log to return a 404 error if the user requests a topic or entry that doesn't belong to them. You've probably seen some 500 server errors (internal errors) by this point as well. A 404 error usually means your Django code is correct, but the object being requested doesn't exist; a 500 error usually means there's an error in the code you've written, such as an error in a function in *views.py*. Currently, Django returns the same generic error page in both situations. But we can write our own 404 and 500 error page templates that match Learning Log's overall appearance. These templates must go in the root template directory.

Making Custom Templates

In the outermost *learning_log* folder, make a new folder called *templates*. Then make a new file called *404.html*; the path to this file should be *learning_log /templates/404.html*. Here's the code for this file:

404.html
```
{% extends "learning_logs/base.html" %}

{% block page_header %}
  <h2>The item you requested is not available. (404)</h2>
{% endblock page_header %}
```

This simple template provides the generic 404 error page information but is styled to match the rest of the site.

Make another file called *500.html* using the following code:

500.html

```
{% extends "learning_logs/base.html" %}

{% block page_header %}
  <h2>There has been an internal error. (500)</h2>
{% endblock page_header %}
```

These new files require a slight change to *settings.py*.

settings.py

```
--snip--
TEMPLATES = [
    {
        'BACKEND': 'django.template.backends.django.DjangoTemplates',
        'DIRS': [os.path.join(BASE_DIR, 'templates')],
        'APP_DIRS': True,
        --snip--
    },
]
--snip--
```

This change tells Django to look in the root template directory for the error page templates.

Viewing the Error Pages Locally

If you want to see what the error pages look like on your system before pushing them to Heroku, you'll first need to set Debug=False on your local settings to suppress the default Django debug pages. To do so, make the following change to *settings.py* (make sure you're working in the part of *settings.py* that applies to the local environment, not the part that applies to Heroku):

settings.py

```
--snip--
# SECURITY WARNING: don't run with debug turned on in production!
DEBUG = False
--snip--
```

Now request a topic or entry that doesn't belong to you to see the 404 error page. To test the 500 error page, request a topic or entry that doesn't exist. For example, the URL *http://localhost:8000/topics/999/* should generate a 500 error unless you've generated 999 example topics already!

When you're finished checking the error pages, set the local value of DEBUG back to True to further develop Learning Log. (Make sure you don't change the way DEBUG is handled in the section that manages settings in the Heroku environment.)

NOTE   *The 500 error page won't show any information about the user who's logged in, because Django doesn't send any context information in the response when there's a server error.*

Pushing the Changes to Heroku

Now we need to commit the error page changes we just made, and push them live to Heroku:

```
❶ (ll_env)learning_log$ git add .
❷ (ll_env)learning_log$ git commit -am "Added custom 404 and 500 error pages."
   3 files changed, 15 insertions(+), 10 deletions(-)
   create mode 100644 templates/404.html
   create mode 100644 templates/500.html
❸ (ll_env)learning_log$ git push heroku master
   --snip--
   remote: Verifying deploy.... done.
   To https://git.heroku.com/learning-log.git
      d5075a1..4bd3b1c  master -> master
   (ll_env)learning_log$
```

We issue the git add . command at ❶ because we created some new files in the project, so we need to tell Git to start tracking these files. Then we commit the changes ❷ and push the updated project to Heroku ❸.

Now when an error page appears, it should have the same styling as the rest of the site, making for a smoother user experience when errors arise.

Using the get_object_or_404() Method

At this point, if a user manually requests a topic or entry that doesn't exist, they'll get a 500 server error. Django tries to render the nonexistent page, but it doesn't have enough information to do so, and the result is a 500 error. This situation is more accurately handled as a 404 error, and we can implement this behavior using the Django shortcut function get_object_or_404(). This function tries to get the requested object from the database, but if that object doesn't exist, it raises a 404 exception. We'll import this function into *views.py* and use it in place of get():

views.py
```
from django.shortcuts import render, redirect, get_object_or_404
from django.contrib.auth.decorators import login_required
--snip--
@login_required
def topic(request, topic_id):
    """Show a single topic and all its entries."""
    topic = get_object_or_404(Topic, id=topic_id)
    # Make sure the topic belongs to the current user.
    --snip--
```

Now when you request a topic that doesn't exist (for example, *http://localhost:8000/topics/999/*), you'll see a 404 error page. To deploy this change, make a new commit and then push the project to Heroku.

Ongoing Development

You might want to further develop Learning Log after your initial push to a live server or develop your own projects to deploy. There's a fairly consistent process for updating projects.

First, you'll make any changes needed to your local project. If your changes result in any new files, add those files to the Git repository using the command git add . (be sure to include the dot at the end of the command). Any change that requires a database migration will need this command, because each migration generates a new migration file.

Second, commit the changes to your repository using git commit -am "commit message". Then push your changes to Heroku using the command git push heroku master. If you migrated your database locally, you'll need to migrate the live database as well. You can either use the one-off command heroku run python manage.py migrate, or open a remote terminal session with heroku run bash and run the command python manage.py migrate. Then visit your live project, and make sure the changes you expect to see have taken effect.

It's easy to make mistakes during this process, so don't be surprised when something goes wrong. If the code doesn't work, review what you've done and try to spot the mistake. If you can't find the mistake or you can't figure out how to undo the mistake, refer to the suggestions for getting help in Appendix C. Don't be shy about asking for help: everyone else learned to build projects by asking the same questions you're likely to ask, so someone will be happy to help you. Solving each problem that arises helps you steadily develop your skills until you're building meaningful, reliable projects and you're answering other people's questions as well.

The SECRET_KEY Setting

Django uses the value of the SECRET_KEY setting in *settings.py* to implement a number of security protocols. In this project, we've committed our settings file to the repository with the SECRET_KEY setting included. This is fine for a practice project, but the SECRET_KEY setting should be handled more carefully for a production site. If you build a project that's getting meaningful use, make sure you research how to handle your SECRET_KEY setting more securely.

Deleting a Project on Heroku

It's great practice to run through the deployment process a number of times with the same project or with a series of small projects to get the hang of deployment. But you'll need to know how to delete a project that's been deployed. Heroku also limits the number of projects you can host for free, and you don't want to clutter your account with practice projects.

Log in to the Heroku website (*https://heroku.com/*); you'll be redirected to a page showing a list of your projects. Click the project you want to delete. You'll see a new page with information about the project. Click the **Settings** link, and scroll down until you see a link to delete the project. This action can't be reversed, so Heroku will ask you to confirm the request for deletion by manually entering the project's name.

If you prefer working from a terminal, you can also delete a project by issuing the destroy command:

```
(ll_env)learning_log$ heroku apps:destroy --app appname
```

Here, *appname* is the name of your project, which is either something like secret-lowlands-82594 or learning-log if you've renamed the project. You'll be prompted to reenter the project name to confirm the deletion.

NOTE *Deleting a project on Heroku does nothing to your local version of the project. If no one has used your deployed project and you're just practicing the deployment process, it's perfectly reasonable to delete your project on Heroku and redeploy it.*

TRY IT YOURSELF

20-3. Live Blog: Deploy the Blog project you've been working on to Heroku. Make sure you set DEBUG to False, so users don't see the full Django error pages when something goes wrong.

20-4. More 404s: The get_object_or_404() function should also be used in the new_entry() and edit_entry() views. Make this change, test it by entering a URL like *http://localhost:8000/new_entry/999/*, and check that you see a 404 error.

20-5. Extended Learning Log: Add one feature to Learning Log, and push the change to your live deployment. Try a simple change, such as writing more about the project on the home page. Then try adding a more advanced feature, such as giving users the option of making a topic public. This would require an attribute called public as part of the Topic model (this should be set to False by default) and a form element on the new_topic page that allows the user to change a topic from private to public. You'd then need to migrate the project and revise *views.py* so any topic that's public is visible to unauthenticated users as well. Remember to migrate the live database after you've pushed your changes to Heroku.

Summary

In this chapter, you learned to give your projects a simple but professional appearance using the Bootstrap library and the django-bootstrap4 app. Using Bootstrap, the styles you choose will work consistently on almost any device people use to access your project.

You learned about Bootstrap's templates and used the *Navbar static* template to create a simple look and feel for Learning Log. You used a jumbotron to make a home page's message stand out and learned to style all the pages in a site consistently.

In the final part of the project, you learned how to deploy a project to Heroku's servers so anyone can access it. You made a Heroku account and installed some tools that help manage the deployment process. You used Git to commit the working project to a repository and then pushed the repository to Heroku's servers. Finally, you learned to begin securing your app by setting DEBUG=False on the live server.

Now that you've finished Learning Log, you can start building your own projects. Start simple, and make sure the project works before adding complexity. Enjoy your continued learning, and good luck with your projects!

AFTERWORD

Congratulations! You've learned the basics of Python and applied your knowledge to meaningful projects. You've made a game, visualized some data, and made a web application. From here, you can go in a number of different directions to continue developing your programming skills.

First, you should continue to work on meaningful projects that interest you. Programming is more appealing when you're solving relevant and significant problems, and you now have the skills to engage in a variety of projects. You could invent your own game or write your own version of a classic arcade game. You might want to explore some data that's important to you and make visualizations that show interesting patterns and connections. You could create your own web application or try to emulate one of your favorite apps.

Whenever possible, invite other people to try using your programs. If you write a game, let other people play it. If you make a visualization, show it to others and see if it makes sense to them. If you make a web app, deploy it online and invite others to try it out. Listen to your users and try to incorporate their feedback into your projects; you'll become a better programmer if you do.

When you work on your own projects, you'll run into problems that are challenging, or even impossible, to solve on your own. Keep finding ways to ask for help, and find your own place in the Python community. Join a local Python User Group or explore some online Python communities. Consider attending a PyCon near you as well.

You should strive to maintain a balance between working on projects that interest you and developing your Python skills in general. Many Python learning sources are available online, and a large number of Python books target intermediate programmers. Many of these resources will be accessible to you now that you know the basics and how to apply your skills. Working through Python tutorials and books will build directly on what you learned here and deepen your understanding of programming in general and Python in particular. Then when you go back to working on projects after focusing on learning about Python, you'll be capable of solving a wider variety of problems more efficiently.

Congratulations on how far you've come, and good luck with your continued learning!

A

INSTALLATION AND TROUBLESHOOTING

 Python has several versions, and there are a number of ways to set it up on each operating system. Use this appendix to install Python if the approach in Chapter 1 didn't work or if you want to install a different version of Python than the one that came with your system.

Python on Windows

The instructions in Chapter 1 show you how to install Python using the official installer at *https://python.org/*. If you couldn't get Python to run after using the installer, the troubleshooting instructions in this section should help you get Python up and running.

Finding the Python Interpreter

If you've entered the simple command python and get an error, such as *python is not recognized as an internal or external command,* you most likely forgot to select the *Add Python to PATH* option when you ran the installer. In this case, you'll need to tell Windows where to find the Python interpreter. To find it, open your C drive and find the folder that starts with the name *Python* (you might need to enter the word python in the Windows Explorer search bar to find the right folder, because it might be nested further down). Open the folder, and look for a file named *python* in lowercase. Right-click this file and choose **Properties**; the path to this file will be listed under the heading *Location*.

To tell Windows where to find the interpreter, open a terminal window and enter the path followed by the --version command, like so:

```
$ C:\Python37\python --version
Python 3.7.2
```

Your path might look something more like C:\Users\username\Programs \Python37\python on your system. Using this path, Windows should then run the Python interpreter.

Adding Python to Your Path Variable

It's annoying to type the full path each time you want to start a Python terminal session, so let's add the path to the system so you can just use the python command. Open your system's **Control Panel**, click **System and Security**, and then click **System**. Click **Advanced System Settings**. In the window that appears, click **Environment Variables**.

In the box labeled *System variables*, look for a variable called Path. Click the word **Path**, and then click **Edit**. You should see a list of locations that your system searches through when it looks for programs. Click **New**, and paste the path to your *python.exe* file in the text box that appears. If your system is set up like mine, that would be:

```
C:\Python37
```

Notice that we're not including the name of the *python.exe* file; we're just telling the system where to look for it.

Close your terminal window and open a new one. Doing so will load the new Path variable into your terminal session. Now when you enter python --version, you should see the version of Python you just added to your Path variable. You can now start a Python terminal session by just entering python at a command prompt.

NOTE   *If you're using an earlier version of Windows, you might see a box labeled* Variable value *when you click* **Edit***. If you see this box, use the right arrow key to scroll all the way to the right. Be careful not to overwrite the existing variable; if you do, click* **Cancel** *and try again. Add a semicolon and the path to your* python.exe *file to the existing variable:*

```
%SystemRoot%\system32\...\System32\WindowsPowerShell\v1.0\;C:\Python37
```

Reinstalling Python

If you're still unable to run Python, oftentimes uninstalling Python and running the installer again will address any problems that occurred in your first attempt.

To do this, open your system's **Control Panel** and click **Programs and Features**. Scroll down until you see the version of Python you just installed, and select it. Click **Uninstall/Change**, and then click **Uninstall** in the dialog that appears. Then run the installer again using the instructions in Chapter 1, but this time make sure you select the **Add Python to PATH** option and any other settings that are relevant to your system. If you're still running into trouble and aren't sure where to get help, see the suggestions in Appendix C.

Python on macOS

The installation instructions in Chapter 1 use the official Python installer at *https://python.org/*, which I recommend you use unless you have a specific reason not to. Another approach uses Homebrew, a tool you can use to install a variety of software on macOS. If you're already using Homebrew and want to use it to install Python, or if the people you're working with use Homebrew and you want a similar setup to what they're using, you can use the following instructions.

Installing Homebrew

Homebrew depends on some of the command line tools from Apple's Xcode package, so you'll first need to install the Xcode command line tools. Open a terminal and run this command:

```
$ xcode-select --install
```

Click through the confirmation dialogs that appear (this might take a while, depending on your connection speed). Next, install Homebrew by entering the following command:

```
$ /usr/bin/ruby -e "$(curl -fsSL
https://raw.githubusercontent.com/Homebrew/install/master/install)"
```

You can find this command at *https://brew.sh/*. Make sure you include a space between curl -fsSL and the URL.

NOTE *The -e in this command tells Ruby (the programming language Homebrew is written in) to execute the code that's downloaded here. You should only run commands like this from sources you trust.*

To confirm that Homebrew installed correctly, run this command:

```
$ brew doctor
Your system is ready to brew.
```

This output means you're ready to use Homebrew to install packages to your system.

Installing Python

To install the latest version of Python, enter the following command:

```
$ brew install python
```

Check which version was installed by using this command:

```
$ python3 --version
Python 3.7.2
$
```

Now you can start a Python terminal session using the command python3. You can also use the python3 command in your text editor so it runs programs with the version of Python you just installed instead of the system's earlier version. If you need help configuring Sublime Text to use the version you just installed, see the instructions in Chapter 1.

Python on Linux

Python is included by default on almost every Linux system. But if the default version is earlier than Python 3.6, you should install the latest version. The following instructions should work for most apt-based systems.

We'll use a package called deadsnakes, which makes it easy to install multiple versions of Python. Enter the following commands:

```
$ sudo add-apt-repository ppa:deadsnakes/ppa
$ sudo apt-get update
$ sudo apt install python3.7
```

These commands should install Python 3.7 onto your system.

Enter the following command to start a terminal session that runs Python 3.7:

```
$ python3.7
>>>
```

You'll also want to use this command when you configure your text editor and when you run programs from the terminal.

Python Keywords and Built-in Functions

Python comes with its own set of keywords and built-in functions. It's important to be aware of these when you're naming variables: your variable names cannot be the same as these keywords and shouldn't be the same as the function names, or you'll overwrite the functions.

In this section, we'll list Python's keywords and built-in function names, so you'll know which names to avoid.

Python Keywords

Each of the following keywords has a specific meaning, and you'll see an error if you try to use any of them as a variable name.

False	await	else	import	pass
None	break	except	in	raise
True	class	finally	is	return
and	continue	for	lambda	try
as	def	from	nonlocal	while
assert	del	global	not	with
async	elif	if	or	yield

Python Built-in Functions

You won't get an error if you use one of the following readily available built-in functions as a variable name, but you'll override the behavior of that function:

abs()	delattr()	hash()	memoryview()	set()
all()	dict()	help()	min()	setattr()
any()	dir()	hex()	next()	slice()
ascii()	divmod()	id()	object()	sorted()
bin()	enumerate()	input()	oct()	staticmethod()
bool()	eval()	int()	open()	str()
breakpoint()	exec()	isinstance()	ord()	sum()
bytearray()	filter()	issubclass()	pow()	super()
bytes()	float()	iter()	print()	tuple()
callable()	format()	len()	property()	type()
chr()	frozenset()	list()	range()	vars()
classmethod()	getattr()	locals()	repr()	zip()
compile()	globals()	map()	reversed()	__import__()
complex()	hasattr()	max()	round()	

B

TEXT EDITORS AND IDEs

Programmers spend a lot of time writing, reading, and editing code, and using a text editor or an *integrated development environment (IDE)* to make this work as efficient as possible is essential. A good editor will do simple tasks, like highlight your code's structure so you can catch common bugs as you're working. But it won't do so much that it distracts you from your thinking. Editors also have useful features like automatic indenting, markers to show appropriate line length, and keyboard shortcuts for common operations.

An IDE is a text editor with a number of other tools included, like interactive debuggers and code introspection. An IDE examines your code as you enter it and tries to learn about the project you're building. For example, when you start typing the name of a function, an IDE might show you all the arguments that function accepts. This behavior can be very helpful when everything works and you understand what you're seeing. But it can also be overwhelming as a beginner and difficult to troubleshoot when you aren't sure why your code isn't working in the IDE.

I encourage you to use a simple text editor while you're learning to code. Text editors also put a much lighter load on your system; so if you're working on an older machine or one with fewer resources, a text editor will work better than an IDE. If you're already familiar with IDEs or if people around you use an IDE and you want to use a similar environment, by all means try them out.

Don't worry too much about choosing your tools at this point; your time will be better spent digging into the language and working on the projects you're interested in. Once you've mastered the basics, you'll have a better idea what tools work for you.

In this appendix, we'll set up the Sublime Text text editor to help you work more efficiently. We'll also take a brief look at a number of other editors you might consider using or see other Python programmers using.

Customizing Sublime Text Settings

In Chapter 1, you configured Sublime Text to use the Python version you want it to when running your programs. Now we'll configure it to do some of the tasks mentioned at the beginning of this appendix.

Converting Tabs to Spaces

If you use a mix of tabs and spaces in your code, it can cause problems in your programs that are difficult to diagnose. To avoid this, you can configure Sublime Text to always use spaces for indentation, even when you press the TAB key. Go to **View ▸ Indentation** and make sure the **Indent Using Spaces** option is selected. If it's not, select it. Also, make sure the **Tab Width** is set to **4** spaces.

If you already have a mix of tabs and spaces in one of your programs, you can convert all tabs to spaces by clicking **View ▸ Indentation ▸ Convert Tabs to Spaces**. You can also access these settings by clicking **Spaces** at the bottom right of the Sublime Text window.

Now you can use the TAB key to indent lines of code, and Sublime Text will insert spaces automatically to indent those lines.

Setting the Line Length Indicator

Most editors allow you to set up a visual cue, usually a vertical line, to show where your lines should end. In the Python community, the convention is to limit lines to 79 characters or less. To set this feature, select **View ▸ Ruler**, and then click **80**. Sublime Text will place a vertical line at the 80-character mark to help restrict your code lines to an appropriate length.

Indenting and Unindenting Code Blocks

To indent an entire block of code, highlight it and select **Edit ▸ Line ▸ Indent** or press CTRL-], or ⌘-] on macOS. To unindent a block of code, click **Edit ▸ Line ▸ Unindent** or press CTRL-[, or ⌘-[.

Commenting Out Blocks of Code

To temporarily disable a block of code, you can highlight the block and comment it so Python will ignore it. Select **Edit ▸ Comment ▸ Toggle Comment** (CTRL-/ or ⌘-/). The selected lines will be commented out with a hash mark (#) indented at the same level as the line of code to indicate these are not regular comments. When you want to uncomment the block of code, highlight the block and reissue the same command.

Saving Your Configuration

Some of the settings mentioned only affect the current file you're working in. To make your settings affect all files you open in Sublime Text, you'll need to define your user settings. Select **Sublime Text ▸ Preferences ▸ Settings**, and look for the file *Preferences.sublime-settings – User*. Enter the following in this file:

```
{
    "rulers": [80],
    "translate_tabs_to_spaces": true
}
```

Save this file, and your ruler and tab settings will apply to all files you work with in Sublime Text. If you add more settings to this file, make sure each line ends with a comma except the last line. You can look at other users' settings files online and customize your editor to the settings that help you work most efficiently.

Further Customizations

You can customize Sublime Text in many ways to help you work even more efficiently. As you're exploring the menus, keep an eye out for keyboard shortcuts for the menu items you use most often. Every time you use a keyboard shortcut instead of reaching for the mouse or trackpad, you become a bit more efficient. Don't try to learn everything at once; just try to become efficient with the actions you use most, and be on the lookout for other features that might help you develop your own workflow.

Other Text Editors and IDEs

You'll hear about and see people using a number of other text editors. Most of them can be configured to help you in the same way you customized Sublime Text. Here's a small selection of text editors you might hear about.

IDLE

IDLE is a text editor that's included with Python. It's a little less intuitive to work with than Sublime Text, but you'll see references to it in other tutorials aimed at beginners, so you might want to give it a try.

Geany

Geany is a simple text editor that lets you run all of your programs directly from the editor. It displays all of your output in a terminal window, which helps you become comfortable using terminals. Geany has a very simple interface, but it's powerful enough that a significant number of experienced programmers still use it.

Emacs and Vim

Emacs and Vim are two popular editors favored by many experienced programmers because they're designed to be used so your hands never have to leave the keyboard. This makes writing, reading, and modifying code very efficient once you learn how the editor works. It also means both editors have a fairly steep learning curve. Vim is included on most Linux and macOS machines, and both Emacs and Vim can be run entirely inside a terminal. For this reason, they're often used to write code on servers through a remote terminal session.

Programmers will often recommend that you give them a try. But many proficient programmers forget how much new programmers are already trying to learn. It's beneficial to be aware of these editors, but hold off on using them until you're comfortable working with code in a simpler editor that lets you focus on learning to program rather than learning to use an editor.

Atom

Atom is a text editor with some features that you'd normally find in an IDE. You can open an individual file you're working on, or you can open a project folder and Atom will instantly make all the files in that project easily accessible. Atom is integrated with Git and GitHub, so as you start to use version control you'll be able to work with local and remote repositories from within your editor instead of having to do so in a separate terminal.

Atom allows you to install packages as well, so you can extend its behavior in many ways. A number of these packages incorporate behavior that makes Atom behave more like an IDE.

Visual Studio Code

Visual Studio Code, also called VS Code, is another editor that acts more like an IDE. VS Code supports efficient use of a debugger, has integrated version control support, and also offers code completion tools.

PyCharm

PyCharm is a popular IDE among Python programmers because it was built to work specifically with Python. The full version requires a paid subscription, but a free version called the PyCharm Community Edition is also available that many developers find useful.

PyCharm features a *linter*, which checks that your coding style matches common Python conventions, and offers suggestions when you deviate from normal Python formatting. It also has an integrated debugger to help you resolve errors proficiently and modes that help you work efficiently with a number of popular Python libraries.

Jupyter Notebooks

Jupyter Notebook is a different kind of tool than traditional text editors or IDEs in that it's a web app primarily built of blocks; each block is either a code block or a text block. The text blocks are rendered in Markdown, so you can include simple formatting in your text blocks.

Jupyter Notebooks were developed to support the use of Python in scientific applications, but they have since expanded to become useful in a wide variety of situations. Rather than just writing comments inside a *.py* file, you can write clear text with simple formatting, such as headers, bulleted lists, and hyperlinks in between sections of code. Every code block can be run independently, allowing you to test small pieces of your program, or you can run all the code blocks at once. Each code block has its own output area, and you can toggle the output areas on or off as needed.

Jupyter Notebooks can be confusing at times because of the interactions between different cells. If you define a function in one cell, that function is available to other cells as well. This is beneficial most of the time, but it can be confusing in longer notebooks and if you don't fully understand how the Notebook environment works.

If you're doing any scientific or data-focused work in Python, you'll almost certainly see Jupyter Notebooks at some point.

C

GETTING HELP

Everyone gets stuck at some point when they're learning to program. So one of the most important skills to learn as a programmer is how to get unstuck efficiently. This appendix outlines several ways to help you get going again when programming gets confusing.

First Steps

When you're stuck, your first step should be to assess your situation. Before you ask for help from anyone else, answer the following three questions clearly:

- What are you trying to do?
- What have you tried so far?
- What results have you been getting?

Make your answers as specific as possible. For the first question, explicit statements like "I'm trying to install the latest version of Python on my Windows 10 laptop" are detailed enough for others in the Python community to help you. Statements like "I'm trying to install Python" don't provide enough information for others to offer much help.

Your answer to the second question should provide enough detail so you won't be advised to repeat what you've already tried: "I went to *https://python.org/downloads/* and clicked the Download button for my system. Then I ran the installer," is more helpful than "I went to the Python website and downloaded something."

For the third question, it's helpful to know the exact error messages you received so you can search online for a solution or provide them when asking for help.

Sometimes just answering these three questions before you ask for help from others allows you to see something you're missing and get you unstuck without having to go any further. Programmers even have a name for this: it's called *rubber duck debugging*. The idea is that if you clearly explain your situation to a rubber duck (or any inanimate object), and ask it a specific question, you'll often be able to answer your own question. Some programming shops even keep a real rubber duck around to encourage people to "talk to the duck."

Try It Again

Just going back to the start and trying again can be enough to solve many problems. Say you're trying to write a for loop based on an example in this book. You might have only missed something simple, like a colon at the end of the for line. Going through the steps again might help you avoid repeating the same mistake.

Take a Break

If you've been working on the same problem for a while, taking a break is one of the best tactics you can try. When we work on the same task for long periods of time, our brains start to zero in on only one solution. We lose sight of the assumptions we've made, and taking a break helps us get a fresh perspective on the problem. It doesn't need to be a long break, just something that gets you out of your current mind-set. If you've been sitting for a long time, do something physical: take a short walk or go outside for a bit; perhaps drink a glass of water or eat a light and healthy snack.

If you're getting frustrated, it might be worth putting your work away for the day. A good night's sleep almost always makes a problem more approachable.

Refer to This Book's Resources

The online resources for this book, available at *https://nostarch.com/pythoncrashcourse2e/*, include a number of helpful sections about setting up your system and working through each chapter. If you haven't done so already, take a look at these resources and see if there's anything that helps your situation.

Searching Online

Chances are that someone else has had the same problem you're having and has written about it online. Good searching skills and specific inquiries will help you find existing resources to solve the issue you're facing. For example, if you're struggling to install the latest version of Python on Windows 10, searching for *install python windows 10* and limiting the results to resources from the last year might direct you to a clear answer.

Searching the exact error message can be extremely helpful too. For example, say you get the following error when you try to start a Python terminal session:

```
> python
'python' is not recognized as an internal or external command,
operable program or batch file
>
```

Searching for the full phrase "python is not recognized as an internal or external command" will probably yield some good advice.

When you start searching for programming-related topics, a few sites will appear repeatedly. I'll describe some of these sites briefly, so you'll know how helpful they're likely to be.

Stack Overflow

Stack Overflow (*https://stackoverflow.com/*) is one of the most popular question-and-answer sites for programmers, and will often appear in the first page of results on Python-related searches. Members post questions when they're stuck, and other members try to give helpful responses. Users can vote for the responses they find most helpful, so the best answers are usually the first ones you'll find.

Many basic Python questions have very clear answers on Stack Overflow, because the community has refined them over time. Users are encouraged to post updates too, so responses tend to stay relatively current. At the time of this writing, over one million Python-related questions have been answered on Stack Overflow.

The Official Python Documentation

The official Python documentation (*https://docs.python.org/*) is a bit more hit or miss for beginners, because its purpose is more to document the language than to provide explanations. The examples in the official documentation should work, but you might not understand everything shown. Still, it's a good resource to check when it comes up in your searches and will become more useful to you as you continue building your understanding of Python.

Official Library Documentation

If you're using a specific library, such as Pygame, Matplotlib, Django, and so on, links to the official documentation for that project will often appear in searches—for example, *https://docs.djangoproject.com/* is very helpful. If you're planning to work with any of these libraries, it's a good idea to become familiar with their official documentation.

r/learnpython

Reddit is made up of a number of subforums called *subreddits*. The *r/learnpython* subreddit (*https://reddit.com/r/learnpython/*) is fairly active and supportive. Here you can read others' questions and post your own.

Blog Posts

Many programmers maintain blogs and share posts about the parts of the language they're working with. You should skim the first few comments on a blog post to see what reactions other people have had before taking any advice. If no comments appear, take the post with a grain of salt. It's possible no one else has verified the advice.

Internet Relay Chat

Many programmers interact in real time through Internet Relay Chat (IRC). If you're stuck on a problem and searching online isn't providing answers, asking in an IRC channel might be a good option. Most people who hang out in these channels are polite and helpful, especially if you can be specific about what you're trying to do, what you've already tried, and what results you're getting.

Making an IRC Account

To create an account on IRC, go to *https://webchat.freenode.net/*. Choose a nickname, fill out the CAPTCHA box, and click **Connect**. You'll see a message welcoming you to the freenode IRC server. In the box at the bottom of the window, enter the following command:

```
/msg nickserv register password email
```

Enter your own password and email address in place of *password* and *email*. Choose a password that you don't use for any other account. You'll receive an email with instructions to verify your account. The email will provide you with a command like this:

```
/msg nickserv verify register nickname verification_code
```

Paste this line into the IRC site with *nickname* as the name you chose earlier and a value for *verification_code*. Now you're ready to join a channel.

If you have trouble logging into your account at some point, you can issue the following command:

```
/msg nickserv identify nickname password
```

Replace *nickname* and *password* with your own nickname and password. This will authenticate you on the network, and you'll be able to access channels that require an authenticated nickname.

Channels to Join

To join the main Python channel, enter **/join #python** in the input box. You'll see a confirmation that you joined the channel and some general information about the channel.

The channel *##learnpython* (with two hashtags) is usually quite active as well. This channel is associated with *https://reddit.com/r/learnpython/*, so you'll see messages about posts on *r/learnpython* too. You might want to join the *#django* channel if you're working on web applications.

After you've joined a channel, you can read the conversations other people are having and ask your own questions as well.

IRC Culture

To get effective help, you should know a few details about IRC culture. Focusing on the three questions at the beginning of this appendix will definitely help guide you to a successful solution. People will be happy to help you if you can explain precisely what you're trying to do, what you've already tried, and the exact results you're getting. If you need to share code or output, IRC members use external sites made for this purpose, such as *https://bpaste.net/+python*. (This is where #python sends you to share code and output.) This keeps the channels from being flooded with code and also makes it much easier to read the code that people share.

Being patient will always make people more likely to help you. Ask your question concisely, and then wait for someone to respond. Often, people are in the middle of many conversations, but usually someone will address you in a reasonable amount of time. If few people are in the channel, it might take a while to get a response.

Slack

Slack is like a modern-day reinvention of IRC. It's often used for internal company communications, but there are also many public groups you can join. If you want to check out Python Slack groups, start with *https://pyslackers.com/*. Click the **Slack** link at the top of the page, and enter your email address to get an invitation.

Once you're in the Python Developers workspace, you'll see a list of channels. Click **Channels**, and then choose the topics that interest you. You might want to start with the *#learning_python* and *#django* channels.

Discord

Discord is another online chat environment with a Python community where you can ask for help and follow Python-related discussions.

To check it out, head to *https://pythondiscord.com/* and click the **Chat Now** link. You should see a screen with an automatically generated invitation; click **Accept Invite**. If you already have a Discord account, you can log in with your existing account. If you don't have an account, enter a username and follow the prompts to complete your Discord registration.

If this is your first time visiting the Python Discord, you'll need to accept the rules for the community before participating fully. Once you've done that, you can join any of the channels that interest you. If you're looking for help, be sure to post in one of the Python Help channels.

D

USING GIT FOR VERSION CONTROL

Version control software allows you to take snapshots of a project whenever it's in a working state. When you make changes to a project—for example, when you implement a new feature—you can revert back to a previous working state if the project's current state isn't functioning well.

Using version control software gives you the freedom to work on improvements and make mistakes without worrying about ruining your project. This is especially critical in large projects, but can also be helpful in smaller projects, even when you're working on programs contained in a single file.

In this appendix, you'll learn to install Git and use it for version control in the programs you're working on now. Git is the most popular version control software in use today. Many of its advanced tools help teams collaborate on large projects, but its most basic features also work well for solo developers. Git implements version control by tracking the changes made to every file in a project; if you make a mistake, you can just return to a previously saved state.

Installing Git

Git runs on all operating systems, but there are different approaches to installing it on each system. The following sections provide specific instructions for each operating system.

Installing Git on Windows

You can download an installer for Git at *https://git-scm.com/*. You should see a download link for an installer that's appropriate for your system.

Installing Git on macOS

Git might already be installed on your system, so try issuing the command `git --version`. If you see output listing a specific version number, Git is installed on your system. If you see a message prompting you to install or update Git, simply follow the onscreen directions.

You can also visit *https://git-scm.com/*, where you should see a download link for an appropriate installer for your system.

Installing Git on Linux

To install Git on Linux, enter the following command:

```
$ sudo apt install git-all
```

That's it. You can now use Git in your projects.

Configuring Git

Git keeps track of who makes changes to a project, even when only one person is working on the project. To do this, Git needs to know your username and email. You must provide a username, but you can make up a fake email address:

```
$ git config --global user.name "username"
$ git config --global user.email "username@example.com"
```

If you forget this step, Git will prompt you for this information when you make your first commit.

Making a Project

Let's make a project to work with. Create a folder somewhere on your system called *git_practice*. Inside the folder, make a simple Python program:

hello_git.py
```
print("Hello Git world!")
```

We'll use this program to explore Git's basic functionality.

Ignoring Files

Files with the extension *.pyc* are automatically generated from *.py* files, so we don't need Git to keep track of them. These files are stored in a directory called *__pycache__*. To tell Git to ignore this directory, make a special file called *.gitignore*—with a dot at the beginning of the filename and no file extension—and add the following line to it:

.gitignore

```
__pycache__/
```

This file tells Git to ignore any file in the *__pycache__* directory. Using a *.gitignore* file will keep your project clutter free and easier to work with.

You might need to modify your text editor's settings so it will show hidden files in order to open *.gitignore*. Some editors are set to ignore filenames that begin with a dot.

Initializing a Repository

Now that you have a directory containing a Python file and a *.gitignore* file, you can initialize a Git repository. Open a terminal, navigate to the *git_practice* folder, and run the following command:

```
git_practice$ git init
Initialized empty Git repository in git_practice/.git/
git_practice$
```

The output shows that Git has initialized an empty repository in *git_practice*. A *repository* is the set of files in a program that Git is actively tracking. All the files Git uses to manage the repository are located in the hidden directory *.git*, which you won't need to work with at all. Just don't delete that directory, or you'll lose your project's history.

Checking the Status

Before doing anything else, let's look at the project's status:

```
git_practice$ git status
❶ On branch master

No commits yet

❷ Untracked files:
    (use "git add <file>..." to include in what will be committed)

    .gitignore
    hello_git.py

❸ nothing added to commit but untracked files present (use "git add" to track)
git_practice$
```

In Git, a *branch* is a version of the project you're working on; here you can see that we're on a branch named master ❶. Each time you check your project's status, it should show that you're on the branch master. You then see that we're about to make the initial commit. A *commit* is a snapshot of the project at a particular point in time.

Git informs us that untracked files are in the project ❷, because we haven't told it which files to track yet. Then we're told that there's nothing added to the current commit, but untracked files are present that we might want to add to the repository ❸.

Adding Files to the Repository

Let's add the two files to the repository, and check the status again:

```
❶ git_practice$ git add .
❷ git_practice$ git status
  On branch master

  No commits yet

  Changes to be committed:
    (use "git rm --cached <file>..." to unstage)

❸     new file:   .gitignore
      new file:   hello_git.py

  git_practice$
```

The command git add . adds all files within a project that aren't already being tracked to the repository ❶. It doesn't commit the files; it just tells Git to start paying attention to them. When we check the status of the project now, we can see that Git recognizes some changes that need to be committed ❷. The label *new file* means these files were newly added to the repository ❸.

Making a Commit

Let's make the first commit:

```
❶ git_practice$ git commit -m "Started project."
❷ [master (root-commit) ee76419] Started project.
❸  2 files changed, 4 insertions(+)
   create mode 100644 .gitignore
   create mode 100644 hello_git.py
❹ git_practice$ git status
  On branch master
  nothing to commit, working tree clean
  git_practice$
```

We issue the command git commit -m "*message*" ❶ to take a snapshot of the project. The -m flag tells Git to record the message that follows ("Started project.") in the project's log. The output shows that we're on the master branch ❷ and that two files have changed ❸.

When we check the status now, we can see that we're on the master branch, and we have a clean working tree ❹. This is the message you want to see each time you commit a working state of your project. If you get a different message, read it carefully; it's likely you forgot to add a file before making a commit.

Checking the Log

Git keeps a log of all commits made to the project. Let's check the log:

```
git_practice$ git log
commit a9d74d87f1aa3b8f5b2688cb586eac1a908cfc7f (HEAD -> master)
Author: Eric Matthes <eric@example.com>
Date:   Mon Jan 21 21:24:28 2019 -0900

    Started project.
git_practice$
```

Each time you make a commit, Git generates a unique, 40-character reference ID. It records who made the commit, when it was made, and the message recorded. You won't always need all of this information, so Git provides an option to print a simpler version of the log entries:

```
git_practice$ git log --pretty=oneline
ee76419954379819f3f2cacafd15103ea900ecb2 (HEAD -> master) Started project.
git_practice$
```

The --pretty=oneline flag provides the two most important pieces of information: the reference ID of the commit and the message recorded for the commit.

The Second Commit

To see the real power of version control, we need to make a change to the project and commit that change. Here we'll just add another line to *hello _git.py*:

hello_git.py
```
print("Hello Git world!")
print("Hello everyone.")
```

When we check the status of the project, we'll see that Git has noticed the file that changed:

```
git_practice$ git status
❶ On branch master
```

```
Changes not staged for commit:
  (use "git add <file>..." to update what will be committed)
  (use "git checkout -- <file>..." to discard changes in working directory)
```
❷ modified: hello_git.py

❸ no changes added to commit (use "git add" and/or "git commit -a")
git_practice$

We see the branch we're working on ❶, the name of the file that was
modified ❷, and that no changes have been committed ❸. Let's commit the
change and check the status again:

```
❶ git_practice$ git commit -am "Extended greeting."
[master 51f0fe5] Extended greeting.
 1 file changed, 1 insertion(+), 1 deletion(-)
❷ git_practice$ git status
On branch master
nothing to commit, working tree clean
❸ git_practice$ git log --pretty=oneline
51f0fe5884e045b91c12c5449fabf4ad0eef8e5d (HEAD -> master) Extended greeting.
ee76419954379819f3f2cacafd15103ea900ecb2 Started project.
git_practice$
```

We make a new commit, passing the -am flags when we use the command git commit ❶. The -a flag tells Git to add all modified files in the
repository to the current commit. (If you create any new files between
commits, simply reissue the git add . command to include the new files in
the repository.) The -m flag tells Git to record a message in the log for this
commit.

When we check the project's status, we see that we once again have a
clean working directory ❷. Finally, we see the two commits in the log ❸.

Reverting a Change

Now let's look at how to abandon a change and revert back to the previous
working state. First, add a new line to *hello_git.py*:

hello_git.py
```
print("Hello Git world!")
print("Hello everyone.")

print("Oh no, I broke the project!")
```

Save and run this file.
We check the status and see that Git notices this change:

```
git_practice$ git status
On branch master
Changes not staged for commit:
  (use "git add <file>..." to update what will be committed)
```

```
         (use "git checkout -- <file>..." to discard changes in working directory)

❶       modified:   hello_git.py

no changes added to commit (use "git add" and/or "git commit -a")
git_practice$
```

Git sees that we modified *hello_git.py* ❶, and we can commit the change
if we want to. But this time, instead of committing the change, we'll revert
back to the last commit when we knew our project was working. We won't
do anything to *hello_git.py*: we won't delete the line or use the Undo feature
in the text editor. Instead, enter the following commands in your terminal
session:

```
git_practice$ git checkout .
git_practice$ git status
On branch master
nothing to commit, working tree clean
git_practice$
```

The command git checkout allows you to work with any previous commit. The command git checkout . abandons any changes made since the
last commit and restores the project to the last committed state.

When you return to your text editor, you'll see that *hello_git.py* has
changed back to this:

```
print("Hello Git world!")
print("Hello everyone.")
```

Although going back to a previous state might seem trivial in this simple project, if we were working on a large project with dozens of modified
files, all the files that had changed since the last commit would be reverted.
This feature is incredibly useful: you can make as many changes as you want
when implementing a new feature, and if they don't work, you can discard
them without affecting the project. You don't have to remember those
changes and manually undo them. Git does all of that for you.

NOTE   *You might have to refresh the file in your editor to see the previous version.*

Checking Out Previous Commits

You can check out any commit in your log, not just the most recent, by
including the first six characters of the reference ID instead of a dot. By
checking out and reviewing an earlier commit, you can then return to the
latest commit or abandon your recent work and pick up development from
the earlier commit:

```
git_practice$ git log --pretty=oneline
51f0fe5884e045b91c12c5449fabf4ad0eef8e5d (HEAD -> master) Extended greeting.
```

```
ee76419954379819f3f2cacafd15103ea900ecb2 Started project.
git_practice$ git checkout ee7641
Note: checking out 'ee7641'.
```

❶ You are in 'detached HEAD' state. You can look around, make experimental
changes and commit them, and you can discard any commits you make in this
state without impacting any branches by performing another checkout.

If you want to create a new branch to retain commits you create, you may
do so (now or later) by using -b with the checkout command again. Example:

```
  git checkout -b <new-branch-name>
```

```
HEAD is now at ee7641... Started project.
git_practice$
```

When you check out a previous commit, you leave the master branch
and enter what Git refers to as a *detached HEAD* state ❶. *HEAD* is the current
committed state of the project; you're *detached* because you've left a named
branch (master, in this case).

To get back to the master branch, you check it out:

```
git_practice$ git checkout master
Previous HEAD position was ee76419 Started project.
Switched to branch 'master'
git_practice$
```

This command brings you back to the master branch. Unless you want
to work with some more advanced features of Git, it's best not to make any
changes to your project when you've checked out an old commit. However,
if you're the only one working on a project and you want to discard all of
the more recent commits and go back to a previous state, you can reset the
project to a previous commit. Working from the master branch, enter the
following:

❶ git_practice$ **git status**
On branch master
nothing to commit, working directory clean
❷ git_practice$ **git log --pretty=oneline**
51f0fe5884e045b91c12c5449fabf4ad0eef8e5d (HEAD -> master) Extended greeting.
ee76419954379819f3f2cacafd15103ea900ecb2 Started project.
❸ git_practice$ **git reset --hard ee76419**
HEAD is now at ee76419 Started project.
❹ git_practice$ **git status**
On branch master
nothing to commit, working directory clean
❺ git_practice$ **git log --pretty=oneline**
ee76419954379819f3f2cacafd15103ea900ecb2 (HEAD -> master) Started project.
git_practice$

We first check the status to make sure we're on the master branch ❶.
When we look at the log, we see both commits ❷. We then issue the git

reset --hard command with the first six characters of the reference ID of the commit we want to revert to permanently ❸. We check the status again and see we're on the master branch with nothing to commit ❹. When we look at the log again, we see that we're at the commit we wanted to start over from ❺.

Deleting the Repository

Sometimes you'll mess up your repository's history and won't know how to recover it. If this happens, first consider asking for help using the methods discussed in Appendix C. If you can't fix it and you're working on a solo project, you can continue working with the files but get rid of the project's history by deleting the *.git* directory. This won't affect the current state of any of the files, but it will delete all commits, so you won't be able to check out any other states of the project.

To do this, either open a file browser and delete the *.git* repository or delete it from the command line. Afterwards, you'll need to start over with a fresh repository to start tracking your changes again. Here's what this entire process looks like in a terminal session:

```
❶ git_practice$ git status
  On branch master
  nothing to commit, working directory clean
❷ git_practice$ rm -rf .git
❸ git_practice$ git status
  fatal: Not a git repository (or any of the parent directories): .git
❹ git_practice$ git init
  Initialized empty Git repository in git_practice/.git/
❺ git_practice$ git status
  On branch master

  No commits yet

  Untracked files:
    (use "git add <file>..." to include in what will be committed)

    .gitignore
    hello_git.py

  nothing added to commit but untracked files present (use "git add" to track)
❻ git_practice$ git add .
  git_practice$ git commit -m "Starting over."
  [master (root-commit) 6baf231] Starting over.
   2 files changed, 4 insertions(+)
   create mode 100644 .gitignore
   create mode 100644 hello_git.py
❼ git_practice$ git status
  On branch master
  nothing to commit, working tree clean
  git_practice$
```

We first check the status and see that we have a clean working tree ❶. Then we use the command rm -rf .git to delete the *.git* directory (rmdir /s .git on Windows) ❷. When we check the status after deleting the *.git* folder, we're told that this is not a Git repository ❸. All the information Git uses to track a repository is stored in the *.git* folder, so removing it deletes the entire repository.

We're then free to use git init to start a fresh repository ❹. Checking the status shows that we're back at the initial stage, awaiting the first commit ❺. We add the files and make the first commit ❻. Checking the status now shows us that we're on the new master branch with nothing to commit ❼.

Using version control takes a bit of practice, but once you start using it you'll never want to work without it again.

INDEX

G

games. *See* Alien Invasion project;
    Pygame
Geany, 476
GET requests, 412
getting help
    Discord, 484
    IRC (Internet Relay Chat),
        482–483
    official Python documentation,
        481
    online resources, 480
    r/learnpython, 482
    rubber duck debugging, 480
    Slack, 483
    Stack Overflow, 481
    three main questions, 479
Git, 360, 450
    branches, 452, 488
    commits, 360, 450
        checking out, 491–493
        making, 452, 457, 460, 488,
            490, 493
    configuring, 451, 486
    detached HEAD, 492
    files
        adding, 452, 460, 488, 493
        ignoring, 451, 487
    HEAD, 492
    installing, 450, 486
    log, checking, 489
    repositories, 360
        deleting, 493
        initializing, 452, 487, 493
    reverting changes, 490
    status, checking, 452, 457,
        487–493
GitHub, 360
greater than (>), 75
greater than or equal to (>=), 75
greeter.py, 114, 130–131
greet_users.py, 143
gunicorn package, 448

H

Hacker News, 372
hash mark (#), for comments, 29
head, of an HTML file, 440
HEAD (Git), 492
Hello World, 9
hello_git.py, 486–491
hello_world.py, 10, 15–19
Heroku, 437. *See also* Django; Git;
    Learning Log project
    Bash shell, 454
    CLI, installing, 448
    commands
        config, 458
        destroy, 462
        login, 453
        open, 453
        ps, 453
        rename, 455
        run, 454
        set, 458
    databases, setting up, 454
    django-heroku package, 448
    documentation, 453
    environment variables, setting,
        456–458
    error pages, custom, 458–460
    free plan, limitations of,
        448, 456
    making an account, 448
    Procfile, 450
    projects
        deleting, 461
        pushing to Heroku,
            452–453, 457
        viewing live, 453
    Python runtime, specifying, 449
    requirements.txt, 448–449
    securing, 456
    settings.py, modifying for, 450,
        456, 459
    superuser, creating, 454–455
    URLs, user-friendly, 455
hidden files, 451

Python Crash Course, 2nd Edition is set in New Baskerville, Futura, Dogma, and The Sans Mono Condensed. The book was printed and bound by Sheridan Books, Inc. in Chelsea, Michigan. The paper is 60# Finch Offset, which is certified by the Forest Stewardship Council (FSC).

The book uses a layflat binding, in which the pages are bound together with a cold-set, flexible glue and the first and last pages of the resulting book block are attached to the cover. The cover is not actually glued to the book's spine, and when open, the book lies flat and the spine doesn't crack.

RESOURCES

Visit *https://nostarch.com/pythoncrashcourse2e/* for resources, errata, and more information.

More no-nonsense books from **NO STARCH PRESS**

SERIOUS PYTHON

Black-Belt Advice on Deployment, Scalability, Testing, and More
by JULIEN DANJOU
DECEMBER 2018, 240 PP., $34.95
ISBN 978-1-59327-878-6

PYTHON FLASH CARDS

Syntax, Concepts, and Examples
by ERIC MATTHES
JANUARY 2019, 101 CARDS, $27.95
ISBN 978-1-59327-896-0
full color

MATH ADVENTURES WITH PYTHON

An Illustrated Guide to Exploring Math with Code
by PETER FARRELL
JANUARY 2019, 304 PP., $29.95
ISBN 978-1-59327-867-0
full color

IMPRACTICAL PYTHON PROJECTS

Playful Programming Activities to Make You Smarter
by LEE VAUGHAN
NOVEMBER 2018, 424 PP., $29.95
ISBN 978-1-59327-890-8

LEARN ROBOTICS WITH RASPBERRY PI

Build and Code Your Own Moving, Sensing, Thinking Robots
by MATT TIMMONS-BROWN
JANUARY 2019, 240 PP., $24.95
ISBN 978-1-59327-920-2
full color

MISSION PYTHON

Code a Space Adventure Game!
by SEAN MCMANUS
OCTOBER 2018, 280 PP., $29.95
ISBN 978-1-59327-857-1
full color

1.800.420.7240 or 1.415.863.9900 | sales@nostarch.com | www.nostarch.com